CORRECTING COURSE

POVERTY AND
SHARED PROSPERITY
2022

CORRECTING
COURSE

WORLD BANK GROUP

ISBN (paper): 978-1-4648-1893-6
ISBN (electronic): 978-1-4648-1894-3
DOI: 10.1596/978-1-4648-1893-6

Cover design: Bill Pragluski, Critical Stages, LLC
Interior design: Ricardo Echecopar, Beyond SAC

Library of Congress Control Number: 2022947109.

Contents

Foreword   *xiii*

Acknowledgments   *xv*

About the Team   *xvii*

Main Messages   *xxi*

Abbreviations   *xxv*

Overview   1

Introduction   1

Part 1. Progress on poverty and shared prosperity   2

Part 2. Fiscal policy for an inclusive recovery   9

Notes   22

References   23

Part 1. Progress on Poverty and Shared Prosperity   27

1 Global Poverty: The Biggest Setback in Decades   29

Summary   29

Setting the scene: Poverty on the eve of the pandemic   30

Poverty over the pandemic period: The nowcast   46

Implications for reaching the 3 percent global poverty target by 2030   56

Notes   58

References   60

2 Shared Prosperity and Inequality: Uneven Losses and an Uneven Recovery   63

Summary   63

Introduction   64

Shared prosperity and inequality, 2014–19   66

Shared prosperity and inequality during COVID-19   74

Global inequality   83

Notes   88

References   88

3 Beyond the Monetary Impacts of the Pandemic: A Lasting Legacy **91**

Summary 91

Introduction 92

Multidimensional poverty on the eve of the pandemic 94

Pandemic impacts from a multidimensional perspective 98

Notes 108

References 109

Part 2. Fiscal Policy for an Inclusive Recovery **111**

Why focus on fiscal policy? 114

What is in part 2? 114

Note 116

References 116

4 Protecting Households with Fiscal Policy: Learning from COVID-19 **117**

Summary 117

The nature of the fiscal response to the COVID-19 crisis 118

The impact of the fiscal response on household welfare 121

Factors that influenced the impact of fiscal policy 137

Conclusion 142

Notes 142

References 144

5 Taxes, Transfers, and Subsidies: Improving Progressivity and Reducing the Cost to the Poor **151**

Summary 151

Introduction 152

The impact of taxes and transfers on short-term poverty and inequality 155

Taxation and distribution 162

Transfers and distribution 171

Economies of all income levels and capacities can achieve progressive fiscal policy 177

Conclusion 180

Notes 182

References 184

6 Fiscal Policy for Growth: Identifying High-Value Fiscal Policies **187**

Summary 187

Introduction 187

Measuring the value of fiscal policies 188

Using information on the value of policies to inform policy choices 191

High-value policies that support growth 195

Constraints on investing in high-value policies 201

Increasing the value of policies through increased efficiency of spending 202

Conclusion 204

Notes 205

References 205

7 Putting It All Together: Better Fiscal Policy for Reducing Poverty and Increasing Shared Prosperity 211

Summary 211

Accelerating progress with better fiscal policy: Different options for different countries 211

Spending for faster growth 213

Positioning fiscal policy to protect households against future crises 215

Raising revenue 221

Data and evidence for better fiscal decision-making 229

Can better fiscal policy put progress back on track? The need for global action 231

Notes 235

References 235

Boxes

O.1 Introducing the new 2017 PPP-based poverty lines 3

O.2 Measuring poverty in India 5

O.3 Tools that help to prioritize fiscal policies 17

1.1 How the new international poverty lines were derived 31

1.2 New data now available to measure poverty in India 35

1.3 Predicting changes in poverty with nowcasts 46

1.4 The impacts of rising global food and energy prices on poverty 54

2.1 Data coverage: A growing challenge for measuring shared prosperity, particularly for poorer countries 64

2.2 Inequality and top incomes 71

2.3 Experiences on the ground with shared prosperity 73

2.4 High-frequency phone surveys 77

3.1 Poverty-adjusted life expectancy: An index aggregating poverty and mortality 99

3.2 Lifecycle foundations for multidimensional comparisons in terms of years of life 103

4.1 COVID-19 cash transfers in Togo 131

5.1 The CEQ framework: An integrated approach to fiscal incidence analysis 153

5.2 Different types of tax instruments 163

5.3 Incidence curves, concentration shares, and fiscal progressivity 165

5.4 Chile: The distributional impact of commonly missing CEQ fiscal instruments 170

5.5 Uruguay: The impact of indirect taxes and direct transfers 178

5.6 Bolivia and Ethiopia: Fiscal system impact on poverty and inequality 179

6.1 Calculating the value of a policy using the MVPF 190

6.2 The progressivity of spending on education and health 196

7.1 Digitalization can improve the efficiency of fiscal administration, but not without challenges   227
7.2 Nudging tax compliance: How behavioral science tools can improve

compliance at low financial and political costs   228
7.3 Using evidence and data to expand COVID-19 social protection in South Africa   229

Figures

O.1 The COVID-19 pandemic triggered a historic shock to global poverty   2
O.2 Recent global inequality trends were reversed in 2020   4
O.3 Poverty reduction resumed slowly in 2021 but may stall in 2022   7
O.4 A widespread reduction in poverty across countries in 2020, followed by a nascent and uneven recovery   8
O.5 Progress in poverty reduction has been altered in lasting ways   9
O.6 The interplay of shocks, policy, and poverty affects workplace mobility   11
O.7 Fiscal policy reduced the impact of the COVID-19 crisis on poverty but less so in poorer economies   12
O.8 Delivering support on time and to those in most need was challenging   14
O.9 In poorer economies, poorer households are more likely to be left with less money after taxes have been paid and transfers received   15
O.10 Poorer economies rely more on indirect taxes, which are less progressive   16
O.11 Poorer economies spend less on transfers than on subsidies, which benefit the poor less   16
1.1 Global extreme poverty has continued to fall but at a slower rate in recent years   30
B1.1.1 Poverty lines expressed in constant 2017 US$ 32
1.2 The global extreme poor are concentrated in Sub-Saharan Africa   36
1.3 From 1990 to 2019, poverty fell in all regions except the Middle East and North Africa   37
1.4 Poverty rates are higher among children in every region   39
1.5 The extreme poor were less connected online going into the pandemic   40
1.6 Global poverty at higher poverty lines continued to fall, slowly   41
1.7 At the higher poverty lines, the regional distribution of the global poor changes   42

1.8 The cost of basic needs increases as countries grow   43
1.9 Progress has been made in reducing the societal poverty rate in recent years   44
B1.3.1 Cross-checking poverty derived using various methods, change in poverty, 2019–20   48
1.10 The COVID-19 pandemic was a historic shock to global poverty   50
1.11 Poverty increased across income groups in 2020 and displayed an uneven recovery in 2021–22   51
1.12 Poverty reduction stalled at all poverty lines in 2022   53
1.13 Poorer households spend more on food   56
1.14 Progress in poverty reduction has been altered in lasting ways   57
2.1 From 2014 to 2019, the vast majority of economies made substantial progress in shared prosperity   67
2.2 Significant differences occured in shared prosperity across regions and country income groups   68
2.3 Median income growth and shared prosperity are highly correlated   70
2.4 Within-country inequality was as likely to fall as to increase before the pandemic, but reductions in inequality were likely to be larger than increases   72
2.5 The pandemic led to large income losses among the bottom 40   75
2.6 Employment and income losses arising from the pandemic were severe, with certain groups being hit harder   78
2.7 The pandemic likely harmed the quality of jobs among those who continued to work   80
2.8 In selected countries, the probability of income loss was greater for the bottom 40 than the top 60, especially in urban areas   81
2.9 Projected changes in the Gini index show no clear pattern across countries with different income levels, with increases and decreases equally likely   82

2.10 The decline in global inequality before the pandemic reflects the strong income growth of the global middle class, whereas those in the bottom and the middle lost the most during the pandemic 84

2.11 The pandemic caused the largest increase in global inequality since World War II, after a steady decline over the past two decades 85

2.12 An increase in between-country inequality was mainly responsible for the reversal in global inequality 86

2.13 The increase in between country inequality was driven by larger countries with large income shocks 87

2.14 The bottom 40 suffered a larger shock from the pandemic and is recovering more slowly than the top 60 88

3.1 Widespread learning losses were reported, especially among low-income countries during the COVID-19 crisis 93

3.2 Meals skipped were highest at the start of the COVID-19 crisis and in lower-income countries 94

3.3 Almost 40 percent of the multidimensionally poor are not monetarily poor 97

B3.1.1 Lower-income economies have experienced larger reductions in poverty-adjusted life expectancy 101

B3.1.2 Reduction in poverty-adjusted life expectancy was driven by learning loss in lower-income countries and by increased mortality in higher-income countries 102

3.4 The pandemic's impact on well-being through additional current and future poverty and excess mortality varies substantially across economies 107

4.1 COVID-19 elicited an unprecedented, but highly unequal, fiscal response 119

4.2 Health spending increased, but the share of spending on education fell in many countries 119

4.3 Nearly all countries provided support to households and firms, but the type of support varied by income group 120

4.4 Household and firm outcomes are strongly correlated in low- and middle-income countries 121

4.5 Fiscal support received by households and firms was lower in poorer economies 122

4.6 Support provided to households had significant impact 125

4.7 Households quickly employed coping strategies in response to lower labor incomes 127

4.8 Countries announced fiscal support quickly at the outset of pandemic 127

4.9 Fiscal support often arrived after needs emerged 128

4.10 In 2022, the fiscal response to rising food and energy prices was much smaller and focused on subsidies 130

4.11 Countries implemented more broad-based support than targeted support during COVID-19 131

4.12 A breakdown by country income group reveals it was challenging to direct support to need 134

4.13 In simulations, fiscal policy reduced the impact of the COVID-19 crisis on poverty but less so in poorer economies 136

4.14 Fiscal policy reduced poverty more when more was spent 138

4.15 A higher credit rating was correlated with a larger fiscal response and increased external borrowing 138

4.16 Support reached more households in formal economies and in countries with high prepandemic rates of social assistance 140

B5.1.1 CEQ framework: Fiscal policy impacts on household income through taxes and transfers 153

5.1 Taxes, transfers, and subsidies reduce inequality in all economies, but in different ways, from different starting positions, and to different degrees 157

5.2 Taxes, transfers, and subsidies increase short-term poverty in a majority of non-HICs 160

5.3 Taxes, transfers, and subsidies increase consumable income for the poorest households at all income levels except LICs 161

5.4 Developing economies rely on indirect taxes for a majority of revenues; as economies get richer, they collect more through direct taxes, the main source of OECD revenues 162

5.5 Direct taxes collect a higher percentage of income from richer households, but indirect taxes collect more relative to incomes from poorer households 164

B5.3.1 Progressive, neutral, and regressive incidence curves 166

B5.3.2 Inequality-reducing and inequality-increasing concentration shares 167

5.6 Poorer households buy more from informal vendors, reducing their effective indirect tax rates 168

5.7 Richer economies spend more on education, health, and social protection 171

5.8 Subsidies are expensive in many developing economies, often exceeding social protection budgets 173

5.9 Most transfers go to poorer households and provide strong income support; most subsidies go to richer households and provide little support to poorer ones 175

5.10 The indirect tax burden usually exceeds the benefit of direct transfers for the poor in all but HICs 177

B5.5.1 Net incidence of transfers and indirect taxes in Uruguay 178

B5.6.1 Net incidence of transfers and indirect taxes in Bolivia 179

B5.6.2 Net incidence of transfers and indirect taxes in Ethiopia 180

6.1 Fiscal policy trade-offs 192

B6.2.1 Education and health concentration shares, by income category and decile 196

6.2 Average MVPF of policies in the United States, and of two policies targeted to children in low- and middle-income countries 197

7.1 Some countries are facing the dual challenge of stimulating recovery and coping with limited access to external finance 213

7.2 Improving fiscal policy can help recover the losses of 2020, but it requires historic efforts and does not result in ending extreme poverty by 2030 233

7.3 Many countries cannot recover the losses of 2020 by 2030, despite historic fiscal efforts 234

Map

1.1 In 2019, countries with the highest poverty rate at the US$2.15-a-day poverty line were mostly in Sub-Saharan Africa 37

Tables

B1.1.1 Derivation of global poverty lines, 2011 PPPs versus 2017 PPPs 32

B1.3.1 Method used for nowcasting global poverty in 2020 47

B2.1.1 Data coverage summary, shared prosperity, circa 2014–19 65

2.1 Summary, shared prosperity and shared prosperity premium, 78 economies 69

2.2 Within-country inequality tended to decrease but with variations across world regions, 2014–19 73

3.1 Deprivations in education and infrastructure raise the multidimensional poverty measure above monetary poverty 96

3.2 Multidimensional poverty declined in recent years, along with monetary poverty 98

3.3 Declines across all dimensions of the multidimensional poverty measure are apparent even when restricting comparison to a consistent set of economies over time 98

3.4 Years lost to premature mortality exceed increase in years lived in poverty in about half of economies 105

3.5 Years lost to premature mortality and the increase in years of future poverty exceed the increase in years of current poverty in most economies 108

CONTENTS

4.1 Cross-country correlations highlight
    the importance of access to external
    borrowing   139
5.1 Number of fiscal incidence
    studies, by region and income
    category   155

6.1 Cash transfers are higher value and
    better targeted than subsidies   195
7.1 Comparison of risk financing
    instruments   217
7.2 Progressive fiscal policy strategies
    are available to all countries   222

Foreword

COVID-19 marked the end of a phase of global progress in poverty reduction. During the three decades that preceded its arrival, more than 1 billion people escaped extreme poverty. The incomes of the poorest nations gained ground.

By 2015, the global extreme-poverty rate had been cut by more than half. Since then, poverty reduction has slowed in tandem with subdued global economic growth. The economic upheavals brought on by COVID-19 and later the war in Ukraine produced an outright reversal in progress. It became clear that the global goal of ending extreme poverty by 2030 would not be achieved. Given current trends, 574 million people—nearly 7 percent of the world's population—will still be living on less than US$2.15 a day in 2030, with most in Africa.

In 2020 alone, the number of people living below the extreme poverty line rose by over 70 million. That is the largest one-year increase since global poverty monitoring began in 1990. Looking at poverty more broadly, nearly half the world—over 3 billion people—lives on less than US$6.85 per day, which is the average of the national poverty lines of upper-middle-income countries. Using that measure, poverty persists well beyond Africa. The prevalence and persistence of poverty darken the outlook for billions of people living around the world.

The data confirm that the income losses of the poorest 40 percent of world's population were twice as high as those of the richest 20 percent. Global median income declined by 4 percent in 2020—the first decline since our measurements of median income began in 1990. This decline represents a major setback for the goal of shared prosperity. The poorest also suffered disproportionate setbacks in education and health, with massive learning losses and shortened lifespans. These setbacks, if left unaddressed by policy action, will have lasting consequences for people's lifetime income prospects and for development more broadly.

This latest *Poverty and Shared Prosperity* report offers the first comprehensive look at the global landscape of poverty in the aftermath of COVID-19 and the war in Ukraine. It outlines the limits of current fiscal policies for poverty reduction in low- and lower-middle-income economies, and points to the importance of reviving economic growth. It also shows the potential of fiscal-policy reforms to help reduce poverty and support broad-based growth and development.

Strong fiscal policy measures made a notable difference in reducing COVID-19's impact on poverty. In fact, the average poverty rate in developing economies would have been 2.4 percentage points higher without a fiscal response. Yet government spending proved far more beneficial to poverty reduction in the wealthiest countries, which generally managed to fully offset COVID-19's impact on poverty through fiscal policy and other emergency support measures. Developing economies had fewer resources and therefore spent less and achieved less: upper-middle-income economies offset just 50 percent of the poverty impact, and low- and lower-middle-income economies offset barely a quarter of the impact.

The rise in poverty in poorer countries reflects economies that are more informal, social protection systems that are weaker, and financial systems that are less developed. Yet several developing economies achieved notable successes during COVID-19. Helped by digital cash transfers, India managed to provide food or cash support to a remarkable 85 percent of rural households and 69 percent of urban households. South Africa initiated its biggest expansion of the social safety net in a generation, spending US$6 billion on poverty relief that benefited nearly 29 million people. And Brazil managed to reduce extreme poverty in 2020 despite an economic contraction, primarily using a family-based digital cash-transfer system.

In short, fiscal policy—prudently used and considering the initial country conditions in terms of fiscal space—*does* offer opportunities for policy makers in developing economies to step up the fight against poverty and inequality. To realize the potential of fiscal measures, the report calls for action on three fronts:

- *Choose targeted cash transfers instead of broad subsidies.* Half of all spending on energy subsidies in low- and middle-income economies went to the richest 20 percent of the population, who also happen to consume more energy. Targeted cash transfers are a far more effective mechanism for supporting poor and vulnerable groups: more than 60 percent of spending on cash transfers goes to the bottom 40 percent. Cash transfers also have a larger impact on income growth than subsidies.
- *Prioritize public spending for long-term growth.* COVID-19 has underlined how progress achieved over decades can vanish suddenly. High-return investments in education, research and development, and infrastructure projects should be made now. Governments need to improve their preparation for the next crisis. They also should improve the efficiency of their spending. Better procurement processes and incentives for public sector managers can boost both the quality and efficiency of government spending.
- *Mobilize tax revenues without hurting the poor.* This can be done by introducing property taxes, broadening the base of personal and corporate income taxes, and reducing regressive tax exemptions. If indirect taxes need to be raised, their design should minimize economic distortions and negative distributional impacts, and they should be accompanied with targeted cash transfers protecting the incomes of the most vulnerable households.

Restoring progress in poverty reduction is possible when helped by strong and broad-based economic growth—not only in the poorest economies but in middle-income economies as well. The policy reforms outlined in this report can help in achieving the necessary course corrections, recognizing that it will likely require stronger global growth and focused policy adjustments.

David Malpass
President
World Bank Group

Acknowledgments

The preparation of this report was co-led by Jed Friedman and Ruth Hill. The core team included Jessica Adler, Pierre Bachas, Katy Bergstrom, Ben Brunckhorst, Benoit Decerf, Uche Ekhator-Mobayode, Yeon Soo Kim, Christoph Lakner, Daniel Gerszon Mahler, Marta Schoch, Mahvish Shaukat, Mariano Sosa, Samuel Kofi Tetteh-Baah, Matthew Wai-Poi, and Nishant Yonzan. The extended team included, Evie Calcutt, Andres Castaneda, Mark Conlon, Leif Jensen, Jose Ernesto Lopez-Cordova, Arthur Galego Mendes, Rose Mungai, Minh Cong Nguyen, Stephen Michael Pennings, Tatiana Skalon, Veronica Montalva Talledo, Marika Verulashvili, Martha Viveros, and Kushan Sanuka Weerakoon, all of whom provided key inputs. Jessica Adler was project coordinator, and Anna Regina Rillo Bonfield, Karem Edwards, and Claudia Gutierrez provided general support to the team.

The authors are especially appreciative of the Poverty and Inequality Data Team; the Data for Goals (D4G) Team, in particular Carolina Diaz-Bonilla, Minh Cong Nguyen, and Rose Mungai; and the regional statistical teams for their tireless work to ensure consistency and accuracy in global poverty monitoring and projections. The authors benefitted from discussions with the staff of the International Comparison Program Global Office at the World Bank, particularly Maurice Nsabimana, Marko Olavi Rissanen, and Mizuki Yamanaka.

This work was conducted under the general direction of Deon Filmer, Haishan Fu, and Carolina Sánchez-Páramo, with additional input from Benu Bidani, Luis Felipe Lopez-Calva, Berk Ozler, and Umar Serajuddin. The team is also grateful for the overall guidance received from Indermit Gill, Aart Kraay, and Carmen Reinhart.

The report would not have been possible without the communications, editorial, and publishing teams. Elizabeth Howton, Anugraha Palan, and Joe Rebello led the communications strategy and engagement, with support from Paul Blake, Paul Gallagher, Nicholas Nam, Inae Riveras, Shane Kimo Romig, Torie Smith, and Nina Vucenik. The report was edited by Gwenda Larsen, Catherine Lips, Sabra Ledent, Honora Mara, and Sara Proehl, and designed by Ricardo Echecopar and Bill Pragluski. Alberto Cairo and Divyanshi Wadhwa provided data visualization services. Mary Fisk, Amy Lynn Grossman, Patricia Katayama, and Yaneisy Martinez from the World Bank Group's Publishing Program managed the editing, design, typesetting, translation, and printing of the report.

The team gratefully acknowledges the advice from peer reviewers and external advisers. Peer reviewers for this report included Paloma Anos Casero, Dean Jolliffe, Ambar Narayan, Norbert Schady, and Celine Thevenot. External advisers included Stefan Dercon, Nathan Hendren, and Nora Lustig. Patrick Heuveline also provided expert guidance. In addition, the team would like to thank the many World Bank colleagues who provided comments during the preparation of this report. In particular, the team is grateful for comments from Alan Fuchs, Ugo Gentilini, Alvaro Gonzalez, Chadi Bou Habib, Alaka Holla, Gabriela Inchauste, Maria Ana Lugo, Johan Mistiaen, Yuko Okamura, Pierella Paci, and Rinku Murgai. The team also benefited from many helpful discussions with teams across the World Bank Group, including the Office of the Chief Economist of the Human Development Global Practice.

The report is a joint project of the Development Data and Development Research Groups in the Development Economics Vice Presidency, and the Poverty and Equity Global Practice in the Equitable Growth, Finance and Institutions Vice Presidency of the World Bank. Financing from the government of the United Kingdom helped support analytical work through the Data and Evidence for Tackling Extreme Poverty Research Programme.

ukaid
from the British people

About the Team

Co-Leads of the Report

Jed Friedman is a lead economist in the Development Research Group (Poverty and Inequality Team) at the World Bank. His research interests include the measurement of well-being and poverty as well as the evaluation of health and social policies. His current work involves investigating the effectiveness of health financing reforms, assessing the nutritional and development gains from early life investment programs, and incorporating new approaches to survey-based well-being measurement. Jed's previous work has appeared in the *Journal of the European Economic Association*, the *Review of Economics and Statistics*, the *Journal of Development Economics*, the *Journal of Human Resources, The Lancet*, and other outlets. Jed holds a BA in philosophy from Stanford University and a PhD in economics from the University of Michigan.

Ruth Hill is a lead economist in the Global Unit of the Poverty and Equity Global Practice at the World Bank. Previously, she worked in the Sub-Saharan Africa and South Asia units on rural income diagnostics, poverty assessments, systematic country diagnostics, and an urban safety net project. From 2019 to 2021, Ruth was on external service as the chief economist at the UK government's Centre for Disaster Protection. Before joining the World Bank in 2013, she was a senior research fellow at the International Food Policy Research Institute, where she conducted impact evaluations on insurance, credit, and market interventions. Ruth has published in the *Journal of Development Economics, World Bank Economic Review, Economic Development and Cultural Change, Experimental Economics,* the *American Journal of Agricultural Economics,* and *World Development*. She has a DPhil in economics from the University of Oxford.

Core Team

Jessica Adler is a senior operations officer in the World Bank's Global Unit of the Poverty and Equity Global Practice. She supports the delivery of the Poverty and Equity work program, including strategy and program design, operational advice, quality assurance, portfolio management, and results monitoring. Jessica also serves as the program manager for the Umbrella Facility for the Poverty and Equity trust fund. She holds a BA in international economics from George Washington University and an MPP from George Mason University.

Pierre Bachas is an economist in the Development Research Group (Macroeconomics and Growth Team) at the World Bank. His research focuses on public finance in developing countries, in particular, on optimal tax design and challenges to tax collection faced by low- and middle-income countries as a result of tax evasion, informality, and differences in economic structure. Prior to joining the World Bank, Pierre was a postdoctoral researcher at Princeton University. He holds a PhD in economics from the University of California, Berkeley.

Katy Bergstrom is an economist in the World Bank's Development Research Group (Poverty and Inequality Team). Her research interests lie at the intersection of public and development economics, specifically in optimal taxation and redistribution in developing countries, the determinants of income inequality, and investment differentials among children. Katy holds a BS in economics and mathematics from the University of Canterbury, New Zealand, and a PhD in economics from Stanford University.

Ben Brunckhorst is a consultant in the Global Unit of the Poverty and Equity Global Practice at the World Bank. His research interests include climate change and poverty, disaster risk finance, and public infrastructure investment. Before joining the World Bank, he was a research assistant at the University of Oxford and the UK government's Centre for Disaster Protection. Ben holds bachelor degrees in engineering and economics from the University of Queensland, and an MSc in economics for development from the University of Oxford.

Benoit Decerf is a research economist in the Development Research Group at the World Bank. He is an applied micro-theorist whose research interests include poverty measurement, welfare economics, and mechanism design. His current research on poverty measurement focuses on the design of poverty indicators aggregating different dimensions of deprivation, for example, combining subsistence and social participation, or combining poverty and mortality. Benoit holds an MS from the Katholieke Universiteit Leuven and a PhD from the Université Catholique de Louvain, both in Belgium.

Uche Ekhator-Mobayode is a World Bank Young Professional in the Global Unit of the Poverty and Equity Global Practice. She was previously an assistant professor of economics at the University of Pittsburgh at Bradford. Her previous World Bank experience includes one year with the pioneer cohort of the Forced Displacement Research Fellowship in 2018, and as a consultant on the Gender Dimensions of Forced Displacement project with the Global Gender Unit. Uche completed her PhD in economics at Northern Illinois University.

Yeon Soo Kim is a senior economist in the Global Unit of the Poverty and Equity Global Practice, where she co-leads the global program on the distributional impact of the COVID-19 crisis. She previously worked in the Europe and Central Asia and South Asia regions and was based in the Sri Lanka country office from 2018 to 2021. Yeon Soo has led and contributed to reports on a wide range of topics, including poverty, inequality, fiscal incidence, informality, and spatial disparities. Before joining the World Bank, she was an associate research fellow at the Korea Development Institute, where she worked on labor and health issues. She holds a PhD in economics from the University of Maryland, College Park.

Christoph Lakner is a senior economist in the Development Data Group at the World Bank. His research interests include inequality, poverty, and labor markets in developing countries. In particular, he has been working on global inequality, the relationship between inequality of opportunity and growth, the implications of regional price differences for inequality, and the income composition of top incomes. He is also involved in the World Bank's global poverty monitoring. Christoph leads the Poverty and Inequality Data Team, which publishes the Poverty and Inequality Platform, the home of the World Bank's global poverty numbers. He holds a BA in economics, an MPhil, and a DPhil from the University of Oxford.

Daniel Gerszon Mahler is an economist in the Development Data Group, where he is part of the Sustainable Development Statistics Team and the team behind the Poverty and Inequality Platform. Prior to joining the World Bank, he was a visiting fellow at Harvard University's Department of Government and worked for the Danish Ministry of Foreign Affairs. He holds a PhD in economics from the University of Copenhagen. Daniel conducts research related to the measurement of poverty, inequality, and well-being.

Marta Schoch is a consultant in the Development Data Group at the World Bank, contributing to the group's work on global poverty and inequality measurement. Her research interests are in political economy, inequality, and poverty, with a focus on the formation of political preferences and its link with inequality. Since she joined the World Bank in 2020, she worked on the *Poverty and Shared Prosperity Report 2020* and contributed to the *Nigeria Poverty Assessment 2022*. Previously, she worked for the University of Sussex, the Migrating out of Poverty Research consortium, and the Imperial College London. Marta holds a PhD in economics from the University of Sussex.

Mahvish Shaukat is an economist in the World Bank's Development Research Group (Macroeconomics and Growth Team). Her research studies issues in governance, political economy, and public finance, with the goal of understanding how institutions and incentives shape state efficacy and citizen welfare. Mahvish holds a PhD in economics from the Massachusetts Institute of Technology.

Mariano Sosa is a consultant for the Global Unit of the Poverty and Equity Global Practice at the World Bank. His research interests include public finance and fiscal policy. His areas of expertise are fiscal incidence analysis, social policy, and the redistributive impact of fiscal policy in developing countries. Before joining the World Bank, Mariano was a research fellow for the Research Department of the Inter-American Development Bank. He holds an MPA in international development from Harvard Kennedy School.

Samuel Kofi Tetteh-Baah is a consultant in the Development Data Group at the World Bank, Washington, DC. He generally works on the empirical analysis of poverty and inequality. He has primarily been assessing the impact of purchasing power parity data on global poverty estimates. He holds a PhD in development economics from the Swiss Federal Institute of Technology, Zürich, Switzerland.

Matthew Wai-Poi is a lead economist in the World Bank's Poverty and Equity Global Practice, where he supports the regional work program in East Asia and Pacific on understanding and addressing poverty and inequality, as well as on topics such as the middle class, top incomes, female labor force participation, and the distributional impacts of climate change. He is also global lead for the Distributional Impacts of Fiscal and Social Policies. Previously, also at the World Bank, he worked on poverty and inequality issues in the Middle East and North Africa, including the role of gender and displacement, and was based in Jakarta for eight years. He was co-editor of the recent flagship report on *Targeting in Social Assistance* and has published in the *Journal of Political Economy* and *American Economic Association Papers and Proceedings,* among others. Matthew has a PhD in economics from Columbia University and degrees in law and business. He worked in management consulting before joining the World Bank.

Nishant Yonzan is a consultant for the Development Data Group (Poverty and Inequality Data Team) at the World Bank, contributing to the group's global agenda on measuring poverty and inequality. His research interests include the measurement and the causes and consequences of economic poverty and inequality. Some of his work has highlighted the role of institutions in shaping economic distributions and civil conflict, the impact of COVID-19 on poverty and inequality, the effect of cash transfers on fertility, and the differences in top incomes captured in survey and tax data. Nishant holds a PhD in economics from the Graduate Center of the City University of New York.

Main Messages

The World Bank's latest *Poverty and Shared Prosperity* report provides the first comprehensive look at global poverty in the aftermath of an extraordinary series of shocks to the global economy.

The COVID-19 pandemic dealt the biggest setback to global poverty in decades. The pandemic increased the global extreme poverty rate to an estimated 9.3 percent in 2020—up from 8.4 percent in 2019. That indicates that more than 70 million people were pushed into extreme poverty by the end of 2020, increasing the global total to over 700 million.

2020 marked a historic turning point—an era of global income convergence gave way to global divergence. The world's poorest people bore the steepest costs of the pandemic. Incomes in the poorest countries fell much more than incomes in rich countries. As a result, the income losses of the world's poorest were twice as high as the world's richest, and global inequality rose for the first time in decades.

The poorest also suffered disproportionately in many other areas that directly affect their well-being. For example, they faced large setbacks in health and education, with devastating consequences, including premature mortality and pronounced learning losses. These setbacks, if left unaddressed by policy action, will have lasting consequences for people's lifetime income prospects.

The economic recovery from the COVID-19 pandemic has been uneven. The richest economies have recovered from the pandemic at a much faster pace than low- and middle-income economies. Rising food and energy prices—fueled by climate shocks and conflict among the world's biggest food producers—have hindered a swift recovery. By the end of 2022, as many as 685 million people could still be living in extreme poverty. This would make 2022 the second-worst year for poverty reduction in the past two decades (after 2020).

These setbacks occurred when the speed of progress toward poverty reduction was already slowing. In the five years leading up to the pandemic, poverty reduction had slowed to 0.6 percentage point per year. Before 2020, the world was already significantly off course on the global goal of ending extreme poverty by 2030. This report projects that 7 percent of the world's population—roughly 574 million people—will still struggle in extreme poverty in 2030. That is far short of the global goal of 3 percent in 2030. Further, the report shows that in 2019 nearly half of the world's population (47 percent) lives in poverty when this is measured as living on less than US$6.85 a day.

These setbacks call for a major course correction. Despite difficult global and domestic circumstances, policy makers must redouble their efforts to grow their economies in the coming years—while paying careful attention to who benefits from that growth. The need for growth that boosts the incomes of the poorest could not be greater than it is today.

Resilient recovery will depend on a wide range of policies. This report focuses on fiscal policy—a key area at the center of pandemic and postpandemic responses. Fiscal policy concerns how governments raise revenue and spend public resources. This report offers new analysis on how fiscal policy was used during the first year of the pandemic. It also sheds light on the impact of taxes, transfers, and subsidies on poverty and inequality in 94 countries before 2020, providing important new insights into the impacts of fiscal policy—not only during crises but also during normal conditions.

Fiscal policy made a noticeable difference in reducing the pandemic's impact on poverty. Without it, the average poverty rate in developing economies, assessed at national poverty lines, would have been 2.4 percentage points higher than it was. Yet fiscal policy was much less protective in poorer economies than in richer ones. Most high-income economies fully offset the pandemic's impacts on poverty through the use of fiscal policy, and upper-middle-income economies offset one-half of the impact. However, low- and lower-middle-income economies offset only one-quarter of the impact. The differences in effectiveness reflected more limited access to finance, weaker delivery systems, and higher levels of informality, which made protecting jobs much more challenging.

In general, low- and middle-income economies tend to be less successful than high-income ones in ensuring that the combination of taxes, transfers, and subsidies benefit the poor. Taxes finance spending on core services and investments, and transfers and subsidies can offset their impact on household incomes. But in two-thirds of low- and middle-income economies, the income of poor households falls by the time taxes have been paid and transfers and subsidies have been received. This divergence is due in part to the larger share of the informal sector in those economies. As a consequence, taxes are predominantly collected indirectly—through sales and excise taxes—and income transfers are often too low to compensate.

Given these structural challenges, this report identifies three key priority actions for fiscal policy in the coming years, as countries work to correct course:

1. ***Reorient spending away from subsidies toward support targeted to poor and vulnerable groups.*** Subsidies are often poorly targeted. For example, one-half of all spending on energy subsidies in low- and middle-income economies goes to the richest 20 percent of the population, who consume more energy. In contrast, programs like targeted cash transfers are far more likely to reach poor and vulnerable groups. More than 60 percent of spending on cash transfers goes to the bottom 40 percent. Cash transfers also tend to have a larger impact on income growth than subsidies.

2. ***Increase public investment that supports long-run development.*** Some of the highest-value public spending—such as investments in the human capital of young people or investments in infrastructure and research and development—can have a beneficial impact on growth, inequality, or poverty decades later. Amid crises, it is difficult to protect such

investments, but it is essential to do so. The COVID-19 pandemic has shown that hard-won progress achieved over decades can suddenly vanish. Designing forward-looking fiscal policies today can help countries to be better prepared and protected against future crises.

3. ***Mobilize revenue without hurting the poor.*** This can be accomplished through property and carbon taxes and by making personal and corporate income taxes more progressive. If indirect taxes need to be raised, cash transfers can be simultaneously used to offset their effects on the most vulnerable households.

Reforming fiscal policy will be an essential element of correcting course, but we must be realistic about how much we can expect it to do. Despite the promise of fiscal reforms, simulations suggest it will take heroic efforts toward more effective fiscal policy choices to restore the pandemic-related losses in the next four to five years. Successful fiscal reform will require the support of sufficiently powerful domestic coalitions interested in pursuing these types of policy goals, as well as stepped-up global cooperation.

Accelerating global poverty reduction, and progress toward the Sustainable Development Goals, will require more comprehensive policy action. This will involve a broader set of policies to stimulate the kind of growth that can benefit people across all income levels—but particularly those at the bottom. Correcting course is both urgent and difficult. Even if the course correction proves insufficient to end extreme poverty by 2030, it must begin now—for the sake of a lasting recovery from the overlapping crises of today.

Abbreviations

BPS	business pulse surveys
CCT	conditional cash transfer
CEA	cost-effectiveness analysis
CEQ	Commitment to Equity
CIT	corporate income tax
CPHS	Consumer Pyramids Household Survey
GDP	gross domestic product
GDSP	Global Database of Shared Prosperity
GIC	growth incidence curve
GMD	Global Monitoring Database
HFPS	high-frequency phone surveys
HIC	high-income country
IMF	International Monetary Fund
LIC	low-income country
LMIC	lower-middle-income country
MCPF	marginal cost of public funds
MEB	marginal excess burden
MIC	middle-income country
MPM	multidimensional poverty measure
MSME	micro, small, and medium enterprises
MVPF	marginal value of public funds
NCD	noncommunicable disease
NSS	National Sample Survey
OECD	Organisation for Economic Co-operation and Development
PALE	poverty-adjusted life expectancy
PDI	pensions as deferred income
PFP	pay-for-performance (program)
PGT	pensions as government transfer
PIP	Poverty and Inequality Platform
PIT	personal income tax
PPP	purchasing power parities
R&D	research and development
SPP	shared prosperity premium

SPL	societal poverty line
TCC	tax compliance costs
UCT	unconditional cash transfer
UMIC	upper-middle-income country
VAT	value added tax
WHO	World Health Organization

Overview

Introduction

The COVID-19 pandemic triggered a pronounced setback in the fight against global poverty—likely the largest setback since World War II. Many low- and middle-income countries have yet to see a full recovery. High indebtedness in many countries has hindered a swift recovery, while rising food and energy prices—fueled in part by the Russian Federation's invasion of Ukraine and climate shocks among the world's biggest food producers—have made a return to progress on poverty reduction more challenging than ever. These setbacks have altered the trajectory of poverty reduction in large and lasting ways, sending the world even further off course on the goal of ending extreme poverty by 2030.

The year 2020 marked a historic turning point—an era of global income convergence gave way to global divergence as the world's poorest people were hardest hit. The richest people have recovered from the pandemic at a faster pace, further exacerbating differences. These diverging fortunes between the global rich and poor ushered in the first rise in global inequality in decades.

COVID-19, along with surging relative hikes in food and energy prices, have affected every economy around the world. Yet the impact has not been uniform across countries. In fact, it has been a function of the policy choices made during the crisis. Similarly, a range of policies and actions today will be critical to a resilient recovery tomorrow. This report focuses on fiscal policy: how governments raise revenue and spend public resources.

Fiscal policy is a main instrument used by governments to address immediate needs and promote long-term growth, with wide-ranging impacts on poverty and inequality. For many countries, fiscal policy is currently under considerable pressure. The fiscal demands of responding to a sustained crisis have left little fiscal space for additional spending, given that many countries already had little fiscal space at the onset of the pandemic (a result of years of lower growth and high debt). History shows that the fiscal choices that governments make in these moments can act as a lifeline for poor and vulnerable households—or they can further impoverish and increase inequality. This report offers new analysis of how fiscal policy was used during the first year of the pandemic. It also sheds light on the impact of taxes, transfers, and subsidies on poverty and inequality in 94 countries before 2020, providing important new insights into the impacts of fiscal policy not only during crises but also under normal conditions.

The analysis shows that the ability of fiscal policy to protect welfare during crises is limited in poorer countries. Fiscal policies fully offset the impact of COVID-19 on poverty in high-income countries (HICs), but they offset barely a quarter of the impact in low-income countries (LICs) and lower-middle-income countries (LMICs). Improving support to households as crises continue will require reorienting protective spending away from generally regressive and inefficient subsidies and toward a direct transfer support system—a first key priority. Reorienting fiscal spending toward supporting growth should be a second key priority. Some of the highest-value public spending—such as investments in the human capital of young citizens or investments in infrastructure and research and development (R&D)—often pays out decades later. Amid crises, it is difficult to protect such investments, but it is essential to do so. Finally, it is not enough just to spend wisely—when additional revenue does need to be mobilized, it must be done in a way that minimizes reductions in poor people's incomes. Exploring underused forms of progressive taxation (such as property, health, or carbon taxes) and increasing the efficiency of tax collection can help in this regard.

What follows is a description of the two parts of this report, the first part painting in broad strokes the poverty and inequality trends since 2020, and the second part describing the possible role of fiscal policy in addressing the current crisis and putting poverty reduction back on track.

Part 1. Progress on poverty and shared prosperity

Three decades of successful global poverty and inequality reduction hit the pandemic wall in 2020

The onset of the COVID-19 pandemic in 2020 marked a turning point in the 30-year pursuit of successful poverty reduction. Global poverty had declined from more than one in three persons (38 percent of the global population) in 1990 to less than one in 10 persons (8.4 percent) by 2019.[1]

The pandemic, delivering a broad-based shock to the global economy, triggered the first increase in extreme poverty in more than two decades (figure O.1). Because of a lack of official

FIGURE O.1

The COVID-19 pandemic triggered a historic shock to global poverty

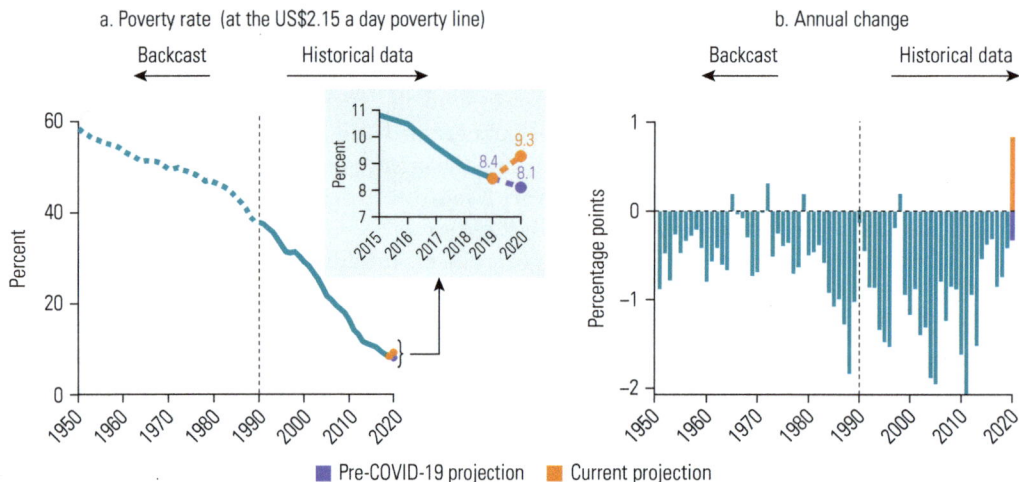

Sources: World Bank estimates based on Mahler, Yonzan, and Lakner, forthcoming; World Bank, Poverty and Inequality Platform, https://pip .worldbank.org; World Bank, Global Economic Prospects database, https://databank.worldbank.org/source/global-economic-prospects.
Note: Panel a shows the global poverty headcount rate at the US$2.15 a day poverty line for 1950–2020. "Historical data" for the period 1990–2019 are from the Poverty and Inequality Platform. "Backcast" estimates are extrapolated backward from the 1990 lineup using growth in national accounts. National accounts data before 1990 are from World Bank, World Development Indicators database, https://databank .worldbank.org/source/world-development-indicators; International Monetary Fund, World Economic Outlook, https://www.imf.org/en /Publications/SPROLLs/world-economic-outlook-databases; Bolt and van Zanden 2020. "Current projection" uses the nowcast methodology outlined in chapter 1 and a variety of data sources to project the latest 2019 lined-up estimate to 2020. "Pre-COVID-19 projection" extrapolates the 2019 lineup to 2020 using per capita gross domestic product (GDP) growth forecasts from the January 2020 Global Economic Prospects database. Panel b shows the annual percentage point change in the global poverty headcount rate.

survey data in many countries, uncertainty does exist around the poverty estimates for 2020, and they will continue to be updated as more information becomes available. The survey work on which poverty numbers rely was halted or conducted by phone (rather than via the usual in-person interviews) during the peak of the crisis in the second quarter of 2020. Nevertheless, survey-informed assessments are now possible for an increasing number of countries. Taken together, they point to an increase in poverty that is large by historic standards. The incomes of the poorest 40 percent of the world's population likely fell by 4 percent in 2020. As a result, the number of people living in extreme poverty likely increased by 11 percent in 2020—from 648 million to 719 million. This increase pushed the extreme poverty rate 1.2 percentage points higher than projections going into the year (extreme poverty had been expected to fall).

This is a historic setback in the fight against global poverty. Although data prior to 1990 are largely imputed based on national growth rates, and thus are more uncertain, the global scale of the pandemic shock likely renders the current shock the largest since 1945. Typically, past shocks (such as the 1997 Asian financial crisis, which resulted in a 0.2 percentage point increase in global poverty) tended to affect particular countries or regions. The current economic shock has led to widespread losses in employment and income as people stopped working and reduced consumption in every region of the world. Data collected by the World Bank using high-frequency phone surveys during the COVID-19 crisis found that, on average, 23 percent of respondents in the countries surveyed reported that they stopped working from April to June 2020, and 60 percent reported losing income.

This report documents these trends using new poverty lines based on the 2017 round of International Comparison Program (ICP) price data collected to generate estimates of purchasing power parity (PPP) (see box O.1). All poverty estimates in this report use the 2017 PPP-based

---

BOX 0.1

Introducing the new 2017 PPP-based poverty lines

The 2019 poverty numbers are the first to adopt the new estimates of global prices from the 2017 round of purchasing power parities (PPPs) that enable international comparisons of living standards across countries. With the new PPPs, the international poverty lines were revised. International poverty lines are calculated as the median of national poverty lines in low-income countries (LICs), lower-middle-income countries (LMICs), and upper-middle-income countries (UMICs), converted to US dollars using PPP exchange rates. The extreme poverty line of US$1.90 (2011 PPP) increased to US$2.15 (2017 PPP). The higher poverty line typically used to measure poverty in LMICs was updated from US$3.20 (2011 PPP) to US$3.65 (2017 PPP) and in UMICs from US$5.50 (2011 PPP) to US$6.85 (2017 PPP).

This change, however, does not mean the new extreme poverty line is now higher, and therefore more people will be counted as living in extreme poverty. The increase in the international poverty line from US$1.90 to US$2.15 primarily reflects the difference between 2017 and 2011 nominal dollar values. The change in the global poverty rate due to these updated poverty lines is thus negligible. As a result, the new extreme poverty line does not dramatically change the number of people living in extreme poverty in 2019. Extreme poverty decreases slightly, by 0.3 percentage point, to 8.4 percent, reducing the global count of the extreme poor by 20 million. This is also true of the increase from US$3.20 to US$3.65 for LMICs, and thus the poverty rate also increases slightly at the global level by 0.5 percentage point.

In UMICs, the national poverty lines have increased in real terms, on average, so the change in the international poverty line from US$5.50 to US$6.85 represents an increase in real as well as nominal terms. The global poverty rate at this line increased from 43 percent to 47 percent.

poverty lines. This updated approach changes the specification of the extreme-poverty line from US$1.90 (2011 PPP) to US$2.15 (2017 PPP), as well as the specification of other international poverty lines.

The rise in global poverty is not limited to extreme poverty measured at the international poverty line. At the US$3.65 poverty line, the line for the typical LMIC, global poverty increased by about 1.3 percentage points—from 23.5 percent in 2019 to 24.8 percent in 2020. At the US$6.85 poverty line, the line for the typical upper-middle-income country (UMIC), the poverty headcount rate also increased by 1.2 percentage points in 2020 (equivalent to 134 million more poor people).

The pandemic also increased global inequality. In terms of lost income, the world's poor paid the highest price for the pandemic: the percentage income losses of the poorest were estimated to be double those of the richest. The global Gini coefficient increased by a little over 0.5 points during the pandemic, from 62 points in 2019 to an estimated 62.6 points in 2020 (figure O.2). By contrast, earlier years had seen a shrinking gap between the global poor and others. For example, the global Gini coefficient dropped by around 0.5 points every year between 2003 and 2013. The Asian financial crisis previously brought a cumulatively large increase in global inequality in the late 1990s. It is yet to be seen what the full impact of the current crisis will be on global inequality, but diverging recoveries since 2020 suggest the impact may be large.

FIGURE O.2

Recent global inequality trends were reversed in 2020

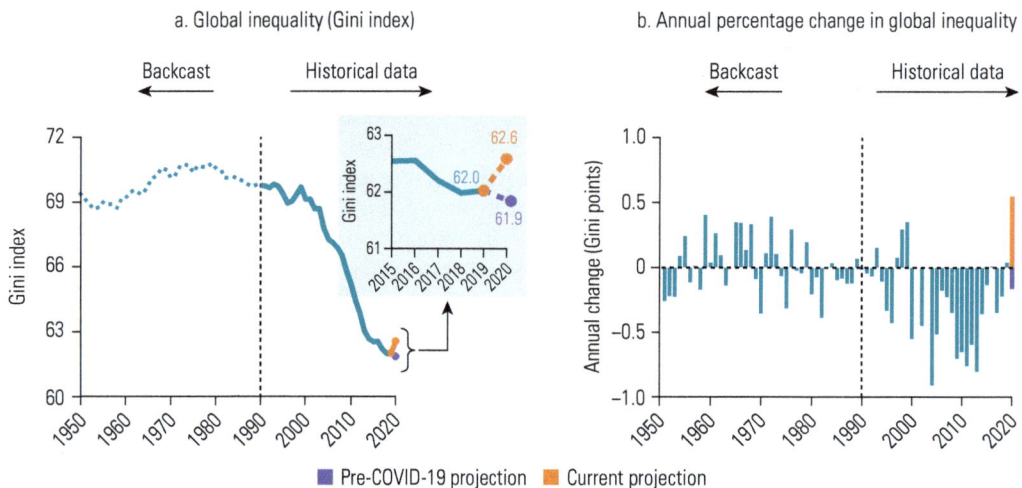

Sources: World Bank estimates based on Mahler, Yonzan, and Lakner, forthcoming; World Bank, Poverty and Inequality Platform, https://pip.worldbank.org; World Bank, Global Economic Prospects database, https://databank.worldbank.org/source/global-economic-prospects. Note: Panel a shows the global Gini index for 1950 to 2020. "Historical data" for the period 1990–2019 are from the Poverty and Inequality Platform. "Backcast" estimates are extrapolated backward from the 1990 lineup using growth in national accounts. National accounts data before 1990 are from World Bank, World Development Indicators database, https://databank.worldbank.org/source/world-development-indicators; International Monetary Fund, World Economic Outlook, https://www.imf.org/en/Publications/SPROLLs/world-economic-outlook-databases; Bolt and van Zanden 2020. "Current projection" uses the nowcast methodology outlined in chapter 1 and a variety of data sources to project the latest 2019 lined-up estimate to 2020. "Pre-COVID-19 projection" extrapolates the 2019 lineup to 2020 using per capita gross domestic product (GDP) growth forecasts from the January 2020 Global Economic Prospects database. Panel b shows the annual change in the global Gini Index, in Gini points.

Most countries experienced increases in poverty, but not always higher inequality

The estimated increase in global poverty of 71 million people is heavily influenced by the most populous countries because each individual in the world is weighted equally. Although large, China is home to a small share of the global extreme poor and had a moderate economic shock in 2020; as a result, China does not contribute to the global increase in extreme poverty in 2020. The global and regional poverty estimates presented in this report include new data for India for 2015–19 (see box O.2). This represents an improvement over the previous edition of this report, in which the absence of recent data for India severely limited the measurement of poverty in South Asia. In 2020, India experienced a pronounced economic contraction. Because 2020 poverty estimates from household survey data for India are still being finalized, there is considerable uncertainty over the estimates of poverty increases in India in 2020. A national accounts–based projection implies an increase of 23 million, whereas initial estimates using the data described in box O.2 suggest an increase of 56 million—this latter number is used for the global estimate. While the final number could be higher or lower, all indications suggest the global shock to poverty reduction as a result of the pandemic was historically large. Although smaller in population, Nigeria and the Democratic Republic of Congo are still relatively large countries and home to a large share of the global extreme poor; however, they had relatively mild economic shocks in 2020 and so contribute less to the global increase in extreme poverty, about three million and half a million, respectively.

Another way to explore the global scope of this crisis period is to note the number of countries that experienced substantive changes in poverty and inequality. Poverty increases were widespread across regions and income groups (figure O.4). With the exception of 19 countries that reduced poverty through generous transfers, nearly all countries saw poverty increases, often quite large, at the poverty line relevant to their income group. The effects were much larger in some countries than in others, highlighting the fact that a country's economic structure and policy response mediated the welfare effects of the common global crisis. In aggregate, in terms

Measuring poverty in India

This report publishes global and regional estimates based on new data for India available for 2015–19. The source of the data is the Consumer Pyramids Household Survey (CPHS), conducted by the Centre for Monitoring Indian Economy, a private data company. India has not published official survey data on poverty since 2011. Given the country's size and importance for global and regional poverty estimates, the CPHS data help fill an important gap.

The household consumption data used for poverty monitoring is based on an analysis by Sinha Roy and van der Weide (2022) in which the CPHS sample is re-weighted to more closely resemble a nationally representative survey and the consumption aggregate is adjusted to more closely match the consumption aggregate used in the official series. Other methods have been used to estimate the evolution of poverty in India since 2011. The methodological differences between the national accounts–based approach of Bhalla, Bhasin, and Virmani (2022) and Sinha Roy and van der Weide (2022) have been outlined elsewhere (Ravallion 2022; Sandefur 2022). Given widespread agreement that microdata from household surveys are necessary for credibly measuring poverty, this report uses the CPHS.

The CPHS was also conducted during 2020. Although the full analysis required to ensure consistency between this survey and previous surveys has not been completed, initial analysis indicates that the CPHS serves as a useful source of data on the trends in consumption in 2020.

of extreme poverty, the largest increases were observed in LICs and LMICs. In UMICs, poverty actually fell in 2020, driven in part by fiscal support in large UMICs, such as Brazil and South Africa, that mitigated the impact of the crisis on poverty (and even reduced poverty in some cases).

Although global inequality rose, this rise did not stem from widespread within-country increases in inequality. In fact, within-country inequality actually fell in many countries, thereby somewhat mitigating the increase in global inequality. The increase in global inequality would be 37 percent higher if within-country inequality changes are not taken into account. Because the change in inequality at the national level is mixed as well as small in most cases, the increase in country poverty rates is largely driven by declines in average income at the country level.

The nonmonetary dimensions of the pandemic and its impacts may ultimately prove to be more costly than the monetary dimensions

The costs of the pandemic go beyond monetary impacts. These broader costs principally include the lost learning of students unable to attend school and significantly higher global mortality rates. In fact, the world experienced the first decline in global life expectancy since the end of World War II: life expectancy fell by almost two full years (Heuveline 2022). Significant increases in pandemic-related mortality, both directly from COVID-19 infections and indirectly from factors such as declines in health care use, have afflicted every region of the world. The countries with the largest mortality burdens were middle-income countries (MICs) that confronted large economic shocks and social disruptions, but also had a relatively high share of older adults in the population who were more vulnerable to COVID-19 (WHO 2022).

As for the learning of young students today, many countries enforced social distancing measures to curtail the spread of the illness. Measures included closing schools for extended periods. From the onset of the pandemic until October 2021, the formal school system was closed for an entire school year, on average, across all countries, and even for a longer period in MICs. As a result, multidimensional poverty, which includes an educational dimension, increased in the short run. Perhaps more important, the learning loss will have significant long-term consequences for today's students and even the wider society if students are unable to make up their losses. This is because the growth potential of economies over the long term will be lower. Poverty will be prolonged for millions of people, especially the students of today who have borne the brunt of extended school closures and are now likely to earn less over their lifetime.

A comparison of the poverty shock in 2020 and 2021 with the impact of the current learning losses on long-run poverty simulations suggests that the persistence of poverty from learning losses will exceed the contemporaneous crisis-induced poverty shock for many countries.[2] The reason is that the drag on growth could persist for decades if unaddressed—even though the implications of learning loss for aggregate growth may appear modest within any one year. In LICs, the crisis increased the number of years spent in poverty by 6.1 per 100 persons for the two-year period 2020–21, whereas the loss in learning may lead to an additional total of 13.3 years in poverty per 100 persons, distributed over the longer 2022–50 period. The same metrics for LMICs and UMICs are 6.6 and 4.5 years in poverty now (2020–21) and 11.8 and 12.9 years in poverty over the future (2022–50), respectively. In 80 percent of the countries studied, the simulated future poverty increase due to learning loss exceeds the measured short-run increase in poverty.

These simulations are a point-in-time comparison that projects current conditions into the future. To the extent that the losses of 2020 can be reversed through policies addressing learning loss, the projected declines can be corrected and a comeback could even be quite rapid. But such outcomes will depend in part on the policy choices of today, including those discussed in this report and in the World Bank's forthcoming report *Collapse and Recovery: How the COVID-19 Pandemic Eroded Human Capital and What to Do About It* (World Bank, forthcoming b).

2021–22: The great divergence and a stalled recovery

Since 2020, progress in poverty reduction has been slow. Poverty estimates for 2021 and 2022 have been "nowcasted"—that is, gross domestic product (GDP) growth rates have been used to forecast household incomes, assuming all households experience equal growth. Nowcast estimates suggest that poverty reduction resumed in 2021, but only at the slow rate of progress seen prior to the crisis (figure O.3).

Projections for 2022 are that the pace of poverty reduction will further stall as global growth prospects dim with the war in Ukraine, a growth slowdown in China, and higher food and energy prices. High food price inflation can in the short run have especially detrimental impacts on poorer households, which spend a larger share of their income on food. To highlight the additional negative impact of food prices in the short run, poverty simulations are also presented for a downside scenario that assumes maximum impact, as reflected by the price data and consumption choices of poorer households.[3] In the long run, households may adapt to higher prices by changing their consumption patterns to at least partly lessen the impacts, and wages in certain sectors can adjust. For many poor rural households engaged in agriculture, higher food prices can be a source of income growth. World Bank poverty assessments conducted after the 2008 and 2011 food price crises in Bangladesh, Cambodia, Ethiopia, India, and Uganda showed the important role that higher food prices, which led to higher agricultural income growth and higher agricultural wages, played in raising the incomes of poor households. However, increases in food prices will hurt some poor—such as poor urban households—much more than others. The impacts on the urban poor can lead to unrest in cities (as in earlier food price crises) and require a strong policy response.

At least 667 million people were expected to be in extreme poverty by 2022. That is 70 million more than the forecast would have been without the lingering effects of COVID-19 and the Russian invasion of Ukraine. In a worst-case scenario, up to 685 million people could be in extreme poverty—89 million more than would have otherwise been the case. At these levels, the number of people forecasted to move out of poverty in 2022 could be as low as 5 million.

FIGURE O.3

Poverty reduction resumed slowly in 2021 but may stall in 2022

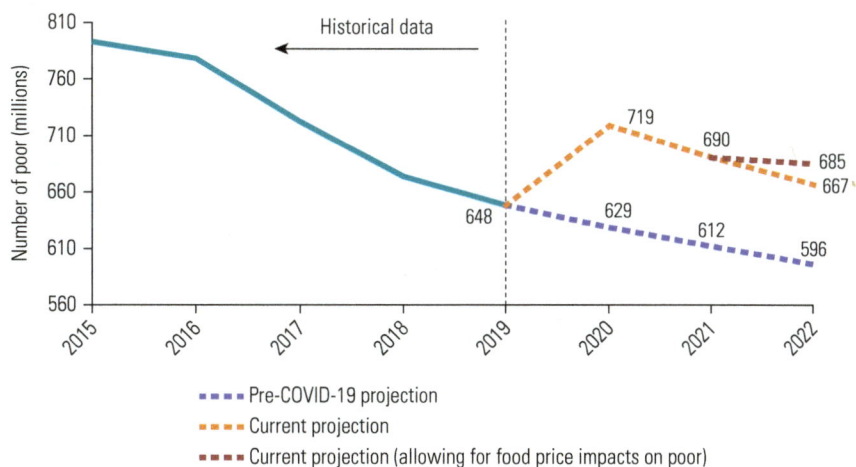

Sources: World Bank estimates based on Mahler, Yonzan, and Lakner, forthcoming; World Bank, Poverty and Inequality Platform, https://pip.worldbank.org; World Bank, Global Economic Prospects database, https://databank.worldbank.org/source/global-economic-prospects.
Note: The figure shows the number of poor at the US$2.15 a day poverty line. For 2022, nowcasts are reported for the "Current projection" and for the "Current projection (allowing for food price impacts on poor)."

This finding places 2022 on track to be the second-worst year for poverty reduction in the last 22 years (after 2020). Global poverty rates are projected to be just as high in 2022 as they were in 2019, indicating several years of lost progress.

The pathways countries have followed since the pandemic have exacerbated global inequality, with richer countries recovering faster than poor countries. Figure O.4 shows the change in the number of extreme poor, by year, for three income groups. Recovery is estimated to have been lower in LICs, with 11 of 27 countries still estimated to have poverty increases in 2021 and full recovery expected in only six. Although recovery was more widespread in LMICs in 2021, it is estimated that most countries had not reversed the substantial increase in poverty seen in 2020. In UMICs, recovery was stronger but not by much. From 2020 to 2022, because of differences in between-country growth rates, the incomes of the world's richest 20 percent likely grew by 3.3 percent. By contrast, the rate for the bottom four quintiles was 2.1 percent to 2.5 percent.

Taken together, the threats to poverty reduction noted in this report have set back progress by at least four years (figure O.5). By 2030, the global extreme poverty rate will be 7 percent. The goal of reducing global poverty to 3 percent by 2030 was difficult enough to achieve before the current crises. The recent setbacks have put this target nearly out of reach—and there is an urgent need to correct course.

These projections mask substantial differences in projections between regions. Extreme poverty is projected to become increasingly concentrated in Sub-Saharan Africa. Other regions will likely reach the 2030 target of less than 3 percent extreme poverty by 2030, but poverty is projected to remain well above target in Sub-Saharan Africa. Achieving the 3 percent goal by 2030 would require Sub-Saharan Africa to achieve growth rates about eight times higher than historical rates between 2010 and 2019.

The compounding pressure of the overlapping crises experienced over the past two years has created an elevated risk profile for the world. Government policies play a critical role in shielding societies from the worst outcomes of crises. Fiscal policy is a key instrument of such policies. Unfortunately, many countries, especially LICs, entered the pandemic with fiscal systems unable to fully confront or deal with the challenges they faced. The coming years present new opportunities and challenges. The second part of this report discusses how fiscal policy can be employed to promote a robust and inclusive recovery.

FIGURE O.4

A widespread reduction in poverty across countries in 2020, followed by a nascent and uneven recovery

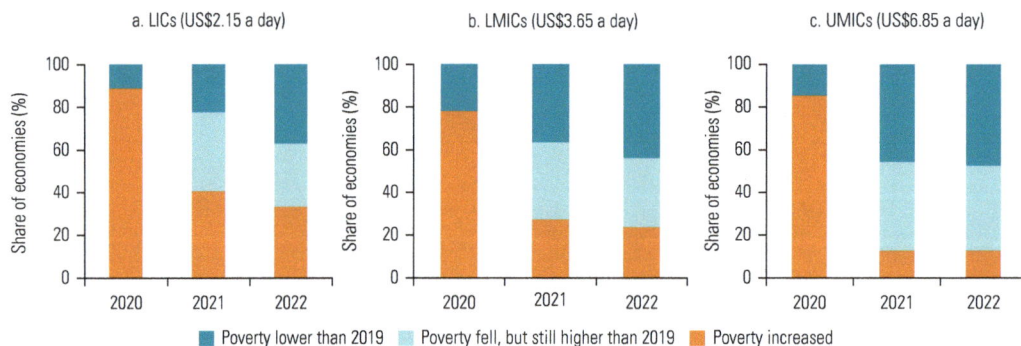

Sources: World Bank estimates based on Mahler, Yonzan, and Lakner, forthcoming; World Bank, Poverty and Inequality Platform, https://pip .worldbank.org; World Bank, Global Economic Prospects database, https://databank.worldbank.org/source/global-economic-prospects.
Note: The figure shows the share of economies where the poverty rate has decreased or increased relative to the prior year and relative to 2019, by income group. Economies where poverty increased include those where poverty did not change. LICs = low-income countries; LMICs = lower-middle-income countries; UMICs = upper-middle-income countries.

FIGURE O.5

Progress in poverty reduction has been altered in lasting ways

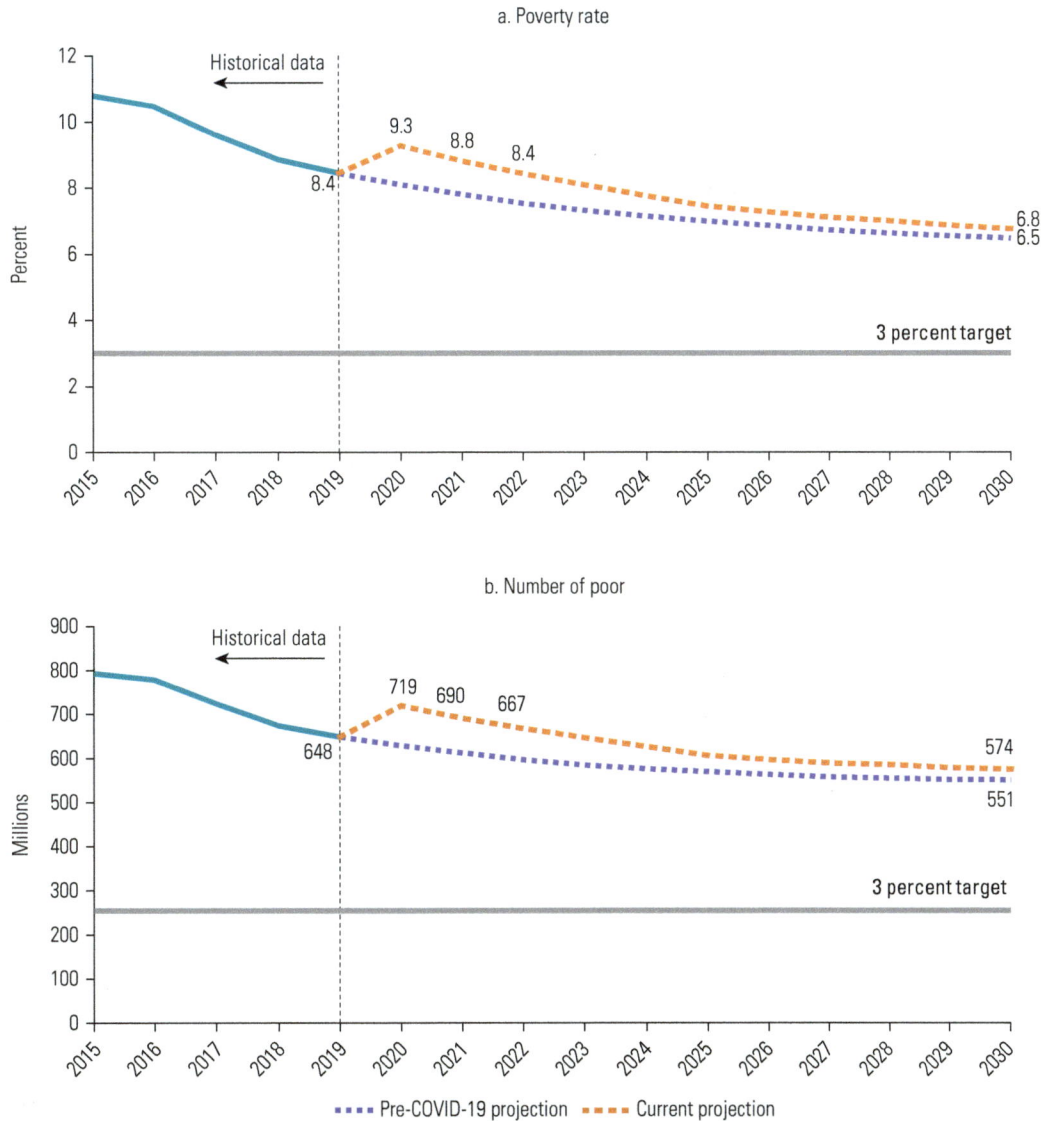

a. Poverty rate

b. Number of poor

····· Pre-COVID-19 projection ····· Current projection

Sources: World Bank estimates based on Mahler, Yonzan, and Lakner, forthcoming; World Bank, Poverty and Inequality Platform, https://pip .worldbank.org; World Bank, Global Economic Prospects database, https://databank.worldbank.org/source/global-economic-prospects.
Note: Two growth scenarios are considered: the "Current projection" uses growth rates from the June 2022 Global Economic Prospects (GEP) database to project poverty up to 2024. The "Pre-COVID-19 projection" uses the January 2020 GEP growth rate to project poverty to 2022. Both scenarios use the country-level average annual historical (2010–19) growth rate to project poverty in the remaining years. The "3 percent target" line in panel b is based on the estimate of the number of poor in 2030—255 million.

Part 2. Fiscal policy for an inclusive recovery

During the COVID-19 crisis, various public health policies—such as stay-at-home directives as well as new and existing monetary, financial, and fiscal policies—affected the dynamics of disease transmission and altered growth, poverty, and learning outcomes. These outcomes were also shaped by the economic and social conditions of the country and the particular mix of policies chosen. Many of these policies were adopted in an environment of economic stress, with great uncertainty about the ultimate impacts they might have.

The effects of some of those policy choices are now on view amid the current food and energy price crisis. Today, food-export bans risk further exacerbating food price volatility, as they did during the 2006–08 food price crisis (Martin and Anderson 2011). Monetary, trade, and fiscal policies (such as lower food tariffs and protective cash transfers) tailored to specific country conditions offer the potential to soften the impacts. However, the dominant policy choice has been subsidies, implemented by 93 percent of the countries that took early fiscal action in response to the food and energy price crisis, even though such subsidies are often not well targeted to need and can be detrimental in the long run.

The second part of this report starts with the recognition that the same policy can have very different effects in different countries. Higher-income economies are more resilient in the face of shocks (World Bank 2013) because their households and firms are endowed with wealth and superior health and education systems and thus are able to adapt to changing circumstances. Governments in LICs and MICs face policy options with more limited effectiveness during a crisis than richer countries because of the structure of their economies (Loayza 2020). A stay-at-home order will be largely futile if people are compelled by necessity to work outside the home. Financial sector policy is less effective when it cannot reach a large informal sector. And fiscal policy cannot achieve much if fiscal space is constrained and the structure of an economy limits the reach of standard fiscal policy instruments. Various features of an economy can amplify the impact of any shock and limit the impact of policies to address it.

This interplay of shocks, policy impact, and poverty is well illustrated in figure O.6 (Aminjonov, Bargain, and Bernard 2021). The figure depicts average workplace mobility (based on smartphone data) across 43 low- and middle-income countries. Stay-at-home directives and private decisions to avoid exposure to COVID-19 drove a dramatic reduction in mobility in March 2020. Reductions in mobility were large in both high- as well as low-poverty regions in countries. The reductions in mobility, however, were larger in the regions with lower poverty and in those that received income support. Mobility fell further in those areas that were better able to accommodate a stay-at-home order by virtue of the prevailing nature of work and the relative ability of the well-off to stay home. The difference in mobility in places with and without income support exceeds the difference in mobility in places with low and high poverty rates. As a result, income support policies also had a larger impact on mobility in higher-poverty areas than in lower-poverty areas. This finding underscores the fact that policies that promote development enable more resilience in the face of crises.

The focus on fiscal policy

Fiscal policy consists of the decisions governments make on how to raise revenue and spend public resources. Part 2 of this report focuses on how fiscal policy affects poverty and inequality. Fiscal choices affect growth, employment, and wages, as well as the services available, the prices people pay, and the income people have left after taxes are paid and transfers are received.

In many countries, fiscal policy is currently under considerable pressure. Even as governments decide which fiscal policies are the most suitable for achieving an inclusive recovery and long-run growth, they must deal with rising fiscal deficits and debt burdens and with little space for fiscal policy to support the recovery and prepare for ongoing and future crises. LICs and MICs are significantly more indebted today than two years ago. In 2020, more emerging economies experienced credit rating downgrades than over the entire 2010–19 period (Kose et al. 2022). Even as countries saw their revenues drop because of the COVID-19 crisis, they had to pursue expansionary fiscal policy if they wanted to mitigate the worst impacts of the downturn. Many countries now need to raise revenue, reduce spending, or both to escape debt distress. Historically, such fiscal policy decisions have often hurt the poor—not only in the immediate

The interplay of shocks, policy, and poverty affects workplace mobility

First COVID-19 income support

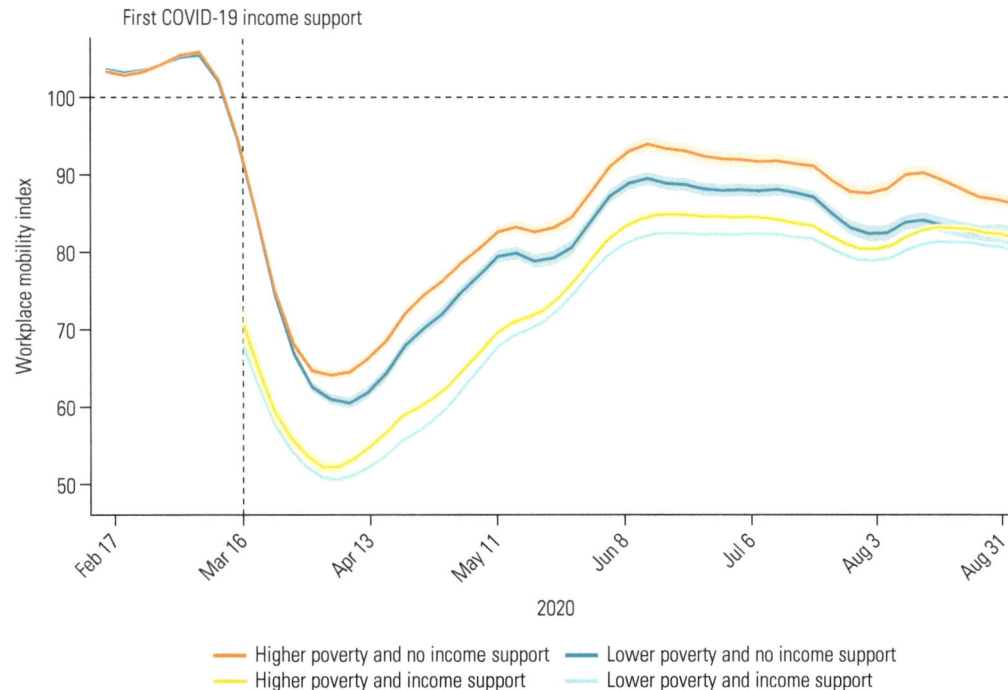

2020

— Higher poverty and no income support — Lower poverty and no income support
— Higher poverty and income support — Lower poverty and income support

Source: Based on data from Aminjonov, Bargain, and Bernard 2021.
Note: The figure depicts workplace mobility in 2020 (based on smartphone data) across subnational regions with high and low poverty rates and with and without income support in 43 low- and middle-income countries. The data points reflect the calculations by Aminjonov, Bargain, and Bernard (2021) based on Google mobility data (change in visits to workplaces relative to the daily median from January 3 to February 6, 2020); poverty data from national statistical offices and estimates by Aminjonov, Bargain, and Bernard (2021) using household surveys; and Oxford COVID-19 Government Response Tracker data on COVID-19 income support. The figure shows the local polynomial fit with a 95 percent confidence interval of daily mobility across regions, weighted by 1 divided by the number of regions in the corresponding country. Poverty is measured as the share of people living below national or international poverty lines in a subnational region. Poverty is defined as lower (higher) if a region's poverty rate is below (above) the country's median regional poverty rate. COVID-19 income support shows the daily status of whether the government provides any income support to those who cannot work or who have lost their jobs because of the COVID-19 pandemic (country-day variation in income support).

term, but also limiting the longer-term opportunities available to them. Policy makers must navigate the current challenges in ways that do not further impoverish the poor today or reduce the opportunities they might enjoy tomorrow.[4]

Fiscal policy, poverty, and inequality: Three findings

1. In low- and middle-income countries, fiscal policy can protect people's welfare in a crisis—but with limits

During the early stages of the pandemic, fiscal policy effectively prevented some vulnerable households from slipping into poverty. Microsimulations in LICs and MICs suggest poverty would have been, on average, 2.4 percentage points higher without a fiscal response (figure O.7). However, even though fiscal policy nearly fully offset the impact of the pandemic on poverty in HICs, it offset only half of the impact in UMICs and just over a quarter of the impact in LICs and LMICs.

There are some lessons to learn from this global experience—not only how to improve fiscal policy in the years to come but also how to be clear-eyed about the limits of protecting poor

FIGURE O.7

Fiscal policy reduced the impact of the COVID-19 crisis on poverty but less so in poorer economies

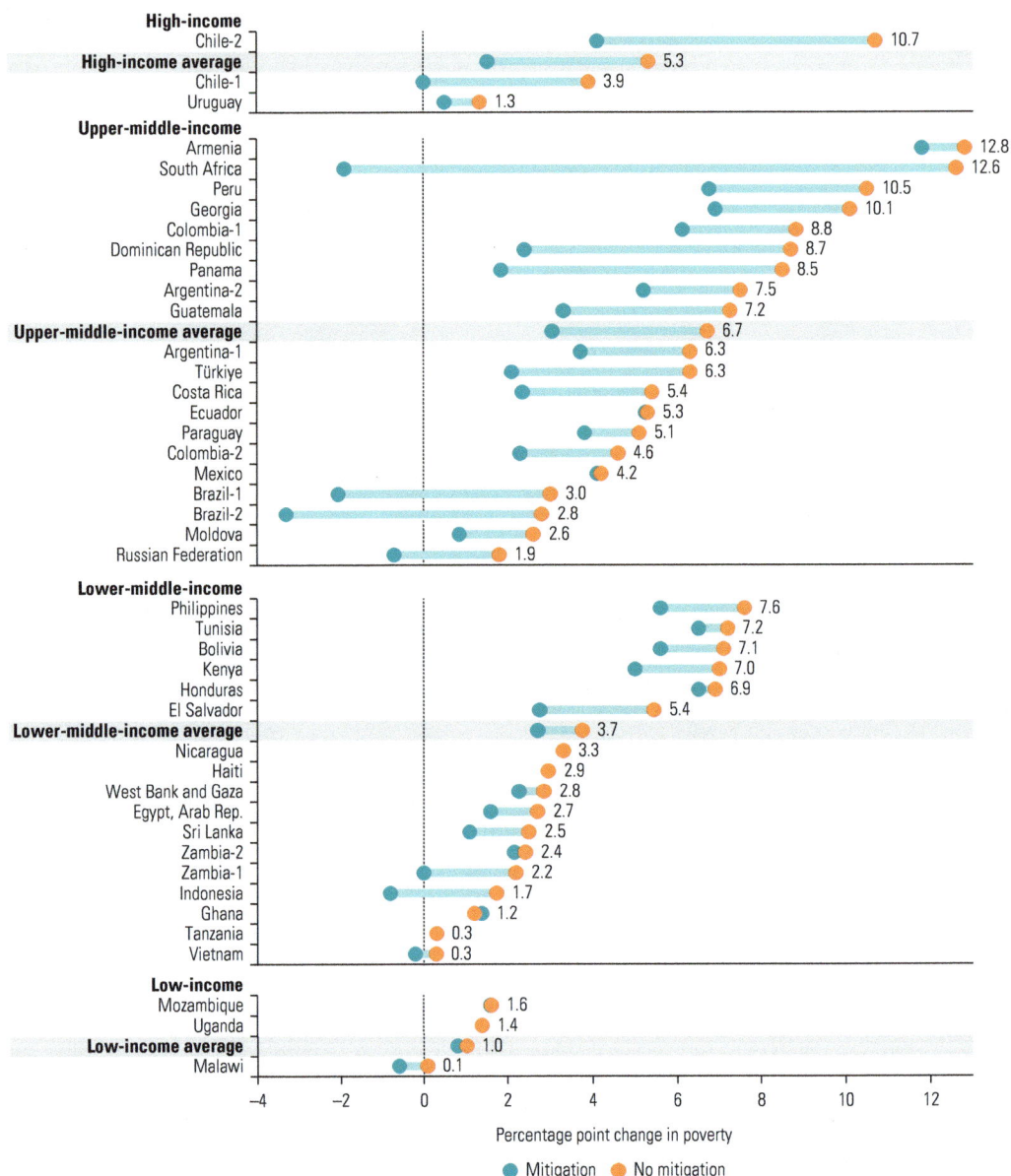

Sources: Estimates collected from published and World Bank microsimulation studies. See chapter 4 of the report for a full list.
Note: The figure shows the results of two simulations from each economy study: one showing the increase in poverty that would have occurred had no fiscal response been present (no mitigation), and one showing the increase in poverty taking into account the fiscal response (mitigation). The increase in poverty is measured against the national poverty line or the global poverty line appropriate to the economy income category. For some economies, more than one study is available, as indicated by the use of "1" or "2" after the economy name in the figure. Full details of the data used are in chapter 4 online annex, annex 4A, table 4A.1, available at http://hdl.handle.net/10986/37739.

and vulnerable households through fiscal policy. High borrowing costs limited the scale of the COVID-19 fiscal response in many low- and lower-middle-income countries. In survey results reported in *World Development Report 2022: Finance for an Equitable Recovery* (World Bank 2022b), 83 percent of LIC policy makers indicated they were concerned about debt sustainability or access to external borrowing for financing their fiscal response to the crisis. Many LIC and LMIC policy makers were even more concerned about access to international financial support. LICs relied almost entirely (95 percent) on international support to finance a fiscal response. Such financing was also a major source of support for LMICs (73 percent) and for UMICs (50 percent). Going into the crisis, more than half of International Development Association (IDA) countries were in debt distress, so could not borrow much. Their main source of external finance was highly-concessional flows from multilateral development banks. This highlights the importance of access to finance in a crisis response.

The structure of the economy also limited the type and impact of fiscal policy tools that could be used. Providing firms with the support needed to save jobs was almost impossible in countries with large informal sectors. The share of workers at firms receiving wage subsidy support was larger in countries with a greater share of formal workers in the economy prior to the crisis— even when controlling for the overall level of spending and GDP per capita. This finding is troubling because emerging evidence suggests that spending to protect jobs may have been more impactful in hastening economic recovery, increasing employment, and reducing poverty than income support measures (World Bank, forthcoming a).

Faced with widespread uncertainty about the impact of the crisis on household incomes and the widespread losses across poor, vulnerable, and middle-class households, most countries were under considerable political pressure to quickly provide broad income support. HICs and UMICs were more likely to provide this support through universal transfers, whereas LMICs and LICs were more likely to implement subsidies alongside targeted transfers. Although subsidies were similarly universal and often rapidly introduced, they came with several disadvantages. A greater share of subsidy support went to the better-off, and subsidies distorted the prices that households faced.

On average, almost three months passed after lockdowns began before transfers reached recipients in LICs and MICs, even though income losses and rising food insecurity took hold immediately—see Beazley, Marzi, and Steller (2021) and figure O.8. Delivery was much quicker when digital payment systems were present. Transfers did target poorer households in general. However, reaching vulnerable households with income losses who were not the usual beneficiaries of social protection systems proved more challenging, especially in LICs and LMICs. Nevertheless, there are standout examples of innovation in reaching well-targeted beneficiaries during challenging times, such as South Africa and Togo (discussed in further detail in the report). In summary, the experience of delivering support during the pandemic highlights the importance of investing in delivery systems for transfers that—when needed—can deliver timely support beyond a narrowly targeted group.

2. In poorer countries, poor households often have less income after taxes are paid and transfers are received

The lack of fiscal space in many poorer countries going into the COVID-19 crisis and the limited delivery systems available to deliver direct transfers to poor and vulnerable households reflected fiscal choices made in the run-up to the crisis. This report brings together for the first time analysis of the impact of taxes, transfers, and subsidies on household income in 94 LICs and MICs (including 55 LICs and LMICs). This analysis assesses the degree to which taxes are raised equitably and transfers and subsidies reach poor and vulnerable households.

Taken together, taxes, transfers, and subsidies reduce inequality in all countries while financing spending on security, health, education, and investments for growth and poverty reduction. HICs are effective at ensuring that taxes, transfers, and subsidies do not reduce the disposable income of

FIGURE O.8

Delivering support on time and to those in most need was challenging

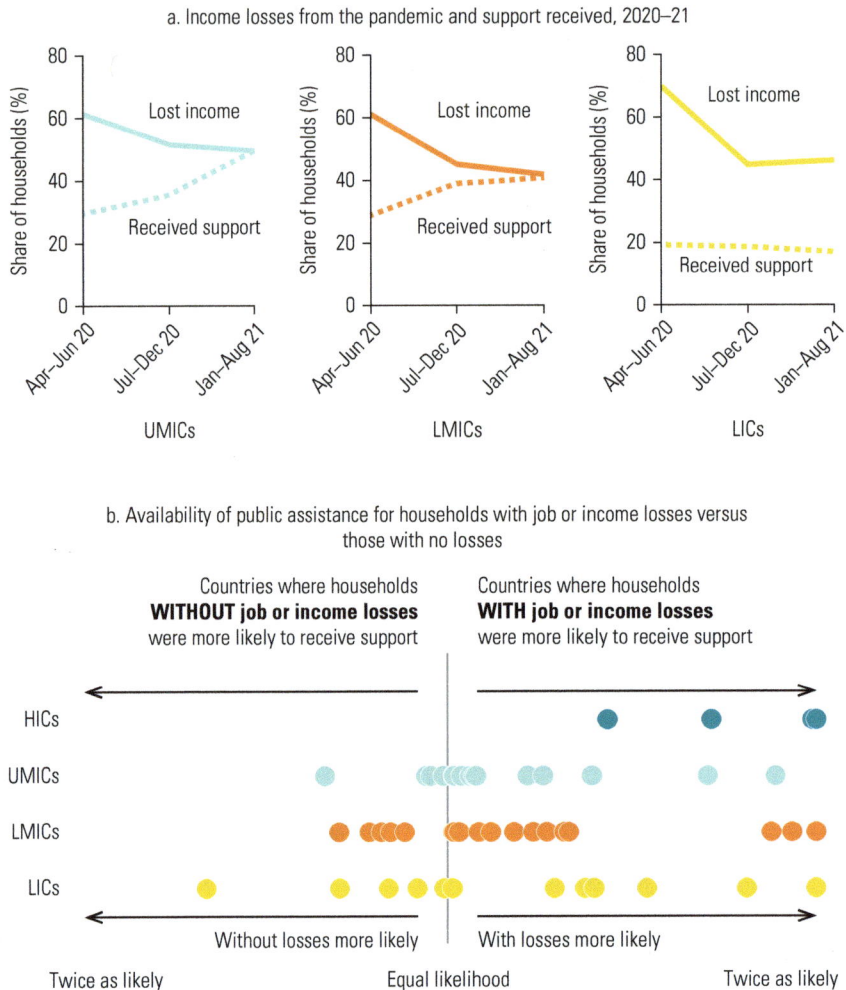

a. Income losses from the pandemic and support received, 2020–21

b. Availability of public assistance for households with job or income losses versus those with no losses

Source: World Bank estimates based on data from World Bank COVID-19 high-frequency phone surveys.
Note: Panel a shows the share of households in each income group that lost income and the share of households that received support across three periods during the pandemic (averaging across economies in each income category). Panel b shows the difference between the share of households that received support and lost income or a job and the share of households that received support but did not lose income or a job (each dot represents an economy). Economies are weighted equally. HICs = high-income countries; LICs = low-income countries; LMICs = lower-middle-income countries; UMICs = upper-middle-income countries.

poor households. However, this is not the case for LICs and MICs. In two-thirds of those countries, the income of poor households falls by the time taxes have been paid and transfers and subsidies have been received (figure O.9). In LICs the income of all households is lower after taxes, transfers and subsidies. The informal sector accounts for a large share of the economy in LICs and MICs. As a consequence, taxes are predominantly collected indirectly, and income transfers are often too low to compensate for the offsetting impact of indirect taxes on poor and vulnerable households. Encouragingly, though, across all income levels some countries are able to reduce both inequality and poverty. The highest performers in each category tend to reduce poverty by 6 to 8 percentage points at the poverty line relevant to their income category. On average, however, reducing poverty becomes much less likely for countries in lower income categories. All HICs reduce poverty by

FIGURE O.9

In poorer economies, poorer households are more likely to be left with less money after taxes have been paid and transfers received

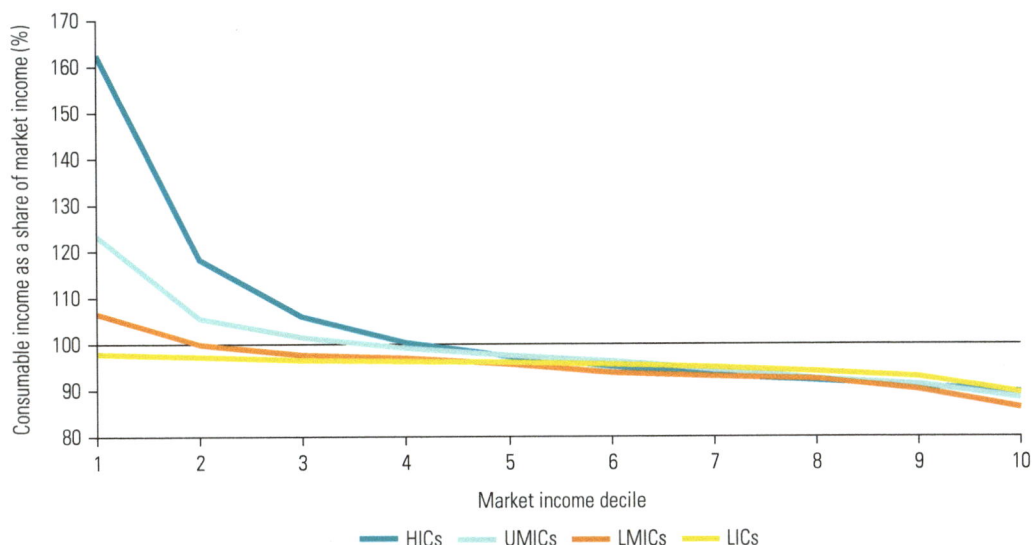

Sources: Original estimates based on data from CEQ Institute, CEQ Data Center on Fiscal Redistribution, https://commitmentoequity.org /datacenter; Organisation for Economic Co-operation and Development data; World Bank data.
Note: The figure shows consumable income (income after direct and indirect taxes have been paid and cash transfers and subsidies have been received) as a percentage of market income (income before any taxes have been paid or transfers or subsidies received), by market income decile, aggregated by income group using the median. The sample includes 5 HICs, 19 UMICs, 16 LMICs, and 3 LICs. HICs = high-income countries; LICs = low-income countries; LMICs = lower-middle-income countries; UMICs = upper-middle-income countries.

more than 1 percentage point, compared with only six of the 23 UMICs and only one of the 24 LICs and LMICs. It is thus a challenge to raise revenue without increasing poverty in a country with a large informal sector and limited safety net coverage.

Poorer countries collect less tax revenue and primarily collect taxes in the least progressive way—64 percent of taxes are from indirect taxes (value added, excise, and trade taxes). By contrast, just 28 percent of tax revenue in Organisation for Economic Co-operation and Development (OECD) member countries is derived from these sources (figure O.10). In richer countries, more taxes are collected from direct taxes: personal income tax and other taxes on income such as social security contributions. Direct taxes are typically more progressive because they can be designed to increase with income, unlike taxes on goods that everyone must purchase regardless of income level. In informal economies where income is not easily observed, recorded, and taxed, there is a greater reliance on indirect taxes. Because of this reliance, a significant share of revenue is collected from the poor.[5]

In LICs and LMICs, spending on direct transfers is low on average, and it is dwarfed by spending on subsidies. Figure O.11 compares spending on energy and agricultural subsidies with all social protection spending. In HICs, spending on social protection far exceeds spending on subsidies. In UMICs, spending on energy and agricultural subsidies is equal to spending on social protection, whereas in LMICs and LICs social protection spending is less than one-half and one-tenth of spending on energy and agricultural subsidies, respectively. Only 20 percent of spending on subsidies reaches the bottom 40 percent in each country, and this, combined with low spending on transfers, means there is little compensation for the reduction in income and consumption brought about by indirect taxes. Subsidies are widespread, in part, because they are popular, providing support to many interest groups on whom governments

15

FIGURE O.10

Poorer economies rely more on indirect taxes, which are less progressive

a. Tax revenue as a share of GDP

b. Direct and indirect taxes as a share of market income, by income decile

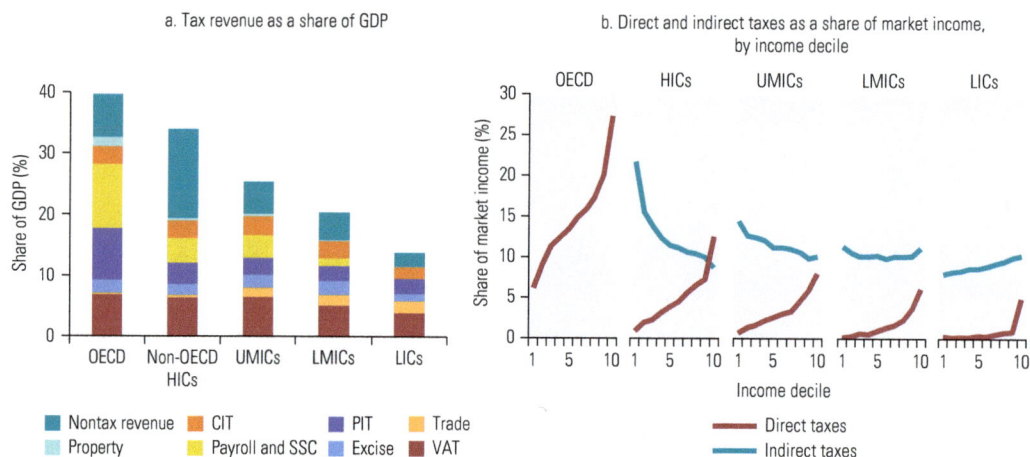

Legend (panel a):
- Nontax revenue
- Property
- CIT
- Payroll and SSC
- PIT
- Excise
- Trade
- VAT

Legend (panel b):
- Direct taxes
- Indirect taxes

Sources: International Centre for Tax and Development, https://www.ictd.ac/; CEQ Institute, CEQ Data Center on Fiscal Redistribution, https://commitmentoequity.org/datacenter; OECD data; World Bank data.
Note: Panel a shows each type of government revenue as a percentage of gross domestic product (GDP), aggregated by income group. Panel b shows direct and indirect taxes as a percentage of total market income by market income decile, aggregated by income group. Indirect tax incidence is not available for OECD countries. CIT = corporate income tax; GDP = gross domestic product; HICs = high-income countries; LICs = low-income countries; LMICs = lower-middle-income countries; OECD = Organisation for Economic Co-operation and Development; PIT = personal income tax; SSC = social security contribution; UMICs = upper-middle-income countries; VAT = value added tax.

FIGURE O.11

Poorer economies spend less on transfers than on subsidies, which benefit the poor less

a. Subsidy and social protection spending as a share of GDP

b. Cash transfers and subsidies as a share of total benefits, by income decile

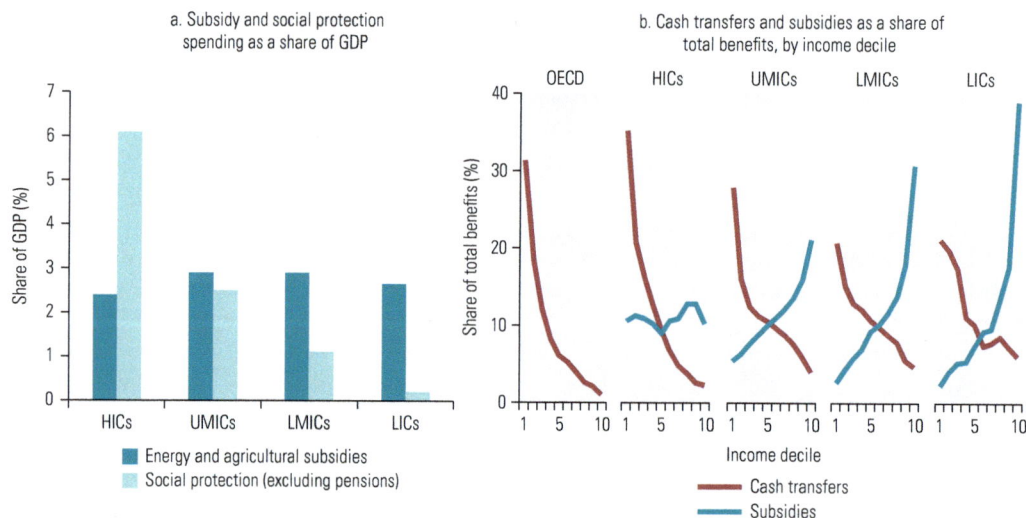

Legend (panel a):
- Energy and agricultural subsidies
- Social protection (excluding pensions)

Legend (panel b):
- Cash transfers
- Subsidies

Sources: Agricultural subsidies: International Organisations Consortium for Measuring the Policy Environment for Agriculture database, http://www.ag-incentives.org/; energy subsidies: International Institute for Sustainable Development, https://www.iisd.org/; social protection: World Bank, BOOST Open Budget Portal, https://www.worldbank.org/en/programs/boost-portal, and International Monetary Fund, Government Finance Statistics database, https://data.imf.org/gfs; cash transfers and subsidies as a share of total benefits: CEQ Institute, CEQ Data Center on Fiscal Redistribution, https://commitmentoequity.org/datacenter; OECD data; World Bank data.
Note: Panel a compares spending on energy and agricultural subsidies with spending on social protection (excluding pensions) as a share of gross domestic product (GDP), aggregated by income group. Panel b shows transfers and subsidies as a share of total benefits by market income decile, aggregated by income group. Subsidy incidence is not available for OECD countries. GDP = gross domestic product; HICs = high-income countries; LICs = low-income countries; LMICs = lower-middle-income countries; OECD = Organisation for Economic Co-operation and Development; UMICs = upper-middle-income countries.

16

depend for support in contrast to targeted transfers. However, the high share of benefits that goes to the rich points to the need to develop systems that can deliver transfers more broadly. Increasingly, LMICs and LICs are developing stronger transfer systems that can reach more households, and important advances were made during the response to COVID-19.

3. Prioritizing effective fiscal spending, particularly in a fiscally constrained environment, is challenging

Some of the highest-impact fiscal decisions made by governments involve how to allocate spending to support long-run income growth for households. Good examples are investments in health, education, roads, electricity, and R&D—especially investments that the private sector cannot or will not make. These investments usually attempt to address market failures or provide public goods. When these policies benefit households at the bottom of the income distribution, their impact on poverty and inequality is large. Conversely, revenue can be raised in a way that negatively affects long-run growth and thus has a negative impact on poverty (see box O.3).

Recent work underscores this point and shows that the highest-value policies are often those with long-run impacts. For example, spending that invests in a child's early development can be transformative and can set the stage for a lifetime of higher earnings (Hendren and Sprung-Keyser 2020; Holla et al. 2021). Delaying the Green Revolution for 10 years would have produced a cumulative loss equivalent to one year of global GDP (Gollin, Hansen, and Wingender 2021). Recent work also highlights that context matters. The value of investing in a cash transfer, for example, depends on the return to beneficiaries' subsequent investments in, for example, children's education; on the impacts of transfers on economic activity in the local economy; and on the ability of the government to capture through taxes a share of any income growth that ultimately results from higher educational attainment.

BOX O.3

Tools that help to prioritize fiscal policies

Anyone assessing the impact of any given fiscal policy—both tax and spending—on poverty and equity must seek answers to two key questions:

1. Who is benefiting from or paying for a given fiscal policy and to what degree? Answering this question is an essential first step in assessing the distributional implications of fiscal policy. In this report, the results from the Commitment to Equity (CEQ) methodology used to conduct fiscal incidence analysis are collated and analyzed for 94 countries.
2. What is the value of this spending in terms of its long-term benefits for beneficiaries, nonbeneficiaries, and government revenue? The concept of the marginal value of public funds (MVPF), a systematic way of determining this value, has resurfaced in recent years and is being applied to a vast range of policies in the United States. It is now also being used more broadly, and in this report it is applied to selected interventions in low- and middle-income settings.

Often, a discussion of the impacts of fiscal policies on poverty and inequality focuses only on answering the first question, but answers to both questions are needed to properly assess the full set of welfare impacts. This information helps governments choose policies. A welfare judgment is needed as well: how much does a society value an additional dollar in the hands of the beneficiaries of one policy versus the beneficiaries of another? In some cases, the trade-off appears quite straightforward: it is between a policy with a high MVPF appropriately targeting the poor versus a policy with a low MVPF targeting the rich. The choice is not always this clear, but even when it is the high-MVPF policy is not always chosen, perhaps reflecting the challenge of incorporating long-run benefits into policy decisions or the specific political economy of a given country.

However, beneficial policies can be hard to prioritize precisely because their benefits accrue over the long term and are not realized immediately. For politicians, this time frame does not align with their political realities—they need to show immediate results to stay in power. So they often underinvest in areas such as health, education, and R&D. Similarly, it is hard for governments to give priority to preparing for the next crisis, even though this can be a cost-effective way of safeguarding progress. Politicians receive greater political gain from showcasing their support during a crisis instead of investing to avoid or mitigate the next one.

In a constrained fiscal space, focusing on high-value policies becomes even more important. In times of crisis and high interest rates, it is difficult to prioritize spending with long-run gains. For that reason, health and education spending are often cut during crises (Al-Samarrai et al. 2021; Mohseni-Cheraghlou 2016). Selecting and protecting high-value spending and tax policies are essential to ensuring that fiscal policy maximizes its welfare impact.

Three sets of policy priorities

This report concludes with a discussion of three policy priorities that reflect both the lessons learned from this analysis as well as the urgent need to foster a robust and inclusive recovery.

1. Spending for today: Reorienting spending away from subsidies to provide income support and stimulate growth

Avoiding overly rapid withdrawal of income support

In 2021 and early 2022, it became clear that income support had been withdrawn too quickly from some vulnerable groups for whom employment and earnings were still much lower than before the COVID-19 crisis. Higher food and energy prices were hurting many of these same households, such as the urban poor. The average duration of COVID-19 support programs was four and a half months, but the majority of programs lasted less than three months, and nearly half of new programs were one-off transfers. Gentilini et al. (2022) estimate that only 21 percent of programs were still active in early 2022. In Brazil, emergency transfers were reduced significantly in 2021. This drop, combined with a labor market that had not yet fully recovered, resulted in an increase in poverty of 6 percentage points from 2020 to 2021 (World Bank 2022a). In Indonesia, although a second round of fiscal support measures was introduced in 2021, reaching more households than the support provided in 2020, the size of the transfers was less generous and the impact on poverty more muted.

Income support is typically needed until growth recovers. However, such support need not involve much greater total spending, provided the effectiveness of social spending can be improved. Reorienting spending away from subsidies to more targeted forms of social protection will have a big impact on those who need it most. Subsidies may appear to be a solution to the current challenge of rising food and energy prices and their impacts on the poor. Subsidies can also be politically popular because the benefits tend to be widely distributed. However, this popularity makes subsidies an expensive way of targeting support to poor households. Fiscal incidence analysis across low- and middle-income countries shows that about half of spending on energy subsidies goes to the richest 20 percent, who consume more energy and receive larger per capita benefits.

Cash transfers are a more effective mechanism for supporting poor and vulnerable groups affected by high energy prices: more than 60 percent of spending on cash transfers goes to the bottom 40 percent (figure O.11, panel b). Like subsidies, cash transfers, which have a broader beneficiary base, can have greater political support—but also a higher price tag—than very targeted programs. However, unlike subsidies, the benefit values do not increase for richer households. That limits the diversion of scarce resources to those not in need. Furthermore, there is little evidence that subsidies offer long-run beneficial impacts, but increasing evidence that cash transfers can help households make crucial long-run investments—such as in educating children. Transfers may also stimulate local economic activity and increase government revenue through higher indirect tax revenue in both the short and long run. Implementing this reorientation is possible. Indonesia, for example, successfully reoriented its social assistance away from subsidies and toward an expanded conditional cash transfer program with a greater redistributive impact. The path to reform was not always straight, but progress was accompanied by political coalition-building and increasingly successful upticks in direct support to poor and vulnerable households (Beaton, Lontoh, and Wai-Poi 2017). Analysis of subsidy reforms in the Dominican Republic, Ghana, and Jordan also highlights the importance of political maneuvering and establishing direct transfer delivery systems for use upon the removal of subsidies (Inchauste and Victor 2017).

Kick-starting income growth

Spending and investments to immediately kick-start economic growth in countries struggling to recover from the COVID-19 crisis—many of which were experiencing low growth prior to the crisis—is an urgent priority. Again, such support need not imply spending more if more effective spending is pursued. Often fiscal spending to promote income growth in the short run is in the form of subsidies to firms and farmers. However, spending that directly addresses market failures is often more cost-effective in the long run than subsidizing behavior. Two examples illustrate this.

Increasing productivity and employment in enterprises should be a priority to address employment losses, particularly in urban areas. Fiscal support of firms in LICs and MICs often takes the form of tax expenditures—indeed, 40 percent of tax expenditures go to firms in LICs and MICs (Redonda, von Haldenwang, and Aliu 2021). However, the evidence on the effectiveness of tax expenditures is mixed. Recent evaluations of support to small and medium enterprises reveal that customized business services and management training can have a high immediate and sustained impact on firms' profits when implemented well (McKenzie 2021; McKenzie et al. 2021; Quinn and Woodruff 2019).

Increasing agricultural production in the face of rising input prices can yield important benefits. Input subsidies increase agricultural production in the short run, but they distort incentives and come with long-run costs for the natural resource base. In MICs, agricultural input subsidies are large, amounting to about 5 percent of the value of agricultural production (FAO, UNDP, and UNEP 2021). However, farmers' investments are based not only on anticipated input prices, but also on output prices, knowledge of how best to invest, and access to credit, insurance, and labor markets (Duflo, Kremer, and Robinson 2008; Rosenzweig and Udry 2020). As a result, well-designed policies in extension and marketing support can increase investment and productivity among smallholder farmers in LICs and MICs (Bridle et al. 2019). Unlike spending on subsidies, these fiscal policies can result in long-run increases in agricultural income.

2. Spending for tomorrow: Prioritizing spending with long-run impacts (even in crisis times)

When fiscal space is tight, it is essential to focus on high-value policies that help countries implement their social welfare contract (box O.3). The right policy choices will differ across contexts, but long-run benefits should factor into those choices, even during a fiscal crisis, despite the fact that benefits will only be realized later.

Investing in long-run growth

COVID-19 has imposed heavy costs on the next generation's quality of life. Reducing these future costs must be an immediate priority. Although specific interventions to remediate these negative effects are discussed elsewhere (see, for example, World Bank, forthcoming b), the influence of learning losses on future income growth suggests high returns to policies that promote learning catch-up. In addition, investments in R&D and some high-value infrastructure can yield very high long-run returns.

Preparing for the next crisis

Spending today on preparing for future crises can also yield long-run benefits. The pandemic has demonstrated tragically that years of progress in reducing poverty can disappear quickly when countries cannot mount a good fiscal response to a major reversal. Crisis financial planning will equip countries with a strategic plan for unleashing the financial tools—contingency instruments, reserve funds, and budget reallocation plans—that can deliver the amount and timing of financing required in a crisis. Key elements of such a plan include the following:

- *Expand the reach of automatic stabilizers.* In countries where the informal sector is large, stabilizers may take the form of employment guarantee schemes (if the supply of work in these schemes can be scaled up) and transfers indexed to weather or prices, such as in the Kenya Livestock Insurance Program, which protects pastoralists in northern Kenya from drought.

- *Set up adaptive cash transfer programs.* Such programs can be scaled up automatically through preapproved protocols backed by social registries, open enrollment protocols, and digital payment systems in response to a crisis trigger. But scaling up will require data that capture the severity of a crisis as it unfolds and should complement data in social registries that identify not just the near-poor, but also those affected by the crisis. Examples of these data are not only traditionally defined economic measures, but also data that convey important features such as population mobility or satellite-based ground cover data that can relay information on flooding and soil moisture.

Investing in data and research to guide future investments

Better data—especially on the costs of policy implementation—are needed to prioritize well-targeted, high-value fiscal spending. Greater investments in evaluations of priority policies implemented at scale are also needed—particularly, long-run evaluations or evaluations that use good proxy indicators of long-run outcomes (Athey, Imbens, and Kang 2019). More fiscal incidence analysis is also needed, especially of productive investments such as in infrastructure, corporate subsidies and tax exemptions, and sectoral specific spending (such as on agriculture). In addition, gaps in the tax incidence analysis of the informal sector, top incomes, corporate tax, property tax, and tariffs should be closed wherever possible.

3. When needed, raise revenue without making the poor worse off

Greater mobilization of domestic resources is also important and can contribute to increased fiscal space in the short run. Poorer countries collect far less tax revenue than richer countries. LICs collect 11 percent of GDP in taxes—well below the 32 percent of GDP collected by OECD high-income countries. Differences in tax revenue reflect differences in state capacity and development (Besley and Persson 2013).[6] Likewise, public spending rates are much lower in poorer countries.

What steps can countries take to raise revenue in a way that reduces inequality while not increasing poverty? Because the level of tax a state can collect is partly determined by trust in the state and the level and quality of the services it delivers, the state cannot change tax revenue sources quickly. However, some fiscal reforms do offer increasingly feasible options for raising revenue, in part due to improvements in digital technology. If implemented well, these reforms can be high value and not put the poor out of pocket. The approach for each country will depend on its income level and economic structure, but there are three options countries can pursue:

1. *Increase property taxation and newer forms of progressive taxation—such as health and carbon taxes.*

- Property taxes are seldom collected in LICs and MICs, even though they play a big role in advanced economies. These taxes typically have little impact on poor people because they target property owners. But in countries in which poor households do own property (such as farmers who own a small plot of land), the rates can be designed to have little impact on the poor. Increasing property taxation requires cadaster investments, new valuation methods, and coordination between local and central governments. These, in turn, can require large up-front investments in implementation capacity, which reduces the initial net revenue gain. Technology can help. In Kigali, Rwanda, for example, drones have been used to update urban cadasters.

- Health taxes that take the form of indirect taxes on tobacco, alcohol, and sugary beverages may seem regressive and small, but they are actually progressive over a taxpayer's lifetime and offer large fiscal gains once health benefits are factored in. These taxes are also relatively easy to implement.

- Finally, the urgency stemming from climate change implies that fiscal policies to reduce carbon dioxide emissions and encourage clean energy use should be considered. There is strong evidence—mostly from HICs—that carbon taxes reduce emissions, and little evidence that they negatively affect GDP growth and employment (Dussaux 2020; Martin, de Preux, and Wagner 2014; Metcalf and Stock 2020; Misch and Wingender 2021; Schroder 2021). Cross-country analysis suggests that carbon taxes can raise revenue without increasing inequality in low- and middle-income countries (Dorband et al. 2019), but poor households must also pay them, so transfers are needed to compensate. Each of these tax categories will disproportionately affect some groups (such as urban property owners, alcohol beverage producers, and carbon-intensive industries), and so implementing these reforms will not always be easy.

2. *Improve the progressivity of the personal income tax (PIT) and corporate tax.* In some UMICs, increasing the progressivity of PIT could be as straightforward as revising tax rates and could be implemented in the short run. In many low- and middle-income countries, increasing the PIT's progressivity would require investing in administrative data systems and long-term monitoring to observe all the income sources of those at the top of the income distribution (including entrepreneurial activity and capital income). A corporate income tax is likely to be progressive and is an important backstop to the PIT, which is already in place in many LICs and MICs. In all countries, it may be more useful to reassess the tax incentives offered to large firms and multinationals and to formalize medium-size informal firms. Tax incentives are the product of negotiations between large firms and governments, and so they can be large, hard to change, and not always of high social value.

3. *Consider indirect taxation and accompanying direct transfers that offset negative effects.* In the short run, LICs and MICs will be unable to generate much tax income from the second option because of the high levels of informality in the economy. Although development of a more vibrant formal sector is important in these economies, increasing revenue in the short run will often require higher indirect taxation (if the rates are not too high). Even though these indirect sources of taxation are less regressive in LICs, they still constitute a large share of the income of the poor, and they do not help address inequality. Increases in indirect taxes will have to be accompanied by increases in direct transfers to offset the effects of tax increases on poverty. As direct transfers are increased, it is essential that they target households at the bottom end of the consumption distribution to offset the impact of any increases in indirect taxation.

In the long run, better debt management will be essential to increase countries' fiscal space for recovery from the pandemic and for responding to ongoing and future crises. *World*

Development Report 2022: Finance for an Equitable Recovery describes steps that can be adopted for debt management. These include taking action to proactively reduce exposure to risks that threaten to worsen public debt, such as pursuing regulatory reform in financial markets, improving debt transparency, and implementing a common framework for debt restructuring or relief (World Bank 2022b).

Finally, increasing the efficiency of spending is also essential. More-efficient public administration (such as improvements in procurement processes and incentives for public sector managers) can increase, in turn, the efficiency and quality of public spending and raise the value delivered for every expenditure.

Good fiscal policy is essential to correct course, but more will be needed

If implemented today, ambitious fiscal reforms designed to promote growth while also reducing inequality could eventually return poverty reduction efforts to the prepandemic trend. In general, increasing the progressivity of tax and spending is more effective for extreme poverty reduction in UMICs than in LMICs and LICs. In other words, a switch to more progressive fiscal policy will enable most UMICs to return to the prepandemic trajectory. For LICs, however, promoting growth through fiscal choices likely achieves more rapid poverty reduction over the medium run. Given the limits of fiscal policy, other national policy reforms will be needed to stimulate growth—particularly to boost the incomes of the poorest households. Supportive global actions will be needed as well. Even if the course correction proves insufficient to end extreme poverty by 2030, the shift must begin now for the sake of a lasting recovery from the overlapping crises of today.

Notes

1. The report presents official poverty numbers for 2019 for the first time and shows that the world entered the COVID-19 crisis in a weak position from the point of view of global poverty reduction. The global poverty headcount rate fell to 8.4 percent in 2019. Although continuing to fall, the drivers of progress that reduced the count of poor people in the world by more than 1 billion from 1990 to 2013 are no longer present, such as the fast growth in countries with a large share of the global poor during this period—in particular, China. Extreme poverty reduction progressed more slowly from 2014 to 2019. Although the pace of poverty reduction remained constant at higher poverty lines, that meant negligible progress on reducing the *number* of poor against the upper-middle-income country poverty line of US$6.85.

2. This exercise was conducted for 60 countries with diverse characteristics, using the country-specific societal poverty lines.

3. The details of these simulations are in Mahler et al. (2022) and use results from Artuc et al. (2022).

4. The report focuses on the fiscal topics of raising revenue in the short and medium term and reorienting spending toward protection and long-run growth. Technical feasibility is a key prism through which policy is recommended. However, the true feasibility of sustained and effective reform is reliant on ensuring political support. Although this report does not delve into what makes a reform politically feasible (something that has to be determined on a country-by-country basis), the analysis and tools discussed here allow a clear identification of winners and losers from any reform.

5. This occurs even though indirect taxes are far less regressive (and can even be progressive) in countries with large informal economies since, in informal economies, purchases are often not recorded so the amount that can be collected from indirect taxes is also lower.

6. For this reason, there is no clear optimal tax-to-GDP ratio across all countries, although some evidence suggests a tipping point between 12 and 13 percent of GDP above which growth and poverty reduction are faster (Gaspar, Jaramillo, and Wingender 2016).

References

Al-Samarrai, Samer, Pedro Cerdan-Infantes, Aliya Bigarinova, Juanita Bodmer, Marianne Joy Anacleto Vital, Manos Antoninis, Bilal Fouad Barakat, et al. 2021. *Education Finance Watch 2021* (English). Washington, DC: World Bank Group.

Aminjonov, U., O. Bargain, and T. Bernard. 2021. "Gimme Shelter: Social Distancing and Income Support in Times of Pandemic." IZA Discussion Paper No. 14967, Institute of Labour Economics, University of Bonn, Germany.

Artuc, Erhan, Guillermo Falcone, Guido Porto, and Bob Rijkers. 2022. "War-Induced Food Price Inflation Imperils the Poor." *VOX EU CEPR* (blog), April 1, 2022. https://voxeu.org/article/war-induced-food-price-inflation-imperils-poor.

Athey, S., R. Chetty, G. W. Imbens, and H. Kang. 2019. "The Surrogate Index: Combining Short-Term Proxies to Estimate Long-Term Treatment Effects More Rapidly and Precisely." NBER Working Paper 26463, National Bureau of Economic Research, Cambridge, MA.

Beaton, Chris, Lucky Lontoh, and Matthew Wai-Poi. 2017. "Indonesia: Pricing Reforms, Social Assistance, and the Importance of Perceptions." In *The Political Economy of Energy Subsidy Reform*, edited by Gabriela Inchauste and David Victor. Washington, DC: World Bank.

Beazley, Rodolfo, Marta Marzi, and Rachael Steller. 2021. *Drivers of Timely and Large-Scale Cash Responses to COVID-19: What Does the Data Say?* Social Protection Approaches to COVID-19: Expert Advice (SPACE). London: DAI Global UK Ltd.

Besley, T., and T. Persson. 2013. "Taxation and Development." In *Handbook of Public Economics*, vol. 5, edited by A. J. Auerbach, R. Chetty, M. Feldstein, and E. Saez. Amsterdam: North Holland.

Bhalla, Surjit, Karan Bhasin, and Arvind Virmani. 2022. "Pandemic, Poverty, and Inequality: Evidence from India." IMF Working Paper No. 2022/069, International Monetary Fund, Washington, DC.

Bolt, Jutta, and Jan Luiten van Zanden. 2020. "Maddison Style Estimates of the Evolution of the World Economy: A New 2020 Update." Maddison-Project Working Paper WP-15. https://www.rug.nl/ggdc/historicaldevelopment/maddison/publications/wp15.pdf.

Bridle, Leah, Jeremy Magruder, Craig McIntosh, and Tavneet Suri. 2019. "Experimental Insights on the Constraints to Technology Adoption." Working paper, Agricultural Technology Adoption Initiative, Abdul Latif Jameel Poverty Action Lab, Massachusetts Institute of Technology, Cambridge, MA; and Center for Effective Global Action, University of California, Berkeley.

Dorband, Ira, Michael Jakob, Matthias Kalkuhl, and Jan Christoph Steckel. 2019. "Poverty and Distributional Effects of Carbon Pricing in Low- and Middle-Income Countries: A Global Comparative Analysis." *World Development* 115: 246–57.

Duflo, Esther, Michael Kremer, and Jonathan Robinson. 2008. "How High Are Rates of Return to Fertilizer? Evidence from Field Experiments in Kenya." *American Economic Review* 98 (2): 482–88.

Dussaux, D. 2020. "The Joint Effects of Energy Prices and Carbon Taxes on Environmental and Economic Performance: Evidence from the French Manufacturing Sector." OECD Environment Working Paper 154, Organisation for Economic Co-operation and Development, Paris.

FAO (Food and Agriculture Organization), UNDP (United Nations Development Programme), and UNEP (United Nations Environment Programme). 2021. "A Multi-Billion-Dollar Opportunity—Repurposing Agricultural Support to Transform Food Systems." Rome: FAO. https://doi.org/10.4060/cb6562en.

Gaspar, Vitor, Laura Jaramillo, and Philippe Wingender. 2016. "Tax Capacity and Growth: Is There a Tipping Point?" IMF Working Paper 16/234, International Monetary Fund, Washington, DC.

Gentilini, Ugo, Mohamed Bubaker, Alsafi Almenfi, T. M. M. Iyengar, Yuko Okamura, John Austin Downes, Pamela Dale, et al. 2022. *Social Protection and Jobs Responses to COVID-19:*

A Real-Time Review of Country Measures. Washington, DC: World Bank.

Gollin, D., C. W. Hansen, and A. M. Wingender. 2021. "Two Blades of Grass: The Impact of the Green Revolution." *Journal of Political Economy* 129 (8): 2344–84.

Hendren, Nathaniel, and Ben Sprung-Keyser. 2020. "A Unified Welfare Analysis of Government Policies." *Quarterly Journal of Economics* 135 (3): 1209–1318.

Heuveline, Patrick. 2022. "Global and National Declines in Life Expectancy: An End-of-2021 Assessment." *Population and Development Review* 48 (1): 31–50.

Holla, Alaka, Magdalena Bendini, Lelys Dinarte, and Iva Trako. 2021. "Is Investment in Preprimary Education Too Low? Lessons from (Quasi) Experimental Evidence across Countries." Policy Research Working Paper 9723, World Bank, Washington, DC.

Inchauste, Gabriela, and David Victor. 2017. *The Political Economy of Energy Reform.* Washington, DC: World Bank.

Kose, M. Ayhan, Franziska Ohnsorge, Carmen M. Reinhart, and Kenneth S. Rogoff. 2022. "The Aftermath of Debt Surges." *Annual Review of Economics* 14.

Loayza, Norman V. 2020. "Costs and Trade-Offs in the Fight against the COVID-19 Pandemic: A Developing Country Perspective." Research and Policy Brief 35, World Bank, Washington, DC.

Mahler, Daniel Gerszon, Nishant Yonzan, Ruth Hill, Christoph Lakner, Haoyu Wu, and Nobuo Yoshida. 2022. "Pandemic, Prices, and Poverty." *Data Blog,* April 2022, World Bank, Washington, DC.

Mahler, Daniel Gerszon, Nishant Yonzan, and Christoph Lakner [randomized order]. Forthcoming. "The Impact of COVID-19 on Global Inequality and Poverty." World Bank, Washington DC.

Martin, Ralf, Laure B. de Preux, and Ulrich J. Wagner. 2014. "The Impact of a Carbon Tax on Manufacturing: Evidence from Microdata." *Journal of Public Economics* 117: 1–14.

Martin, Will, and Kym Anderson. 2011. "Export Restrictions and Price Insulation during Commodity Price Booms." Policy Research Working Paper 5645, World Bank, Washington, DC.

McKenzie, David. 2021. "Small Business Training to Improve Management Practices in Developing Countries: Reassessing the Evidence for 'Training Doesn't Work.'" *Oxford Review of Economic Policy* 37 (2): 276–301.

McKenzie, David, Christopher Woodruff, Kjetil Bjorvatn, Miriam Bruhn, Jing Cai, Juanita Gonzalez-Uribe, Simon Quinn, et al. 2021. "Training Entrepreneurs." *VoxDevLit* 1 (2).

Metcalf, Gilbert E., and James H. Stock. 2020. "Measuring the Macroeconomic Impact of Carbon Taxes." *American Economic Review Papers and Proceedings* 110: 101–06.

Misch, Florian, and Philippe Wingender. 2021. "Revisiting Carbon Leakage." Working Paper No. 2021/207, International Monetary Fund, Washington, DC.

Mohseni-Cheraghlou, A. 2016. "The Aftermath of Financial Crises: A Look on Human and Social Wellbeing." *World Development* 87: 88–106.

Quinn, Simon R., and Christopher Woodruff. 2019. "Experiments and Entrepreneurship in Developing Countries." *Annual Review of Economics* 11: 225–48.

Ravallion, Martin. 2022. "Filling a Gaping Hole in the World Bank's Global Poverty Measures: New Estimates of Poverty in India since 2011." Centre for Global Development Notes, Centre for Global Development, Washington, DC. https://www.cgdev.org/publication/filling-gaping-hole-world-banks-global-poverty-measures-new-estimates-poverty-india#:~:text=Ravallion%20(2016)%20proposes%20that%20the,zero%20at%20the%20poverty%20line.

Redonda, Agustin, Christian von Haldenwang, and Flurim Aliu. 2021. "Companion Paper to the Global Tax Expenditures Database." Global Tax Expenditures Database, German Development Institute.

Rosenzweig, Mark R., and Christoper Udry. 2020. "External Validity in a Stochastic World: Evidence from Low-Income Countries." *Review of Economic Studies* 87 (1): 343–81.

Sandefur, Justin. 2022. "The Great Indian Poverty Debate, 2.0." *Centre for Global Development Blog,* April 19, 2022. https://www.cgdev.org/blog/great-indian-poverty-debate-20.

Schroder, C. 2021. "Regime-Dependent Environmental Tax Multipliers: Evidence from

75 Countries." Policy Research Working Paper 9640, World Bank, Washington, DC.

Sinha Roy, Sutirtha, and Roy van der Weide. 2022. "Poverty in India Has Declined over the Last Decade but Not as Much as Previously Thought." Policy Research Working Paper 9994, World Bank, Washington, DC.

WHO (World Health Organization). 2022. "Global Excess Deaths Associated with COVID-19, January 2020–December 2021." https://www.who.int/data/stories/global-excess-deaths-associated-with-covid-19-january-2020-december-2021.

World Bank. 2013. *World Development Report 2014: Risk and Opportunity—Managing Risk for Development.* Washington, DC: World Bank.

https://openknowledge.worldbank.org/handle/10986/16092.

World Bank. 2022a. *Brazil Poverty and Equity Assessment: Looking Ahead of Two Crises.* Washington, DC: World Bank.

World Bank. 2022b. *World Development Report 2022: Finance for an Equitable Recovery.* Washington, DC: World Bank.

World Bank. Forthcoming a. *Europe and Central Asia Economic Update, Fall 2022: Social Protection for Recovery.* Europe and Central Asia Economic Update 14. Washington, DC: World Bank.

World Bank. Forthcoming b. *Collapse and Recovery: How the COVID-19 Pandemic Eroded Human Capital and What to Do About It.* Washington, DC: World Bank.

Part 1.
Progress on Poverty and Shared Prosperity

Global Poverty: The Biggest Setback in Decades

Summary

Poverty and Shared Prosperity 2020: Reversals of Fortune *predicted that the COVID-19 pandemic would be a once-in-a-generation shock, causing the first increase in global poverty in at least 25 years and reversing decades of global poverty reduction (World Bank 2020a). Two years later, this chapter draws on a considerable body of data to show that 2020 was indeed a historic reversal in global progress on reducing extreme poverty and inequality. The number of people living in extreme poverty likely rose by 11 percent in 2020, pushing poverty 1.2 percentage points higher than projections going into the year (extreme poverty had been expected to fall). Thus 90 million more people were living in extreme poverty in 2020 than had been forecast.*

Since 2020, progress in reducing poverty has been slow and highly uneven. Nowcasts reveal that poverty reduction resumed in 2021, but only at prepandemic rates and not fast enough to recover the ground lost in 2020. Projections in 2022 suggest the pace of poverty reduction will further stall as the global growth prospects dim because of the Russian invasion of Ukraine and a growth slowdown in China. Higher food and energy prices hurt the poor in the short run and may increase the number of poor, although higher prices may have positive income effects in the long run because many poor households are net producers of food or earn their income in the agriculture sector.

In presenting the World Bank's first official global poverty estimates for 2019, this chapter describes how the world entered the COVID-19 crisis already in a weak position from a global poverty reduction perspective. The target of ending poverty in 2030 was already slipping out of reach, and extreme poverty reduction progressed more slowly between 2014 and 2019 than previously. The substantial shock in 2020 and the weak recovery of losses since then have further set back progress by four years. By 2030, the poverty rate is expected to be 7 percent, much higher than the target of 3 percent. Reaching the target looks increasingly hard. There is an urgent need to correct course.

Chapter 1 online annexes available at http://hdl.handle.net/10986/37739:
1A. PIP Data and Methodology for the Measurement of Extreme Poverty; 1B. Additional Results on the Shift to 2017 PPPs; 1C. Global, Regional, and Country Estimates at the US$2.15 Poverty Line; 1D. Global and Regional Estimates at Higher Poverty Lines: US$3.65 and US$6.85 a Day; 1E. Societal Poverty; 1F. Nowcasts of Global Poverty; and 1G. Nowcasting Poverty in 2020 in India.

Setting the scene: Poverty on the eve of the pandemic

Extreme poverty was falling at a slower place

The world has changed dramatically during the last two years, and these changes have profoundly affected the breadth and depth of poverty. The starting point for documenting these impacts is the World Bank's official regional and global poverty estimates for 2019, the eve of the pandemic. According to these estimates, 8.4 percent of the global population (648 million people) lived in extreme poverty prior to the start of the pandemic. On average, each person living in extreme poverty lived on 30 percent less income per day than the international poverty line. These numbers represent lives lived in great hardship, and at the start of the pandemic these numbers were well above where they had to be to eradicate the scourge of extreme poverty by 2030.[1]

Although too high, these numbers represent a continued decline in global poverty. Global poverty was 1.2 percentage points lower in 2019 than in 2017. However, these numbers reveal that progress was slowing before the pandemic hit. From 1990 to 2013, the global poverty rate declined from 37.8 percent to 11.7 percent, corresponding to over a billion fewer people living in extreme poverty. The end of this period recorded strong poverty reduction: the poverty rate fell, on average, by 1.4 percentage points per year between 2008 and 2013, or 86 million people per year. However, the pace of poverty reduction began to slow around 2014 (figure 1.1). Between 2014 and 2019, the pace of poverty reduction slowed to only 0.6 percentage point per year, or 33 million people per year (see table 1C.1, panel a, in online annex 1C) with South Asia as the only region that maintained a rapid rate of poverty reduction.[2] Thus the pandemic hit a world that was seeing slowing progress toward the 2030 goal of eradicating poverty, as discussed in the 2018 and 2020 editions of *Poverty and Shared Prosperity* (World Bank 2018, 2020a).

The global estimates presented in this edition of *Poverty and Shared Prosperity* incorporate two key updates to the calculations of the global poverty number. First, the report adopts the 2017 purchasing power parities (PPPs), as announced by the World Bank in May 2022 (Filmer, Fu, and Sánchez-Páramo 2022; Jolliffe et al. 2022; Tetteh Baah et al. 2022). The new PPPs use more recent price data for converting country-level household welfare measures into an international

FIGURE 1.1

Global extreme poverty has continued to fall but at a slower rate in recent years

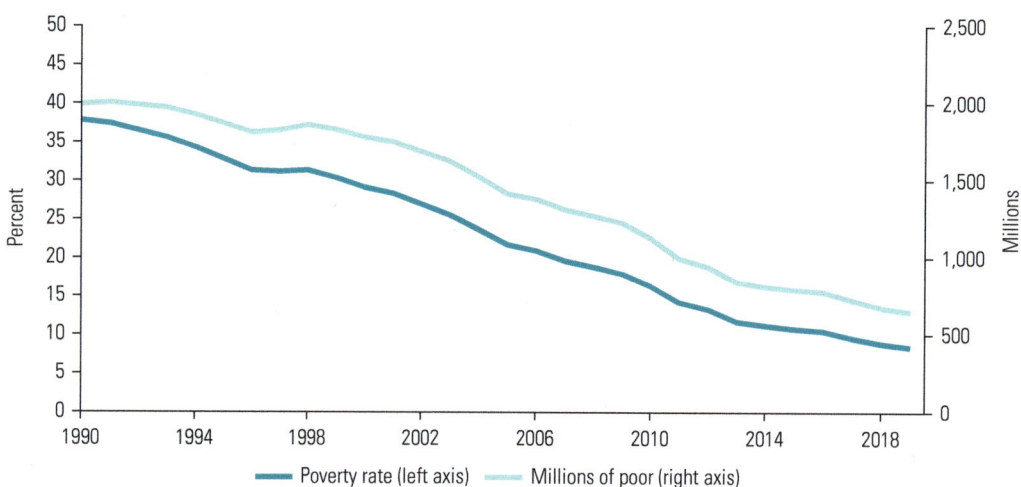

Source: World Bank, Poverty and Inequality Platform, https://pip.worldbank.org.
Note: The figure shows the poverty rate and number of poor at the international poverty line of US$2.15 (2017 PPP) per person, per day. See box 1.1 for more details on the adoption of 2017 PPPs that are used for monetary poverty measures throughout the chapter. PPP = purchasing power parity.

price standard and thus contribute to a better understanding of current living standards around the world. Adopting the 2017 PPPs also affects the derivation of the international poverty line. The global and regional poverty rates in this chapter use the new value of the international poverty line, US$2.15 (revised from the US$1.90 value used with the 2011 PPPs in previous editions of this report). Box 1.1 provides more information on the shift to the 2017 PPPs, and online annex 1B discusses in greater detail the changes in the global and regional poverty estimates stemming from adoption of the new international poverty line. The increase in the international poverty line from US$1.90 to US$2.15 primarily reflects the difference between 2017 and 2011 nominal dollar values. The change in the global poverty rate due to the change in poverty line is thus negligible. Extreme poverty decreases slightly, by 0.3 percentage point, to 8.4 percent, reducing the global count of the extreme poor by 20 million. The trends in global and regional

BOX 1.1

How the new international poverty lines were derived

In May 2020, the International Comparison Program (ICP) released new purchasing power parities (PPPs) based on price data collected in 176 economies in 2017 (World Bank 2020b). Poverty estimates are often updated with new PPP data to reflect new information on price differences across countries. Related statistics such as gross domestic product (GDP) are similarly updated with new PPPs. When switching to a different base year (in this case, 2017), two revisions are made. First, the consumption aggregate of each household is converted into dollars of the new base year using the new price information. Second, the poverty line used to assess whether a household is poor is also updated to the new base year. This box is an overview of the new poverty lines, and further details are available in Jolliffe et al. (2022).

What is the international poverty line?

The international poverty line is a standard that has been used to shape key policy actions on global poverty—see, for example, Sustainable Development Goal 1 (United Nations 2017). In 1990, the World Bank introduced the dollar-a-day poverty line and has since followed the approach of basing the international poverty line on the national poverty lines of some of the poorest countries in the world, expressed in PPPs (World Bank 1990). The global line has been revised each time the ICP has released a new round of PPPs—from US$1.00 (1985 PPP) to US$1.08 (1993 PPP) to US$1.25 (2005 PPP) to US$1.90 (2011 PPP).

The starting point of deriving the international poverty line and the higher absolute poverty lines is a new set of national poverty lines calculated around 2017 and converted to 2017 PPPs.[a] The international poverty line is derived as the median of the national poverty lines of low-income countries (LICs), while the higher absolute poverty lines are the median national poverty lines of lower-middle-income countries (LMICs) and upper-middle-income countries (UMICs). In 2011 PPPs, US$1.90 was the median for LICs, US$3.20 for LMICs, and US$5.50 for UMICs.[b] In 2017 PPPs, US$2.15 was the median national poverty line for LICs; US$3.65 was the median line for LMICs; and US$6.85 was the median for UMICs (see table B1.1.1). The change in the line for UMICs was relatively large, driven by an increase in the real value of national poverty lines in UMICs between 2011 and 2017.[c] One way to show this change in poverty lines is to express the US$1.90, US$3.20, and US$5.50 poverty lines in constant 2017 US dollars and observe real changes in their value between 2011 and 2017. Figure B1.1.1 illustrates the fact that the lower lines are virtually unchanged in real terms, whereas the UMIC line increases significantly, reflecting a *real* increase in the value of the line.

The selection of US$2.15 as the international poverty line is robust to several methodological choices, as Jolliffe et al. (2022) explain in detail. It is robust to using the method that underpinned

(continued)

BOX 1.1

How the new international poverty lines were derived *(continued)*

TABLE B1.1.1

Derivation of global poverty lines, 2011 PPPs versus 2017 PPPs

Country income group	2011 PPPs			2017 PPPs		
	Median (US$)	Rounded (US$)	Number of observations	Median (US$)	Rounded (US$)	Number of observations
Low-income	1.91	1.90	33	2.15	2.15	28
Lower-middle-income	3.21	3.20	32	3.63	3.65	54
Upper-middle-income	5.47	5.50	32	6.85	6.85	37
Total			**97**			**119**

Source: Jolliffe et al. 2022.
Note: PPPs = purchasing power parities.

FIGURE B1.1.1

Poverty lines expressed in constant 2017 US$

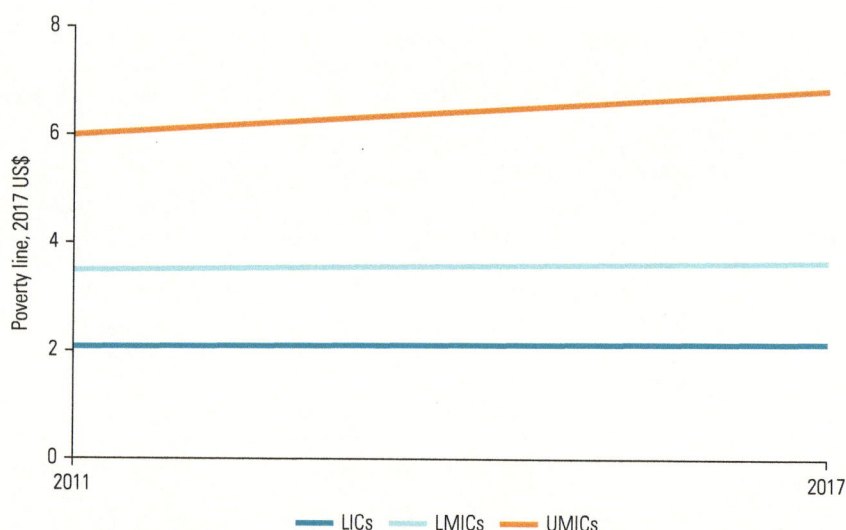

Source: Original calculations based on Jolliffe et al. 2022.
Note: The figure compares the 2011 purchasing power parity (PPP) and 2017 PPP poverty lines when the former are expressed in 2017 US dollars using US inflation from 2011 to 2017. It shows how much of the increase in the lines can be explained by US inflation alone. Note that this does *not* reveal whether the real value of the lines between the two PPP rounds is constant, because changes in the purchasing power of the US relative to other countries from 2011 to 2017 are unaccounted for. For details, see Jolliffe et al. (2022). LICs = low-income countries; LMICs = lower-middle-income countries; UMICs = upper-middle-income countries.

the choice of the US$1.90 line in 2011 PPPs. That method used the national poverty lines from the same set of poorest 15 countries that was used with the 2005 PPPs.[d] This method with the 2017 PPPs results in a poverty line of US$2.10. The current method has several advantages, and it offers a consistent way of deriving the international poverty lines as well as the higher absolute poverty lines.[e] The value of US$2.15 is also robust to choosing different sets of poorest countries.

(continued)

BOX 1.1

How the new international poverty lines were derived *(continued)*

As described in detail in online annex 1B, switching from the 2011 PPPs to the 2017 PPPs and updating the poverty lines accordingly slightly change the estimates of the poverty headcount rate at the global and regional levels. Yet these modifications mask much larger changes in country-level poverty estimates. This issue disproportionately affects countries in western and central Africa—the region in which the largest share of the population lives in countries where the PPPs and consumer price indexes moved very differently between 2011 and 2017, and poverty estimates therefore changed significantly.[f] The 2017 PPP data generally are of higher quality than the 2011 PPP data (Jolliffe et al. 2022; World Bank 2020b). Some countries were affected by severe shocks—including the Ebola crisis and the collapse of commodity prices—when the 2017 PPP data were being collected. For these countries, additional analysis using the detailed microdata that underpin the PPPs may be needed to understand what drives the differences between the 2011 PPPs and 2017 PPPs, as well as the knock-on effects on poverty estimates.

Complementary measures of poverty

The adoption of the new 2017 PPPs also affects two other official poverty measures used by the World Bank: the societal poverty line (SPL) and the multidimensional poverty measure (MPM).[g]

The SPL combines elements of absolute and relative poverty measures, and it captures the notion that the definition of poverty evolves as countries get richer. Jolliffe and Prydz (2021) derive the SPL with the 2011 PPPs as *max*(1.90, \$1.00 + 0.5*Median), where *Median* denotes median income or consumption of the country. With the 2017 PPPs, the SPL is updated to *max*(2.15, \$1.15 + 0.5*Median). The international poverty line remains the floor of the SPL, the intercept term changes from US\$1.00 (2011 PPP) to US\$1.15 (2017 PPP), and the slope parameter remains unchanged.[h] The MPM goes beyond monetary poverty by including two nonmonetary dimensions of well-being in classifying households as multidimensionally poor: access to basic infrastructure and access to education—see chapter 4 in World Bank (2018) and box 1.1 in World Bank (2020a). In the MPM, the international poverty line is used as an indicator for the monetary dimension. Thus a person will be considered poor in the monetary dimension if that person lives on less than US\$2.15 (2017 PPP) a day (an analysis of multidimensional poverty appears in chapter 3).

a. The methodology uses the implicit poverty line approach, first proposed by Jolliffe and Prydz (2016). The authors rely on a data set of survey-based national poverty lines harmonized so they are all in per capita units. The harmonization process involves retrieving the percentiles from income or consumption distributions expressed in PPP per capita terms that correspond to national poverty rates. The national poverty rates are reported in the World Bank's World Development Indicators database (https://databank.worldbank.org/source/world-development-indicators) and rely on countries' own definitions of poverty. Thus the resulting international poverty line reflects the standard of poverty in the poorest countries, but it is also calculated using comparable national poverty measures. Jolliffe and Prydz then selected for each country in this harmonized data set the survey-based poverty line that is closest to the ICP reference year, thereby limiting the sensitivity of the international poverty line to changes in historical consumer price index data. Eighty-four percent of selected surveys were conducted after 2011, and 43 percent were conducted in 2017. More than three-quarters of selected surveys were conducted within three years of 2017. Finally, the subset of national poverty lines is aggregated by income group based on the World Bank's income classification in the survey year. The international poverty line is derived as the median line of all low-income countries.
b. The poverty lines based on 2011 PPPs were derived using two different methodologies. More details can be found in Tetteh Baah et al. (2022) and Jolliffe et al. (2022).
c. The revisions to the lines can be explained not only by PPP updates but also by changes in national poverty lines, changes in income classifications of countries, revisions of welfare aggregates, and the inclusion of new countries and data. The change in the UMIC line is largely explained by real upward shifts in the national poverty lines of those countries after controlling for the other factors. The PPP updates solely explain the changes in the international poverty line and the LMIC line.

(continued)

BOX 1.1

How the new international poverty lines were derived *(continued)*

d. The US$1.90 poverty line was based on national poverty lines of 15 poor countries with data from the 1980s and 1990s (Ferreira, Jolliffe, and Prydz 2015; Ferreira et al. 2016; Ravallion, Chen, and Sangraula 2009). The US$1.90 line is the arithmetic mean of the 15 PPP-based national poverty lines updated from 2005 PPPs to 2011 PPPs.
e. The methodology used to derive the new official poverty lines also addresses some of the concerns raised by experts and scholars after past revisions of the poverty line (Deaton 2010; Klasen et al. 2016; Reddy and Pogge 2010). The first concern was that it may be hard to argue that the sample of countries traditionally used to derive the international poverty line is representative of the poorest countries in the world in more recent years. Moreover, the selection of the 15 countries in the sample lacks statistical support. The selection was based on the empirical finding that, for countries with such low levels of consumption, national poverty lines are not correlated with the per capita household final consumption expenditure. For countries with higher incomes, there is a positive relationship between national poverty lines and per capita household income. With more recent data, however, national poverty lines (in logs) and per capita household final consumption expenditure (in logs) are positively correlated at all levels on consumption (Jolliffe and Prydz 2016). The second concern was that the derivation of the US$1.90 poverty line was highly sensitive to the consumer price indexes available for those countries, which are used to deflate to the ICP reference year. The third concern was that the national poverty lines of the 15 poor countries were not expressed in comparable units, with some in per capita terms and others in adult-equivalent. Finally, expressing the US$1.90 international poverty line as the mean, as opposed to the median, across national poverty lines of a reference group of poorest countries makes it vulnerable to outliers.
f. See Ferreira et al. (2013) and Joliffe et al. (2022) for details.
g. See World Bank (2018, 2020a) for more details on these poverty measures.
h. The analysis in Jolliffe et al. (2022) shows an intercept parameter of US$1.15 and a slope parameter of 50 percent when the same regression model used to derive the original societal poverty line parameters (in 2011 PPPs) is reestimated using more recent data (for circa 2017) in 2017 PPPs. Furthermore, the intercept is expected to change because it is expressed in PPP dollars—see Jolliffe et al. (2022) for details and the impact on global and regional profiles of societal poverty.

poverty using the 2017 PPPs are the same as the trends using the 2011 PPPs. All trends discussed in this chapter are based on the 2017 PPPs.

Second, the global and regional poverty estimates presented in this chapter include new data for India for 2015–19—see box 1.2 and Castaneda Aguilar et al. (2022b) for technical details. Inclusion of these data represents an improvement over the previous edition of this report, where the absence of recent data for India severely limited the measurement of poverty in South Asia.[3] According to the latest poverty estimates for the region, poverty reduction continued between 2014 and 2019. The poverty headcount rate declined from 18 percent in 2014 to 9 percent in 2019—a smaller decline in poverty reduction than what was previously estimated for global poverty measurement purposes and a revision of the global poverty trend (see box 1.2).

These two methodological changes are reflected in the analysis presented in this report. This chapter now turns to analysis of the regional distribution of the poor to better place in context the geographic impacts of the pandemic as well as the differential impacts by income group.

Among regions, extreme poverty remained highly concentrated in Sub-Saharan Africa

In 2019, extreme poverty remained highly concentrated in Sub-Saharan Africa (figure 1.2 and map 1.1) and in fragile and conflict-affected economies. Sub-Saharan Africa accounted for 60 percent of the global poor at the US$2.15 poverty line in 2019 (figure 1.2). Thirty-five percent of the population (389 million) in the region lived below the international poverty line (figure 1.3). People residing in fragile and conflict-affected economies represented about 10 percent of the global population, but almost 40 percent of the global poor—see table 1C.3 in online annex 1C and Corral et al. (2020) for an extensive analysis.

BOX 1.2

New data now available to measure poverty in India

The most recent survey data released by the National Sample Survey Office of India used to measure poverty is the 2011/12 National Sample Survey (NSS). The government decided not to release the 2017/18 NSS round because of concerns about data quality—see box 1.2 in World Bank (2020a). Because of India's size, the lack of recent survey data for the country significantly affects the measurement of global poverty, as was evident in *Poverty and Shared Prosperity 2020*.

This report includes global and regional poverty estimates based on the new household survey data for India for 2015/16, 2016/17, 2017/18, 2018/19, and 2019/20 from the Consumer Pyramids Household Survey (CPHS) conducted by the Centre for Monitoring Indian Economy, a private data company. The household consumption data used for poverty monitoring are based on an analysis by Sinha Roy and van der Weide (2022).

The main advantage of the CPHS data is that they facilitate the measurement of poverty in India for the period 2015–19, thereby considerably improving estimation of poverty in the country and the world in recent years. However, the CPHS data do have some limitations and differ from the official NSS data traditionally used for global poverty monitoring. For example, concerns have been raised about the sampling and the fact that the consumption aggregate is not directly comparable with the NSS (Dreze and Somanchi 2021).

To address these issues, Sinha Roy and van der Weide (2022) make several adjustments to the CPHS data. They reweight the data with the objective of transforming the CPHS into a nationally representative survey and correcting for the sampling biases.[a] In addition, they transform the measured CPHS consumption into an NSS-type consumption measure for each year of data. Sinha Roy and van der Weide also compare their results with a wide range of supplementary data that show broadly similar trends.

Other methods have been employed to estimate the state of poverty in India since 2011. Bhalla Bhasin, and Virmani (2022) use a mixed approach, largely relying on the gross domestic product growth rate along with corollary assumptions to project poverty from the 2011/12 NSS. The methodological differences between Bhalla, Bhasin, and Virmani (2022) and Sinha Roy and van der Weide (2022) have been outlined elsewhere (Ravallion 2022; Sandefur 2022). Because there is widespread agreement that microdata from household surveys are necessary to credibly measure poverty, this report uses the Sinha Roy and van der Weide (2022) methodology. Other published analyses also use the CPHS for assessing recent changes in welfare in India (for example, Gupta, Malani, and Woda 2021). Meanwhile, the National Sample Survey Office is conducting a household survey in 2022 that will provide updated official statistics on poverty for India.

The data reveal that poverty has declined in India since 2011, driven by a larger poverty reduction in rural areas (Sinha Roy and van der Weide 2022). Even though overall poverty has declined, it is by less than what earlier estimates used for global poverty measurement would suggest. Previous estimates suggested a poverty headcount rate at the US$1.90 poverty line of 10.4 percent in 2017, with a 95 percent confidence interval of between 8.1 and 11.3 (World Bank 2020a). The latest estimate based on Sinha Roy and van der Weide (2022) shows that poverty at the US$1.90 poverty line was 13.6 percent in 2017.

The estimates used for this report adopt the 2017 purchasing power parities and show that the national poverty headcount rate at the US$2.15 poverty line in India was 10 percent in 2019/20—12 percent in rural areas and 6 percent in urban areas (see table 1C.2 in online annex 1C).[b] The new data for India also allow the South Asia trend to be published and drive a revision in the poverty trend for South Asia. The poverty headcount rate at the US$2.15 poverty line was 9 percent in South Asia in 2019.

a. The CPHS sample has evolved over time but settled after the first round of data collection in 2014/15. For this reason, the first round of CPHS data covering the period 2014/15 was not added to the World Bank's Global Monitoring Database. Only CPHS-based poverty estimates for survey years in or after 2015/16 are part of the survey data available in the Poverty and Inequality Platform for global poverty monitoring and underlie the regional and global poverty estimates in this report.
b. The lined-up estimate for India that underpins the global and regional poverty aggregates in 2019 is 9.5 percent—10.9 in rural areas and 6.7 percent in urban areas.

FIGURE 1.2

The global extreme poor are concentrated in Sub-Saharan Africa

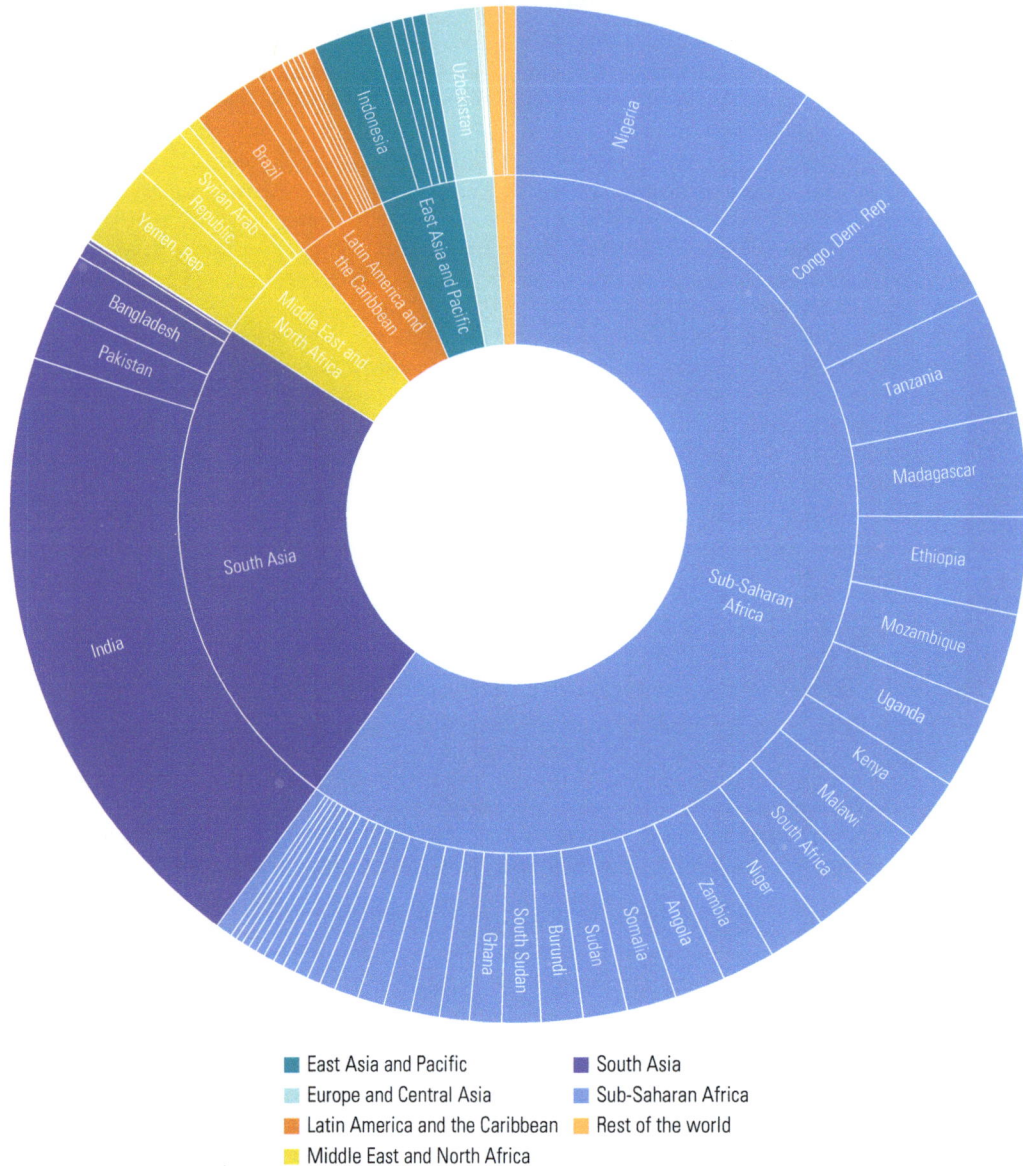

Source: World Bank, Poverty and Inequality Platform, https://pip.worldbank.org.
Note: The figure shows the distribution of the poor population at the US$2.15-a-day poverty line in 2019, by region and economy. For each economy, the number of poor is calculated using the economy-level poverty estimate that underlies the global poverty estimate (see section "Calculating global and regional poverty" in online annex 1A to see how this is calculated) and the population in 2019.

In 2019, countries with the highest poverty rate at the US$2.15-a-day poverty line were mostly in Sub-Saharan Africa

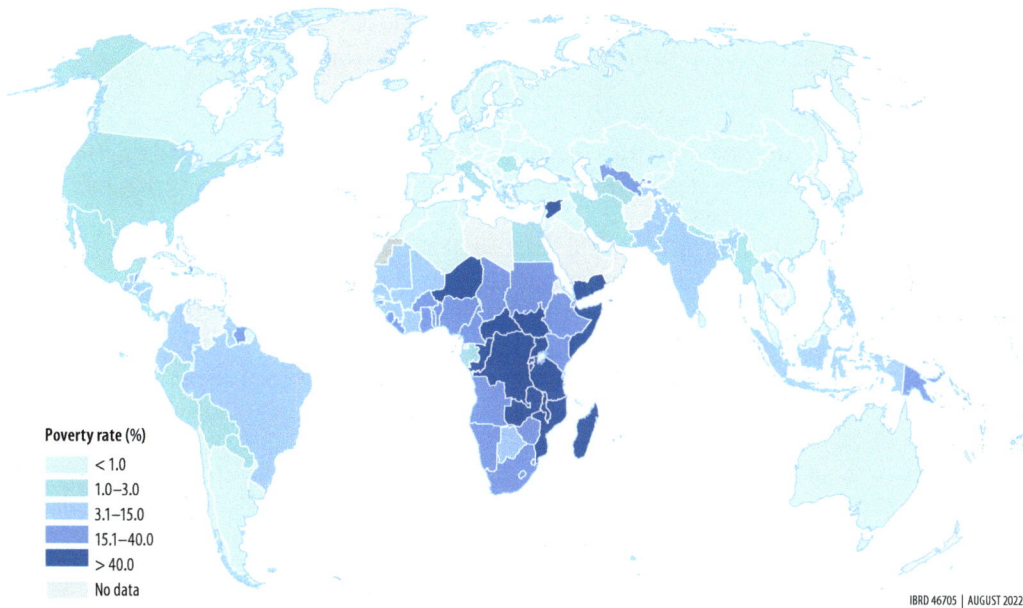

Poverty rate (%)
- < 1.0
- 1.0–3.0
- 3.1–15.0
- 15.1–40.0
- > 40.0
- No data

IBRD 46705 | AUGUST 2022

Source: World Bank, Poverty and Inequality Platform, https://pip.worldbank.org.
Note: The map shows each economy's poverty headcount rate at the US$2.15-a-day poverty line for 2019. Economies without survey data available in the Poverty and Inequality Platform are shown in gray.

From 1990 to 2019, poverty fell in all regions except the Middle East and North Africa

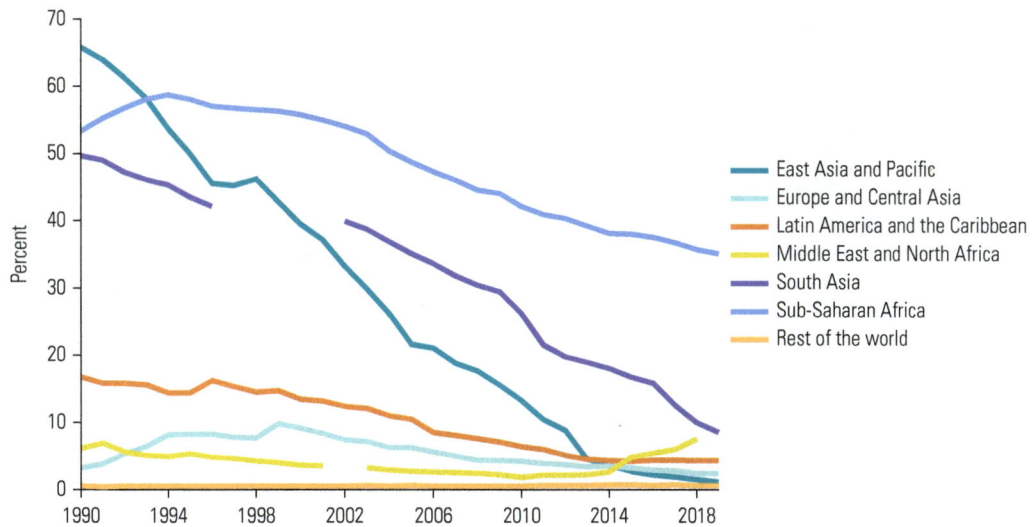

Legend:
- East Asia and Pacific
- Europe and Central Asia
- Latin America and the Caribbean
- Middle East and North Africa
- South Asia
- Sub-Saharan Africa
- Rest of the world

Source: World Bank, Poverty and Inequality Platform, https://pip.worldbank.org.
Note: The figure shows poverty trends at the US$2.15-a-day poverty line, by region, 1990–2019. Poverty estimates are not reported when regional population coverage is below 50 percent within a three-year period before and after the reference year (see online annex 1A).

The regional poverty rate in Sub-Saharan Africa is lower than what was previously reported (Castaneda Aguilar et al. 2022a; World Bank 2020a). The lower rate is largely driven by adoption of the new 2017 PPPs, which reduce the regional poverty rate in 2019 by about 3 percentage points (see online annex 1B). Sub-Saharan Africa shows the largest changes in the levels of poverty when moving from the 2011 PPPs to the 2017 PPPs (Jolliffe et al. 2022).[4] Nevertheless, poverty remains highly concentrated in Sub-Saharan Africa, with a poverty rate that is about four times higher than that of the second-poorest region in the world, and the evidence on the pace of poverty reduction in the region is unaffected. The poverty headcount rate continues to fall, from 37 percent in 2017 to 35 percent in 2019 (figure 1.3). This masks considerable heterogeneity in poverty reduction across countries in Africa, with some countries seeing poverty increasing and others falling. However, high population growth in the region means that the number of people in poverty has increased, from 385 million to 389 million (see table 1C.1, panel c, in online annex 1C).

Sub-Saharan Africa is also the region in which the largest share of the population lives in countries in which the PPPs and consumer price indexes moved very differently between 2011 and 2017, requiring further scrutiny (box 1.1). More generally, analysis of poverty in Sub-Saharan Africa remains affected by issues of data availability and quality. Although new data for Nigeria and newly available data for 2018 for 10 countries in West Africa significantly improve the understanding of poverty in West Africa (Castaneda Aguilar et al. 2022a; Lain, Schoch, and Vishwanath 2022), data have become less available in other parts of the region. As a result, overall the share of the population in Sub-Saharan Africa living in a country with a survey within a three-year period declined from 79 percent in 2017 to 55 percent in 2019 (see table 1C.4 in online annex 1C).[5] Ensuring timely, high-quality data collection across Africa will become increasingly important for the assessment of global extreme poverty because a larger share of the global extreme poor continues to reside in the region.

The implications of data scarcity for global poverty and monitoring progress toward the 2030 goal are severe and are a recurrent topic of discussion in this chapter and chapter 2. In addition, for better survey coverage in Sub-Saharan Africa, survey coverage in fragile and conflict-affected situations is increasingly important. Data coverage of this group improved between 2017 and 2019. In 2017, 43 percent of the population in this group lived in a country with a survey. By 2019, this share had gone up to 50 percent (see table 1C.4 in online annex 1C).

Because of missing data, a regional estimate for 2019 for the Middle East and North Africa cannot be reported. With this caveat in mind, the Middle East and North Africa is the only region where, driven mostly by the situation in fragile and conflict-affected economies, the poverty headcount rate has been increasing since 2014 (figure 1.3). The rate in the region was 7.5 percent in 2018, or three times higher (at 2.6 percent) than in 2014 (see table 1C.1, panel b, in online annex 1C). However, as noted before, these estimates are subject to a high degree of uncertainty because of lack of recent data on the Syrian Arab Republic and the Republic of Yemen.

As discussed later in the section on nowcasting, additional COVID-19–related disruptions of the household survey data collection process present a challenge in data availability everywhere. Surveys conducted during 2020 confirm that the pandemic has had an impact on data collection methods and on the definition of the household welfare measure.[6] Those impacts pose an additional challenge for this report because they limit the availability of household survey data for 2020.[7] Of the 169 countries with survey data used to calculate the global and regional poverty estimates presented in the report, only 20 countries so far have an official estimate for 2020 in the World Bank's Poverty and Inequality Platform (PIP).[8] By contrast, 85 countries have survey data available for 2018 and 61 for 2019. Moreover, the available surveys are not equally distributed across regions. Of the 20 available surveys for 2020, 12 are for countries in Latin America and the Caribbean, six are for countries in Europe and Central Asia, and two more surveys are available for Indonesia and Thailand.

Extreme poverty was high among children, and the poor were less connected online

Poverty and Shared Prosperity 2020 provides a detailed assessment of the characteristics of poor people using data from the Global Monitoring Database (GMD), which combines information on the poverty status of households with characteristics of those households (World Bank 2020a). These characteristics change very slowly over time. Analysis using the updated GMD finds a very similar pattern in 2019 to that in 2017: extreme poor households are more likely than other households to live in rural areas, are more likely to be engaged in agriculture, and are more likely to have more children, but are not more likely to have a larger share of women (see online annex 1C).

One of the most striking findings of the analysis in *Poverty and Shared Prosperity 2020* was the high levels of poverty among children. Figure 1.4 shows children 17 years and younger as a share of those living in extreme poverty and as a share of the total population. In every region of the world, children are more likely to be poor, and this difference is particularly pronounced in the East Asia and Pacific, Latin America and the Caribbean, and Middle East and North Africa regions. Because of the very differential impacts of the COVID-19 crisis on people of different age groups, this difference will be subject to analysis later in this chapter.

Another characteristic of households is their access to electricity and telecommunications. During the COVID-19 crisis, access to online content and services became particularly important as people avoided face-to-face contact. Figure 1.5 shows the degree to which the extreme poor had access to electricity and mobile phones on the eve of the crisis in 2019. Access to electricity was significantly lower among extreme poor households: 37 percent, compared with 78 percent, on average, globally. A similar pattern is observed for mobile phones. Although 84 percent of the world's population lived in a household with at least one mobile phone, only 55 percent of people living in extreme poverty did. The figures show very clearly the disadvantage faced by those in extreme poverty in accessing goods and services during periods of social distancing.

FIGURE 1.4

Poverty rates are higher among children in every region

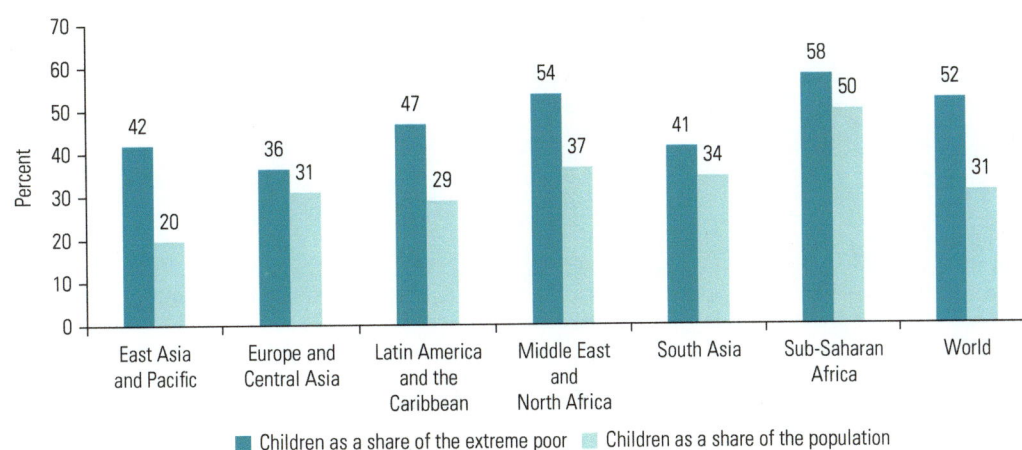

Source: World Bank, Global Monitoring Database (GMD).
Note: The figure shows the share of children among the extreme poor and among the total population in 2019. "Extreme poor" is the population living below the US$2.15-a-day poverty line. Children are defined as between 0 and 17 years old. See chapter 3 in World Bank (2020b) and box 5.2 in World Bank (2018) for more details on the GMD data.

FIGURE 1.5

The extreme poor were less connected online going into the pandemic

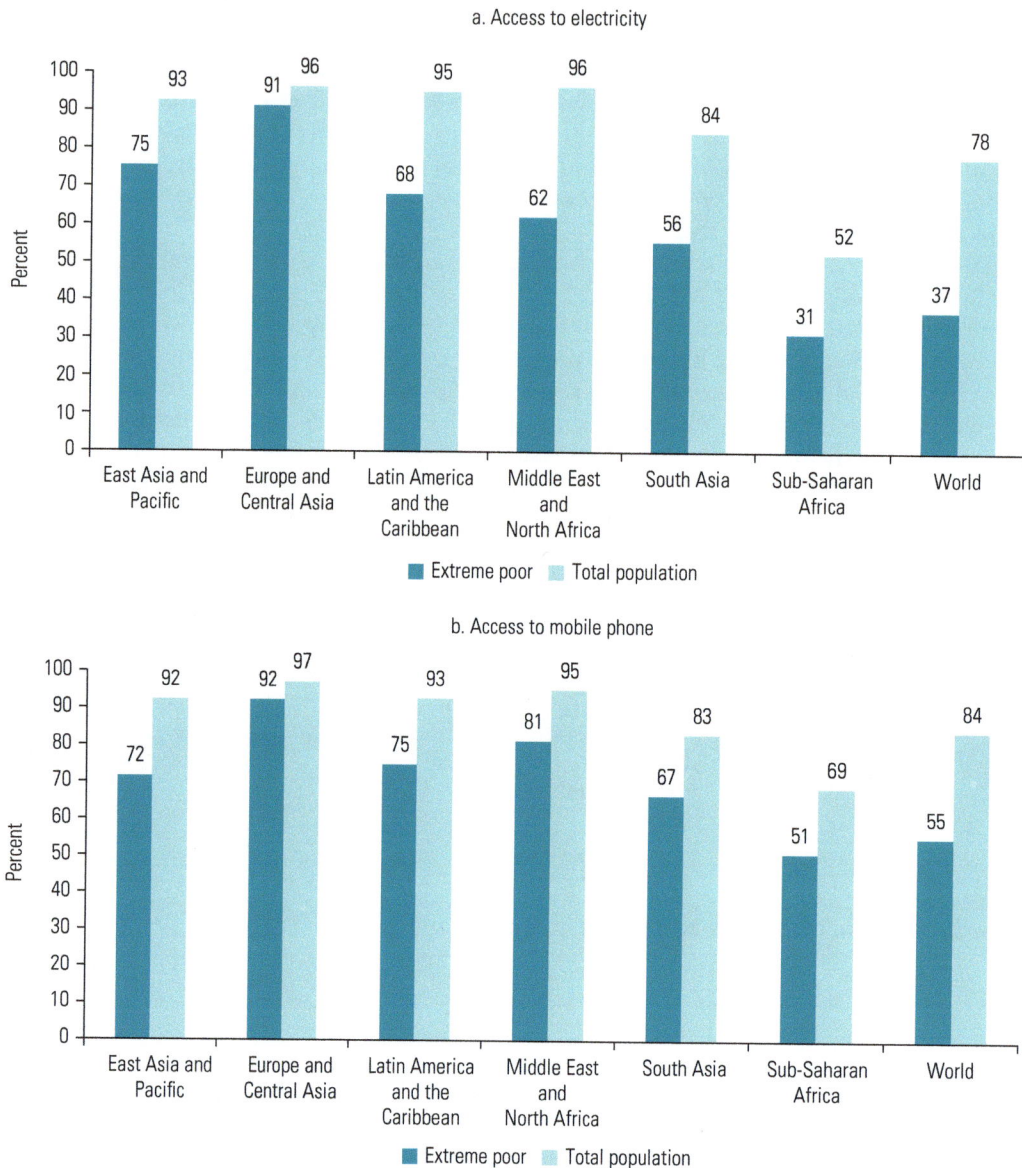

a. Access to electricity

■ Extreme poor ■ Total population

b. Access to mobile phone

■ Extreme poor ■ Total population

Source: World Bank, Global Monitoring Database (GMD).
Note: The figure shows the share of the extreme poor and of the total population with access to electricity (panel a) and to mobile phones (panel b) in 2019. "Extreme poor" is the population living below the US$2.15-a-day poverty line. See chapter 3 in World Bank (2020b) and box 5.2 in World Bank (2018) for more details on the GMD data.

At higher poverty lines, poverty continued to fall at the same (slow) pace

As noted in previous editions of *Poverty and Shared Prosperity*, in half of countries extreme poverty is at or below 3 percent, but that does not mean the fight to eradicate poverty is over in these countries (World Bank 2018). In 2018, the World Bank introduced two higher poverty lines typical of standards among lower-middle-income countries (LMICs) and upper-middle-income countries

(UMICs) to help monitor poverty as living standards improve as countries grow. With the adoption of the 2017 PPPs, the two measures reflecting the poverty definitions in LMICs and UMICs were revised to US$3.65 and US$6.85, respectively (see box 1.1).[9] These lines are designed to complement, not replace, the US$2.15 international poverty line. Such poverty measures are becoming progressively more relevant as a larger share of the global population lives in LMICs and UMICs. In 2019, 75 percent of the global population lived in middle-income countries, whereas only 9 percent of the global population lived in low-income countries (see table 1C.3 in online annex 1C).

In 2019, almost a quarter of the global population, 23 percent, lived below the US$3.65 poverty line and almost a half, 47 percent, lived below the US$6.85 poverty line (see figure 1.6). For both lines, poverty continued to fall from 2017 to 2019, but the percentage of the world's population living beneath the UMIC line (US$6.85) is higher than the share published in *Poverty and*

FIGURE 1.6

Global poverty at higher poverty lines continued to fall, slowly

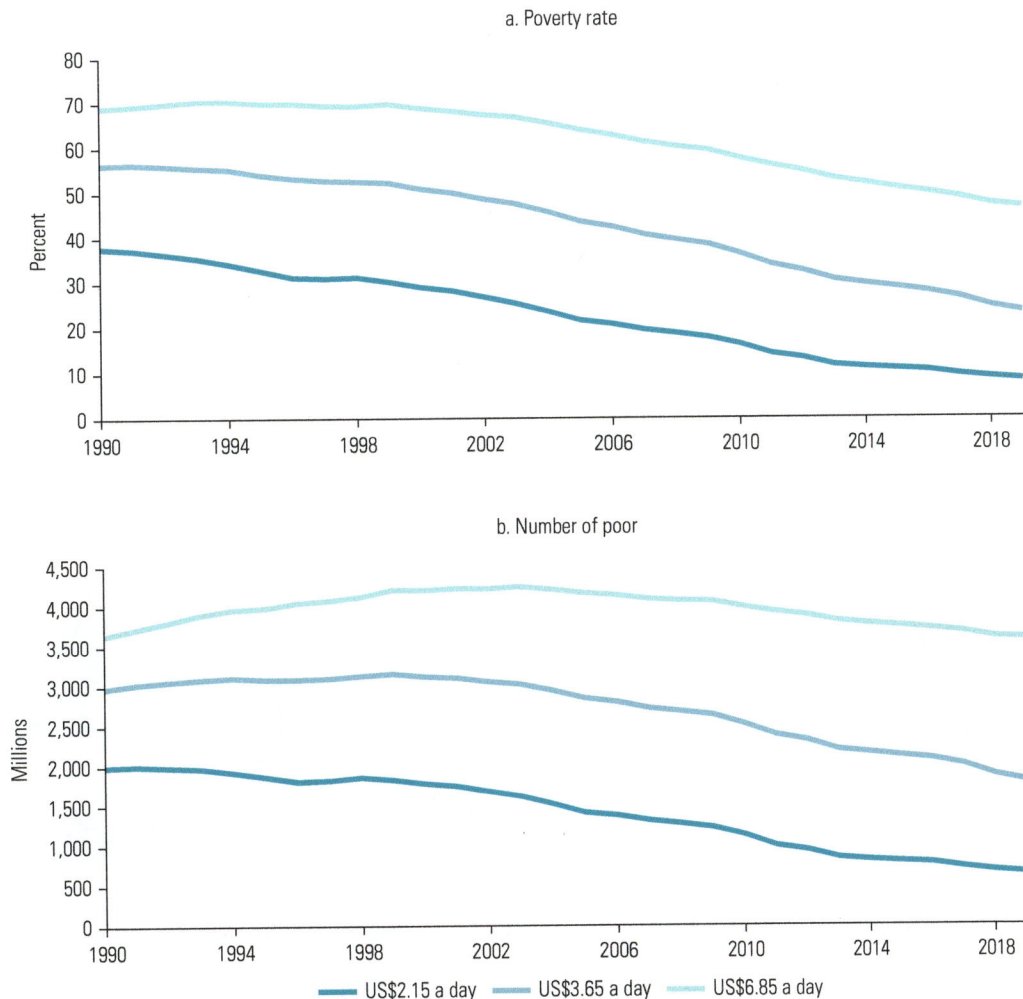

a. Poverty rate

b. Number of poor

US$2.15 a day   US$3.65 a day   US$6.85 a day

Source: World Bank, Poverty and Inequality Platform, https://pip.worldbank.org.
Note: The figure shows the poverty rate (panel a) and number of poor (panel b) at the US$2.15-a-day, US$3.65-a-day, and US$6.85-a-day poverty lines.

Shared Prosperity 2020 using the 2011 PPPs. The reasons are that adoption of the 2017 PPPs was accompanied by a real increase in the poverty line typical of UMICs (see box 1.1) and the availability of more recent survey data. For example, recent data for China and Mexico reveal a higher poverty rate in these countries in 2019 relative to what was suggested by extrapolating older data available at the time in *Poverty and Shared Prosperity 2020*. The result is higher poverty rates in the East Asia and Pacific and Latin America and the Caribbean regions (see Castaneda Aguilar et al. 2022a).[10]

The slowdown in poverty reduction observed at the US$2.15 line has not been observed at higher lines; poverty has continued to decline at a relatively constant rate in recent years. However, the reduction in the poverty rate and number of poor at the US$6.85 poverty line has been slower than at the US$3.65 poverty line (figure 1.6). The number of poor at the US$3.65 poverty line decreased, on average, by 71 million per year between 2014 and 2019, while only by 37 million at the US$6.85 poverty line.

Most of the extreme poor live in Sub-Saharan Africa, but not at the US$3.65 and US$6.85 poverty lines (figure 1.7). In 2019, South Asia had the highest share of the global poor at both the US$3.65 (43 percent) and US$6.85 (42 percent) poverty lines. The share of the global poor who live in the East Asia and Pacific region is also significant at the US$6.85 poverty line (19 percent in 2019). A large number of the global poor at these higher lines live in India (where 595 million people live on less than US$3.65 a day) and China (where 348 million people live on less than US$6.85 a day).

For regions that have low extreme poverty rates, trends in progress are more relevant at these higher lines. Twenty-eight percent of the population in Latin America and the Caribbean (180 million people) lives below the US$6.85 poverty line. The poverty headcount rate at the US$6.85 poverty line has been declining at 0.5 percentage point per year, on average, since 2014. The East Asia and Pacific region saw a reduction of 3 percentage points per year at the same line and over the same period, with the poverty rate declining from 47 percent to 32 percent between 2014 and 2019. The pace of poverty reduction in that region was even faster at the US$3.65 poverty line.

FIGURE 1.7

At the higher poverty lines, the regional distribution of the global poor changes

a. Number of poor, US$2.15   b. Number of poor, US$3.65   c. Number of poor, US$6.85

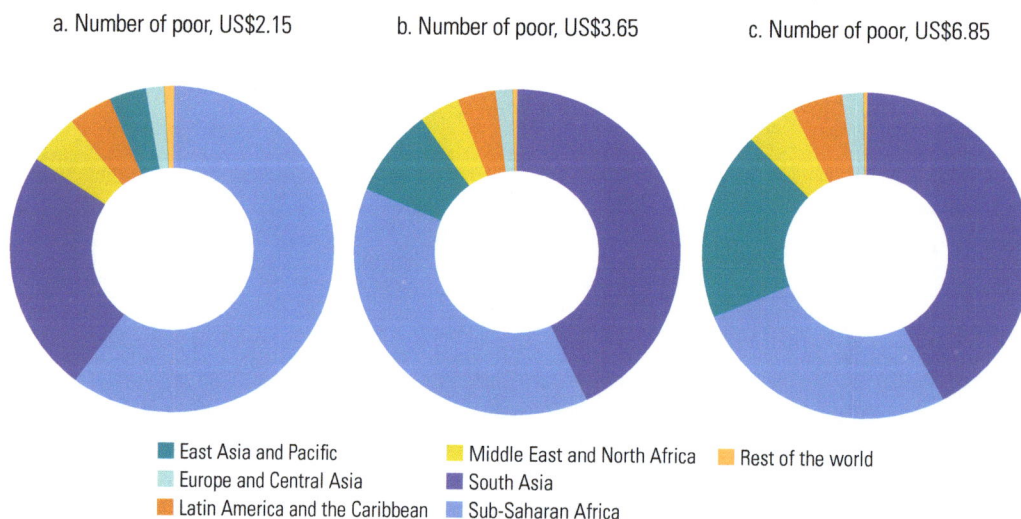

- East Asia and Pacific
- Europe and Central Asia
- Latin America and the Caribbean
- Middle East and North Africa
- South Asia
- Sub-Saharan Africa
- Rest of the world

Source: World Bank, Poverty and Inequality Platform, https://pip.worldbank.org.
Note: The figure shows the distribution of the global poor at the US$2.15-a-day (panel a), US$3.65-a-day (panel b), and US$6.85-a-day (panel c) poverty lines, by region, in 2019.

In South Asia, the decline in the share of the population living below the US$3.65 poverty line accelerated after 2016, but 42 percent of the population of South Asia remained in poverty at this value of the line (see table 1D.1, panel b, in online annex 1D).

The societal poverty rate fell

Analysis of poverty at the higher lines of US$3.65 and US$6.85 reveals how the picture of progress and setbacks in poverty reduction changes when incorporating poverty measures meant to monitor poverty in richer countries (see figure 1.8). Yet, together with the international poverty line, these are absolute poverty measures—that is, they use a poverty threshold that remains fixed across countries and within countries over time. In 2018, the World Bank introduced the societal poverty line (SPL), an indicator that combines elements of absolute and relative poverty measures.[11] In contrast to the absolute poverty lines presented in this chapter, the SPL varies across countries and within a country over time, increasing with the level of income as captured

FIGURE 1.8

The cost of basic needs increases as countries grow

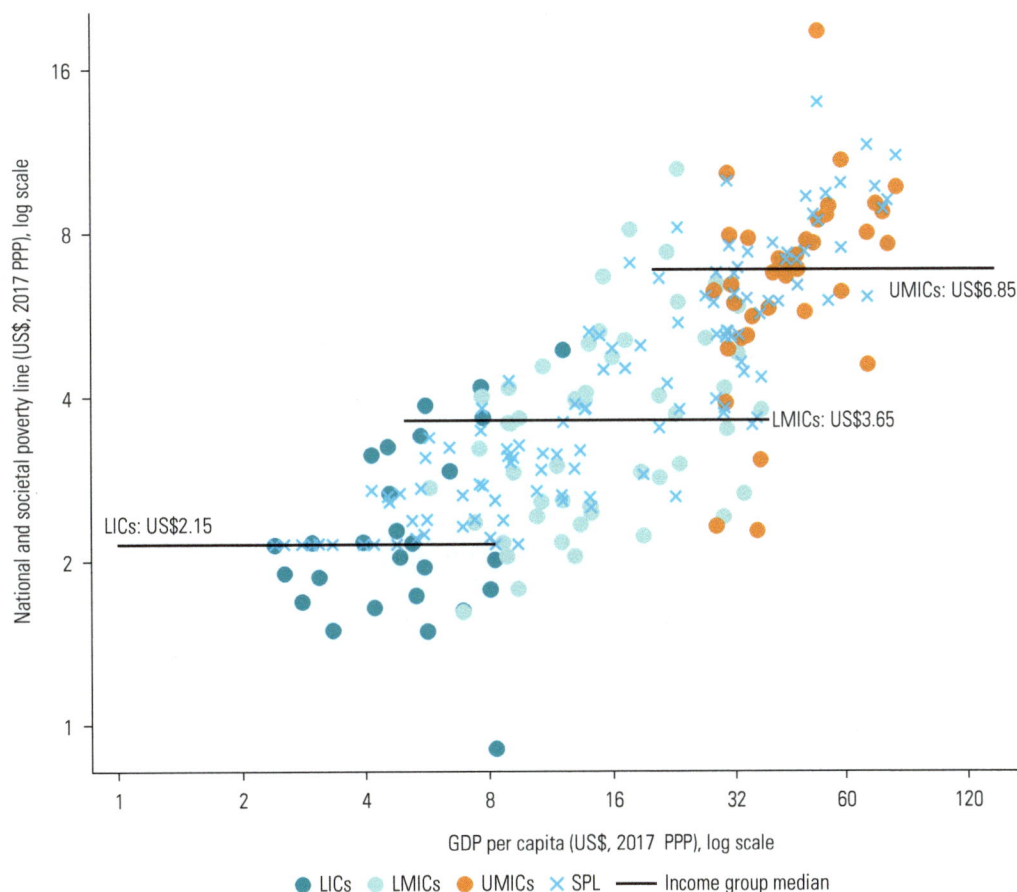

Source: Original calculations based on Jolliffe et al. 2022.
Note: The figure plots national and societal poverty lines against GDP per capita per day. There is one national and one societal poverty line per country; the line closest in time to 2017 is displayed. All variables are expressed in daily per capita terms. GDP = gross domestic product; LICs = low-income countries; LMICs = lower-middle-income countries; PPP = purchasing power parity; SPL = societal poverty line; UMICs = upper-middle-income countries.

by median income or consumption.[12] The relative portion of the SPL can be considered a measure of inequality. For this reason, the SPL is a relevant poverty measure even in high-income countries (HICs).

As with the other measures of poverty in this report, the country-level SPLs have been revised to reflect the introduction of the 2017 PPPs (see box 1.1). This revision led, in turn, to an upward revision of the average global value of the SPL, which for 2019 was US$8.20 (see table 1E.1, panel a, in online annex 1E).

In 2019, 27 percent of the global population lived below their country's SPL (figure 1.9). This represents an ongoing decline in societal poverty since 2017, underscoring that global progress on poverty reduction before 2020 was not limited to progress on reducing absolute deprivation but also included progress in reducing relative deprivation. Although progress in reducing the global societal poverty rate has continued, figure 1.9 shows that the number of societal poor has largely remained the same over time at about 2 billion people. The geographical distribution of the societal poor is also different from other poverty lines considered in this chapter. According to figure 1.9, panel c, the number of societal poor in 2019 is very similar in South Asia and Sub-Saharan Africa. It also shows that societal poverty captures poverty in HICs under "rest of the world." In 2019, 167 million people lived in societal poverty in HICs (15.1 percent of the population of HICs).[13] This figure highlights the relevance of the SPL as countries become richer.

FIGURE 1.9

Progress has been made in reducing the societal poverty rate in recent years

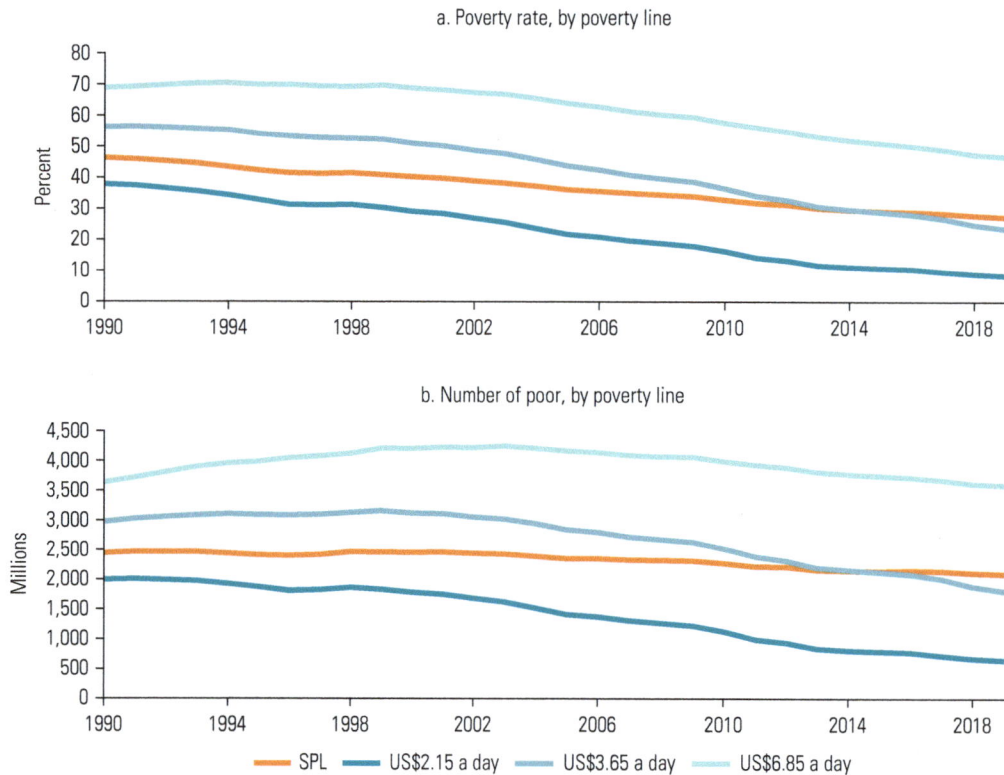

a. Poverty rate, by poverty line

b. Number of poor, by poverty line

SPL ▬ US$2.15 a day ▬ US$3.65 a day ▬ US$6.85 a day

(continued)

44

FIGURE 1.9
Progress has been made in reducing the societal poverty rate in recent years *(continued)*

c. Number of societal poor, by region, 2019

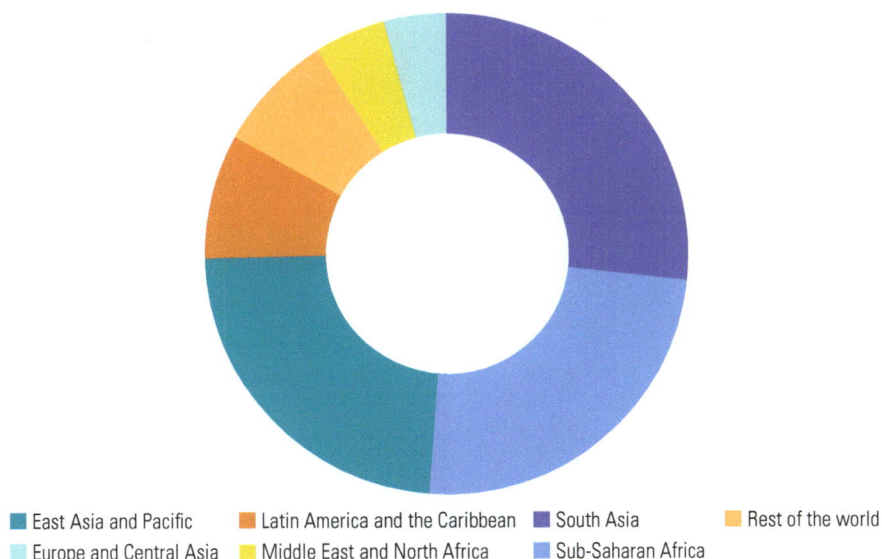

- East Asia and Pacific
- Latin America and the Caribbean
- South Asia
- Rest of the world
- Europe and Central Asia
- Middle East and North Africa
- Sub-Saharan Africa

Source: World Bank, Poverty and Inequality Platform, https://pip.worldbank.org.
Note: Global societal poverty is calculated using a population-weighted average of country-specific societal poverty rates. The treatment of missing countries is identical to the other monetary poverty measures (see online annex 1E for the complete series of yearly lined-up estimates). SPL = societal poverty line.

The levels of poverty in HICs at the three absolute poverty lines of US$2.15, US$3.65, and US$6.85 were 0.6 percent, 0.8 percent, and 1.4 percent, respectively.

New data available for India also allow the construction of societal poverty estimates after 2015 for South Asia for the first time since 2018 (World Bank 2018). The societal poverty head-count rate in 2019 was 30 percent in the region, or more than three times higher than the poverty headcount at the international poverty line. Societal poverty in the region fell from 37 percent to 30 percent between 2014 and 2019. Although this was a more moderate decrease than that for extreme poverty, which decreased from 18 percent to 9 percent over the same period, the region outperformed many other regions where societal poverty rates stagnated or increased during this period: Europe and Central Asia, Latin America and the Caribbean, Middle East and North Africa, and the rest of the world. The East Asia and Pacific and Sub-Saharan Africa regions were the only other two in which the rate of societal poverty fell from 2014 to 2019 (see table 1E.1, panel b, in online annex 1E).

In summary, on the eve of the pandemic in 2019, poverty continued to fall against the global poverty lines of US$2.15, US$3.65, and US$6.85 in almost all regions. However, there was a slow-down in global poverty reduction at the US$2.15 line and a persistence of high poverty rates at higher values of the poverty line and under the societal poverty definition, even in regions where extreme poverty has largely been eradicated. The chapter now turns to the analysis of global poverty between 2020 and 2022.

Poverty over the pandemic period: The nowcast

Poverty and Shared Prosperity 2020, published just as the economic impacts of the COVID-19 pandemic were emerging, highlighted the three C's that were threatening global progress on poverty: COVID-19, climate, and conflict. Two years after the onset of the pandemic, this report documents more fully the substantial shocks that COVID-19 has imposed, identifies those for whom the shocks have been particularly large or long-lived, and describes how climate and conflict shocks have stalled the recovery.

The pandemic induced a historic increase in poverty

Poverty and Shared Prosperity 2020 predicted that the COVID-19 pandemic would be a once-in-a-generation shock, causing the largest increase in global poverty since 1990 and reversing decades of continued global poverty reduction (World Bank 2020a). Based on the additional data collected over the last two years, it is now clearer that the COVID-19 pandemic has indeed triggered the most pronounced setback in the fight against global poverty since 1990, and most likely since World War II.

Box 1.3 details the data and methods used in putting this picture together. During the peak of the crisis (in the second quarter of 2020), the survey work on which poverty numbers rely was halted or conducted by phone rather than by the usual in-person interviews. Although many countries do not have official poverty statistics for 2020, the poverty estimates for 2020 are informed

BOX 1.3

Predicting changes in poverty with nowcasts

Nowcasting and forecasting poverty are a challenge.[a] Mahler, Castaneda Aguilar, and Newhouse (forthcoming) suggest that, in general, when predicting current or future changes in poverty, growth of the per capita gross domestic product (GDP) performs nearly as well as 1,000 other development indicators combined.[b] This is one reason global poverty nowcasts use per capita GDP growth to estimate the growth in household income.[c] Because such nowcasts assume that the same growth rate in national accounts is experienced by all households in the distribution, they assume distribution neutrality within a country.

How nowcasts are estimated in this report

The method just described is used for the nowcasts presented for 2021 and 2022 in keeping with previous editions of *Poverty and Shared Prosperity*. However, unlike in previous editions, the 2020 nowcast in this report incorporates many sources of data now available to allow for an estimate that both takes into account the impact of growth contraction on incomes (as is usually done for nowcasts) and considers that the pandemic had differential impacts on groups within a country. Survey-based estimates are preferred to extrapolations using national accounts given that the former are based on microdata collected by national statistical offices for the purpose of measuring poverty and inequality within a country.

The approach used is set out in full in Mahler, Yonzan, and Lakner (forthcoming). Nowcasting begins with the same country-level data underlying the 2019 global poverty estimate. These data are available for 168 countries in the World Bank's Poverty and Inequality Platform, or PIP (see online annex 1A).[d] The next step is to estimate a household welfare distribution for each country in 2020. As mentioned earlier, survey data—the preferred data source for measuring poverty in a country—are available for only 20 countries in 2020. Thus the nowcast uses a variety of data sources ranked in order of preference as follows:

(continued)

BOX 1.3

Predicting changes in poverty with nowcasts *(continued)*

1. Household survey data: available for 20 countries.
2. Tabulated 2020 income statistics reported by national statistical offices (NSOs): available for an additional 8 countries.
3. High-frequency phone surveys (HFPS) collected by the World Bank in collaboration with NSOs.[e] These phone surveys provide information on whether a household has lost, gained, or experienced no change in its income since the start of the pandemic (see box 2.4 in chapter 2 for more information on these surveys).[f] After mapping the information from the HFPS to the 2019 welfare distribution, the size of the change in income gains and losses is estimated using sectoral growth rate estimates available from the World Bank's April 2022 Macro Poverty Outlook.[g] This approach is available for 37 countries.
4. For the remaining countries, the nowcast uses a variety of alternative data sources, where available: (1) estimates based on microsimulations from the literature or from World Bank teams; (2) sectoral growth estimates from national accounts; and (3) per capita GDP growth rates applied to all households. For the 3 percent of the global population with no survey data in PIP, the regional average distributions are used (table B1.3.1).

This approach, which includes survey-based estimates of mean growth for many countries and allows for within-country distributional effects, slightly increases overall poverty numbers. Using GDP per capita growth rates to project poverty changes for all countries for 2020 would instead result in an estimated 18 million fewer people living in extreme poverty in 2020. For 2021 and 2022, distribution-neutral per capita GDP-based projections are then used.

Testing the accuracy of the 2020 nowcasts

For the 20 countries with survey data, it is possible to compare survey-based estimates with results from two approaches: (1) poverty derived using per capita GDP growth–based, distribution-neutral projections; and (2) for a subset of 13 countries, poverty derived using HFPS. Although the nowcast just discussed above uses survey microdata for the 20 countries, comparison with distribution-neutral and phone survey–based projections would provide some sense of how the poverty rates might be the same as or differ from poverty calculated using actual microdata. It is important to remember that, for countries in the nowcast that rely on methods (1) and (2), survey microdata are not available. Of the 20 available surveys for 2020, 18 are for countries in either Latin America and the Caribbean or Europe and Central Asia, covering 14 percent of the global population. Therefore, the extent to which the findings can be generalized to countries in other regions or at other levels of development is unknown.

TABLE B1.3.1

Method used for nowcasting global poverty in 2020

Data source (preferred order)	Countries		Population	
	Number	Share (%)	Number (millions)	Share (%)
Household survey data	20	9	1,096	14
Tabulated data from NSOs	8	4	2,146	28
High-frequency phone survey data and sectoral growth rates	37	17	1,027	13
Estimates from literature and World Bank teams	26	12	2,091	27
Sectoral growth rates	56	26	1,035	13
Per capita GDP growth rates	21	10	155	2
Regional average	50	23	211	3
Total	**218**	**100[a]**	**7,762[a]**	**100**

Source: Mahler, Yonzan, and Lakner, forthcoming.
Note: GDP = gross domestic product; NSOs = national statistical offices.
a. Any discrepancies in the sum are due to rounding.

(continued)

BOX 1.3

Predicting changes in poverty with nowcasts *(continued)*

FIGURE B1.3.1

Cross-checking poverty derived using various methods, change in poverty, 2019–20

a. Per capita GDP growth

b. High-frequency phone survey

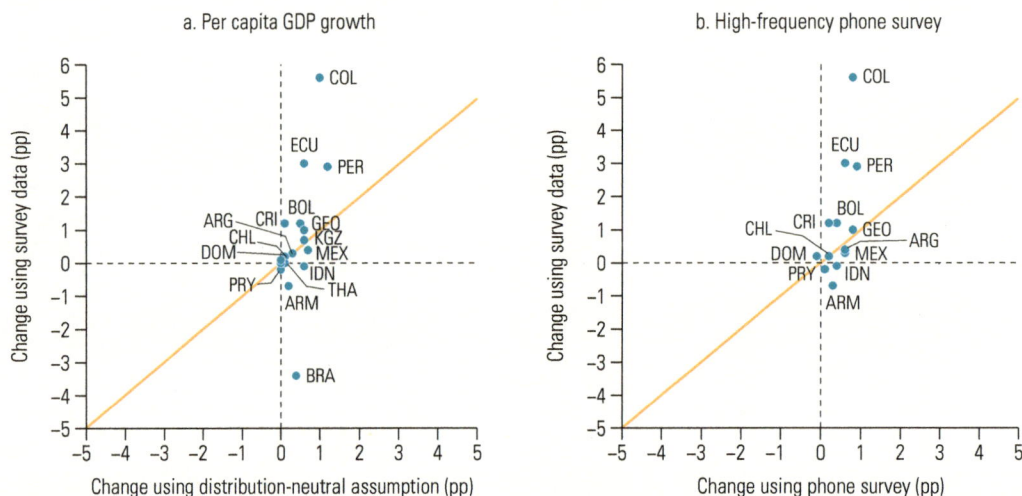

Sources: Original calculations based on Mahler, Yonzan, and Lakner, forthcoming; World Bank, Poverty and Inequality Platform, https://pip.worldbank.org.

Note: The figure compares the percentage point change in poverty at the US$2.15 poverty line in various countries from 2019 to 2020, calculated using actual survey data and the projection based on per capita GDP growth (panel a) or on the high-frequency phone survey (panel b). Countries with no change in poverty using both the survey and distribution-neutral assumption are not labeled in panel a. For a list of country codes, go to https://www.iso.org/obp/ui/#search/code/. GDP = gross domestic product; pp = percentage point.

Figure B1.3.1, panel a, shows the correlation of the percentage point change in extreme poverty from 2019 to 2020 between poverty calculated using the actual survey data and poverty derived using per capita GDP growth–based, distribution-neutral projections. For 13 countries, panel b compares the change in poverty using actual survey data with the change in poverty using phone surveys.

Both panels show that, for most countries in the sample, the change in poverty derived from survey microdata is often, but not always, close to estimates derived using per capita GDP growth and phone surveys. Poverty levels derived using survey data are, on average, 0.25 percentage point higher than projections based on per capita GDP growth and 0.72 percentage point higher than projections based on phone surveys. As for changes, the mean absolute change in poverty from 2019 to 2020 in actual surveys is 0.76 percentage point higher than in those using per capita GDP growth and 0.95 percentage point higher than in those using phone surveys. The correlation coefficient of poverty changes is 0.60 between survey data and per capita GDP growth–based projections and 0.62 between survey data and phone survey–based projections. At one extreme, the change in poverty is 4.6 percentage points higher in Colombia in survey data than in the per capita GDP growth–based projection and 4.8 percentage points higher than in the phone survey–based projection. At the other extreme, survey data estimate for Brazil poverty lower by 3.8 percentage points than the per capita GDP growth projection. The lower poverty in Brazil in the survey data is primarily due to the extraordinarily large social protection measures implemented during the pandemic—measures that are discussed later in the report (Lara Ibarra and Campante Cardoso Vale 2022).

The global poverty numbers are largely influenced by the most populous countries—such as China or India—because each individual in the world is weighted equally. Tabulated data published by the National Bureau of Statistics of China is used to inform the nowcast

(continued)

48

BOX 1.3

Predicting changes in poverty with nowcasts *(continued)*

for China. Although large, China is home to a small share of the global extreme poor and had a moderate economic shock in 2020; as a result, China does not contribute to the global increase in extreme poverty in 2020. There is a large difference in the 2020 poverty estimates for India depending on the method used. The Consumer Pyramids Household Survey (CPHS) used to monitor poverty in India (see box 1.2) was collected throughout 2020, but the 2020 poverty estimates from these data are yet to be finalized. A per capita GDP growth rate projection implies an increase of 23 million poor people in India in 2020 (at the US$2.15 extreme poverty line), while initial estimates using the CPHS (implementing a survey-to-survey imputation method - method 1 - in Sinha Roy and van der Weide 2022) suggest an increase of 56 million poor people. This report uses these initial estimates from the CPHS for the purposes of the 2020 global nowcast, putting India under the category of "Estimates from literature and World Bank teams" in table B1.3.1 (for details of how these estimates were calculated see online annex 1G). However, as online annex 1G indicates the final number may be higher or lower than this. The importance of the India numbers in the global poverty estimate for 2020 underscores the uncertainty that still surrounds this estimate. Despite this uncertainty, the finding that 2020 was a historically bad year for progress on poverty reduction remains: even taking the lower bound on the India poverty number, 2020 is likely still the year with the largest increase in poverty since World War II. Although smaller in population, Nigeria and the Democratic Republic of Congo are still relatively large countries and home to a large share of the global extreme poor, however they had relatively mild economic shocks in 2020 and so contribute less to the global increase in extreme poverty, about three million and half a million, respectively.

a. The term *nowcast* refers to global poverty projections beyond 2019—that is, for 2020, 2021, and 2022. For 2020, realized growth rates from the World Bank's World Development Indicators database (https://databank .worldbank.org/source/world-development-indicators) are used. Estimated growth rates for 2021 and the data on projected growth rates in national accounts for 2022 come from the June 2022 *Global Economic Prospects* (World Bank 2022b).
b. Mahler, Castaneda Aguilar, and Newhouse (forthcoming) evaluate the performance of alternative predictors using past surveys. To maintain the conclusion that per capita GDP growth performs nearly as well as 1,000 other development indicators, this report assumes that this relationship also holds during the current crisis period. In general, it is difficult to evaluate poverty changes during crises because there are often breaks in survey comparability. For example, in those countries conducting a survey in 2020, data collection switched from traditional face-to-face interviews to phone interviews. Questionnaires were also shortened, especially to accommodate the addition of COVID-19–related questions. In Brazil, Colombia, and Peru, among others, the welfare aggregate captured by the survey data includes onetime cash transfers that in other years would not have been included. See Castaneda Aguilar et al. (2022a) for details.
c. Not all the growth in per capita GDP translates into the growth of mean consumption of households (see Deaton 2005; Prydz, Jolliffe, and Serajuddin 2022; Ravallion 2003). The rate of transfer of growth, also known as the pass-through rate, is 70 percent when consumption is used to measure household welfare and 100 percent when income is used instead (Mahler, Castaneda Aguilar, and Newhouse, forthcoming). For nowcasts and projections, this report adjusts the growth in per capita GDP by a factor of 0.7 when the last household survey of the country uses a consumption aggregate. This method differs from that used in *Poverty and Shared Prosperity 2020*, which used a pass-through rate of 0.85 for all countries, regardless of the welfare measure used.
d. Although survey microdata are available for 169 countries in PIP, growth data are only available until 2014 for República Bolivariana de Venezuela. Thus regional and global poverty estimates after 2014 are calculated by assigning the population-weighted average of the Latin America and the Caribbean region to República Bolivariana de Venezuela, following the methodology used for countries missing data (see online annex 1A).
e. These surveys, as their name indicates, are conducted over the phone and are therefore less comprehensive than traditional household surveys. Yet, because of the mode of data collection, they can be conducted even during strict quarantines and government shutdowns. In many countries, phone surveys are some of the only national surveys available since 2020. As of 2022, such surveys had been conducted in 72 countries across all developing regions. More than 100 indicators have been harmonized across countries from these surveys.
f. Twenty-four countries report an income change measure. An additional 13 countries that do not record change in income report whether households experienced a loss in consumption.
g. World Bank, Macro Poverty Outlook, https://www.worldbank.org/en/publication/macro-poverty -outlook#:~:text=The%20Macro%20Poverty%20Outlook%20(MPO,and%20the%20International%20 Monetary%20Fund. See Mahler, Yonzan, and Lakner (forthcoming) for technical details.

by surveys for a large number of countries and territories and so constitute a much more detailed analysis of the impact of COVID-19 on poverty than has been presented to date using traditional nowcasting methods. That said, more uncertainty surrounds these numbers than those presented for poverty trends until 2019. Results have been triangulated where possible and robustness checks carried out for the main messages, as is discussed in box 1.3 and described in much more detail in Mahler, Yonzan, and Lakner (forthcoming), but this uncertainty should be kept in mind. The numbers will continue to be updated as more information becomes available.

According to the nowcast of global poverty, 71 million more people were likely living in extreme poverty in 2020 than in 2019—a 11 percent increase. This increase in global poverty, an increase from 8.4 to 9.3 percent, is the largest increase since 1990 and likely the largest increase since World War II (see figure 1.10).[14] The last increase in the global headcount poverty rate occurred during the Asian financial crisis, when between 1997 and 1998 the global poverty headcount rate at the international poverty line increased by 0.2 percentage point, equivalent to 37 million more poor people. The magnitude of the COVID-19–induced increase is more than four times larger than the Asian financial crisis–induced increase after controlling for differences in global population.

To isolate the impact of the pandemic in 2020, figure 1.10 compares the nowcast with a counterfactual series estimated using prepandemic GDP growth forecasts for 2020. This series shows where the nowcasted series would have been without the crisis. The net effect is the difference between where the world is (the COVID-19 nowcast or "Current projection") and where the world would have been ("Pre-COVID-19 projection").[15] Poverty had been projected to decline in 2020, prior to the pandemic. Taking this projection into account reveals that poverty was 1.2 percentage points higher than projections going into 2020 (extreme poverty had been expected to fall by 4 percent), which translates to 90 million additional poor people—the net impact of the pandemic.

FIGURE 1.10

The COVID-19 pandemic was a historic shock to global poverty

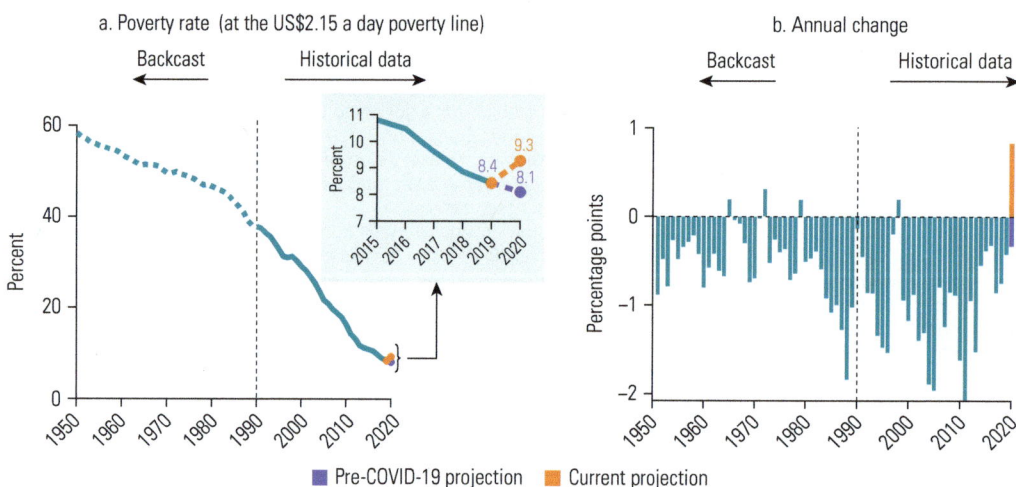

Sources: Original calculations based on Mahler, Yonzan, and Lakner, forthcoming; World Bank, Poverty and Inequality Platform, https://pip .worldbank.org; World Bank 2022b.
Note: Panel a shows the global poverty headcount rate at the US$2.15-a-day poverty line for 1950 to 2020. "Historical data" for the period 1990–2019 are from the Poverty and Inequality Platform. "Backcast" estimates are extrapolated backward from the 1990 line-up using growth in national accounts. National accounts data before 1990 are from the World Development Indicators, the World Economic Outlook, and Bolt and van Zanden 2020. "Current projection" uses the nowcast methodology outlined in this section and a variety of data sources to project the latest 2019 lined-up estimate to 2020. "Pre-COVID-19 projection" extrapolates the 2019 lineup to 2020 using per capita GDP growth forecasts from the January 2020 *Global Economic Prospects* database. Panel b shows the annual percentage point change in the global poverty headcount rate.

Unlike other recent crises, the pandemic shock was truly global in its impact, increasing poverty in most low- and middle-income countries.

The majority of the additional poor people at the US$2.15 poverty line live in South Asia (see table 1F.1 in online annex 1F for a regional breakdown of the projection). Sub-Saharan Africa and the East Asia and Pacific region follow. As discussed in more detail in box 1.3, different data and assumptions for India alter the number of additional poor in 2020. However, under all assumptions the increase in global poverty was concentrated in South Asia, which is consistent with the observed gross domestic product (GDP) per capita shock. The contraction in GDP per capita in 2020 for the three countries with the highest share of extreme poor was –7.5 percent for India, –4.3 percent for Nigeria, and –1.4 percent for the Democratic Republic of Congo.[16] At the higher poverty lines, South Asia still contributes the largest share to the global numbers, but the increase in poverty in the East Asia and Pacific region becomes much more substantial and a higher contribution to the global total (table 1F.1 in online annex 1F).

Figure 1.11 shows how country income groups fared against the poverty line relevant to their income category. Panels a, b, and c of figure 1.11 show the share of countries that experienced

FIGURE 1.11

Poverty increased across income groups in 2020 and displayed an uneven recovery in 2021–22

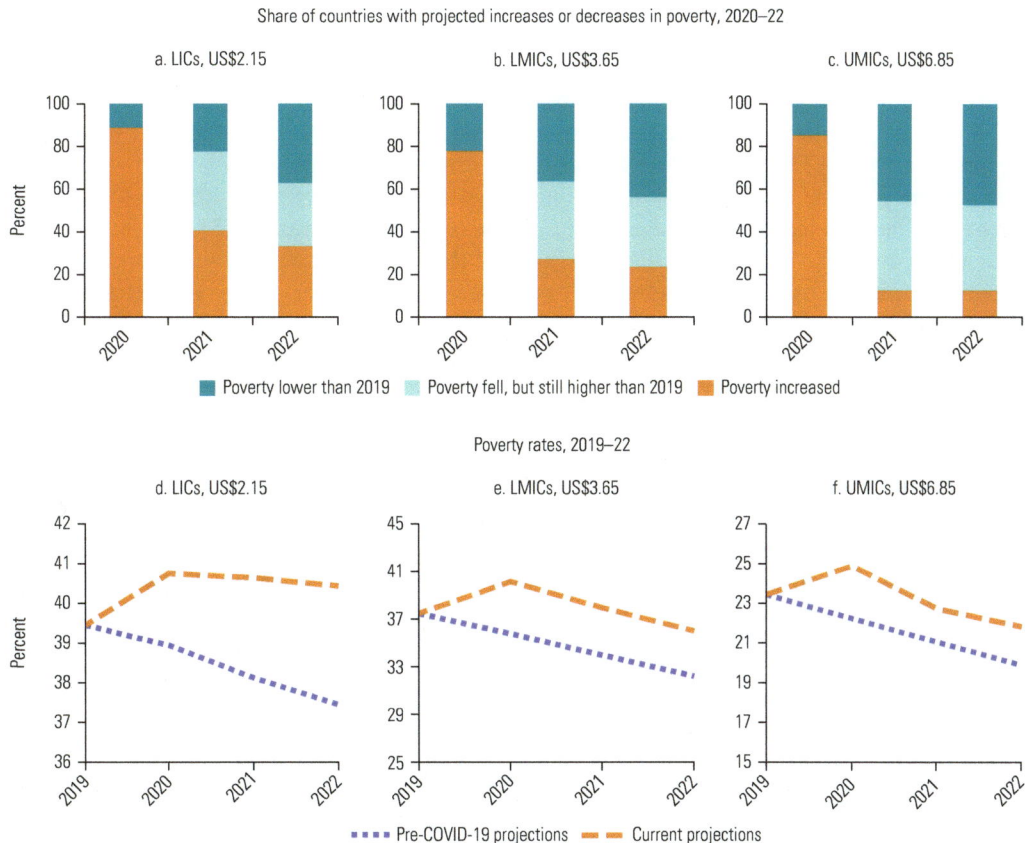

Share of countries with projected increases or decreases in poverty, 2020–22

a. LICs, US$2.15   b. LMICs, US$3.65   c. UMICs, US$6.85

■ Poverty lower than 2019   ■ Poverty fell, but still higher than 2019   ■ Poverty increased

Poverty rates, 2019–22

d. LICs, US$2.15   e. LMICs, US$3.65   f. UMICs, US$6.85

▪▪▪▪ Pre-COVID-19 projections   ▬ ▬ Current projections

Sources: Original calculations based on Mahler, Yonzan, and Lakner, forthcoming; World Bank, Poverty and Inequality Platform, https://pip .worldbank.org; World Bank 2022b.
Note: Panels a–c show the share of countries where the poverty rate has decreased or increased relative to the prior year and relative to 2019, by income group. Countries where poverty increased include countries where poverty did not change. Panels d–f show the poverty rate between 2019 and 2022 at the income group–relevant poverty line. See also figure 1.10. LICs = low-income countries; LMICs = lower-middle-income countries; UMICs = upper-middle-income country.

increases or decreases in poverty, and panels d, e, and f show the projected poverty rates (as well as the prepandemic projection). In 2020, nearly all low-income countries (LICs) and LMICs saw increases in poverty. The size of the increase was particularly large in LMICs, where the poverty rate at the US$3.65 poverty line increased by 2.7 percentage points between 2019 and 2020. Poverty also increased in most UMICs. However, the substantial fiscal support received by households in large UMICs such as Brazil and South Africa mitigated the impact of the crisis on poverty and even reduced poverty in some cases (see chapter 4 for a fuller discussion).

A slow and uneven recovery in 2021

Indonesia is the only country for which survey microdata are available for 2021. For the remaining countries in 2021, the nowcast starts with the 2020 distribution presented in the previous section and uses growth forecasts available from the World Bank's June 2022 *Global Economic Prospects* (World Bank 2022b) to estimate poverty using the standard method for nowcasting described in box 1.3 (also see World Bank 2018, 2020a). In this method, all households in a country are assumed to experience the same income growth (predicted by the per capita GDP growth for that country). As survey data for 2021 becomes available these estimates will be updated. The nowcast of global poverty for 2021 shows that the global economic recovery in 2021 allowed for some reduction in global poverty (figure 1.12). The global poverty headcount rate fell from 9.3 percent in 2020 to 8.8 percent in 2021. However, the recovery was limited.

The pace of poverty reduction for 2021 has reverted to levels similar to the pre-COVID-19 projections (see figure 1.12). Returning to pre-COVID-19 rates of poverty reduction means that little progress was made on reversing the impact of the devastating shock to global poverty in 2020. As a result, nowcasts suggest that there were still 78 million more poor in 2021 than anticipated prior to COVID-19 (see table 1F.1 in online annex 1F for a regional breakdown). At the US$3.65 poverty line, poverty is set to decline by 1 percentage point from 2020 to 2021, which is progress but still leaves 147 million more people living on less than US$3.65 a day in 2021 than anticipated. The poverty trend looks similar at the US$6.85 poverty line. The poverty rate decreased by about 1 percentage point between 2020 and 2021, but at the end of 2021 there were 140 million more poor than anticipated (figure 1.12).

Recovery has also been highly uneven. Figure 1.11 shows the change in poverty by country income group. Recovery in 2021 was very uneven in LICs. Of 27 countries, poverty increased in almost as many countries (11) as it fell (16), and few countries (6) saw poverty return to 2019 levels. As a result, the aggregate poverty rate stayed almost constant. Recovery in LMICs was stronger, with nearly three-quarters of LMICs recording poverty reductions, but recovery was not strong enough to reverse increases in 2020 in about half of these countries. A higher share of UMICs registered a reduction in poverty in 2021 (87 percent), but again in only half of them was it large enough to offset the increase experienced in the previous year. Chapter 2 discusses in more detail how the pandemic increased global inequality between countries, but this finding already points to diverging fortunes.

Recovery stalled in 2022

Nowcasts suggest this weak recovery will effectively stall in 2022, in part because of the war in Ukraine, which exacerbated high food and energy prices, compounded by a series of climate shocks in the world's largest food producers. Seventy million more people are expected to be living in extreme poverty in 2022 compared with prepandemic projections for 2022 (figure 1.12). Poverty at the US$6.85 poverty line shows an even smaller reduction between 2021 and 2022, declining by just 0.5 percentage point, or half the reduction registered between 2020 and 2021.

Lower growth rates have reduced projected poverty reduction.[17] In the short run, high food price inflation can have particularly detrimental impacts on poorer households, which spend

FIGURE 1.12

Poverty reduction stalled at all poverty lines in 2022

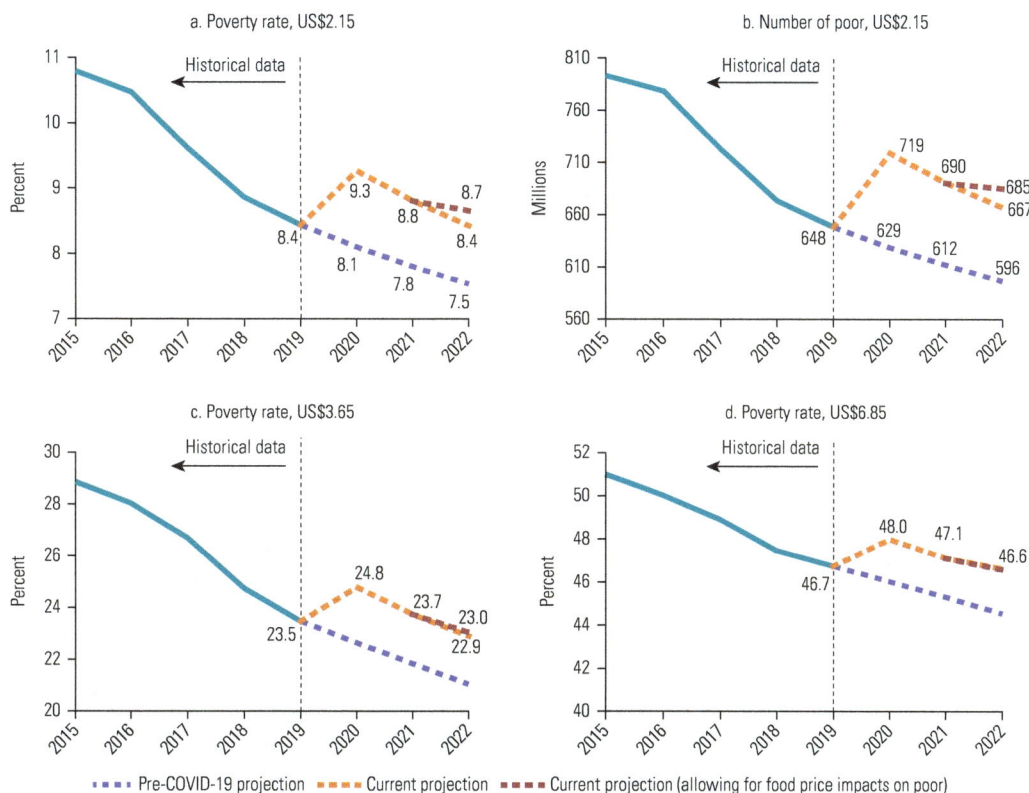

a. Poverty rate, US$2.15

b. Number of poor, US$2.15

c. Poverty rate, US$3.65

d. Poverty rate, US$6.85

∙∙∙∙∙ Pre-COVID-19 projection   ▪▪▪▪ Current projection   ▪▪▪▪ Current projection (allowing for food price impacts on poor)

Sources: Original calculations based on Mahler, Yonzan, and Lakner, forthcoming; World Bank, Poverty and Inequality Platform, https://pip .worldbank.org; World Bank 2022b.
Note: The figure shows the nowcast for the poverty headcount rate (panels a, c, and d) at the three poverty lines—US$2.15, US$3.65, and US$6.85 a day—and for the number of poor at the US$2.15-a-day poverty line (panel b). For 2022, nowcasts are reported for the "Current projection" and for the "Current projection (allowing for food price impacts on poor)."

a larger share of their income on food. In the long run, households can partially adapt to higher prices by changing their consumption patterns to lessen the impact (Friedman and Levinsohn 2002). In addition, higher food prices can be a source of income growth for households producing food on their own farms. For poor households working in agriculture as wage labor, wages can also adjust to the situation (Headey 2018). As a result, analyses and poverty assessments have found higher food prices to be a driver of poverty reduction in the long run. Box 1.4 provides a fuller discussion of this evidence.

However, in the short run the impact of food prices on poverty can be large, particularly for urban poor households who spend a lot of their income on food and who do not benefit from the potential to increase their income. To capture the short-run effect of rising food price inflation on poverty in 2022, it is important to relax the assumption that all households in a country are equally affected by rising prices. To take this factor into account, nowcasts include a pessimistic (or downside) scenario that accounts for the differential short-run impacts of food price inflation on poorer households relative to richer ones. This scenario is based on the results of a simulation of the current food price inflation in 53 countries by Artuc et al. (2022). Their analysis considers the share of food in total spending for households across the income distribution, as well as some immediate income effects as a result of changes in prices (but no changes in production or rural

The impacts of rising global food and energy prices on poverty

Food prices rose by 5 percentage points more than core inflation (estimated as the median of country inflation data) in the two years prior to March 2022 (Ha, Kose, and Ohnsorge 2021). Energy prices rose by 11 percentage points more than core inflation in this period, but they are expected to rise 50 percent in 2022 (Ha, Kose, and Ohnsorge 2021; World Bank 2022a). The increases observed so far are very similar to those during the 2008 food price crisis. The prices of agricultural inputs such as fertilizer also rose dramatically in both periods, increasing 266 percent in the two years prior to June 2008 and 217 percent in the two years prior to March 2022. In 2022, prices of wheat and corn spiked, but rice prices remained relatively unaffected. By contrast, rice prices doubled in 2007, alongside wheat and corn price increases.

Immediate and long-run impacts of higher food prices

The immediate impacts of rising food prices are likely to hit the poor the hardest. However, simulations that focus only on the immediate impacts of higher prices are unlikely to capture the full nature of the price impacts in the long run because they do not consider several factors that may dampen the immediate impact of the food price shock (Minot and Dewina 2015). Consumers seek substitutes for the foods whose relative prices are increasing (Andreyeva, Long, and Brownell 2010; Friedman and Levinsohn 2002), food producers benefit from higher prices in their next sale, wages adjust, and agricultural investment and production increase (Ivanic and Martin 2014; Jacoby 2016; Van Campenhout, Pauw, and Minot 2018). These changes occur within a matter of months, reducing any immediate impact quite quickly.

Analysis of 300 different poverty episodes drawn from the World Bank's global poverty data finds that increases in international food prices are correlated with reductions in poverty over the next one to five years (Headey 2018). The reductions are attributed to the agricultural supply response and, to a lesser extent, to the wage response to higher food prices.

A look back at periods of high food prices and effects on poverty

The remainder of this box looks at poverty assessments that considered the drivers of poverty trends during the periods of high food prices from 2008 to 2011.

In Uganda, Simler (2010) predicted an increase in national poverty of 2.6 percentage points due to higher global food prices in 2008. However, official poverty estimates pointed to an annual 1.6 percentage point reduction in poverty from 2006 to 2013. Good rainfall and prices accounted for two-thirds of the growth in crop income of the bottom 40 percent from 2006 to 2012 (World Bank 2016).

Ivanic and Martin (2008) simulated the short-run impacts of increasing global food prices between 2005 and 2007 in several countries, including Cambodia, and projected a 1.5 percentage point increase in national poverty rates in Cambodia. However, the pace of poverty reduction increased from 2007 to 2009 because of increasing rice prices, which particularly benefited rural poverty reduction (World Bank 2013b). Increases in farmers' incomes as a result of higher goods prices, better rural wages, and higher income from nonfarm self-employment were drivers of poverty reduction in rural areas.

In Bangladesh, the food price spike in 2008 resulted in real wage growth for agricultural workers, reversing the short-term impact of higher prices for rural households (World Bank 2013a). Similarly, Jacoby (2016) found that agricultural wages rose faster in rural Indian districts growing a higher share of crops that experienced larger relative price increases and that the rise in agricultural wages had significant spillover effects on nonagricultural wages as well.

In Ethiopia, poverty fell fastest when and where agricultural growth was strongest, and a driver of agricultural growth was higher food prices (World Bank 2015). However, high food prices hurt

(continued)

BOX 1.4

The impacts of rising global food and energy prices on poverty *(continued)*

agricultural households in the poorest decile in Ethiopia, who produce very little, and unskilled wage workers in urban areas for the four to five months that wages took to adjust to food price increases (Headey et al. 2012). A review in Brazil also found that, although the market income effects of food price increases were positive for the rural poor, they were not positive for urban populations (Ferreira et al. 2013).

Overall, official estimates show reductions in poverty and inequality arising in the long run from high food prices. However, some vulnerable groups—urban households and marginal agricultural households—do not necessarily stand to benefit. This finding points to the need to provide households with quick, time-bound, targeted support immediately after a price crisis. It also points to the need to remove constraints to agricultural investments that will enable realization of the positive impacts of high food prices on production.

wage effects). Artuc and his colleagues do not include any government response to the increase in food prices.

The authors estimate that the bottom 40 percent of each country faces, on average, 3 percentage point higher inflation than the top 60 percent. Across 36 countries in Sub-Saharan Africa, this equates to food price inflation that is roughly twice as high as nonfood price inflation. In the downside scenario, the number of extreme poor increases by over 18 million on top of the estimated 667 million poor in 2022 (figure 1.12, panel b). However, as noted, this impact could be a short-run downside one.

Governments can mitigate such impacts through social protection policies. However, somewhat different from the previous periods of high food price inflation, and as part 2 discusses, governments' finances have been depleted by the various fiscal measures enacted through the COVID-19 crisis. For economies still reeling from the pandemic, these inflationary pressures could not have come at a worse time.

Inflation forecasts are subject to great uncertainty, and it is possible that food and energy prices will rise further. Figure 1.13 shows how the share of food in total consumption changes across the income distribution to highlight why further increases in food prices, beyond what was anticipated, would increase the pressures on poor households in the short run. This analysis uses data on food consumption shares and mean consumption by quintile from household surveys from 71 countries across the income spectrum. The food consumption share is then regressed on log consumption to predict the share for any given consumption level.[18] This analysis based on Mahler et al. (2022) reveals that people living in extreme poverty spend about two-thirds of their resources on food.[19] As online annex 1C reports, 81 percent of people living in extreme poverty live in rural areas, and so for some of these households further increases in food prices may also increase incomes, thereby reducing negative impacts. However, there is significant regional variation in the share of the extreme poor who live in rural areas, ranging from 43 percent in Latin America and the Caribbean to 87 percent in South Asia. Regions in which a large share of poor people live in urban areas (such as Latin America and the Caribbean and Europe and Central Asia) are likely to be more adversely affected by rising food prices.

FIGURE 1.13

FIGURE 1.13

Poorer households spend more on food

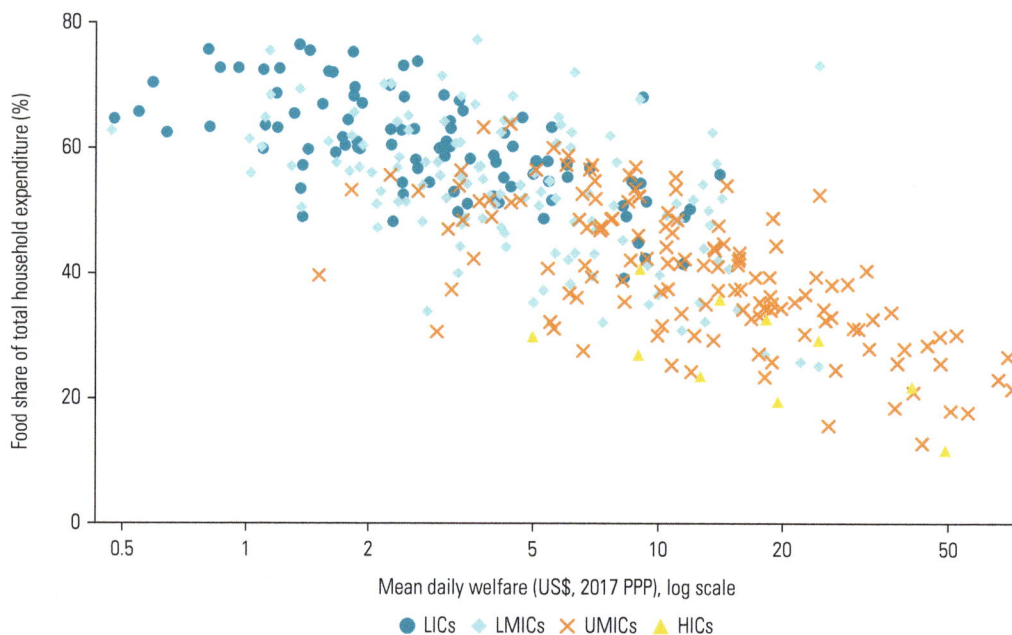

Source: Original calculations based on Mahler et al. 2022.
Note: The figure shows the relationship between food share and average logged consumption for each consumption quintile using household surveys for 71 countries. Each observation is a consumption quintile for a country. Estimates for India are reported by rural and urban quintiles. "Mean daily welfare" captures the average daily income of each country quintile expressed in 2017 PPP US$. HICs = high-income countries; LICs = low-income countries; LMICs = lower-middle-income countries; PPP = purchasing power parity; UMICs = upper-middle-income countries.

Implications for reaching the 3 percent global poverty target by 2030

The United Nations' Sustainable Development Goals call for ending extreme poverty by 2030, and the World Bank's own goal is to reduce global poverty to at most 3 percent by the end of this decade. These goals were set following the successful achievement of the Millennium Development Goal to halve global poverty between 2000 and 2015. The 3 percent target was at the time considered an aspirational target for the global community. The first section of this chapter, however, points to slowing poverty reduction between 2014 and 2019 as poverty became increasingly concentrated in fewer countries with slower growth rates than those countries that drove progress prior to 2014. This and other setbacks, as well as the slow recovery nowcasted for 2020–22, are already raising concerns about whether the world is on track to meet the 2030 target. Indeed, previous editions of this report have highlighted that the target is increasingly challenging to meet, and it will require higher and higher growth rates or reductions in inequality.

World Bank growth forecasts are only available until 2024 (World Bank 2022b), so the projections in figure 1.14 assume that each country grows at its average annual historical per capita GDP growth rate for the period 2025–30. Closely following World Bank (2020a), historical average annual growth rates are derived for each country for the 10-year period (2010–19) before the pandemic. Although growth rates are available for the pandemic period, it is safe to assume that the growth shocks observed during the pandemic are rare enough that they most likely will

FIGURE 1.14

Progress in poverty reduction has been altered in lasting ways

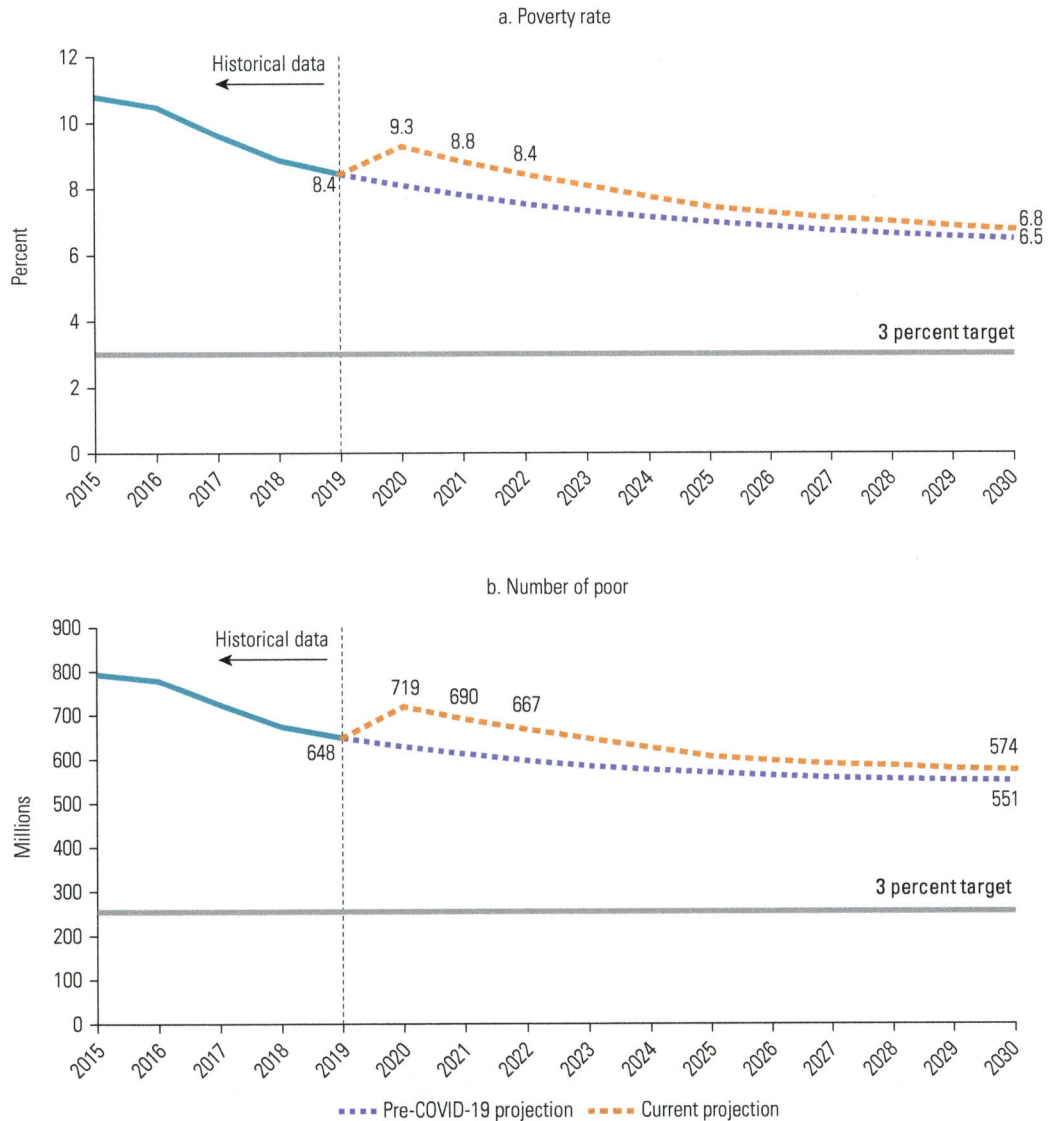

a. Poverty rate

b. Number of poor

Sources: Original calculations based on Mahler, Yonzan, and Lakner, forthcoming; World Bank, Poverty and Inequality Platform, https://pip
.worldbank.org; World Bank 2022b.
Note: Two growth scenarios are considered: the "Current projection" uses growth rates from the June 2022 *Global Economic Prospects* (GEP)
database to project poverty up to 2024. The "Pre-COVID-19 projection" uses the January 2020 GEP growth rate to project poverty to 2022.
Both scenarios use the country-level average annual historical (2010–19) growth rate to project poverty in the remaining years. "3 percent
target" is based on the estimated number of poor in 2030 (255 million).

not recur during the period ending in 2030. Projections are also presented in figure 1.14 for a
pre-COVID-19 scenario to illustrate the setback caused by the pandemic.[20]

Figure 1.14 shows that, even before the pandemic, the world was not set to achieve the World
Bank's goal of reaching 3 percent global extreme poverty by 2030, confirming findings in *Poverty
and Shared Prosperity 2020* (World Bank 2020a). Under the prepandemic scenario, the global
extreme poverty rate would have been 6.5 percent in 2030, equivalent to 551 million poor.[21]

Incorporating the most recent growth scenario, which includes the effect of the pandemic and of the compounding shocks of inflation and conflict for 2022, the global poverty rate for 2030 is projected to be 7 percent, equivalent to 574 million people still living on less than US$2.15 per person per day in 2030.

Under pre-COVID-19 projections, a similar global poverty headcount rate of 7 percent would have been achieved in 2026. In other words, the pandemic, conflict, and inflation are likely responsible for a four-year delay in the progress toward global poverty reduction. A three-year delay was anticipated in the previous edition of this report (World Bank 2020a), highlighting how the still-evolving nature of the current crises could continue pushing the 3 percent goal further into the future. Growth projections from long-run growth models indicate that, even before COVID-19, projected growth was not fast enough to achieve the target of ending poverty in this lifetime.[22] Thus that point at which the world meets the 3 percent goal is now further in the future.

These projections mask substantial differences in projections between regions. As figure 1.3 foretells, extreme poverty is projected to become increasingly concentrated in Sub-Saharan Africa. Other regions will likely reach the 2030 target of less than 3 percent extreme poverty by 2030, but poverty is projected to remain intractably above target in Sub-Saharan Africa. The challenge facing this region is well illustrated by considering the income growth that would have to be achieved to reach the 2030 target. Findings from simulations show that all countries would need to grow 9 percent a year beginning in 2023 to achieve the 3 percent goal by 2030. For Sub-Saharan Africa, which had an average per capita GDP growth rate of 1.2 percent in the decade preceding the pandemic, this would mean achieving growth rates about eight times higher than historical rates between 2010 and 2019. These projections underscore the key findings and messages of the recent trends presented in this chapter: there is an urgent need to correct course.

Notes

1. The first United Nations Sustainable Development Goal calls for a global effort to "end poverty in all its forms everywhere" (United Nations 2017). The World Bank set a target of reducing global poverty to below 3 percent by 2030. Box 1.1 in *Poverty and Shared Prosperity 2018* (World Bank 2018) describes how the World Bank's corporate goals align with the Sustainable Development Goals.

2. This reduction in pace is not just because the percentage point changes are smaller—percentage point changes are smaller at lower rates (Ravallion 2003)—but also because the average annual percentage change in poverty fell from 8 percent to 5 percent.

3. Following the coverage rule of the Poverty and Inequality Platform (PIP), regional estimates for South Asia were only reported until 2014 in *Poverty and Shared Prosperity 2020* (in that report, see box 1.2; in this report see table 1C.4 in online annex 1C).

4. As discussed in online annex 1B, the World Bank will continue to make the 2011 PPPs-based estimates available to users via PIP. The objective is to ensure transparency and replicability and to address the recommendation of the Atkinson Commission on Global Poverty that the World Bank continue to report poverty estimates on the basis of the 2011 PPPs until 2030.

5. Data coverage for 2017 refers to the data available at the time of writing *Poverty and Shared Prosperity 2020*. PIP's data coverage for 2017 for Sub-Saharan Africa is currently 87 percent.

6. For example, several countries collected welfare data via phone interviews, replacing or complementing traditional in-person interviews. Moreover, in several countries the welfare aggregate used to measure poverty has been adapted to better capture the full extent of the COVID-19 shock—see Castaneda Aguilar et al. (2022a) for further details.

7. Because of this limited data availability and the incomparability in household welfare measures collected in 2020 using previous surveys, global and regional poverty estimates for 2020 are not reported in PIP, even though data coverage met PIP's coverage rule (see online annex 1A). Poverty rates for 2020 are presented as nowcasts instead (see the section on nowcasts later in this chapter).

8. The number of available surveys for 2020 may increase in the coming years. However, in 2020 and at the time of writing the 2020 edition of this report, 30 household surveys for 2018 were already available. Country-level lined-up poverty estimates are available in each reporting year between 1990 and 2019 (see online annex 1A).

9. The change in PPPs largely explains the changes in the lower lines, while the change in the UMIC line is partly due to PPP changes and partly due to upward revisions in national poverty lines in real terms (Jolliffe et al. 2022). This result seems intuitive because poverty in UMICs is more likely to reflect the concept of relative poverty, which changes over time with changes in income and consumption patterns.

10. One way to quantify this revision is to compare the lined-up poverty estimate for 2019 from the global poverty data vintage used in *Poverty and Shared Prosperity 2020* with the lined-up estimate for 2019 used in this report. Because the former was expressed in 2011 PPPs, the estimates are calculated using the 2011 PPPs legacy series. The latest data drive an upward revision of 1.7 percentage points in the 2019 lined-up estimate for China and of 3.2 percentage points for Mexico.

11. See chapter 3 in *Poverty and Shared Prosperity 2018* (World Bank 2018) and box 1.1 in *Poverty and Shared Prosperity 2020* (World Bank 2020a).

12. Figure 1.8 captures the relationship between the SPL and higher living standards measured with GDP per capita. GDP per capita is highly correlated with measures of median household income or consumption used to derive the SPL—see figure 3.3 in World Bank (2018).

13. This chapter follows the PIP regional classification, which is different from the regional classifications used by the World Bank. Some economies, mostly high-income economies, are excluded from the geographical regions and are included as a separate group referred to as "rest of the world." See the PIP regional classification available here: https://worldbank .github.io/PIP-Methodology/lineupestimates .html#regionsandcountries.

14. To allow for a historical comparison, household welfare vectors for 1990 are extrapolated back to 1950 using growth in per capita GDP from the national accounts (a *backcast*).

The global poverty estimates for the period 1981–89 in figure 1.10 could differ from the official poverty rates available in PIP (https://pip.worldbank.org). For example, the increase in global poverty between 1989 and 1990 in PIP is driven by a methodological change in the welfare aggregate used to measure poverty in China, changing its survey-based welfare aggregate from a measure of income to a measure of consumption between 1987 and 1990. The backcast series avoids such data incomparability. However, backcasting poverty, similar to nowcasting poverty, imposes strong assumptions that introduce a considerable degree of uncertainty around the backcasted estimates.

15. On the one hand, the counterfactual is a hypothetical scenario and thus requires many assumptions. On the other hand, it allows estimation of the net impact of the pandemic in 2020, as opposed to the overall change from 2019 to 2020. This is an important distinction because, for example, some lower-income countries were expected to experience an increase in poverty in 2020 even without the pandemic (see figure 1.11).

16. World Bank, World Development Indicators (database), https://databank.worldbank.org/source /world-development-indicators.

17. Global average per capita income growth is expected to slow to 2 percent in 2022. Per capita incomes in LICs are expected to grow by only 0.6 percent in 2022. The recovery of LMICs is likely to stall in 2022, with an average per capita income increase of 0.6 percent, which is well short of the 2.4 percent average annual growth they saw for the 2010–19 period. Like the other income groups, UMICs and HICs are also expected to slow down the recovery in 2022 with per capita income increases of 3.1 percent in the upper-middle-income group and 2.9 percent in the high-income group.

18. For technical details, see Mahler et al. (2022).

19. The same figure for a person with a daily income of around US$50—a typical income in HICs—is closer to 25 percent.

20. For the pre-COVID-19 projection series, growth rates from the January 2020 *Global Economic Prospects* are available only until 2022. Thus the pre-COVID-19 projection series uses historical average annual growth rates from 2023 onward. All projections rely

on the same pass-through rates used in the nowcast: 70 percent for countries using a consumption aggregate in their latest survey and a pass-through of 100 percent for countries using income aggregates.

21. This figure is in line with the projected global poverty rate of 6.1 percent (521 million poor) published in *Poverty and Shared Prosperity 2020* (World Bank 2020a). Changes to the projected estimates are due to several changes in the data and methodology between the two editions of the report: adoption of the 2017 PPPs, newly available survey data, changes to the nowcast methodology, and changes to national accounts data, among other things.

22. See chapter 3 for more details on the long-run growth models used. The setback from COVID-19 has put this target even further out of reach.

References

Andreyeva, Tatiana, Michael W. Long, and Kelly D. Brownell. 2010. "The Impact of Food Prices on Consumption: A Systematic Review of Research on the Price Elasticity of Demand for Food." *American Journal of Public Health* 100 (2): 216–22.

Artuc, Erhan, Guillermo Falcone, Guido Porto, and Bob Rijkers. 2022. "War-Induced Food Price Inflation Imperils the Poor." *VOX EU CEPR* (blog), April 1, 2022. https://voxeu.org/article/war-induced-food-price-inflation-imperils-poor.

Bhalla, Surjit, Karan Bhasin, and Arvind Virmani. 2022. "Pandemic, Poverty, and Inequality: Evidence from India." IMF Working Paper No. 2022/069, International Monetary Fund, Washington, DC.

Bolt, Jutta, and Jan Luiten van Zanden. 2020. "Maddison Style Estimates of the Evolution of the World Economy: A New 2020 Update." Maddison-Project Working Paper WP-15. https://www.rug.nl/ggdc/historicaldevelopment/maddison/publications/wp15.pdf.

Castaneda Aguilar, R. Andres, Reno Dewina, Carolina Diaz-Bonilla, Ifeanyi N. Edochie, Tony Fujs, Dean Jolliffe, Jonathan Lain, et al. 2022a. "April 2022 Update to the Poverty and Inequality Platform (PIP): What's New." Global Poverty Monitoring Technical Note Series 20, World Bank, Washington, DC.

Castaneda Aguilar, R. Andres, Carolina Diaz-Bonilla, Tony Fujs, Dean Jolliffe, Christoph Lakner, Daniel G. Mahler, Minh C. Nguyen, Marta Schoch, Samuel K. Tetteh-Baah, Martha C. Viveros Mendoza, and Nishant Yonzan. 2022b. "September 2022 Update to the Poverty and Inequality Platform (PIP): What's New." Global Poverty Monitoring Technical Note Series 24, World Bank, Washington, DC.

Corral, Paul, Alexander Irwin, Daniel Gerzon, and Tara Wishwanath. 2020. *Fragility and Conflict: On the Front Lines of the Fight against Poverty.* Washington, DC: World Bank.

Deaton, Angus. 2005. "Measuring Poverty in a Growing World (or Measuring Growth in a Poor World)." *Review of Economics and Statistics* 8 (1): 1–19. https://doi.org/10.1162/0034653053327612.

Deaton, Angus. 2010. "Price Indexes, Inequality, and the Measurement of World Poverty." *American Economic* 100 (1): 5–34. https://doi.org/10.1257/aer.100.1.5.

Dreze, Jean, and Anmol Somanchi. 2021. "View: New Barometer of India's Economy Fails to Reflect Deprivations of Poor Households." *Economic Times*, June. https://economictimes.indiatimes.com/opinion/et-commentary/view-the-new-barometer-of-indias-economy-fails-to-reflect-the-deprivations-of-poor-households/articleshow/83696115.cms.

Ferreira, Francisco H. G., Shaohua Chen, Andrew Dabalen, Yuri Dikhanov, Nada Hamadeh, Dean Jolliffe, Ambar Narayan, et al. 2016. "A Global Count of the Extreme Poor in 2012: Data Issues, Methodology and Initial Results." *Journal of Economic Inequality* 14 (2): 141–72. https://doi.org/10.1007/s10888-016-9326-6.

Ferreira, Francisco H. G., Anna Fruttero, Phillippe G. Leite, and Leonardo R. Lucchetti. 2013. "Rising Food Prices and Household Welfare: Evidence from Brazil in 2008." *Journal of Agricultural Economics* 64 (1): 151–76.

Ferreira, Francisco H. G., Dean Jolliffe, and Espen Beer Prydz. 2015. "The International Poverty Line Has Just Been Raised to $1.90 a Day, but Global Poverty Is Basically Unchanged. How Is That Even Possible?" World Bank Blogs, October 4, 2015. https://blogs.worldbank.org/developmenttalk/international-poverty-line-has-just-been-raised-190-day-global-poverty-basically-unchanged-how-even.

Filmer, Deon, Haishan Fu, and Carolina Sánchez-Páramo. 2022. "An Adjustment to Global Poverty Lines." *Voices* (blog), May 2, 2022. https://blogs.worldbank.org/voices/adjustment-global-poverty-lines.

Friedman, Jed, and James Levinsohn. 2002. "The Distributional Impacts of Indonesia's Financial Crisis on Household Welfare: A 'Rapid Response' Methodology." *World Bank Economic Review* 16 (3): 397–423.

Gupta, Arpit, Anup Malani, and Bartosz Woda. 2021. "Inequality in India Declined During COVID." NBER Working Paper 29597, National Bureau of Economic Research, Cambridge, MA.

Ha, Jongrim, Ayhan M. Kose, and Franziska Ohnsorge. 2021. "One-Stop Source: A Global Database of Inflation." Policy Research Working Paper 9737, World Bank, Washington, DC.

Headey, Derek D. 2018. "Food Prices and Poverty." *World Bank Economic Review* 32 (3): 676–91.

Headey, Derek, Fantu Bachewe Nisrane, Ibrahim Worku Hassen, and Mekdim Dereje. 2012. "Urban Wage Behavior and Food Price Inflation: The Case of Ethiopia." Working paper, International Food Policy Research Institute, Washington, DC.

Ivanic, Maros, and Will J. Martin. 2008. "Implications of Higher Global Food Prices for Poverty in Low-Income Countries." *Agricultural Economics* 39: 405–16.

Ivanic, Maros, and Will J. Martin. 2014. "Short- and Long-Run Impacts of Food Price Changes on Poverty." Policy Research Working Paper 7011, World Bank, Washington, DC.

Jacoby, Hanan G. 2016. "Food Prices, Wages, and Welfare in Rural India." *Economic Inquiry* 54 (1): 159–76.

Jolliffe, Dean, Daniel Gerszon Mahler, Christoph Lakner, Aziz Atamanov, and Samuel Kofi Tetteh-Baah. 2022. "Assessing the Impact of the 2017 PPPs on the International Poverty Line and Global Poverty." Policy Research Working Paper 9941, World Bank, Washington, DC.

Jolliffe, Dean, and Espen Beer Prydz. 2016. "Estimating International Poverty Lines from Comparable National Thresholds." *Journal of Economic Inequality* 14 (2): 185–98. https://doi.org/10.1007/s10888-016-9327-5.

Jolliffe, Dean, and Espen Beer Prydz. 2021. "Societal Poverty: A Relative and Relevant Measure." *World Bank Economic Review* 35 (1): 180–206. https://doi.org/10.1093/wber/lhz018.

Klasen, Stephan, Tatyana Krivobokova, Friederike Greb, Rahul Lahoti, Syamsul Hidayat, and Pasaribu Manuel. 2016. "International Income Poverty Measurement: Which Way Now?" *Journal of Economic Inequality* 14: 199–225. https://doi.org/10.1007/s10888-016-9324-8.

Lain, Jonathan William, Marta Schoch, and Tara Vishwanath. 2022. "Estimating a Poverty Trend for Nigeria between 2009 and 2019." Policy Research Working Paper 9974, World Bank, Washington, DC. https://doi.org/10.1596/1813-9450-9974.

Lara Ibarra, Gabriel, and Ricardo Campante Cardoso Vale. 2022. "Brazil 2020 Data Update: Methodological Adjustments to the World Bank's Poverty and Inequality Estimates." Global Poverty Monitoring Technical Note 21, World Bank, Washington, DC. https://documents.worldbank.org/en/publication/documents-reports/documentdetail/099815204132219104/idu0cdb267100a24104a010b1ab03dd511e0d135.

Mahler, Daniel Gerszon, R. Andres Castaneda Aguilar, and David Newhouse. Forthcoming. "Nowcasting Global Poverty." *World Bank Economic Review*.

Mahler, Daniel Gerszon, Nishant Yonzan, Ruth Hill, Christoph Lakner, Haoyu Wu, and Nobuo Yoshida. 2022. "Pandemic, Prices, and Poverty." *Data Blog*, April 13, 2022, World Bank, Washington, DC. https://blogs.worldbank.org/opendata/pandemic-prices-and-poverty.

Mahler, Daniel Gerszon, Nishant Yonzan, and Christoph Lakner [randomized order]. Forthcoming. "The Impact of COVID-19 on Global Inequality and Poverty." World Bank, Washington, DC.

Minot, Nicholas, and Reno Dewina. 2015. "Are We Overestimating the Negative Impact of Higher Food Prices? Evidence from Ghana." *Agricultural Economics* 46 (4): 579–93.

Prydz, Espen Beer, Dean Jolliffe, and Umar Serajuddin. 2022. "Disparities in Assessments of Living Standards Using National Accounts and Household Surveys." *Review of Income and Wealth*, May 23, 2022. https://doi.org/10.1111/roiw.12577.

Ravallion, Martin. 2003. "Measuring Aggregate Welfare in Developing Countries: How Well Do

National Accounts and Surveys Agree?" *Review of Economics and Statistics* 85 (3): 645–52.

Ravallion, Martin. 2022. "Filling a Gaping Hole in the World Bank's Global Poverty Measures: New Estimates of Poverty in India since 2011." Centre for Global Development Notes, Centre for Global Development, Washington, DC. https://www.cgdev.org/publication/filling-gaping-hole-world-banks-global-poverty-measures-new-estimates-poverty-india#:~:text=Ravallion%20(2016)%20proposes%20that%20the,zero%20at%20the%20poverty%20line.

Ravallion, Martin, Shaohua Chen, and Prem Sangraula. 2009. "Dollar a Day Revisited." *World Bank Economic Review* 23 (2): 163–84. https://doi.org/10.1093/wber/lhp007.

Reddy, Sanjay G., and Thomas Pogge. 2010. "How Not to Count the Poor." In *Debates on the Measurement of Global Poverty*, edited by Sudhir Anand, Paul Segal, and Joseph E. Stiglitz. New York: Oxford University Press. https://doi.org/10.1093/acprof:oso/9780199558032.001.0001.

Sandefur, Justin. 2022. "The Great Indian Poverty Debate, 2.0." *Centre for Global Development Blog*, April 19, 2022. https://www.cgdev.org/blog/great-indian-poverty-debate-20.

Simler, Kenneth R. 2010. "The Short-Term Impact of Higher Food Prices on Poverty in Uganda." Policy Research Working Paper 5210, World Bank, Washington, DC.

Sinha Roy, Sutirtha, and Roy van der Weide. 2022. "Poverty in India Has Declined over the Last Decade but Not as Much as Previously Thought." Policy Research Working Paper 9994, World Bank, Washington, DC.

Tetteh Baah, Samuel Kofi, Aziz Atamanov, Dean Mitchell Jolliffe, Christoph Lakner, and Daniel Gerszon Mahler. 2022. "Updating the International Poverty Line with the 2017 PPPs." *Data Blog*, May 2, 2022. https://blogs.worldbank.org/opendata/updating-international-poverty-line-2017-ppps.

United Nations. 2017. *The Sustainable Development Goals Report 2017*. New York: United Nations. https://unstats.un.org/sdgs/report/2017/.

Van Campenhout, Bjorn, Karl Pauw, and Nicholas Minot. 2018. "The Impact of Food Price Shocks in Uganda: First-Order Effects versus General-Equilibrium Consequences." *European Review of Agricultural Economics* 45 (5): 783–807.

World Bank. 1990. *World Development Report 1990: Poverty*. Washington, DC: World Bank. https://openknowledge.worldbank.org/handle/10986/5973.

World Bank. 2013a. *Bangladesh Poverty Assessment: Assessing a Decade of Progress in Reducing Poverty, 2000–2010* (English). Washington, DC: World Bank. http://documents.worldbank.org/curated/en/109051468203350011/Bangladesh-Poverty-assessment-assessing-a-decade-of-progress-in-reducing-poverty-2000-2010.

World Bank. 2013b. "Where Have All the Poor Gone? Cambodia Poverty Assessment 2013." World Bank, Washington, DC. https://openknowledge.worldbank.org/handle/10986/17546.

World Bank. 2015. *Ethiopia Poverty Assessment 2014*. Washington, DC: World Bank. https://openknowledge.worldbank.org/handle/10986/21323.

World Bank. 2016. *The Uganda Poverty Assessment Report 2016: Farms, Cities and Good Fortune—Assessing Poverty Reduction in Uganda from 2006 to 2013*. Washington, DC: World Bank. https://openknowledge.worldbank.org/handle/10986/26075.

World Bank. 2018. *Poverty and Shared Prosperity 2018: Piecing Together the Poverty Puzzle*. Washington, DC: World Bank. https://doi.org/10.1596/978-1-4648-1330-6.

World Bank. 2020a. *Poverty and Shared Prosperity 2020: Reversals of Fortune*. Washington, DC: World Bank. https://doi.org/10.1596/978-1-4648-1602-4.

World Bank. 2020b. *Purchasing Power Parities and the Size of World Economies: Results from the 2017 International Comparison Program*. Washington, DC: World Bank. http://hdl.handle.net/10986/33623.

World Bank. 2022a. *Commodity Markets Outlook: The Impact of the War in Ukraine on Commodity Markets, April 2022*. Washington, DC: World Bank.

World Bank. 2022b. *Global Economic Prospects*. Washington, DC: World Bank. https://www.worldbank.org/en/publication/global-economic-prospects.

Shared Prosperity and Inequality: Uneven Losses and an Uneven Recovery

Summary

One of the twin goals of the World Bank Group is to promote shared prosperity, which reflects the extent to which economic growth is inclusive. During the COVID-19 pandemic, large and unequal job and income losses were reported, contributing to concerns about reduced shared prosperity, as well as rising inequality within countries.

Data on shared prosperity for 11 countries in 2020 confirm the declines in income depicted in chapter 1. The average income of the bottom 40 percent of the population fell substantially in most countries. Changes in the income of the bottom 40 are very closely tied to changes in the median income, which also declined by 4 percent globally, with larger relative declines among low- and lower-middle-income countries. The impact of the pandemic stands in stark contrast to the overall positive progress in shared prosperity evident on the eve of the pandemic. Prepandemic growth was, overall, inclusive based on the estimates of shared prosperity for 2014–19. Sixty-five of 78 economies reported positive values (although there was wide variation in shared prosperity across regions and across countries within regions). Thus the pandemic-induced shock in 2020 came as a reversal for many countries.

This chapter draws on official data and projections to show that within countries, changes in inequality in 2020 were mixed. Higher rates of job and income losses among vulnerable households did not necessarily result in relatively larger income losses for the poorest in each country. Some countries saw inequality increase, but regardless of the direction, the estimated changes in inequality are small in magnitude in nearly all cases.

Of global concern, however, the global income Gini index rose by a little more than 0.5 points in 2020 and the recovery to date has also proceeded at different speeds. In 2021, it appeared to have stalled for the poorest countries. The incomes of the bottom 40 of the world income distribution are projected to have remained below precrisis levels in 2021. Meanwhile, those in the top 20 of the world income distribution had already recovered their losses by 2021 and continued to pull ahead in 2022.

Chapter 2 online annexes available at http://hdl.handle.net/10986/37739:
2A. Shared Prosperity Estimates by Economy; 2B. Releases of Data for Shared Prosperity; 2C. Mean and Median Income/Consumption, 2019–22; and 2D. Bottom 40 Profiles.

Introduction

Promoting shared prosperity is one of the twin goals of the World Bank Group (the other is ending extreme poverty). Shared prosperity is defined as the annualized growth rate in average consumption or income of the poorest 40 percent of the population ("the bottom 40"). This indicator measures the extent to which economic growth is inclusive by focusing on household income or consumption growth among the population at the bottom of the income distribution rather than on those near the average or at the top. Specifically, growth in the average income of the bottom 40 is equal to growth in average income *plus* growth in the share of income that goes to the bottom 40 percent. This indicator is meaningful at the country level, but it can also be applied to global incomes to look at the bottom 40 percent of the world income distribution. Because this shared prosperity indicator monitors the progress of the bottom 40 and how the less well-off are able to benefit from the growth process, it is relevant even in higher-income countries, where extreme poverty is much lower.

Shared prosperity is calculated using two household surveys administered approximately five years apart. This greater data requirement results in country coverage smaller than that for extreme poverty, which requires only one survey. In this report, the latest Global Database of Shared Prosperity (GDSP) comprises selected surveys for circa 2014–19, supplemented with surveys from circa 2013–18 to compensate for falling data coverage. The exact survey years vary across countries: for example, the survey period covers 2016–20 for Argentina and Mexico and 2012–17 for the Arab Republic of Egypt and Mauritius. Box 2.1 describes in detail the country coverage of the database used to calculate shared prosperity. Because this period covers a

---

BOX 2.1

Data coverage: A growing challenge for measuring shared prosperity, particularly for poorer countries

The shared prosperity indicator is available for 91 of the world's 218 economies. This is the same number of economies considered in *Poverty and Shared Prosperity 2020,* which examined shared prosperity circa 2012–17 (World Bank 2020, table B2.1.1). However, data coverage is more limited for circa 2014–19, and so this level of indicator coverage is attained only because the data from circa 2014–19 are supplemented with surveys from circa 2013–18 for countries that otherwise would not have data. With this addition, approximately 5.9 billion people in these economies are represented, or 76.9 percent of the world's population in 2019. The Global Database of Shared Prosperity (GDSP) includes coverage of 85 percent or more populations residing in the Europe and Central Asia and Latin America and the Caribbean regions. Population coverage in the East Asia and Pacific region is nearly 96 percent. With India's inclusion (chapter 1, box 1.2), the database now covers about 88 percent of South Asia's population, or over 1.6 billion people.

Despite high representation of the global population, underrepresentation of the poorest and most vulnerable populations continues to be a challenge for monitoring shared prosperity. Compared with coverage in the 2020 report, population coverage in Sub-Saharan Africa has dropped by almost half, from 31 percent to 17 percent. Only nine of the 48 countries in Sub-Saharan Africa are represented in the database. Slightly less than half of the population of the Middle East and North Africa are covered, but only three of the 14 countries in the region. Coverage in fragile and conflict-affected economies remains a challenge because the database represents less than 9 percent of people living in such situations. Only five of 39 fragile and conflict-affected economies reported on shared prosperity in the latest period. By income class, about 12.9 percent of low-income country populations are included in the database, in stark contrast to the 76.5 percent and 92.7 percent of populations residing in lower-middle- and upper-middle-income countries, respectively. Of the 74 International Development Association (IDA) countries, 14 countries have shared prosperity data available, covering less than 30 percent of the corresponding population (table B2.1.1).

(continued)

BOX 2.1

Data coverage: A growing challenge for measuring shared prosperity, particularly for poorer countries *(continued)*

TABLE B2.1.1

Data coverage summary, shared prosperity, circa 2014–19

	Population				Number of economies			
	All economies (millions)	Economies with poverty rate (millions)	Economies with SP (millions)	Economies with SP (%)	All economies	Economies with poverty rate	Economies with SP	Economies with SP (%)
East Asia and Pacific	2,103.8	2,051.4	2,049.0	97.4	26	21	9	34.6
Europe and Central Asia	495.0	494.8	432.6	87.4	31	30	25	80.6
Latin America and the Caribbean	642.2	597.9	561.0	87.4	31	24	15	48.4
Middle East and North Africa	394.4	382.7	188.0	47.7	14	12	3	21.4
South Asia	1,835.8	1,797.7	1,605.5	87.5	8	7	4	50.0
Sub-Saharan Africa	1,107.0	1,102.1	187.8	17.0	48	46	9	18.8
Rest of the world	1,105.3	1,037.8	886.0	80.2	60	28	26	43.3
Fragile and conflict-affected	908.7	831.9	78.1	8.6	39	35	5	12.8
IDA and Blend	1,670.7	1,612.3	482.9	28.9	74	68	14	18.9
Low-income	647.9	580.7	83.3	12.9	27	24	4	14.8
Lower-middle-income	3,285.4	3,268.9	2,514.8	76.5	55	54	21	38.2
Upper-middle-income	2,510.8	2,477.1	2,327.2	92.7	55	48	28	50.9
High-income	1,210.8	1,137.8	984.5	81.3	80	42	38	47.5
Total	**7,683.4**	**7,464.5**	**5,909.9**	**76.9**	**218**	**168**	**91**	**41.7**

Sources: Data for 81 economies from World Bank, Global Database of Shared Prosperity (9th edition, circa 2014–19); data for 10 economies from the Global Database of Shared Prosperity (8th edition, circa 2013–18). https://www.worldbank.org/en/topic/poverty/brief/global-database-of-shared-prosperity.

Note: Population data are from 2019. The list of International Development Association (IDA) countries and economies in fragile and conflict-affected situations is from fiscal year 2022. República Bolivariana de Venezuela is temporarily declassified in the World Bank's income classification due to pending national accounts statistics and not included in the breakdown by income group. "Economies with poverty rate" includes economies that reported poverty estimates in 2012 or later. Blend = IDA-eligible economies but also creditworthy for some borrowing from the International Bank for Reconstruction and Development; SP = shared prosperity.

span of time before the onset of COVID-19 for some countries, and including the COVID-19 years for other countries, the report separates the discussion of trends for those countries with only pre-COVID-19 data from that of countries with data collected in 2020. Online annex 2A provides details on the measurement of the shared prosperity indicator, as well as information on country-level data sets. Online annex 2B lists the number of countries from all releases of the GDSP.

Although shared prosperity indicates how the poorest in each country have fared in recent years, this measure alone does not reveal whether the progress (or setbacks) at the bottom of the distribution is the result of widespread growth benefiting all groups (or widespread contraction that has set back all groups) or whether it is the result of a shift in the distribution of economic gains toward the bottom 40 (Lakner et al. 2022). To distinguish between these possibilities, the shared prosperity premium (SPP) is defined as the difference between shared prosperity and the growth in the mean consumption or income of the population—that is, the growth rate of the share of the bottom 40.

The SPP is one of several ways of measuring changes in inequality. Later in this chapter, other measures of inequality and their change over time are also used. Because of the pandemic, relatively few countries have survey data available to assess how inequality may have changed over this period. Therefore, to better understand how inequality has fared during the pandemic, this analysis uses distribution-sensitive simulations for countries that lack postpandemic survey data.

Shared prosperity and inequality, 2014–19

Substantial gains were made in shared prosperity from 2014 to 2019, but they varied across regions

Substantial progress in shared prosperity occurred for the vast majority of economies measured during the latest shared prosperity period, circa 2014–19. Overall, shared prosperity was positive for 65 of 78 economies. Average shared prosperity—calculated as an unweighted average of annualized income growth rates of the bottom 40 across all countries—stands at 3.2 percent. This is a notable improvement over the results presented in the 2020 report, when the average growth rate was 2.3 percent. However, there was wide variation in the annualized income growth of the bottom 40 as shown in figure 2.1, which plots the annualized income growth of the bottom 40 and of the total population against each other. Twenty-three countries achieved shared prosperity rates of 5.0 percent or more.

Comparing shared prosperity with the growth rate of the entire population, which the SPP does, provides insights into how the benefits of growth are shared across the distribution. A positive SPP indicates faster growth among the bottom 40 than the entire population, implying that economic growth or redistributive policies have favored the poorer segments of the population. A negative SPP indicates that the growth rate of average incomes or consumption exceeded that of the bottom 40. Countries located above the 45-degree line in figure 2.1 have a positive SPP—that is, the incomes of the bottom 40 grew faster than the average. Although the database used in this analysis covers 91 economies, the shared prosperity estimates for 13 economies are discussed in the next section because their shared prosperity ends in 2020 and therefore captures the early stages of the pandemic, which saw steep declines in incomes.

Significant differences in shared prosperity can be seen across regions. The East Asia and Pacific and Europe and Central Asia regions recorded the highest shared prosperity, measuring 4.5 percent and 5.4 percent, on average, respectively. Shared prosperity was positive in almost all countries in both regions, with the exceptions of Kazakhstan and Mongolia. Meanwhile, shared prosperity was negative in all three countries that represent the Middle East and North Africa. Among countries in Sub-Saharan Africa, the performance was mixed, with four of the nine economies recording negative shared prosperity (figure 2.2). By income group, low-income countries (LICs) had the poorest performance, recording almost no change

FIGURE 2.1

From 2014 to 2019, the vast majority of economies made substantial progress in shared prosperity

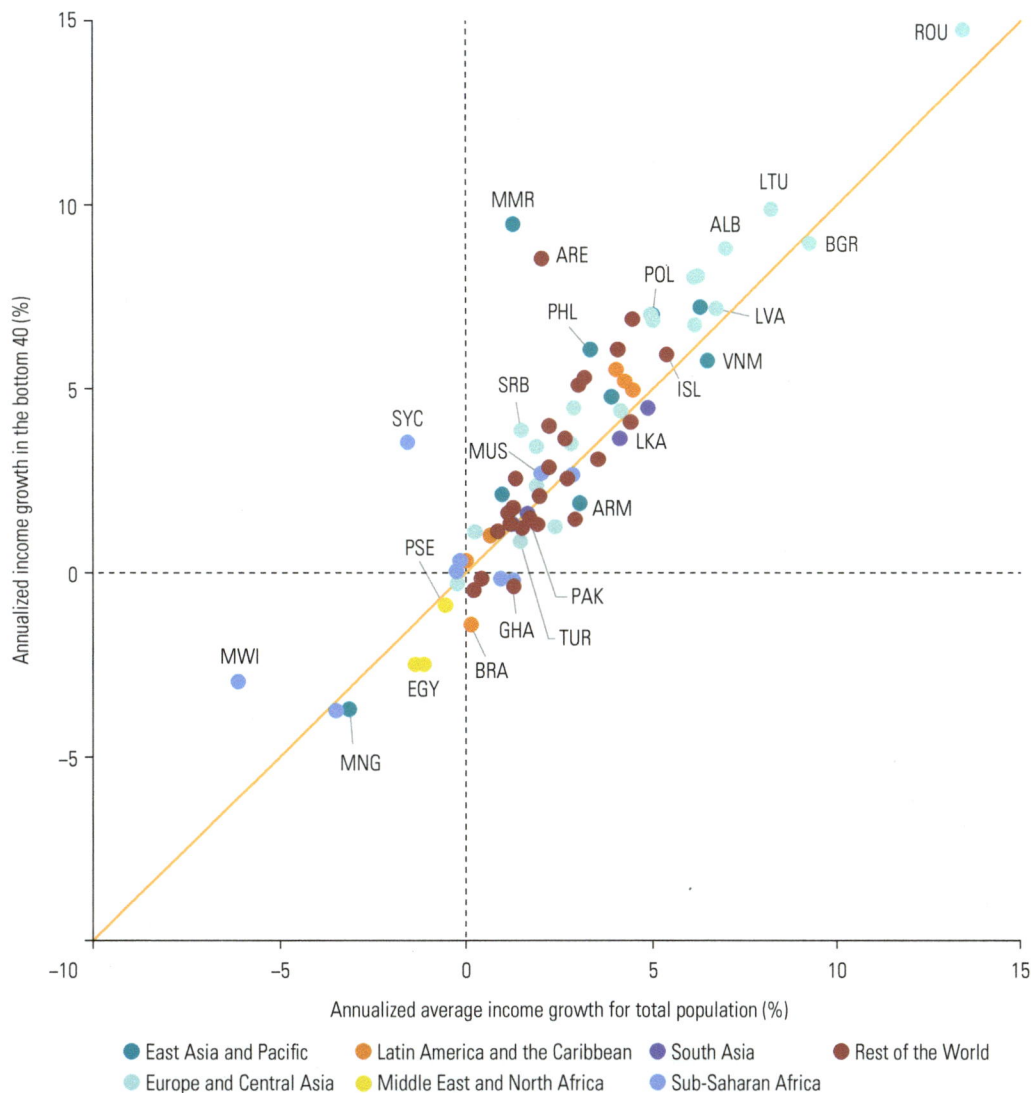

Sources: World Bank, Global Database of Shared Prosperity (9th edition, circa 2014–19, for 68 economies; 8th edition, circa 2013–18, for 10 economies), https://www.worldbank.org/en/topic/poverty/brief/global-database-of-shared-prosperity.
Note: The figure shows the relationship between the annualized average income growth for the total population and the Shared Prosperity measure (annualized income growth in the bottom 40 percent of the income distribution), circa 2014–19 or circa 2013–18. A 45-degree line is shown for reference. The sample includes 78 economies; those with data collected in 2020 are not included. For a list of country codes, go to https://www.iso.org/obp/ui/#search/code/.

in shared prosperity. Upper-middle-income countries (UMICs) had the best performance, with an average bottom 40 income growth of 4.3 percent. Shared prosperity in lower-middle-income countries (LMICs) measured around 1.8 percent (table 2.1).

Globally, the SPP was positive in 48 countries, indicating relative gains among the bottom 40 percent. The average SPP across all countries was also positive but small at

FIGURE 2.2

Significant differences occured in shared prosperity across regions and country income groups

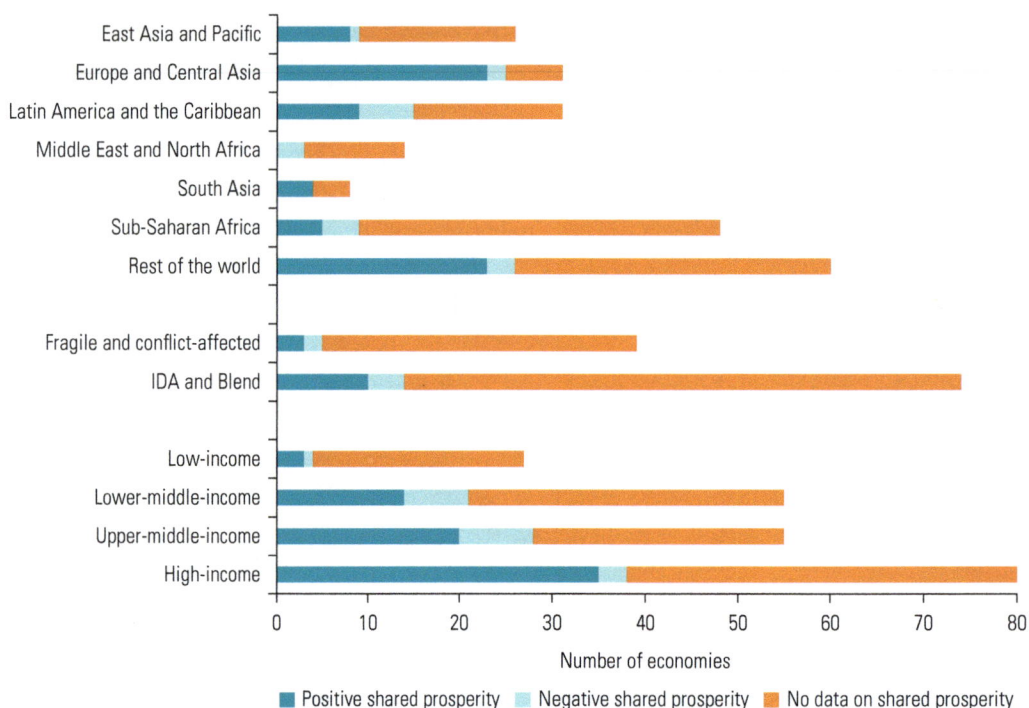

Sources: World Bank, Global Database of Shared Prosperity (9th edition, circa 2014–19, for 81 economies; 8th edition, circa 2013–18, for 10 economies), https://www.worldbank.org/en/topic/poverty/brief/global-database-of-shared-prosperity.
Note: The figure shows the number of economies in each country group with positive (negative) shared prosperity, which indicates positive (negative) income growth of the bottom 40 percent, and with no data on shared prosperity. Blend = IDA-eligible economies but also creditworthy for some borrowing from the International Bank for Reconstruction and Development; IDA = International Development Association.

0.6 percentage points. At the regional level, the average SPP was highest in the East Asia and Pacific region, followed by Europe and Central Asia and Sub-Saharan Africa (table 2.1). However, there is wide variation across countries within these regions. In Sub-Saharan Africa, the SPP ranged from –1.5 percent in Ghana to 5.1 percent in the Seychelles. In the East Asia and Pacific region, the indicator was negative for three of the nine economies. China, the most populous country in the world, reported a shared prosperity rate of 7.2 percent and an SPP of 0.9 percent. The highest SPP was found in Myanmar—8.2 percent. Europe and Central Asia accounted for 18 of the 47 economies that recorded both a positive SPP and a positive shared prosperity indicator, meaning that their bottom 40 experienced positive and faster-than-average income growth. In the Europe and Central Asia region, only a handful of countries had a negative SPP.

The most worrisome trend is in countries with both negative shared prosperity and a negative SPP, suggesting that average incomes declined but that the less well-off were disproportionately affected. Globally, 12 countries fell in this group. In the Middle East and North Africa, the less well-off were disproportionately affected in all three countries for which shared prosperity data were available.

Median income is another indicator of interest, particularly for assessing the welfare of a "representative" individual in a country, and especially when the income distribution is skewed to the right with a long tail, as is typical with income. In the latest shared prosperity

68

TABLE 2.1

Summary, shared prosperity and shared prosperity premium, 78 economies

	Number of economies					Simple average across economies			
	Number of economies with SP	SP > 0	Growth in median > 0	Growth in mean > 0	SPP > 0	Average SP (%)	Average SPP (pp)	Growth of the mean (%)	Growth of the median (%)
East Asia and Pacific	9	8	8	8	6	4.5	1.5	3.0	4.0
Europe and Central Asia	21	20	20	20	17	5.4	0.9	4.4	4.6
Latin America and the Caribbean	6	5	5	5	5	2.6	0.4	2.3	2.8
Middle East and North Africa	3	0	1	0	0	−2.0	−0.9	−1.0	−1.3
South Asia	4	4	4	4	1	2.8	−0.2	3.0	3.0
Sub-Saharan Africa	9	5	7	4	5	0.2	0.8	−0.5	0.5
Rest of the world	26	23	26	26	14	2.7	0.4	2.3	2.3
Fragile and conflict-affected	5	3	4	3	2	1.7	1.4	0.3	1.0
IDA and Blend	13	9	11	9	7	1.1	0.7	0.4	1.1
Low-income	4	3	3	1	3	0.0	0.9	−0.9	0.2
Lower-middle-income	18	11	14	13	6	1.8	0.3	1.5	1.9
Upper-middle-income	19	17	18	18	14	4.3	0.7	3.6	3.8
High-income	37	34	36	35	25	3.6	0.8	2.9	3.1
Total	**78**	**65**	**71**	**67**	**48**	**3.2**	**0.6**	**2.5**	**2.9**

Sources: World Bank, Global Database of Shared Prosperity (9th edition, circa 2014–19, for 68 economies; 8th edition, circa 2013–18, for 10 economies), https://www.worldbank.org/en/topic/poverty/brief/global-database-of-shared-prosperity.

Note: The table shows a summary for 78 economies, excluding those with data for 2020. Population data are from 2020. The list of International Development Association (IDA) countries and economies in fragile and conflict-affected situations is from fiscal year 2022. Blend = IDA-eligible economies but also creditworthy for some borrowing from the Bank for Reconstruction and Development; pp = percentage point; SP = shared prosperity; SPP = shared prosperity premium.

database, median income grew in 71 of 78 economies, at an average of 2.9 percent. Similar to shared prosperity, median income growth was highest in UMICs and lowest in LICs (table 2.1). In fact, the two measures of shared prosperity and median income growth are highly correlated, with a correlation coefficient of 0.97 (figure 2.3). Online annex 2C presents aggregated estimates of mean and median incomes during 2019–22, based on the nowcast methodology in chapter 1.

FIGURE 2.3

Median income growth and shared prosperity are highly correlated

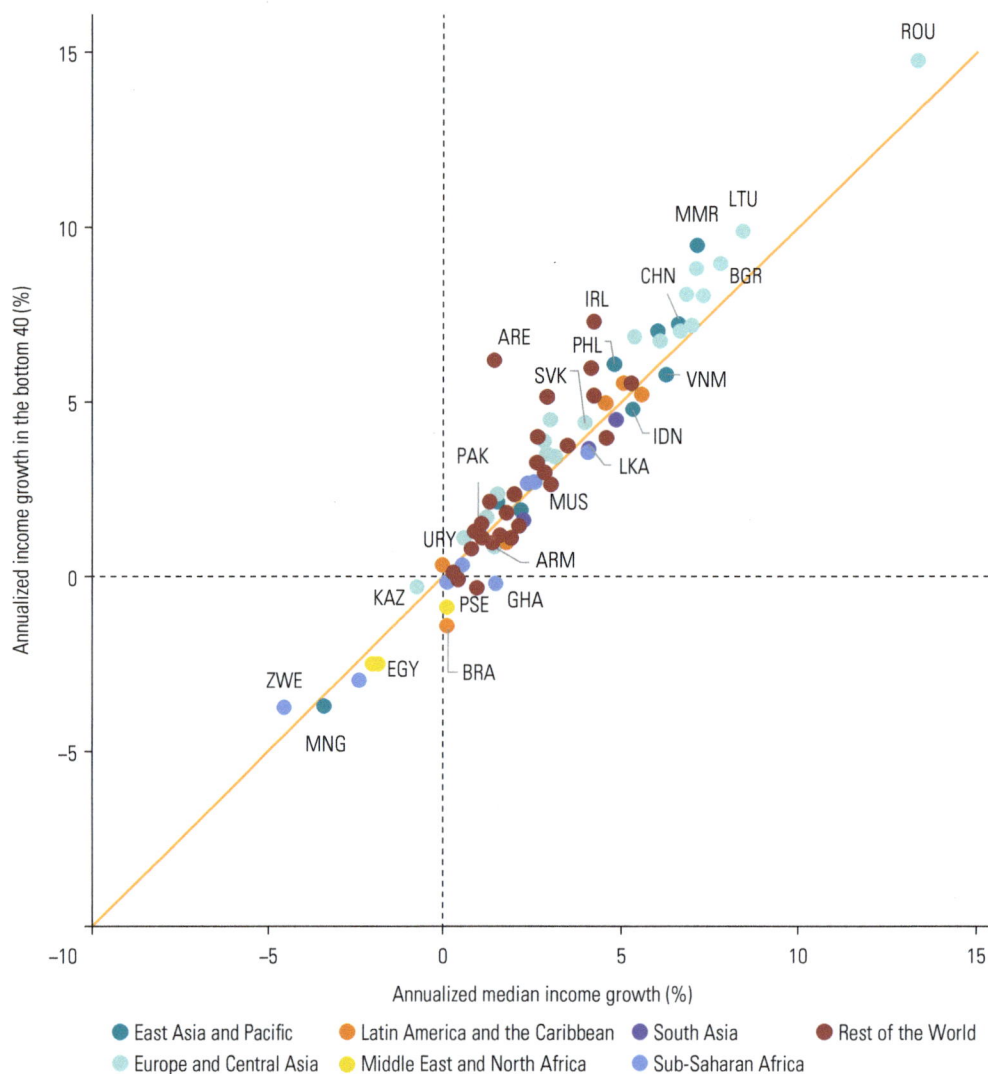

Sources: World Bank, Global Database of Shared Prosperity (9th edition, circa 2014–19, for 68 economies; 8th edition, circa 2013–18, for 10 economies), https://www.worldbank.org/en/topic/poverty/brief/global-database-of-shared-prosperity.
Note: The figure shows the relationship between annualized median income growth and the Shared Prosperity measure (annualized income growth in the bottom 40 percent of the income distribution), circa 2014–19 or circa 2013–18. A 45-degree line is shown for reference. The sample includes 78 economies; those with data collected in 2020 are not included. For a list of country codes, go to https://www.iso.org/obp/ui/#search/code/.

The characteristics of the people in the bottom 40 differ from those in the top 60 of the population ("top 60"). Figure 2D.1 in online annex 2D is a profile of the bottom 40 as an average across regions for economies that conducted a survey in 2014 or later. The figure reports the share of individuals in each group that belongs to the bottom 40. For example, over 40 percent of individuals ages 0–14 are in the bottom 40, indicating that this group is overrepresented in the bottom of the income distribution. Generally, those in the bottom 40 are likely to be younger and less educated and much more likely to live in a rural area. There are also some regional differences. Overall, the group of people age 64 and older is much less likely to be in the bottom 40, whereas the same group in South Asia is about as likely to be in the bottom 40 as in the top 60. Individuals without any formal education are most likely to be in the bottom 40 in Europe and Central Asia. By comparison, the gender distribution among the bottom 40 and the top 60 is fairly even: about 40 percent of both men and women belong to the bottom 40 in all regions.

Within-country inequality was mostly stable or declining prior to the pandemic

Poverty and Shared Prosperity 2016 examined long-term trends in inequality (World Bank 2016). The report pointed out the wide variation in within-country inequality but noted it narrowed in many countries between 1998 and 2013. Countries in Latin America and the Caribbean had achieved a significant reduction in inequality, although after a period of increase in the preceding decades. The average Gini coefficient declined during the same period in most regions except South Asia and the Middle East and North Africa, where data were also more limited. Although the Gini index is a widely recognized measure of inequality, it is less sensitive to changes in the top of the distribution. Such changes are also less accurately measured in standard household surveys, potentially underestimating inequality. Addressing these issues at the global level is difficult because of data limitations, and so they are only acknowledged here (see box 2.2 for details).

Consistent with overall positive progress in shared prosperity, within-country inequality measured by the Gini coefficient was as likely to fall as to increase in the years leading up to the pandemic. However, reductions in inequality were likely to be larger than increases (figure 2.4), particularly in the Latin America and the Caribbean, East Asia and Pacific, and Europe and Central Asia regions. Countries in the Middle East and North Africa were more

---

BOX 2.2

Inequality and top incomes

Survey-based measures of inequality are likely to be underestimated because the incomes of the richest are challenging to capture in household surveys. Possible reasons are underreporting of incomes, refusal to participate in a survey, and the low probability of top-earning households being sampled. Previous research has shown that the likelihood of responding to surveys is negatively correlated with income—see Korinek, Mistiaen, and Ravallion (2007) for the United States. To capture top incomes, some researchers have used administrative tax data, which provide a more accurate account of the incomes of the richest groups. For example, box 2.3 illustrates a case study from Poland, where top-corrected measures of income significantly raised inequality. *Poverty and Shared Prosperity 2016* revealed that the income share of the top 1 percent has risen much more quickly in France, Japan, and the United States since the 1970s if one uses more accurate measures of top incomes (World Bank 2016). However, tax record data are generally very limited in low-income countries and come with other concerns such as tax avoidance or evasion, low coverage of informal sectors, as well as limitations of taxable income as a basis for welfare comparisons (Ravallion 2021).

FIGURE 2.4

Within-country inequality was as likely to fall as to increase before the pandemic, but reductions in inequality were likely to be larger than increases

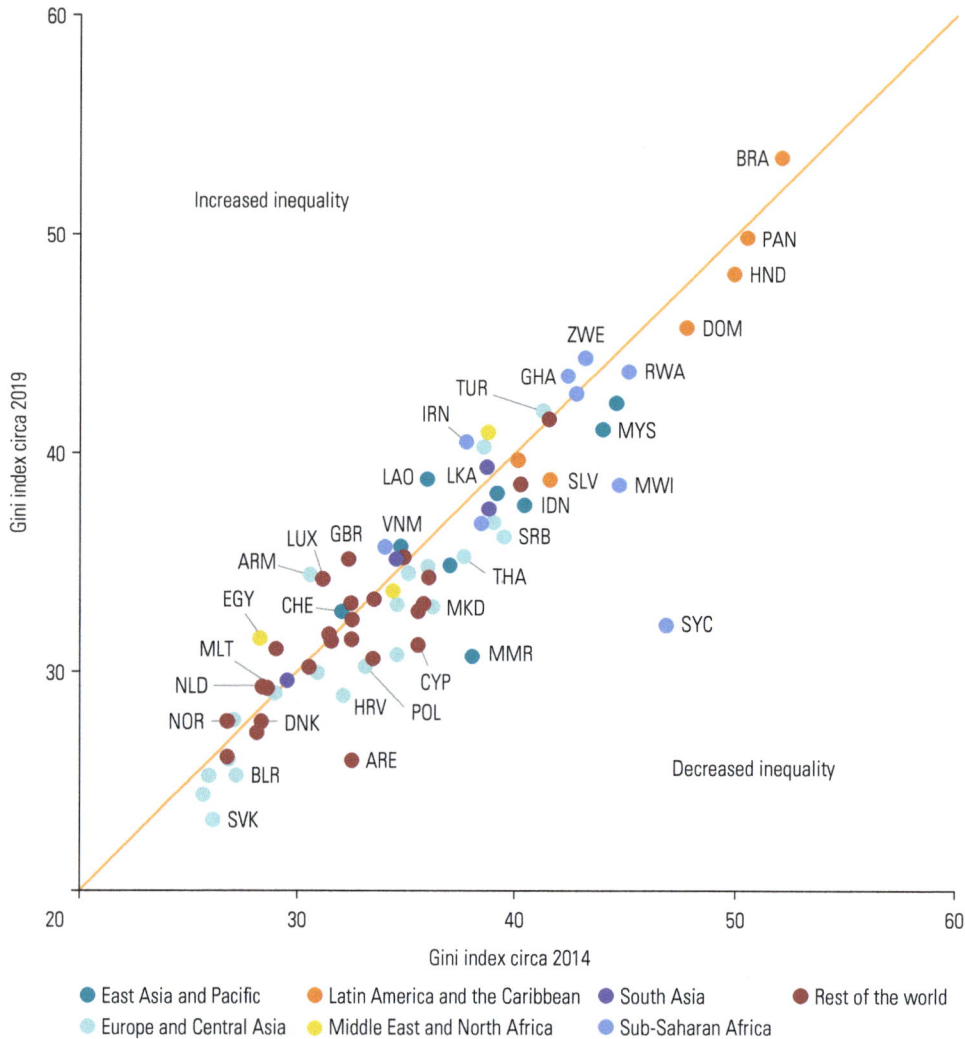

Source: World Bank, Poverty and Inequality Platform, https://pip.worldbank.org.
Note: The figure shows the relationship between the Gini index in the start and end years of the shared prosperity period (circa 2014 and circa 2019). The Gini index decreased (increased) in countries below (above) the 45-degree line. The sample includes 78 economies, those with data collected in 2020 are not included. For a list of country codes, go to https://www.iso.org/obp/ui/#search/code/.

likely to experience an increase in inequality, whereas it was either stable or declining in South Asia. Altogether, in a sample of 78 countries, 34 had falling inequality, compared with 13 with rising inequality. In 31 countries, the Gini index was essentially unchanged; it varied by less than 1 Gini point over time (table 2.2). Box 2.3 features a few country examples that highlight the diversity of experiences with shared prosperity in different settings.

TABLE 2.2

Within-country inequality tended to decrease but with variations across world regions, 2014–19

Region	Number of countries				Mean Gini index	
	Gini index up	Gini index down	Gini index ±	Total number of countries	2014	2019
East Asia and Pacific	1	6	2	9	38.4	36.9
Europe and Central Asia	2	12	7	21	32.7	31.5
Latin America and the Caribbean	3	8	15	26	32.2	31.6
Middle East and North Africa	1	3	2	6	47.0	45.9
South Asia	2	0	1	3	33.8	35.4
Sub-Saharan Africa	0	1	3	4	35.4	35.4
Rest of the world	4	4	1	9	41.7	39.8

Source: World Bank, Poverty and Inequality Platform, https://pip.worldbank.org.
Note: The table shows data points for 78 economies, excluding those with data in 2020. Increases and decreases in the Gini index refer to changes greater than 1 Gini point. The mean Gini index is calculated as the unweighted average of country-level Gini coefficients. Years of measurement are the same as for shared prosperity.

BOX 2.3

Experiences on the ground with shared prosperity

Poland: Rapid economic rise, not evenly shared

Poland has made significant progress in reducing poverty and growing incomes of the bottom 40 of its population. Productivity improvements, a strong labor market, rising wages, and demographically based transfers that reached poorer households have contributed to the progress. However, survey-based measures provide contrasting results about the extent of the progress, depending on the treatment of top incomes, which are poorly captured in survey data. Studies suggest a significant rise after 2000 in the income share going to the richest 10 percent and rising wealth inequality. Bukowski and Novokmet (2021) estimate that the top decile of the income distribution captured 57 percent of estimated gross domestic product (GDP) growth during 1989–2015. Brzeziński, Myck, and Najsztub (2022) combine survey and tax return data to provide top-corrected measures of income inequality and find that the magnitude of this correction is two to three times higher than in other countries.

Romania: Top performer in shared prosperity through fiscal and other reforms

Between 2014 and 2019, the share of Romanians living on less than US$5.50 a day at 2011 purchasing power parity (PPP) prices declined sharply, from 25.6 percent to 9.2 percent. Over the same period, the income growth rate of the bottom 40 surpassed the growth rate of the rest of the population. Most of this progress can be attributed to pro-poor fiscal and other reforms, such as reductions in the flat personal income tax (PIT) rate and value added taxes, an expansion of the PIT exemption coverage, and an increase in the minimum wage. However, over half of PIT relief benefited households at the top of the income distribution, and these reforms put additional pressure on the country's increasing fiscal deficits (Inchauste and Militaru 2018), calling the sustainability of these reforms into question. Meanwhile, a large share of the bottom 40 percent is overwhelmingly concentrated in low-productivity agriculture, disconnected from the drivers of the economy in the booming manufacturing, trade, and information communications and technology sectors.

China: Long-term inequality turnaround

Over the last 40 years, China has lifted over 800 million people out of extreme poverty, accounting for almost three-quarters of the reduction in global poverty since 1980. This reduction was mostly

(continued)

73

Experiences on the ground with shared prosperity *(continued)*

driven by decades of sustained high economic growth, fueled by a massive shift of workers from low-productivity agriculture to higher-productivity industry and, more recently, services. And yet fast growth was accompanied with increasing inequality. The income-based Gini index rose from 30 in the mid-1980s to 49 in 2008. It then began to fall at the end of the 2000s, reaching 46 by 2015. This "great Chinese inequality turnaround" (Kanbur, Wang, and Zhang 2021) was brought about by a shift in public policies toward development of the western and northern regions, the end of agricultural taxation, the rise of social protection investments, and the increase in the minimum wage (Kanbur, Wang, and Zhang 2021). Ravallion and Chen (2021) argue, however, that because the moderation of inequality was driven by specific policies, peak inequality may still lie ahead unless mitigated by policy. Indeed, improvements in income inequality have stalled over the last five years: the Gini Index was still 46 in 2019.

Arab Republic of Egypt: Limited benefits of growth to many households, especially the bottom 40

Egypt's gross per capita GDP growth averaged 1.1 percent per year between 2012 and 2017, but consumption declined at an average rate of −1.1 percent per year during this period, and −2.5 percent per year for the bottom 40 percent. The limited transmission of aggregate growth to household consumption growth reflects long-standing challenges for job creation. The labor market has struggled to absorb Egypt's fast-growing labor force. The share of employed in the working-age population has been low and declining. Women and youth employment rates remain particularly low. In addition, growth has been based on employment opportunities created either in low-value-added sectors or in sectors that experienced a productivity decline while informal employment has also grown. The construction sector, a labor-intensive sector employing many informal workers, saw a boom in employment but low productivity growth. Overall, the economy has had little success in creating well-paying, productive jobs in the private sector.

Shared prosperity and inequality during COVID-19

As chapter 1 documents, the COVID-19 crisis had a profound impact on welfare around the world. This section uses data available for 2020 as well as earlier years to explore the impacts of the crisis on shared prosperity and across the income distribution. The household surveys of 13 economies cover either 2015–20 or 2016–20 and thus the early stages of the COVID-19 crisis. Eleven of these economies also have data for 2019, allowing an assessment of shared prosperity both immediately before and during the pandemic. In addition, high-frequency phone surveys (HFPS) collected information on who lost income and employment and who faced food insecurity over the crisis, providing additional data on the differential impacts of the pandemic on households. Finally, analysis of the official national labor force surveys available for some countries helps contextualize and corroborate information from other sources, including phone surveys, on how the crisis and recovery unfolded across different population groups during the pandemic.

Large income losses among the bottom 40 are recorded in the official data

Only a few countries have the data needed to produce estimates of shared prosperity over the 2019–20 period. This section turns to those countries.

The 13 economies whose shared prosperity survey periods cover either 2015–20 or 2016–20 provide a first estimate of the impact of the COVID-19 crisis on shared prosperity. All of these countries are in Latin America and the Caribbean or Europe and Central Asia, and most conduct annual surveys. To understand the impact of the crisis, estimates of the bottom 40 income growth in the latest shared prosperity period are disaggregated into income growth estimates for 2015–19 (or 2016–19 in the case of Argentina) and 2019–20 for the 11 countries that have annual survey data available. It is then possible to distinguish the COVID-19 impact from the prepandemic trends in shared prosperity.

The comparison shows large income losses among the bottom 40 in these countries during the pandemic. Most of these countries experienced positive shared prosperity trends prior to the COVID-19 crisis (figure 2.5, panel a), only to see those trends followed by steep income losses between 2019 and 2020 (figure 2.5, panel b). In other words, the gains achieved between 2015 and 2019 were often more than offset by large income declines during the crisis. In the worst cases, the bottom 40 in Colombia and Peru lost about a quarter of their income between 2019 and 2020. In the hardest-hit countries—Colombia, Costa Rica, Ecuador, and Peru—the incomes of the bottom 40 declined by more than the average rate of contraction. This large one-year decline led to negative shared prosperity for 2015–20 (2016–20 for Argentina), the survey years captured in the shared prosperity database for these countries. Meanwhile, Bolivia and Paraguay were still able to record positive shared prosperity in 2015–20 because income losses in 2020 were not as dramatic as in these other countries (figure 2.5, panel c). For six of the

FIGURE 2.5

The pandemic led to large income losses among the bottom 40

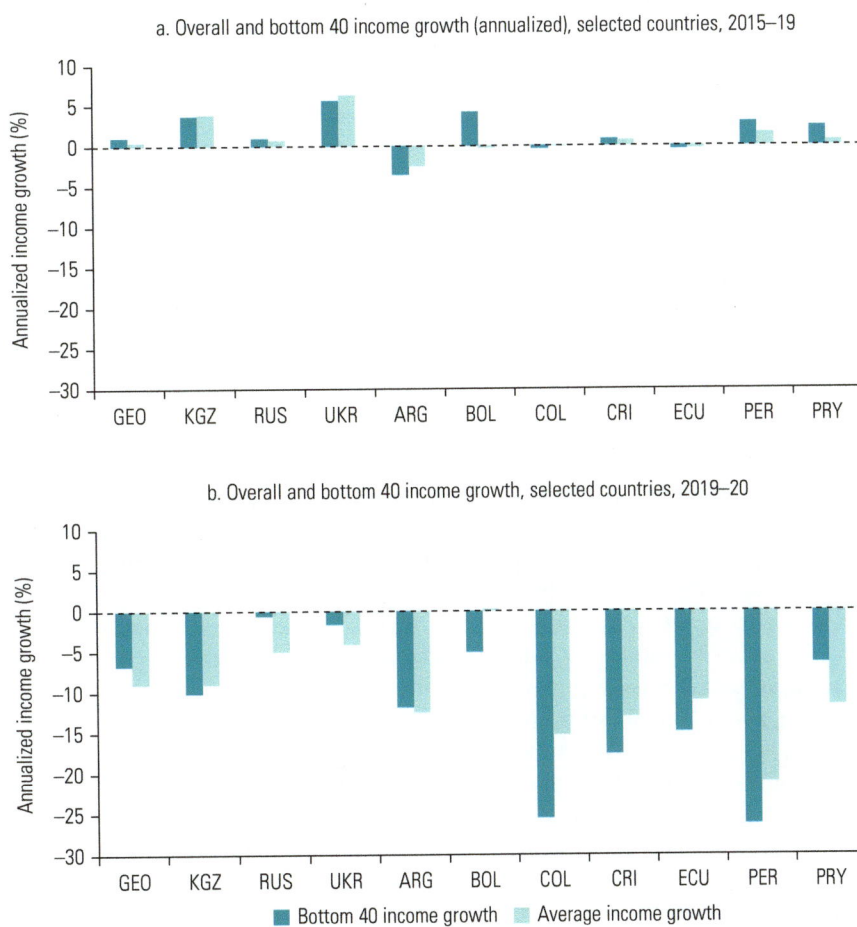

a. Overall and bottom 40 income growth (annualized), selected countries, 2015–19

b. Overall and bottom 40 income growth, selected countries, 2019–20

■ Bottom 40 income growth   ■ Average income growth

(continued)

75

FIGURE 2.5

The pandemic led to large income losses among the bottom 40 *(continued)*

c. Overall and bottom 40 income growth (annualized), selected countries, 2015–20

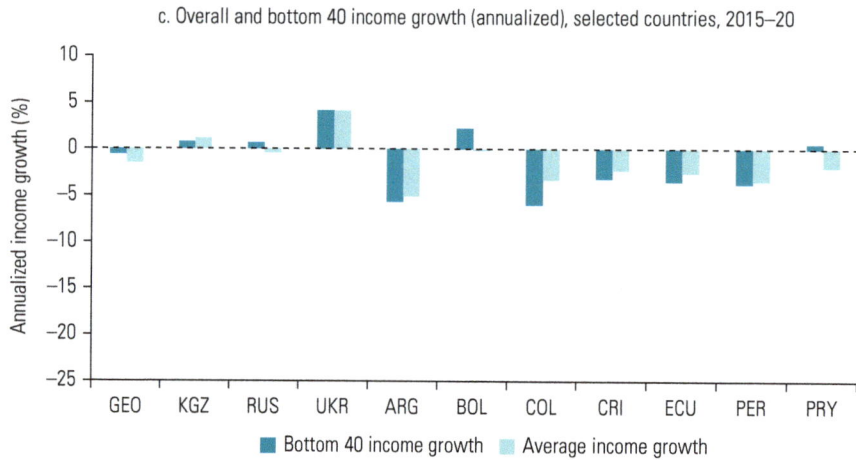

Source: Original estimates based on household surveys for 2015, 2019, and 2020 for all countries except Argentina, which uses survey years 2016, 2019, and 2020.

Note: The figure compares the annualized average income growth in the bottom 40 percent and for the total population for 2015–19 (panel a), 2019–20 (panel b), and 2015–20 (panel c) in selected economies. For a list of country codes, go to https://www.iso.org/obp/ui/#search/code/.

countries studied, the SPP was negative in 2019–20. Together, the negative SPP and the negative shared prosperity indicator confirm that the pandemic hit the poorer populations harder in those countries.

Within countries, job and income losses differed across groups

Worldwide, employment is the main source of income for most households, especially the poorest. Although the previous section explored measured changes to the bottom 40 for 13 countries, analysis of pandemic-induced changes in employment is possible for a larger number of countries. Typically, labor force surveys enable granular analysis of employment changes over time, but relatively few such surveys were available for analysis in the immediate aftermath of the onset of the pandemic. Household phone surveys were conducted, however, in many settings during the pandemic and help to reveal the distributional impact of the crisis.

Because in-person household surveys were interrupted or suspended early in the pandemic, phone surveys emerged as one of the few sources of information on how impacts unfolded at the household level after onset of the pandemic. The World Bank conducted high-frequency phone surveys in 88 mostly low- and middle-income countries, and this section partly draws on this data to investigate welfare losses during the pandemic. Box 2.4 provides details on the design, implementation, and potential biases of these World Bank–supported surveys.

Phone surveys reveal large and sudden increases in the rates of reported job and income losses across countries early in the pandemic (see figure 2.6, as well as Bundervoet, Davalos, and Garcia 2021; Egger et al. 2021; Khamis et al. 2021). Across countries, less educated and female respondents reported larger initial losses in employment and a slow recovery (figure 2.6, panel b). The same was true for urban respondents—not traditionally among the poorest in most countries—reflecting the fact that urban workers were more often affected by mobility restrictions than rural workers.

High-frequency phone surveys

To monitor the impact of the pandemic on households, the World Bank, often in partnership with national institutions, implemented or supported high-frequency phone surveys (HFPS) in 88 countries. The phone surveys were administered in all six World Bank regions, and the majority of countries were low- or middle-income. The questionnaires were based on a global core template and customized for each country. The first surveys were conducted between April and June 2020 in over half of the countries. In some cases, data collection continued into 2022. New modules, such as on attitudes toward vaccine, were added over time to respond to the rapidly evolving nature of the pandemic. Because the exact content of surveys differed by country and across survey waves, responses were carefully harmonized to construct an internationally comparable data set.

The April 2022 vintage of the harmonized data set includes indicators for up to 500,000 respondents from 323 phone survey waves in 88 countries. The indicators range from employment and income outcomes to food security, education, and access to basic services. Country-level indicators are published online on the interactive World Bank COVID-19 Household Monitoring Dashboard. The harmonized microdata set represents a combined population of 4.35 billion and is the basis for most of the analysis using phone surveys in this report.

Phone surveys have the advantage of collecting data rapidly in a relatively cost-effective way. Although the surveys were designed to be nationally representative (using reweighting methods), several limitations arise because of the inherent nature of phone surveys in developing country settings. For example, the sample is representative of the phone-owning population in the country, potentially underrepresenting the poorest population. Furthermore, the survey results may be subject to sampling and selection biases. In most countries, surveys relied on either random digit dialing or used a subsample drawn from a nationally representative survey conducted before the pandemic. For the latter, the sampling frame was likely to overrepresent household heads and underrepresent members who are neither heads nor spouses. As a result, the representativeness of labor market outcomes may be affected by respondent selection within households because the surveys often collected information only about the respondent.

Kugler et al. (2021) investigate the magnitude of potential biases across different population groups by comparing the World Bank's harmonized HFPS database with household surveys in five countries. Using information on all household members, they find that these phone surveys overstate employment rates for the full population because they oversample household heads and produce greater bias for age comparisons of employment trends. However, phone surveys appear to track disparities and changes across gender, education, and urban/rural groups reasonably well. The authors find little evidence that differences in employment outcomes and trends between groups are affected by oversampling household heads. Nevertheless, the employment-related results from phone surveys and their interpretation should be distinguished from standard labor market indicators based on traditional labor force surveys because there are differences in sampling, framing of questions, and timing of surveys. When available, labor force survey data should take precedence over phone survey data to track nationally representative labor market outcomes.

a. World Bank, COVID-19 Household Monitoring Dashboard, https://www.worldbank.org/en/data/interactive/2020/11/11/covid-19-high-frequency-monitoring-dashboard. Indicators for some countries are not published due to issues of data access.

FIGURE 2.6

Employment and income losses arising from the pandemic were severe, with certain groups being hit harder

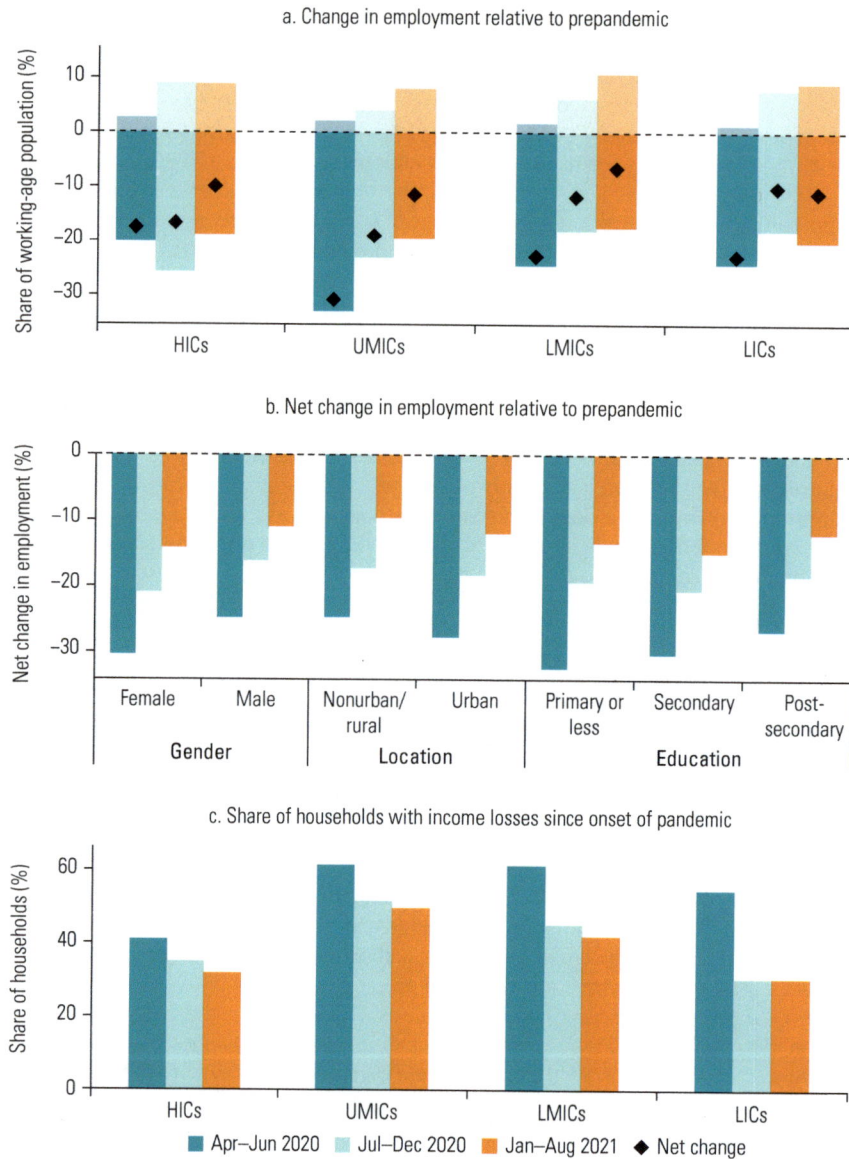

a. Change in employment relative to prepandemic

b. Net change in employment relative to prepandemic

c. Share of households with income losses since onset of pandemic

■ Apr–Jun 2020   ■ Jul–Dec 2020   ■ Jan–Aug 2021   ◆ Net change

Source: Original estimates based on data from COVID-19 high-frequency phone surveys (HFPS).
Note: Panel a shows the share of working-age population that started or stopped working, and the net change in employment relative to prepandemic levels during three periods of the crisis, aggregated by income category. The sample includes 44 economies with employment data from HFPS in multiple periods. Dark bars = stopped working; light bars = started working. Panel b shows the net change in employment relative to the prepandemic level during three periods of the crisis, by population characteristic. The sample includes 69 economies for gender, 66 for location, and 57 for education. Prepandemic employment in panels a and b is based on recall in HFPS. Panel c shows the share of households that reported total income decreased since the pandemic started during three periods of the crisis, aggregated by income category. The sample includes 22 economies with income loss data from HFPS in multiple periods. To account for the fact that the sample of economies with observations changes for each period, panels a and c display the predicted values from a regression with time dummies and economy fixed effects (taking the average of the economy fixed effects for each income category within each period). In all panels, economies are weighted equally. HICs = high-income countries; LICs = low-income countries; LMICs = lower-middle-income countries; UMICs = upper-middle-income countries.

In their study using HFPS data, Bundervoet, Davalos, and Garcia (2021) highlight that within countries the early impact of the pandemic was highly unequal across population groups. Kugler et al. (2021) examine the differential impacts across groups and find that gender gaps in work stoppage were mainly due to differences within sectors rather than across sectors and that the groups that suffered the brunt of the early job losses had partially recovered in 2020. Vulnerable groups were often more affected because the sectors in which they worked typically employed informal daily or temporary workers (Narayan et al. 2022; World Bank 2021). Kim et al. (2021), using phone survey data from East Asian countries, find that employment impacts were widespread across the income distribution when mobility restrictions were stringent, but that it was more difficult for poorer workers to regain employment once restrictions had been relaxed.

In line with job losses, the share of households who reported income losses since the start of the pandemic remained substantial, especially in low- and middle-income countries, where the share was estimated to exceed 40 percent through mid-2021 (figure 2.6, panel c). The fact that more households were reporting income losses than job losses may be attributable to the widespread informal employment in poorer countries, where labor market adjustments during downturns are more likely to occur on the intensive margin (hours or earnings) than the extensive margin (outright job losses).

Disproportionate impacts on vulnerable groups are also found in standard labor force surveys. A World Bank analysis of labor force survey data from 80 high- and middle-income countries confirms a large and heterogeneous employment shock across countries, with the largest drops observed in LMICs (World Bank 2022b). Employment declines were consistently larger among youth and low-skilled workers, while gender impacts were more mixed across countries. In analysis using more recent data, the International Labour Organization (ILO) finds that the gender gap in working hours remained wider in the first quarter of 2022 than before the pandemic in low- and middle-income countries, but it had fully recovered by 2021 in high-income countries (ILO 2022). In Türkiye, Aldan, Çıraklı, and Torun (2021) find lower employment and labor force participation across most population groups but larger effects among women and the less educated. In South Africa, Köhler et al. (2021) find that the impact of the pandemic on the informal sector was three times larger than on the formal sector. In Brazil, job losses were most common among the less educated, informal wage, and own-account workers, and among women, black, and young workers (World Bank 2022a).[1] By contrast, in Vietnam people with low education were less affected, possibly because they tend to work in the agriculture sector (Dang and Nguyen 2020). In India, national-level high-frequency panel data show that while employment for men had recovered by August 2020, for women it continued to be significantly lower than in the prepandemic period (Deshpande 2020). Finally, the Asian Development Bank (ADB) reports that young, female, less skilled workers suffered the brunt of the job losses in Indonesia, Malaysia, the Philippines, Thailand, and Vietnam in the second quarter of 2020 (ADB 2021).

There is also evidence that the crisis may have harmed the quality of jobs among those who were able to maintain employment. A high rate of employment transitions was reported in phone surveys, including moving from the nonagriculture to agriculture sector and changing employment type, from wage employment to self-employment. Over time, these transitions were most common among the less educated (figure 2.7, panel a) and likely suggest that job quality deteriorated for poorer workers because remuneration and other employment characteristics tend to be inferior among self-employed workers and jobs in agriculture. Switching to self-employment or agricultural activities was more strongly associated with income losses reported in phone surveys, compared with other types of employment transitions (figure 2.7, panel b). Finally, the transition from nonagriculture to agriculture sector jobs was, on average, more frequent among rural than urban households, implying that the transition was prompted mainly by workers in rural areas switching from nonfarm to farm activities rather than urban workers migrating back to rural areas to take up farming.

FIGURE 2.7

The pandemic likely harmed the quality of jobs among those who continued to work

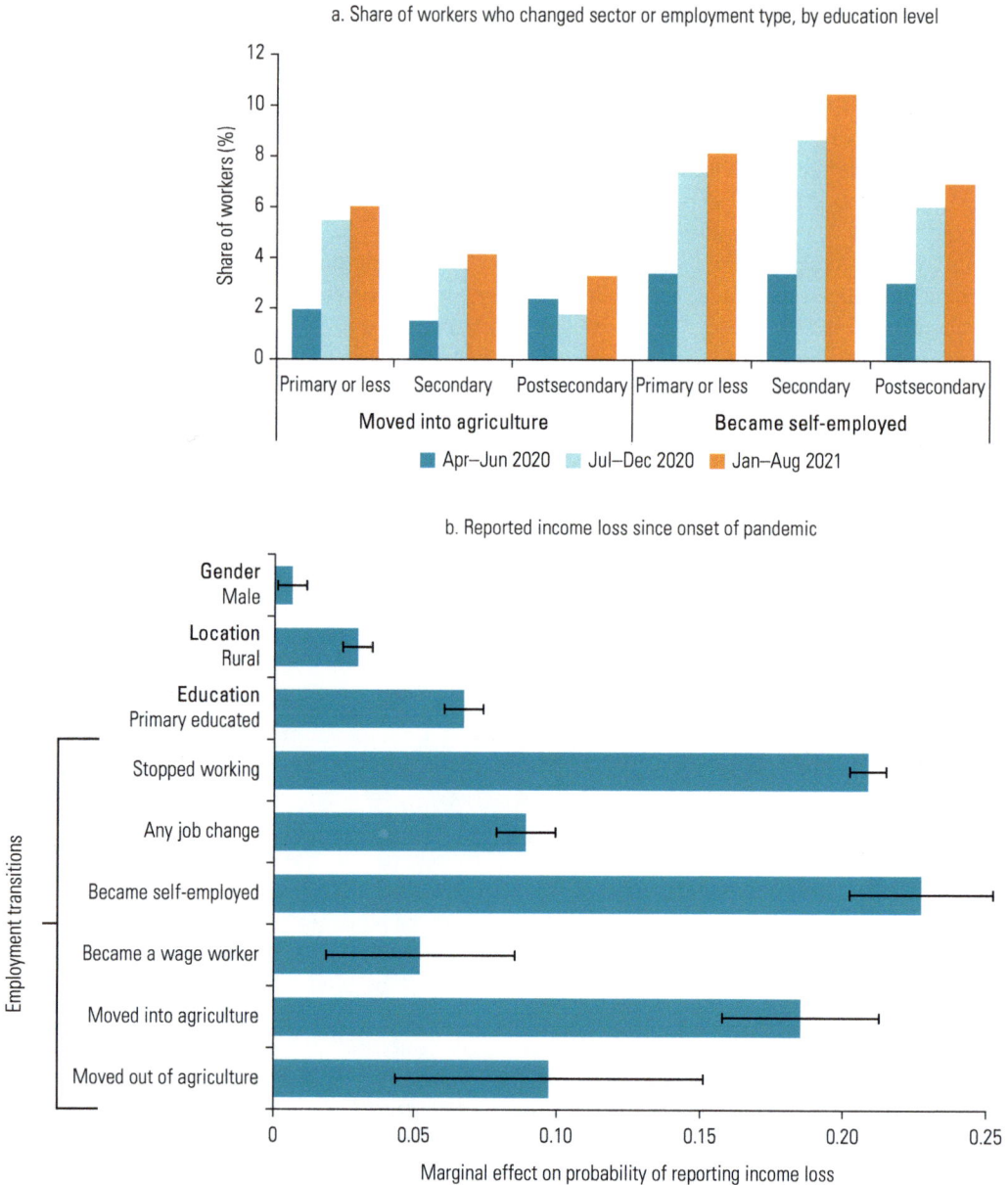

a. Share of workers who changed sector or employment type, by education level

■ Apr–Jun 2020   ■ Jul–Dec 2020   ■ Jan–Aug 2021

b. Reported income loss since onset of pandemic

Source: Original estimates based on data from COVID-19 high-frequency phone surveys.
Note: Panel a shows the share of workers who moved into agriculture (from nonagriculture) and became self-employed (from wage work), by education level. The sample includes 51 economies for sectoral transitions (moved into agriculture) and 33 economies for employment type transitions (became self-employed). Panel b shows the estimated marginal effect of each population characteristic on the probability of reporting income loss using bivariate regressions, with 95 percent confidence intervals. The sample includes between 24 economies (employment type transitions) and 48 economies (gender and education). Economies are weighted equally in both panels.

Changes in inequality within countries are mixed

For countries with both HFPS and prepandemic consumption or income data, the analysis is extended to impute the probability of employment or income loss across the income distribution of each country. An estimate of the differential impact of the crisis across poor and rich households can be used, for example, to estimate the difference in the probability of losing employment for the bottom 40 percent of the population versus the top 60 percent. The distributional impacts have varied across countries—in over two-thirds of countries, income losses were likely greater for the bottom 40 than the top 60 in urban areas, reflecting the findings from the previous section that showed that vulnerable workers were often more affected by the pandemic. However, the sample of countries shown in figure 2.8 is evenly split on whether income

FIGURE 2.8

In selected countries, the probability of income loss was greater for the bottom 40 than the top 60, especially in urban areas

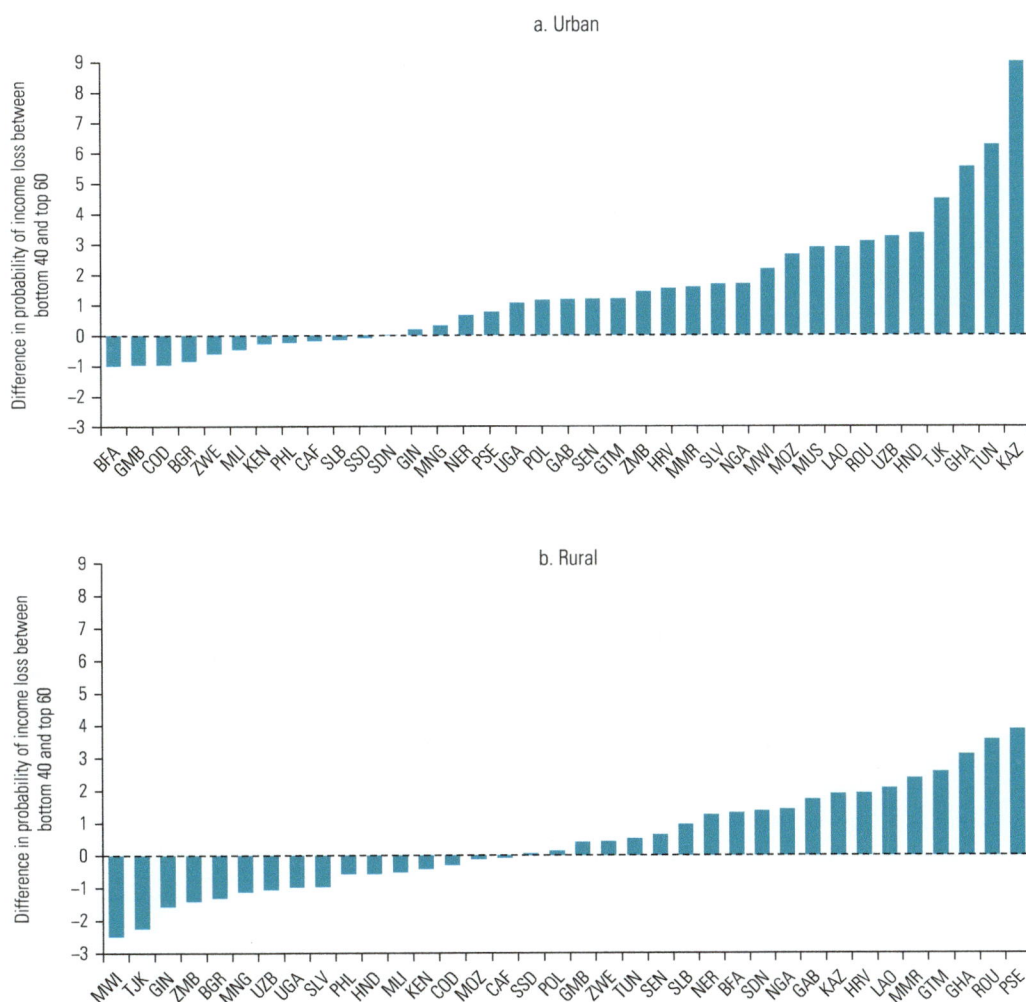

a. Urban

b. Rural

Source: Updated estimates based on Yonzan et al. 2022. https://blogs.worldbank.org/opendata/impact-covid-19-poverty-and-inequality-evidence-phone-surveys.
Note: The figure shows the difference in the share of households in the bottom 40 and top 60 percent of the income distribution that experienced income losses for selected economies, in urban (panel a) and rural (panel b) locations. A positive difference indicates that proportionately more households in the bottom 40 lost incomes during the pandemic. For a list of country codes, go to https://www.iso.org/obp/ui/#search/code/.

81

losses were greater for the bottom 40 or the top 60 in rural areas. Urban households are often better off than rural households, so on aggregate it is not always the case that those that suffered income losses were among the poorest households. When information on income losses is combined with GDP data to estimate the distribution of pandemic period income shocks (see section of chapter 1 on nowcasting), the estimates serve as one source of information to investigate changes in within-country inequality.

From this exercise emerges no clear pattern across countries in changes in within-country inequality during the pandemic. In figure 2.9, the percentage change in the Gini index in 2020 is plotted against the log of mean daily consumption across countries. Countries are only included in this figure when the Gini index is available from estimates based on actual survey data, tabulated income statistics from national statistical offices, imputed values based on data from household surveys and phone surveys, or estimates from the literature. As the figure shows, not only are the results mixed, but the magnitude of change also tends to be small in most cases. The finding that richer countries more likely experienced a decline in inequality in 2020 is consistent with other studies in the literature such as that by Clark, D'Ambrosio, and Lepinteur (2020), which estimates declines in inequality in five European countries. These declines are likely a result of the fiscal response introduced to counteract the anticipated pandemic-related income losses. Some of the largest projected changes in inequality were seen among middle-income countries such as Brazil. The poorest countries were less likely to experience a meaningful decrease in inequality. The largest increase in the Gini index was observed in the Philippines, while the largest decrease occurred in Armenia (figure 2.9).[2] Ultimately, the net impact of the

FIGURE 2.9

Projected changes in the Gini index show no clear pattern across countries with different income levels, with increases and decreases equally likely

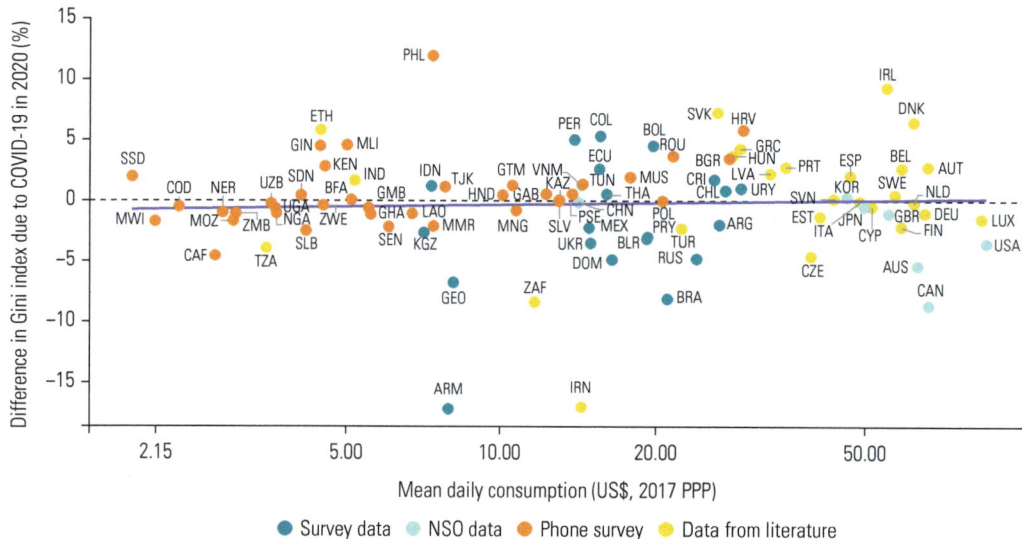

Source: Mahler, Yonzan, and Lakner, forthcoming.
Note: The figure shows the percentage difference in Gini index due to COVID-19 in 2020, with countries ordered by daily mean income or consumption per capita in 2019 on the horizontal axis. The pandemic-induced difference in Gini index is calculated as the difference between the nowcast with the pandemic and the nowcast without the pandemic. The sample includes countries with estimates based on actual survey data, tabulated income data from national statistical offices (NSOs), data from phone surveys, or data from the literature. PPP = purchasing power parity. For a list of country codes, go to https://www.iso.org/obp/ui/#search/code/.

crisis on poverty and well-being would depend on where in the distribution the people most affected are located and the capacity of a country to implement fiscal mitigation measures, such as emergency cash transfers.

Global inequality

The year 2020 saw a reversal in the prepandemic trend of declining global income inequality

Global inequality was trending downward on the eve of the COVID-19 pandemic. When global inequality is decomposed into components of between-country inequality (the differences in mean incomes across countries) and within-country inequality (the differences in incomes within a country), the decline in global inequality over the last decades was primarily due to a convergence in mean incomes across countries.[3] China played a particularly large role in this decline because the fall in global income inequality is mainly attributed to the country's rapid economic growth, which lifted over a billion of its people from the bottom toward the median of the global income distribution (Lakner and Milanovic 2013). As a result, the global Gini index dropped by about half a point every year between 2003 and 2013.[4] The steep decline in global inequality over the last two decades mostly reflects the strong income growth of the global middle class. Indeed, income growth between 2003 and 2013 was consistently strong for those around the median (Lakner and Milanovic 2013; Milanovic 2021). As depicted in figure 2.10, panel a, the decline in global inequality continued in a similar fashion between 2014 and 2019, and income growth was stronger among those roughly between the 20th and 60th percentiles, compared with those in the richer percentiles.

To assess the impact of the pandemic on global inequality, the country income distributions for 2020 that appeared earlier in this chapter and are described in box 1.3 in chapter 1 are extended to 2021 and 2022 for 168 countries using per capita GDP growth rates from national accounts and an assumption of distribution neutrality within countries. These country-level estimates are then compiled to estimate changes in the global income distribution and thus global income inequality. Meanwhile, household survey data are more readily available in the period after 1990, and so to understand global inequality in the period before 1990 the lined-up country income distributions in 1990 are extrapolated backward using GDP growth rates from the Word Bank's World Development Indicators[5] and Bolt and van Zanden (2020)—see chapter 1 for details. This "backcasting" exercise keeps the distribution of welfare within a country constant—that is, inequality within a country is held fixed at the level observed in 1990. As a result, the global inequality estimates reported in figure 2.11 account for only the between-country portion of inequality over the 1950–89 period and again in 2021 and 2022, whereas they account for both within-country and between-country inequality from 1990 to 2020 (inclusive).

The results of this exercise suggest that the COVID-19 pandemic appears to have caused the largest single-year increase in global inequality since World War II. Findings from the simulated global income distribution suggest that the global Gini index increased by a little more than 0.5 points during the pandemic, from a 2019 value of 62.0 to an estimated 62.6 in 2020 (figure 2.11). This reversal of the global inequality trend is historical and particularly striking in view of the continual decline in global income inequality over the last two decades, most notably in the 2000s. The increase in global inequality is also reflected in the global growth incidence curve (GIC) for 2019–20, which finds income losses for almost all percentiles, but greater losses among poorer than richer percentiles, amounting to a reversal of global inequality trends (figure 2.10, panel b). The GIC in figure 2.10, panel a, indicates larger income growth at the middle of the global income distribution over the 2014–19 period and thus a catch-up of the middle relative to the top. By contrast, panel b suggests larger income losses for the middle and bottom of the global income distribution compared with the top for 2020, suggesting greater income dispersion.

83

FIGURE 2.10

The decline in global inequality before the pandemic reflects the strong income growth of the global middle class, whereas those in the bottom and the middle lost the most during the pandemic

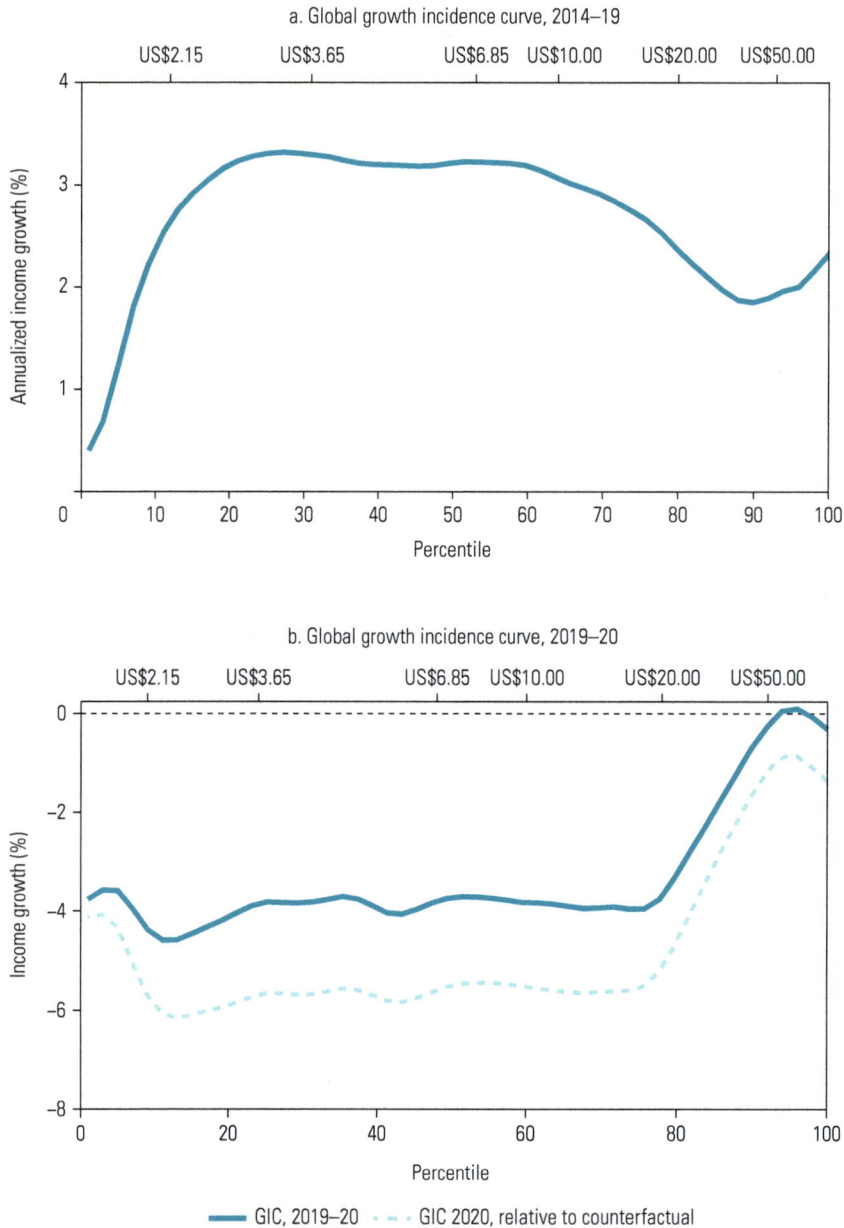

a. Global growth incidence curve, 2014–19

b. Global growth incidence curve, 2019–20

GIC, 2019–20 ··· GIC 2020, relative to counterfactual

Sources: Mahler, Yonzan, and Lakner, forthcoming; World Bank, Poverty and Inequality Platform (PIP), https://pip.worldbank.org.
Note: Panel a shows the annualized income growth for each percentile across the income distribution for 2014–19. In panel b, "GIC, 2019–20" indicates the change in income for each percentile between 2019 and 2020. "GIC 2020, relative to counterfactual" indicates the shortfall in income in 2020 compared with a pre-COVID-19 projection for the same year. GIC = growth incidence curve.

The pandemic caused the largest increase in global inequality since World War II, after a steady decline over the past two decades

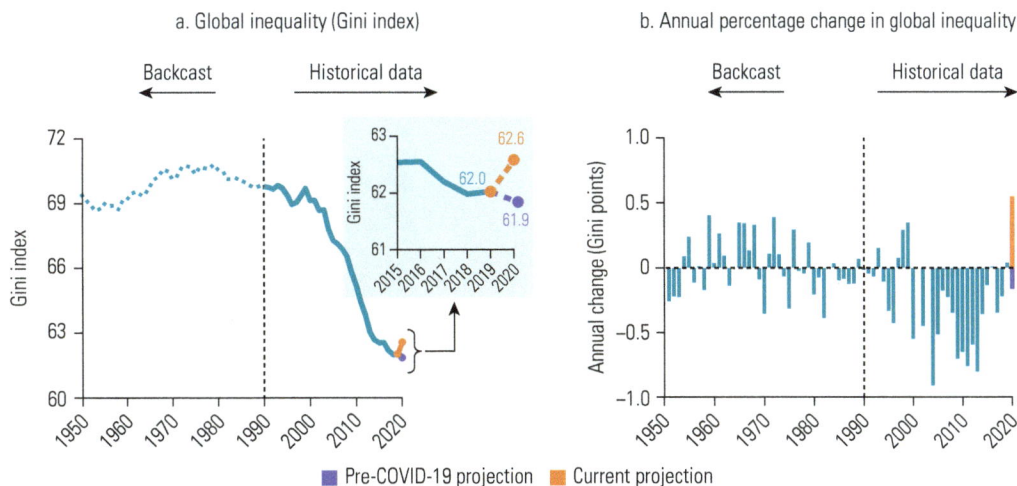

a. Global inequality (Gini index)

b. Annual percentage change in global inequality

■ Pre-COVID-19 projection ■ Current projection

Sources: Original estimates based on Mahler, Yonzan, and Lakner, forthcoming; World Bank, Global Economic Prospects database, https://databank.worldbank.org/source/global-economic-prospects; World Bank, Poverty and Inequality Platform (PIP), https://pip.worldbank.org. *Note:* The figure shows the global Gini index (panel a) and the annual change in Gini points (panel b) from 1950 to 2020. "Historical data" for the period 1990–2019 is from the PIP. "Backcast" estimates are extrapolated backward from the 1990 lineup using GDP growth in national accounts. National accounts data before 1990 are from the World Development Indicators, the World Economic Outlook, and Bolt and van Zanden (2020). "Current projection" uses the nowcast methodology outlined in box 1.3 in chapter 1 and a variety of data sources to project the latest 2019 lined-up estimate to 2020. "Pre-COVID-19 projection" extrapolates the 2019 lineup to 2020 using per capita GDP growth forecasts from the January 2020 *Global Economic Prospects*.

Widening between-country inequality drove the increase in global inequality

The increase in global inequality was not driven by increasing inequality within countries. In fact, as the previous sections have shown, in many countries inequality decreased in 2020. Instead, it was driven by differences between countries in the impact of the pandemic on the average incomes of each country. Figure 2.12 shows that the increase in global inequality was driven by between-country changes, and, in fact, would have been even larger had reductions in inequality in many countries not offset some of the increase.

Countries with large populations and incomes well above or well below the global median are more likely to exert a disproportionate influence on changes to global inequality when they experience large negative shocks to income. For example, although China has a large population, since average incomes are close to the global median, the negative shock in China contributed little to the change in global inequality in 2020 (figure 2.12). Nigeria and the Democratic Republic of Congo, two large economies well below the global median, also had little impact on the change in global inequality because the economic contraction they experienced was relatively mild (figure 2.12). The influence of large countries on the change in global inequality is more easily illustrated using global GICs, which are well suited to examining growth in average incomes by income percentile over time. Consider counterfactual scenarios in which the

FIGURE 2.12

An increase in between-country inequality was mainly responsible for the reversal in global inequality

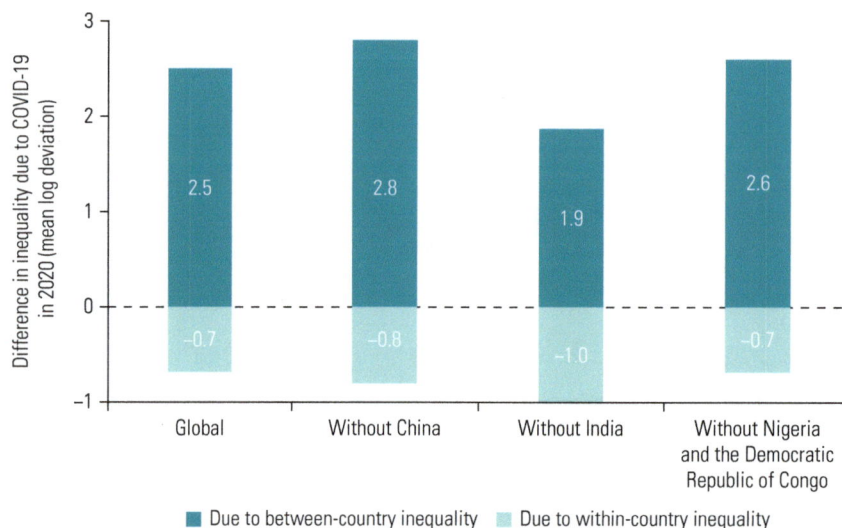

Source: Mahler, Yonzan, and Lakner, forthcoming.
Note: The figure shows the difference in global inequality in 2020 due to COVID-19 that can be attributed to within- and between-country differences for the global distribution and the sample excluding China, India, or Nigeria and the Democratic Republic of Congo. The gap in inequality is calculated as the difference between the inequality estimated with and without the pandemic.

population of China or India or Nigeria and the Democratic Republic of Congo was affected to the same degree as the global average for each income percentile. The global distribution of the income shock from the COVID-19 crisis would have been roughly the same in the China and the Nigeria and Democratic Republic of Congo counterfactual scenarios but smaller for lower global income quintiles in the case of the India counterfactual scenario (figure 2.13). In the India counterfactual scenario, it is the fourth quintile that experiences a a slightly larger shock than other quintiles as opposed to the roughly equal and large shock felt by the bottom four quintiles in the actual global GIC. The finding that between-country inequality widened during the COVID-19 crisis and that a substantial part of this widening was due to India's falling incomes is consistent with other literature (Deaton 2021).

Global inequality may remain higher after 2020

In 2020, the impact of the pandemic on the incomes of the bottom 40 percent of the global income distribution was more than twice as large as the impact on the top 40 percent. Average incomes of the bottom 40 percent in 2020 were about 4 percent lower than in 2019, compared with less than 2 percent lower for the top 40 percent. Median incomes fell by 4 percent.

The recovery since 2020 has not fully offset this increase. Since the large pandemic-induced shock in 2020, there has been a substantial recovery across the global distribution, even for the poorest. The bottom 20 percent of the global distribution lost an average of 4 percent of their incomes in 2020 compared with 2019, but the level of losses has narrowed significantly since then, mostly due to a swift and large growth rebound in India. However, the poorest 20 percent globally have not fully recovered their income losses, while the top 20 percent globally have already more

FIGURE 2.13

The increase in between country inequality was driven by larger countries with large income shocks

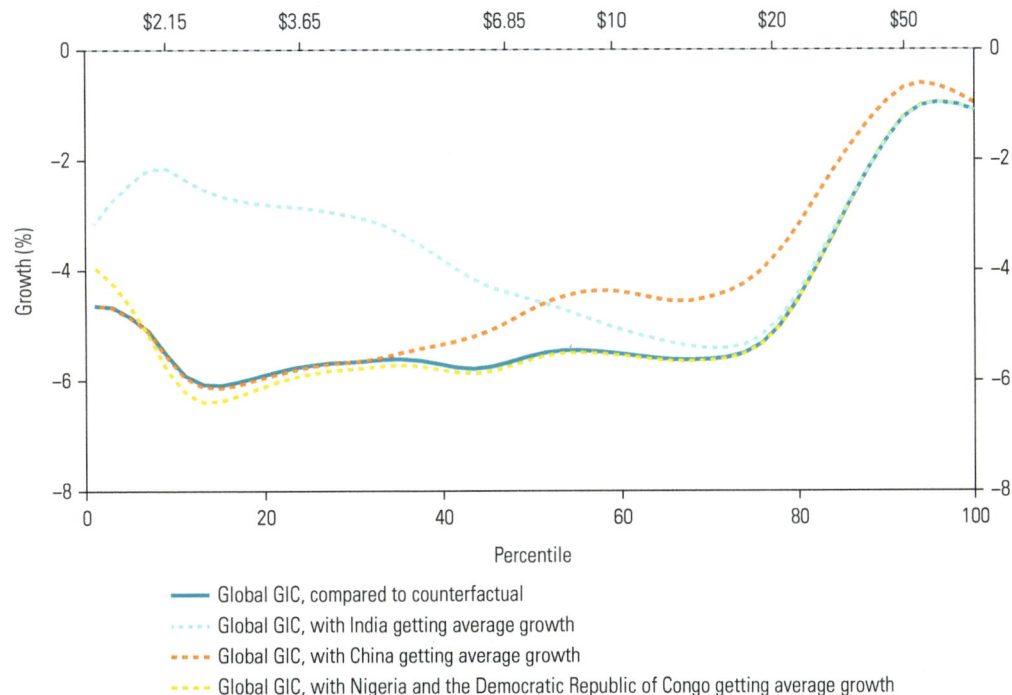

Source: Mahler, Yonzan, and Lakner, forthcoming.
Note: The figure shows the global growth incidence curve for 2020 relative to the pre-pandemic distribution (see figure 2.10) and the counterfactual global growth incidence curve if China, India or Nigeria and the Democratic Republic of Congo had experienced a per capita GDP shock equivalent to the average shock in other countries. GIC = growth incidence curve.

than recovered their initial income loss in 2021. The recovery in incomes is projected to continue at a sluggish pace in 2022 for the poorer populations, while the top 20 percent pull further ahead (figure 2.14).

Although the within-country increases in inequality have not been as bad as initial expectations during the early days of the pandemic, income losses have been large and widespread, and some groups have been more affected than others. The rise in global income inequality after decades of progress is a notable consequence of the COVID-19 crisis. Also of note, the recovery has been uneven across countries, and so the incomes of all but the global top 20 are projected to remain at or below precrisis levels through 2022. This pattern of partial recovery is related, in part, to the fiscal policies in place before the pandemic and the policies enacted in response to it. The role of fiscal policy in mitigating the pandemic shock and fostering recovery is further taken up in part 2 of this report, which also discusses how countries can be better prepared to effectively respond to future crises.

The recovery in 2022 was further hampered by a rapidly unfolding food price crisis. The bottom 40 generally spend a larger share of their budget on food, and estimates indicate that they could face higher inflation than the top 60 (Artuc et al. 2022), which may hurt shared prosperity in the short run. The longer-term impact is difficult to determine, however, and may, in fact, be favorable for many of the poor and bottom 40, particularly for those households that are engaged in the agriculture sector (see box 1.4 in chapter 1).

FIGURE 2.14

The bottom 40 suffered a larger shock from the pandemic and is recovering more slowly than the top 60

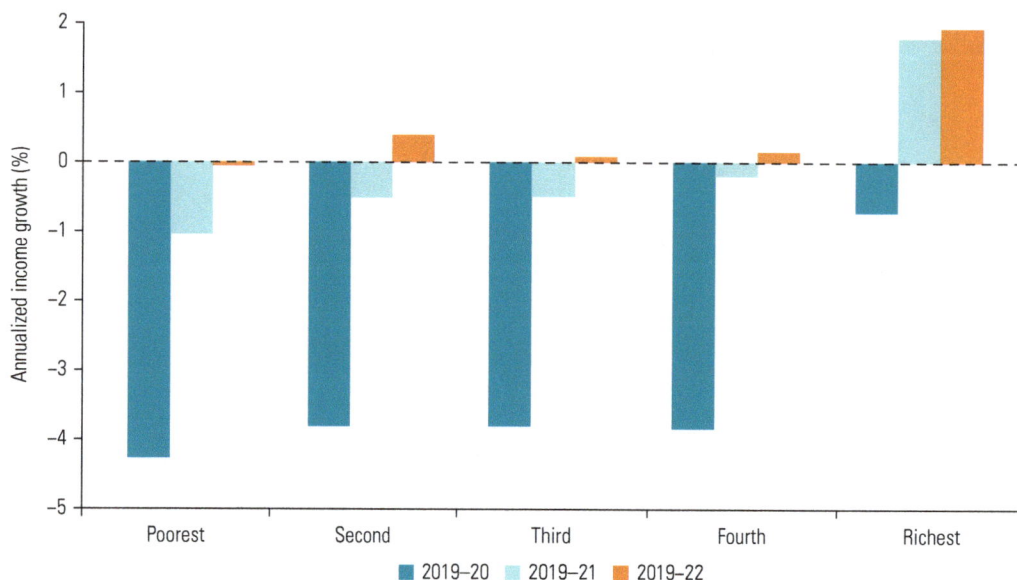

Source: Mahler, Yonzan, and Lakner, forthcoming.
Note: The figure shows the annualized income growth in each income quintile, for 2019–20, 2019–21, and 2019–22.

Notes

1. Despite a large negative labor market shock, well-targeted fiscal support mitigated the impact of the crisis on poverty in both South Africa and Brazil.

2. A comparison of changes in the Gini index based on actual surveys and phone survey–based projections for 13 countries finds that the latter tends to underestimate actual changes in inequality, but even the survey-based estimates turned out to be quite small in magnitude.

3. The decomposition is carried out using the Theil Index, which can be additively decomposed into a between- and within-group component.

4. Three different concepts of global inequality are used in the literature in discussions of global inequality. Concept 1, intercountry inequality, measures inequality between countries' unweighted mean incomes and is typically used in studies of income convergence across countries. Concept 2 measures inequality among countries by weighting them according to their populations. Each person is assigned the per capita income of the country of residence. Within-country inequality is ignored in this case. Concept 3, global interpersonal inequality, measures inequality of all individual incomes in the world (Milanovic 2006). The third concept best fits the purpose of the analysis described in this report.

5. World Bank, World Development Indicators (database), https://databank.worldbank.org /source/world-development-indicators.

References

ADB (Asian Development Bank). 2021. "COVID-19 and Labor Markets in Southeast Asia: Impacts on Indonesia, Malaysia, the Philippines, Thailand, and Viet Nam." ADB, Manila, the Philippines.

Aldan, Altan, Muhammet Enes Çıraklı, and Huzeyfe Torun. 2021. "Covid 19 and the Turkish Labor Market: Heterogeneous Effects across Demographic Groups." *Central Bank Review* 21.

Artuc, Erhan, Guillermo Falcone, Guido Porto, and Bob Rijkers. 2022. "War-Induced Food Price Inflation Imperils the Poor." *VOX EU CEPR* (blog), April 1, 2022. https://voxeu.org/article/war-induced-food-price-inflation-imperils-poor.

Bolt, Jutta, and Jan Luiten van Zanden. 2020. "Maddison Style Estimates of the Evolution of the World Economy: A New 2020 Update." Maddison-Project Working Paper WP-15, Maddison Project, University of Groningen, Groningen, the Netherlands.

Brzeziński, Michal, Michal Myck, and Mateusz Najsztub. 2022. "Sharing the Gains of Transition: Evaluating Changes in Income Inequality and Redistribution in Poland Using Combined Survey and Tax Return Data." *European Journal of Political Economy* 73 (June): 102121.

Bukowski, Paweł, and Filip Novokmet. 2021. "Between Communism and Capitalism: Long-Term Inequality in Poland, 1982–2015." *Journal of Economic Growth* 26 (2): 187–239.

Bundervoet, Tom, Maria E. Davalos, and Natalia Garcia. 2021. "The Short-Term Impacts of COVID-19 on Households in Developing Countries." Policy Research Working Paper 9582, World Bank, Washington, DC.

Clark, Andrew E., Conchita D'Ambrosio, and Anthony Lepinteur. 2020. "The Fall in Income Inequality during COVID-19 in Five European Countries." ECINEQ Working Paper 2020 565, Society for the Study of Economic Inequality, Palma de Mallorca, Spain.

Dang, Hai-Anh H., and Cuong Viet Nguyen. 2020. "Did a Successful Fight against the COVID-19 Pandemic Come at a Cost? Impacts of the Outbreak on Employment Outcomes in Vietnam." IZA Discussion Paper No. 13958, Institute of Labour Economics, University of Bonn, Germany.

Deaton, Angus. 2021. "COVID-19 and Global Income Inequality." NBER Working Paper 28392, National Bureau of Economic Research, Cambridge, MA.

Deshpande, Ashwini. 2020. "The COVID-19 Pandemic and Gendered Division of Paid and Unpaid Work: Evidence from India." IZA Discussion Paper No. 13815, Institute of Labour Economics, University of Bonn, Germany.

Egger, Dennis, Edward Miguel, Shana S. Warren, Ashish Shenoy, Elliott Collins, Dean Karlan, Doug Pakerson, et al. 2021. "Falling Living Standards during the COVID-19 Crisis: Quantitative Evidence from Nine Developing Countries." *Science Advances* 7 (6).

ILO (International Labour Organization). 2022. *ILO Monitor on the World of Work.* Ninth Edition. Geneva: ILO.

Inchauste, Gabriela, and Eva Militaru. 2018. "The Distributional Impacts of Taxes and Social Spending in Romania." Policy Research Working Paper 8565, World Bank, Washington, DC.

Kanbur, Ravi, Yue Wang, and Xiaobo Zhang. 2021. "The Great Chinese Inequality Turnaround." *Journal of Comparative Economics* 49 (2): 467–82.

Khamis, Melanie, Daniel Prinz, David Newhouse, Amparo Palacio-Lopez, Utz Pape, and Michael Weber. 2021. "The Early Labor Market Impacts of COVID-19 in Developing Countries: Evidence from High-Frequency Phone Surveys." Policy Research Working Paper 9510, World Bank, Washington, DC.

Kim, Lydia Y., Maria Ana Lugo, Andrew D. Mason, and Ikuko Uochi. 2021. "Inequality under COVID-19: Taking Stock of High-Frequency Data for East Asia and the Pacific." Policy Research Working Paper 9859, World Bank, Washington, DC.

Köhler, Timothy, Haroon Bhorat, Robert Hill, and Benjamin Stanwix. 2021. "COVID-19 and the Labour Market: Estimating the Employment Effects of South Africa's National Lockdown." Working Paper 202107, Development Policy Research Unit (DPRU), University of Cape Town, South Africa.

Korinek, Anton, Johan A. Mistiaen, and Martin Ravallion. 2007. "An Econometric Method of Correcting for Unit Nonresponse Bias in Surveys." *Journal of Econometrics* 136 (1).

Kugler, Maurice, Mariana Viollaz, Daniel Duque, Isis Gaddis, David Newhouse, Amparo Palacios-Lopez, and Michael Weber. 2021. "How Did the COVID-19 Crisis Affect Different Types of Workers in the Developing World?" Jobs Working Paper 60, World Bank, Washington, DC.

Lakner, Christoph, Daniel Gerszon Mahler, Mario Negre, and Espen Beer Prydz. 2022. "How Much Does Reducing Inequality Matter for Global Poverty?" *Journal of Economic Inequality.* https://doi.org/10.1007/s10888-021-09510-w.

Lakner, Christoph, and Branko Milanovic. 2013. "Global Income Distribution: From the Fall of the Berlin Wall to the Great Recession." Policy Research Working Paper 6719, World Bank, Washington, DC.

Mahler, Daniel Gerszon, Nishant Yonzan, and Christoph Lakner [randomized order]. Forthcoming. "The Impact of COVID-19 on Global Inequality and Poverty." World Bank, Washington, DC.

Milanovic, Branko. 2006. "Global Income Inequality: A Review." *World Economics* 7 (1): 131–57.

Milanovic, Branko. 2021. "After the Financial Crisis: The Evolution of the Global Income Distribution between 2008 and 2013." *Review of Income and Wealth* 68 (1): 43–73.

Narayan, Ambar, Alexandru Cojocaru, Sarthak Agrawal, Tom Bundervoet, Maria Davalos, Natalia Garcia, Christoph Lakner, et al. 2022. "COVID-19 and Economic Inequality: Short-Term Impacts with Long-Term Consequences." Policy Research Working Paper 9902, World Bank, Washington, DC.

Ravallion, Martin. 2021. "Missing Top Income Recipients." NBER Working Paper 28890, National Bureau of Economic Research, Cambridge, MA.

Ravallion, Martin, and Shaohua Chen. 2021. "Is that Really a Kuznets Curve? Turning Points for Income Inequality in China." NBER Working Paper 29199, National Bureau of Economic Research, Cambridge, MA.

World Bank. 2016. *Poverty and Shared Prosperity 2016: Taking on Inequality*. Washington, DC: World Bank.

World Bank. 2020. *Poverty and Shared Prosperity 2020: Reversals of Fortune*. Washington, DC: World Bank.

World Bank. 2021. "Distributional Impacts of COVID-19 in the Middle East and North Africa (MENA) Region." World Bank, Washington, DC.

World Bank. 2022a. *Brazil Poverty and Equity Assessment: Looking Ahead of Two Crises*. Washington, DC: World Bank.

World Bank. 2022b. *Collapse and Recovery: How the COVID-19 Pandemic Eroded Human Capital and What to Do about It*. Washington, DC: World Bank.

Yonzan, Nishant, Alexandru Cojocaru, Christoph Lakner, Daniel Gerszon Mahler, and Ambar Narayan. 2022. "The Impact of COVID-19 on Poverty and Inequality: Evidence from Phone Surveys." World Bank Blogs, January 18, 2022. World Bank, Washington, DC. https://blogs.worldbank.org/opendata/impact-covid-19-poverty-and-inequality-evidence-phone-surveys.

Beyond the Monetary Impacts of the Pandemic: A Lasting Legacy

3

Summary

The COVID-19 pandemic has affected many dimensions of human well-being. Among its negative consequences are lower incomes, higher mortality, school closures and interrupted learning, and disruptions of essential health services. Most countries have suffered multiple impacts across various dimensions, even if to different degrees. But how does one measure the combined extent of these impacts?

Poverty and Shared Prosperity 2018: Piecing Together the Poverty Puzzle (World Bank 2018) introduced the World Bank's multidimensional poverty measure to account for certain nonmonetary dimensions of well-being such as access to education and to core services like electricity and sanitation. This chapter updates that measure with the latest available data, reviews historical changes, and uses it as a lens through which to explore the nonmonetary consequences of the pandemic period.

The chapter then focuses on three dimensions severely affected by the pandemic: excess mortality, monetary poverty, and learning loss. For comparability, all three dimensions are expressed in terms of years of human life: excess mortality—loss of years of life; income loss—additional years spent in poverty over the 2020–21 period; and school closures—permanent learning losses that, if unaddressed, will reduce future earnings and prolong years spent in poverty.

From this analysis emerge two insights. First, losses of well-being from nonmonetary impacts—mortality and learning loss—are heterogeneous across countries but substantial. In fact, the analysis suggests that, for a range of valuations for years of life lost and years of life spent in poverty, the well-being losses from nonmonetary impacts could exceed the well-being losses solely from the current increases in monetary poverty in most countries. Second, the well-being losses are generally smallest on average for high-income countries and largest on average for middle-income countries.

Overall, this chapter confirms that monitoring well-being is a broader undertaking than monitoring monetary poverty alone. Moreover, the pandemic has brought to light potential trade-offs across dimensions of well-being that should be taken into account when calibrating policies. In particular, addressing recent learning loss is likely a key need for many countries, perhaps as important as protecting the poor and vulnerable from the income losses associated with the pandemic.

Chapter 3 online annexes available at http://hdl.handle.net/10986/37739:
3A. Estimating Multidimensional Poverty, circa 2018; 3B. The Pandemic Shock through the Lens of the MPM: The Poverty-Adjusted Life Expectancy Measure; and 3C. A Disaggregated Analysis of the Pandemic Shock.

Introduction

Although the extent and severity of the steep economic costs imposed on the world economy by the COVID-19 crisis have varied widely on the basis of local circumstances and local policy responses, nearly all countries across all income levels have felt these impacts. Many have yet to show signs of a significant recovery more than two years into the pandemic. However, because of the unique nature of the pandemic and the global response, including the adoption of social distancing measures, income losses are far from the only losses confronting policy makers in the recovery period.

A variety of dimensions of human well-being have suffered since March 2020, perhaps none more than life itself. The impact of COVID-19 on excess mortality—mortality above what would be expected on the basis of prepandemic projections—has been so severe that global life expectancy declined for the first time since 1950, the first year for which the United Nations provided a global estimate (Heuveline 2022). The World Health Organization (WHO) estimates that approximately 14.9 million excess deaths occurred between January 1, 2020, and December 31, 2021. This excess mortality captures deaths directly from infection as well as from the widespread indirect impacts on society and health systems, including those from overburdened health systems unable to provide life-saving and life-extending care for other health conditions (WHO 2022a). For example, one analysis of dialysis patients in Rajasthan, India, revealed that, following a month of lockdown, mortality in May 2020 was 64 percent higher than in March 2020 (Jain and Dupas 2022). While this example provides evidence for just one type of health service interruption for a highly-vulnerable group, more generally, pandemic-related health service disruptions in 2020 were estimated to increase child and maternal mortality in 18 countries by 3.6 percent and 1.5 percent, respectively (Ahmed et al., 2022).

The health service disruptions widely documented worldwide have affected not only excess mortality but also many areas of health-related well-being. Essential health services in a large number of countries have experienced comprehensive and sustained disruptions during the pandemic. According to surveys by WHO, use of health services was disrupted in nearly all countries from May 2020 through November 2021. Disruptions in potentially life-saving emergency care and routine child immunizations were increasing toward the end of this period, suggesting that the duration and extent of the health impacts have not yet been fully captured. The predominant reasons reported for overall disruptions in each country were a roughly even mix of declines in spending, intentional service reductions, and fewer individuals seeking care (WHO 2022b). A review of several studies that focused on January–May 2020 found a 37 percent reduction in the use of health care services across 20 economies (Moynihan et al. 2021). Another review of studies investigating use of maternal and child health services in eight Sub-Saharan African countries found disruptions in all assessed countries between March and July 2020, especially in critical services such as child vaccination and antenatal care (Shapira et al. 2021).

School closures, one of the social distancing measures enacted in many countries to limit transmission of the virus, will likely have severe ramifications for the future human capital of current school-age children if not addressed by remedial policy. Two years into the pandemic, empirical studies have begun to document widespread instances of learning loss and dropouts. The magnitude of the documented learning loss, highly variable and at times lower than earlier predictions, is consistently concentrated among the poorest students, regardless of country income level (Moscoviz and Evans 2022). Estimates based on data from the World Bank's high-frequency phone surveys (HFPS) found that the average percentage of students who had stopped learning since school closures in low- and lower-middle-income countries (LICs and LMICs) was highest at the peak of the pandemic, in April–June 2020, and remained elevated, while declining, through August 2021 (figure 3.1). Learning interruptions in upper-middle-income countries (UMICs) over the same period were lower but also increased

FIGURE 3.1

Widespread learning losses were reported, especially among low-income countries during the COVID-19 crisis

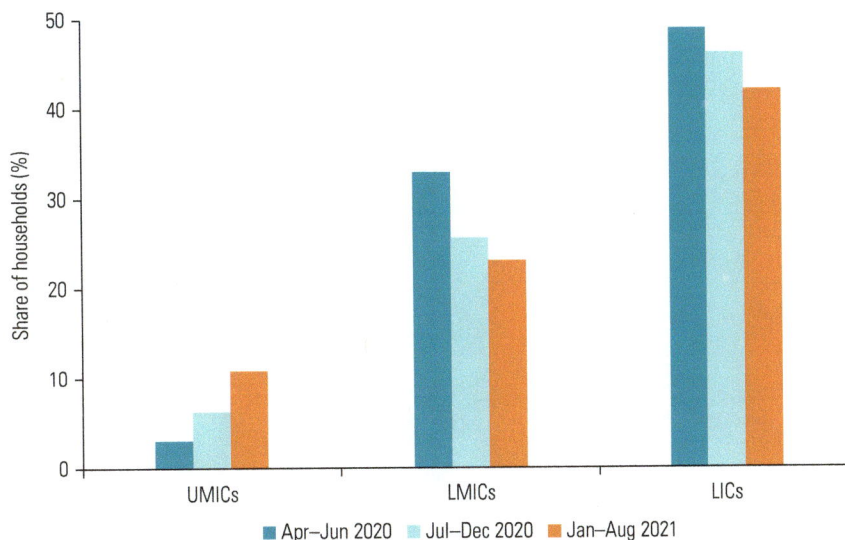

Source: Original estimates based on data from World Bank COVID-19 high-frequency phone surveys.
Note: The figure shows the share of households with children who attended primary or secondary school before the COVID-19 crisis in each income category and calendar period that report children stopped learning during the crisis. To account for the fact that the sample of economies with observations changes for each period, the numbers presented are the predicted values from a regression with time dummies and economy-fixed effects (taking the average of the economy-fixed effects for each income category within each period). The sample includes 29 economies. Economies are weighted equally. LICs = low-income countries; LMICs = lower-middle-income countries; UMICs = upper-middle-income countries.

rather than decreased over time. Averaging across a range of countries reveals what seems to be a one-to-one correspondence between the duration of school closure and a measure of learning loss—that is, for every month of school closure there is a corresponding month lost in learning (World Bank 2022a).

The consequences of such learning loss, if unaddressed by public policy and the private efforts of families, are expected to be severe. Worldwide, school closures could result in an average lifetime reduction of 2–10 percent in annual expected earnings due to learning loss from a single missed academic year for those students affected. Globally, this earnings loss would equate to between US$10 trillion and US$21 trillion, depending on the extent of school closures and effectiveness of mitigation measures (Azevedo et al. 2021; Neidhöfer, Lustig, and Tommasi 2021; Psacharopoulos et al. 2021; Samaniego et al. 2022; World Bank 2022b). The most recent estimates predict losses even exceeding US$21 trillion—Samaniego et al. (2022) project a worst-case scenario of welfare declines due to learning loss equivalent to a one-time loss of 111 percent of current national income in high-income countries (HICs), 89 percent in middle-income countries, and 74 percent in LICs.

Another important dimension of well-being likely widely affected over the pandemic period is the food security of vulnerable households. Food security has been affected primarily by pandemic-induced loss of employment and income, as well as reduced mobility (mandatory or voluntary) and reduced food availability due to multiple supply constraints (Éliás and Jámbor 2021; Picchioni, Goulao, and Roberfroid 2021). Data from the World Bank's HFPS show that the average estimated percentage of adults who skipped one

FIGURE 3.2

Meals skipped were highest at the start of the COVID-19 crisis and in lower-income countries

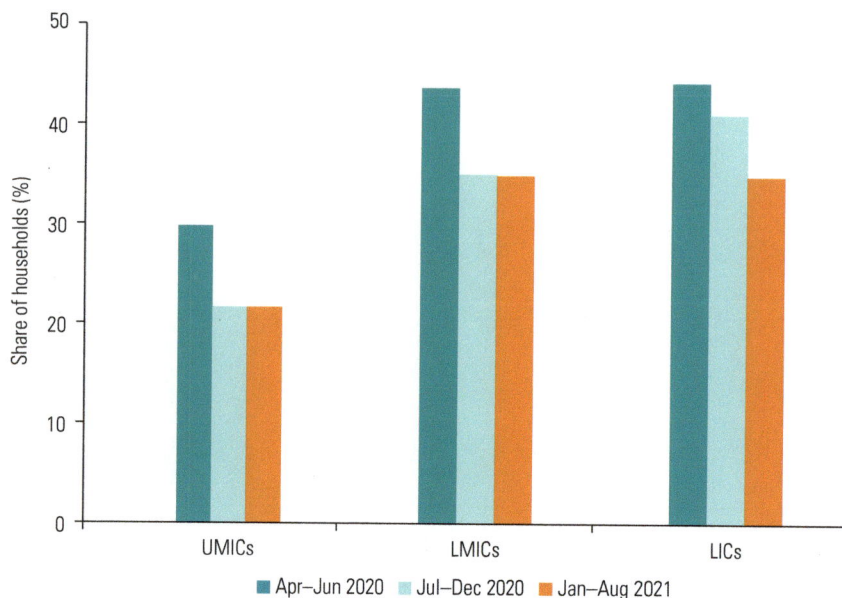

Source: Original estimates based on data from World Bank COVID-19 high-frequency phone surveys.
Note: The figure shows the share of households in each income category and calendar period in which adults skipped a meal in the past 30 days. To account for the fact that the sample of economies with observations changes for each period, the numbers presented are the predicted values from a regression with time dummies and economy-fixed effects (taking the average of the economy-fixed effects for each income category within each period). The sample includes 29 economies. Economies are weighted equally. LICs = low-income countries; LMICs = lower-middle-income countries; UMICs = upper-middle-income countries.

meal in the past 30 days was highest across all country income levels at the peak of the pandemic (figure 3.2). HFPS data also show that households with children have fared worse by some measures of income loss and food insecurity. After controlling for proxies of welfare such as education level and location, 5–7 percent more households with children reported total income loss, and 4 percent reported an adult member who had gone a day without eating because of resource constraints (World Bank and UNICEF 2022). It is possible that more recent data may also indicate challenges with food security after the worldwide rise in food prices that began in March 2022. In addition to the higher risks posed for food intake and nutritional status, increases in intimate partner violence were documented in several countries in the early months of the COVID-19 crisis amid movement restrictions, reduced social support, increased tension, and other risk factors (De Paz Nieves, Gaddis, and Muller 2021; Lausi et al. 2021).

Multidimensional poverty on the eve of the pandemic

Multidimensional poverty outstripped monetary poverty

The recognition that monetary welfare measures are able to capture only a subset of well-being dimensions has spurred a wide body of research on multidimensional poverty measures (Alkire et al. 2015; Bourguignon and Chakravarty 1999). In 2018, the World Bank published its first estimates of a multidimensional poverty measure (MPM), grounded in the notion that a comprehensive view of well-being, even one centered on consumption like the World Bank measure, should include nonmarket goods measured consistently for the same unit of analysis (that is, the household) and in a wide range of countries. The first MPM figures were presented in *Poverty and Shared Prosperity 2018* (World Bank 2018), and subsequent reports update the MPM.

The World Bank's MPM expands the definition of poverty beyond monetary deprivation to include five indicators of well-being under two additional dimensions: access to education and access to basic infrastructure. These indicators are used to produce a household-level multidimensional headcount ratio. The MPM is produced with data (primarily) from the harmonized household surveys in the Global Monitoring Database.[1] A household is considered to be multidimensionally poor if it is below the extreme poverty line or if it cumulates too many deprivations in education and basic infrastructure. For education, the two deprivation indicators are whether a child is not enrolled in school and whether no adult in the household has completed a primary education. For basic infrastructure, the three deprivation indicators are no access to electricity, no access to limited-standard drinking water, and no access to limited-standard sanitation. The methodology for constructing the MPM was documented in detail in the 2018 and 2020 *Poverty and Shared Prosperity* reports (World Bank 2018, 2020) and is summarized in online annex 3A.

As noted, the MPM provides insight into the extent of poverty not captured solely by stand-alone monetary measures. Table 3.1 summarizes the global and regional multidimensional poverty headcount ratios for 2018, the most recent year there is total population data coverage of at least 50 percent. However, as indicated in the table, the East Asia and Pacific and South Asia regions do not reach the 50 percent threshold.

Worldwide, the 2018 multidimensional poverty headcount ratio was 14.7 percent, which is a 65 percent increase over the monetary poverty measure of 8.9 percent. By comparing the monetary poverty dimension with indicators from other dimensions, it is possible to form a picture of how many multidimensionally poor are not captured by monetary poverty, as well as which indicator deprivations most affect well-being in the different regions. Indeed, almost four out of 10 (39 percent) multidimensionally poor persons are not captured by monetary poverty because they are deprived in nonmonetary dimensions alone. Figure 3.3 depicts the extent of the overlap in deprivation across the three dimensions for the world circa 2018 among those who are multidimesionally poor. Almost one out of three (28 percent) is deprived in all three dimensions.

In terms of deprivations in individual indicators, the most prevalent is clearly sanitation, with 22.8 percent of the covered population living with less than adequate sanitation. After sanitation, the most prevalent deprivations occur with adult educational attainment (12.9 percent) and access to electricity (12.7 percent). Consistent with the observations from previous *Poverty and Shared Prosperity* reports (World Bank 2018, 2020), multidimensional poverty in 2018 was concentrated in Sub-Saharan Africa and South Asia. In Sub-Saharan Africa, just over half of all households experienced multidimensional poverty. Sub-Saharan Africa and South Asia have, respectively, the highest and second-highest percentage of population experiencing each of the individual deprivations, except for drinking water. For this indicator, the East Asia and Pacific region has the second-worst performance (although this regional comparison may be complicated by the relatively low population coverage of the East Asia and Pacific and South Asia regions).

TABLE 3.1

Deprivations in education and infrastructure raise the multidimensional poverty measure above monetary poverty

| Region | Monetary | Deprivation rate (% of population) | | | | | Multidimensional poverty headcount ratio (%) | Number of economies | Population coverage (%)[a] |
		Educational attainment	Educational enrollment	Electricity	Sanitation	Drinking water			
East Asia and Pacific	3.8	8.7	1.7	6.6	15.9	8.2	6.0	14	30
Europe and Central Asia	0.3	0.9	2.2	1.7	7.1	4.5	2.1	25	89
Latin America and the Caribbean	3.8	9.4	1.6	1.0	16.6	2.9	4.6	14	87
Middle East and North Africa	1.7	8.6	2.8	0.5	3.1	1.4	2.4	5	51
South Asia	8.2	20.5	19.1	14.8	35.5	5.3	17.4	5	22
Sub-Saharan Africa	32.4	35.7	23.0	48.7	65.1	28.9	52.6	35	73
Rest of the world	0.7	1.0	2.2	0.0	0.2	0.5	1.4	25	78
All regions	**8.9**	**12.9**	**9.7**	**12.7**	**22.8**	**10.1**	**14.7**	**123**	**51[b]**

Source: World Bank, Global Monitoring Database.

Note: The table presents the multidimensional poverty headcount ratio and share of population deprived in each indicator by region and rest of the world circa 2018. "Multidimensional poverty headcount ratio" is the share of the population in each region defined as multidimensionally poor. "Number of economies" is the number of economies in each region for which information is available in the window between 2015 and 2019 for a circa 2018 reporting year. The monetary headcount is based on the international poverty line. Regional and total estimates are population-weighted averages of survey year estimates for 123 economies and are not comparable with those presented in the previous section. The coverage rule applied to the estimates is identical to that used in the rest of the chapter. Details can be found in online annex 3A. Regions without sufficient population coverage are highlighted in purple.

a. Data coverage differs across regions. The data cover as much as 89 percent of the population of Latin America and the Caribbean and as little as 22 percent of the population of South Asia. The coverage for South Asia is low because no household surveys are available for India between 2014 and 2021. Regional coverage is calculated using the same rules as in the rest of this chapter (see online annex 3A). Thus, because of the absence of data on China and India, coverage of the East Asia and Pacific and South Asia regions is insufficient.

b. The table conforms to both coverage criteria for global poverty reporting. Both the global population coverage and the coverage for low-income and lower-middle-income countries are 51 percent.

FIGURE 3.3

Almost 40 percent of the multidimensionally poor are not monetarily poor

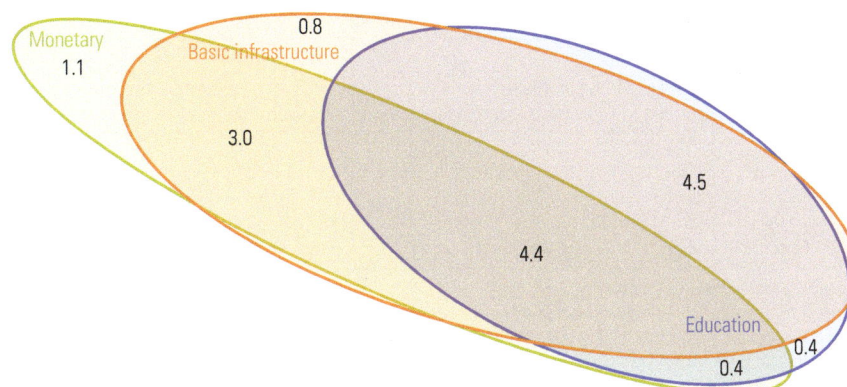

Source: World Bank estimates based on data from World Bank, Global Monitoring Database.
Note: The figure shows the share of population that is multidimensionally poor and the dimensions in which they are deprived. For example, the numbers in the yellow oval add up to 8.9 percent, which is the monetary headcount. Adding up all numbers in the figure results in 14.7 percent, which is the proportion of people who are multidimensionally deprived. Estimates are based on harmonized household surveys in 123 economies, circa 2018.

Before the pandemic, declining trends in multidimensional poverty mirrored declines in monetary poverty

The significant progress in poverty reduction achieved before the onset of COVID-19 applies to nonmonetary dimensions as well. Table 3.2 summarizes the MPM from 2015 to 2018. In parallel with the declines in monetary poverty, the MPM and each individual indicator displayed strong declines at the global level. The overall multidimensional poverty head-count ratio fell 2.9 percentage points from 2015 to 2018, while the monetary poverty figure linked to the same countries fell 2.3 percentage points. Progress was observed in each of the individual dimensions as well. For example, the rate of deprivation in sanitation fell from 25.5 percent to 22.8 percent.

One interpretive difficulty with table 3.2 is that the underlying composition of economies was not constant over the four-year period. For example, the share of the global population covered declined from 57 percent to 51 percent. Therefore, some of the improvements in poverty and multidimensional well-being may be attributable to the changing composition of economies. However, when the analysis is restricted to a smaller set of seven countries in Latin America and the Caribbean that contribute regular and complete data to the estimation of multidimensional poverty, the declining trends in all assessed dimensions remain. Table 3.3 depicts the MPM and the incidence of each indicator as measured annually from 2012 to 2019 for these seven Latin American countries. The monetary poverty rate declined from 5.7 percent to 3.5 percent, while the MPM poverty rate declined from 7.8 percent to 4.6 percent. Gains in other dimensions include a reduction in the proportion of the population deprived of electricity from 4.5 percent to 2.2 percent and the proportion deprived of adequate access to water, falling from 7.9 percent to 4.2 percent.

Finally, in the years before the COVID-19 crisis hit, the world benefited not only from sustained reductions in monetary poverty but also from gains in access to key goods not typically provided through market purchase such as primary education and sanitation services.

TABLE 3.2

Multidimensional poverty declined in recent years, along with monetary poverty

Reporting year	Deprivation rate (% of population)						Multi-dimensional poverty headcount ratio (%)	Population coverage (%)
	Monetary	Educational attainment	Educational enrollment	Electricity	Sanitation	Drinking water		
2015	11.2	13.8	10.3	14.3	25.5	13.1	17.6	57
2016	9.7	13.4	10.5	12.6	24.2	11.5	15.9	56
2017	9.6	13.5	10.4	12.9	24.5	11.0	16.0	54[a]
2018	8.9	12.9	9.7	12.7	22.8	10.1	14.7	51

Source: World Bank, Global Monitoring Database.
Note: The table depicts the global multidimensional poverty headcount ratio and share of population deprived in each indicator, circa 2015–18. The monetary headcount is based on the international poverty line. Estimates are population-weighted averages of survey year estimates for 140 economies for 2015, 138 for 2016, 134 for 2017, and 123 for 2018. Estimates are not comparable with those presented in previous sections due to changes in underlying composition. The multidimensional poverty headcount ratio indicates the share of the population in each region defined as multidimensionally poor. The coverage rule applied to the estimates is identical to that used in the rest of the chapter. Details can be found in online annex 3A.
a. The table conforms with the coverage criteria for global poverty reporting. For reporting year 2017, the global population coverage is 54 percent. In low- and lower-middle-income countries, it is 55 percent. For other reporting years, the coverage figure shown is the same for both populations.

TABLE 3.3

Declines across all dimensions of the multidimensional poverty measure are apparent even when restricting comparison to a consistent set of economies over time

Reporting year	Deprivation rate (% of population)						Multidimensional poverty headcount ratio (%)
	Monetary	Educational attainment	Educational enrollment	Electricity	Sanitation	Drinking water	
2012	5.7	8.5	2.7	4.5	12.5	7.9	7.8
2013	4.9	8.0	2.3	4.0	11.8	7.4	6.8
2014	4.4	7.8	2.4	3.6	12.2	6.4	6.1
2015	4.2	7.3	2.2	3.1	11.1	6.4	5.7
2016	4.2	7.2	2.0	2.8	10.0	5.7	5.7
2017	3.7	7.0	2.1	2.6	10.2	4.3	5.1
2018	3.4	6.9	2.0	2.4	9.3	4.5	4.8
2019	3.5	6.3	2.4	2.2	8.9	4.2	4.6

Source: World Bank, Global Monitoring Database.
Note: The table presents estimates of the multidimensional poverty headcount ratio and share of population deprived in each indicator for Bolivia, Colombia, Costa Rica, the Dominican Republic, Ecuador, Paraguay, and Peru. Estimates are population-weighted averages of survey year estimates and are reported from circa 2012 through circa 2019 for these countries because they have data available for the entire time window. Estimates are not comparable with regional estimates for Latin America and the Caribbean in previous tables that cover 14 economies. The monetary headcount is based on the international poverty line. The multidimensional poverty headcount ratio indicates the share of the population in each region defined as multidimensionally poor. The coverage rule applied to the estimates is identical to that used in the rest of the chapter. Details can be found in online annex 3A.

Pandemic impacts from a multidimensional perspective

Multidimensional impacts indicate long-term consequences

The pandemic has had substantial impacts on poverty and inequality and, as reviewed at the outset of this chapter, on many nonmonetary dimensions of well-being. This section explores the wider range of pandemic impacts and how these losses relate to declines in the more familiar monetary poverty measures. The exercise focuses on two key nonmonetary dimensions: mortality and education. For mortality, every region of the world has suffered elevated death rates during periods of peak COVID-19 transmission. As for education, the closure of schools is a severe challenge to the human capital investments in today's school-age children—a challenge that may have long-lived consequences if the human capital scarring is not remediated.

Although all countries have suffered losses of life, income, and human capital, outcomes of the pandemic have been quite heterogeneous. For example, some countries have suffered high mortality and education losses, but they have been able to limit the impacts of monetary poverty by enacting social protection policies. Other countries have seen limited increases in mortality but have recorded significant monetary poverty or education losses.

Any attempts to compare the well-being impacts of premature mortality, income loss, and learning loss must come with caveats. First, the data available since the outset of the pandemic on these three dimensions are still scarce in many countries. Often, national estimates are derived from research papers that provide estimates in the absence of underlying data. Therefore, the reported impact estimates may capture the order of magnitude of the impact in these three dimensions but may not define precise levels of impact. To mitigate this issue, whenever possible the analysis makes conservative assumptions that often understate the total impact. Second, many important impacts, especially in the health dimension such as quality of life reductions associated with long COVID-19, are not considered. For the purposes of this exercise, COVID-19 affects health only through mortality. Likewise, the analysis considers only the incidence of poverty and thus ignores the depth of poverty. Third, there is considerable uncertainty around the implications of learning loss for future poverty. This uncertainty is due to various reasons, including whether learning loss may be compounded when the affected young cohorts enter the labor market, or whether the losses may instead be alleviated over time with concerted private actions and public policies. The analysis simply extends the given estimated losses into the future, without assuming any mitigation through public or private efforts.

It is possible to aggregate losses across these three dimensions using several different approaches. One approach adopts the framework of the MPM, which already records monetary poverty and education, and combines it with a life expectancy measure, reflecting mortality impacts to generate a poverty-adjusted life expectancy, or PALE (see box 3.1). However, the main analysis in this section adopts a straightforward disaggregated years-of-life framework that

---

BOX 3.1

Poverty-adjusted life expectancy: An index aggregating poverty and mortality

Mortality and poverty are arguably the two major sources of well-being losses at the global level. Poverty reduces the quality of life, while mortality reduces the quantity of life. However, mortality is often not addressed by most measures of well-being. It must be treated in a unique way because of its exclusive nature: one cannot be dead and simultaneously deprived in other dimensions. As shown by Baland, Cassan, and Decerf (2022), a lifecycle perspective provides the justification for aggregating mortality and poverty through the poverty-adjusted life expectancy (PALE) indicator. When considering multidimensional poverty, PALE is defined as

$$PALE = LE\,(1 - \theta * MPM),$$

where *LE* is life expectancy at birth; *MPM* is the multidimensional poverty headcount ratio (numerous definitions of poverty can be used, but this example adopts the MPM); and the normative parameter θ (between 0 and 1) captures the fraction of period utility lost when multidimensionally poor. At one extreme, when θ = 0—that is, when spending one year in multidimensional poverty is considered the same as spending that year out of multidimensional poverty—PALE corresponds to life expectancy at birth. At the other extreme, when θ = 1—that is,

(continued)

BOX 3.1

Poverty-adjusted life expectancy: An index aggregating poverty and mortality *(continued)*

when spending one year in multidimensional poverty is considered the same as losing one year from premature death—PALE can be interpreted as the number of years that a newborn expects to live free from multidimensional poverty *if she were confronted throughout her lifetime with the mortality and MPM poverty observed during the birth year.* For this latter extreme, PALE thus corresponds to the poverty-free life expectancy index initially proposed by Riumallo-Herl, Canning, and Salomon (2018).

Henceforth, it is assumed that θ = 1, a conservative assumption that ascribes a rather small relative weight to mortality. Analyzing the data in this manner is not to normatively equate a year lived in poverty with a year of life lost. Both are distinct and significant forms of deprivation. Rather, it provides a lower bound on the relative weight of premature mortality, which is rooted in the assumption that, if given the choice, people would choose an additional year of life in multidimensional poverty to the loss of a year of life to early mortality. Indeed, 1/θ can alternatively be interpreted as the number of additional years one would be willing to spend in multidimensional poverty to gain one year of life.

PALE provides a lens through which one can analyze some of the main well-being losses of the COVID-19 pandemic. Indeed, excess mortality is captured through its impact on life expectancy, while income losses and school closures are captured through their impact on the MPM. An approach based on the MPM provides the same global standard of deprivation cutoffs and dimensional weights for all countries when aggregating dimensions.

Conducting this analysis requires simulating the changes to the MPM because very few countries already provide postoutbreak MPM data. For each country in the data, the impact of the pandemic on PALE is defined as the difference between a baseline prepandemic value and a pandemic value. The baseline value is computed from the most recent MPM data available for the country, along with the more recent estimate of prepandemic life expectancy at birth. The pandemic value is then simulated off this baseline value on the basis of several assumptions described in online annex 3B.

The baseline value of PALE is plotted against gross domestic product (GDP) per capita in figure B3.1.1. Countries with larger GDP per capita have larger PALE values for two reasons. First, they have higher life expectancy at birth. Second, and more important, they have much less multidimensional poverty. The austere deprivation standards embedded in the MPM frequently bind in a lower-income country, but almost no one is multidimensionally poor in high-income countries.

For two reasons, the absolute reduction of PALE in low- and lower-middle-income countries (LICs and LMICs) over the pandemic period is larger than that in upper-middle or high-income countries (UMICs or HICs), despite starting from a lower baseline PALE estimate. First, the extreme poverty shock is, as expected, larger in LICs and LMICs than in UMICs and HICs. Second, and more important, school closures have a much larger impact on the MPM rate in LICs and LMICs than in UMICs and HICs. This could appear to be surprising because school closures were not shorter in UMICs and HICs than in LICs and LMICs. However, the education shock alone is not sufficient for households to be considered multidimensionally poor when they have no other deprivations. Because of the austere deprivation cutoffs used by the MPM, the vast majority of households in HICs and UMICs face no deprivation and thus would not be rendered multidimensionally poor by school closures alone. By contrast, the large impact of the education shock on the MPM in LICs and LMICs reflects the fact that many households living in these countries already face deprivations in other dimensions; therefore, many of them are pushed into multidimensional poverty when they become also deprived in school enrollment.

(continued)

BOX 3.1

BOX 3.1

Poverty-adjusted life expectancy: An index aggregating poverty and mortality *(continued)*

FIGURE B3.1.1

Lower-income economies have experienced larger reductions in poverty-adjusted life expectancy

a. PALE estimates, by level of GDP per capita

b. Average PALE, by income category

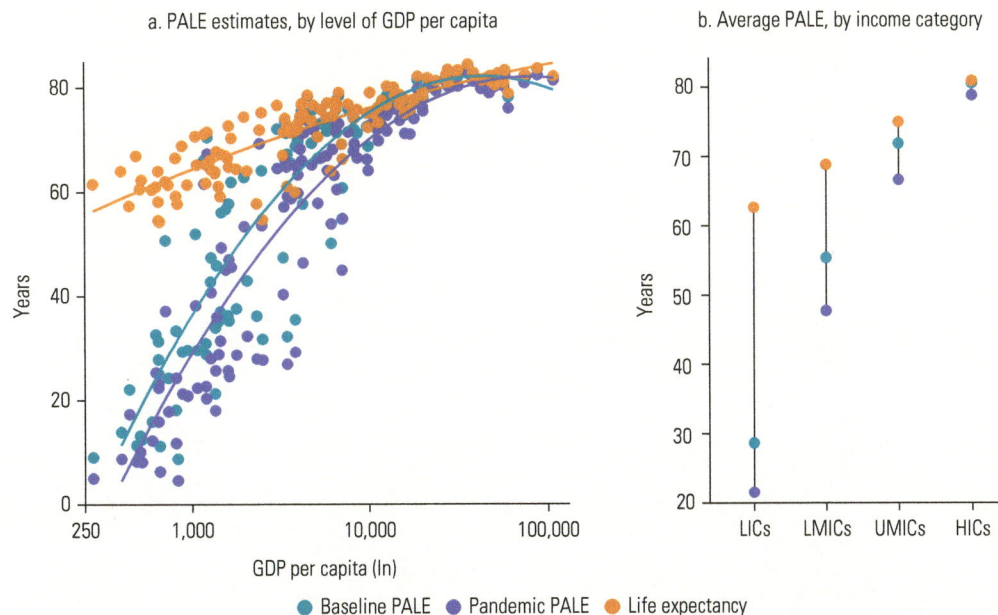

● Baseline PALE ● Pandemic PALE ● Life expectancy

Sources: Original estimates based on multidimensional poverty measure data from World Bank, Global Monitoring Database; mortality data from Heuveline 2022.
Note: Panel a shows the number of years, in each economy, of life expectancy, baseline poverty-adjusted life expectancy (PALE) using prepandemic data, and pandemic PALE using assumptions in online annex 3B. Economies are sorted by GDP per capita on the horizontal axis using a logarithmic scale. The relationship between each measure and log GDP per capita is shown using a quadratic line of best fit. Panel b shows the same metrics aggregated by income category using a simple average (not weighted by population). GDP per capita is for 2019 expressed in 2015 constant US dollars. GDP = gross domestic product; HICs = high-income countries; LICs = low-income countries; LMICs = lower-middle-income countries; ln = logarithm; UMICs = upper-middle-income countries.

Finally, the results suggest that the main drivers of the decline in PALE vary across country income groups. Figure B3.1.2 depicts the fraction of the total reduction in PALE that can be attributed to each dimension, as determined by a Shapley decomposition (see online annex 3B). The rise in mortality risk had the largest impact on PALE in higher-income countries, whereas the restrictions in access to education have the greatest influence on the declines in PALE in lower-income countries. This figure further highlights that the rise in monetary poverty was the least influential of the three factors modeled in determining the sharp declines in PALE.

There are many possible approaches to the aggregation of pandemic impacts across disparate dimensions, and all require interpretation of some normative framework. PALE is one such example grounded in the World Bank's MPM that suggests the largest impacts are experienced by the poorest economies, driven primarily by widespread school closures as well as by elevated mortality and increases in poverty.

(continued)

BOX 3.1

Poverty-adjusted life expectancy: An index aggregating poverty and mortality *(continued)*

FIGURE B3.1.2

Reduction in poverty-adjusted life expectancy was driven by learning loss in lower-income countries and by increased mortality in higher-income countries

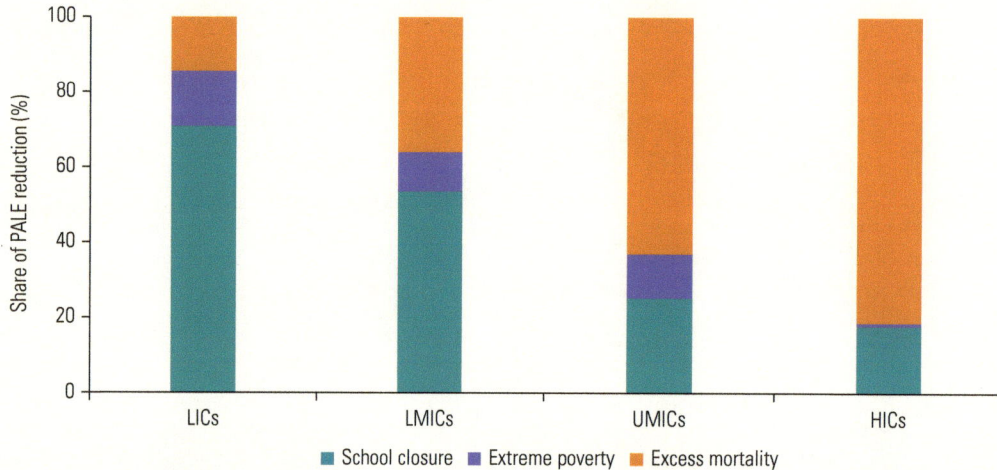

Sources: Original estimates based on multidimensional poverty measure data from World Bank, Global Monitoring Database; mortality data from Heuveline 2022.
Note: The figure shows the share of reduction in poverty-adjusted life expectancy (PALE) in each income category attributable to excess mortality, additional extreme poverty, and school closure, using an average Shapley decomposition. PALE reduction is a simple average of economies in each income category and is not weighted by population. PALE reduction represents the peak value of each shock occurring between 2020 and 2021. HICs = high-income countries; LICs = low-income countries; LMICs = lower-middle-income countries; UMICs = upper-middle-income countries.

allows a policy maker to consider a range of values when assessing the relative importance of the declines in each of these three dimensions.

In the flexible disaggregated years-of-life framework used for the analysis in the remainder of this section, loss estimates in each of the three dimensions—mortality, income, and learning—are measured using the same unit: years of human life. Premature mortality is captured through an estimated number of years of life lost for each individual, depending on the age at death, and these individual-level figures are then aggregated across a population. The immediate monetary impacts lead to additional years of life spent in monetary poverty due to the increase in poverty incidence. Learning losses can also generate additional years of life spent in monetary poverty; however, in contrast to the immediate impacts on poverty, these additional years are realized in the future, stemming from lower productivity and lower long-run growth.

The conceptual foundation for this analysis and the main assumptions sustaining its estimates are presented in box 3.2 (with further explication and estimation details explained in online annex 3C). The goal of the analysis is to compare, at the country level, the magnitudes of the well-being losses generated by the pandemic through its impacts occurring *over the period 2020–21* on excess mortality, monetary poverty, and school closures. Because these impacts materialize over different dimensions of well-being, such a comparison requires the analyst to express these impacts in comparable units—years of life. The years of life spent below the monetary poverty line as a result of the pandemic-induced economic contraction during 2020–21

BOX 3.2

Lifecycle foundations for multidimensional comparisons in terms of years of life

Comparing the size of well-being losses on the basis of three dimensions (excess mortality, monetary poverty, and school closures) requires expressing them in the same units. The analysis considers an extension of the framework of Decerf et al. (2021), which is grounded in a simplified version of lifecycle utility, with period consumption levels reduced to only two states: being poor monetarily or not. The pandemic is assumed to reduce an individual's lifecycle utility in three ways:

- *Mortality.* The excess mortality estimated over the period 2020–21 may have prematurely cost the life of an individual who otherwise would have lived for a certain number of additional years.
- *Current poverty.* The economic recession may have pushed a nonpoor individual into monetary poverty in either 2020 or 2021, or both.
- *Future poverty (school closures).* The school closures over 2020–21 may depress future incomes in such a way that the individual is pushed into poverty for several years (over the period 2020–50, corresponding to the working life of the affected student cohort), whereas this person would not have been poor in the absence of the pandemic.

Under these assumptions, the total well-being losses (WL) over the whole population deriving from the mortality, poverty, and learning detriments observed up to December 2021 are proportional to a weighted sum of years of life either prematurely lost to excess mortality or spent in poverty. In more formal terms,

$$WL = CPY + \alpha \, YLL + FPY,$$

where CPY is the number of additional (current) poverty years spent in 2020 and 2021; YLL is the number of years of life lost due to excess mortality in 2020 and 2021; FPY is the number of additional (future) poverty years due to school closures in 2020 and 2021, whose scarring effects will materialize over the period 2020–50; and α is a normative parameter that expresses the relative weight of mortality in relation to poverty. The parameter α captures how many poverty years generate an equivalent well-being loss as one lost year of life.

The number of current poverty years (CPY) begins with the observation that one additional year spent in poverty constitutes one poverty year. The additional years in poverty are obtained following the information in chapter 1 based on the societal poverty line anchored to its 2019 value. The increase in the fraction of poor is the difference between the nowcasted poverty headcount and the counterfactual poverty headcount based on prepandemic growth rates. CPY is the sum of the additional number of people who were poor in 2020 and 2021.

The number of years of life lost (YLL) derives from estimates of the number of excess deaths in a country over the period 2020–21 (Wang et al. 2022). The number of years of life lost due to a COVID-19–related death corresponds to a country's residual life expectancy at the age at which the excess death takes place. Because data on the age distribution of excess deaths are not available in most countries, the analysis assumes that the age distribution of excess deaths from all causes corresponds to the age distribution of excess deaths arising from COVID-19. This assumption likely underestimates the number of years lost because COVID-19 mortality mostly affects older persons.

The number of future poverty years (FPY) is based on a simulation of the future earning losses caused by learning losses due to school closures observed up to November 2021, using projected declines in national income from a long-term growth model (Loayza et al. 2022; Loayza and Pennings, forthcoming). School closures can lead to widespread learning losses that, in turn, reduce the stock of human capital—a key factor in long-term economic growth—and thus lower national income in the future. The counterfactual growth projections of learning losses are applied to distribution-neutral poverty forecasts, and then the difference between the fraction of poor on

(continued)

BOX 3.2

Lifecycle foundations for multidimensional comparisons in terms of years of life *(continued)*

a baseline growth path (without learning loss) and on a learning loss scenario path is determined. The change in the number of future poverty years is the sum of the additional number of poor individuals over all the years in the period 2020–50.

Estimates of a country's learning loss are derived from data on the duration of its school closure, the quality of its schooling system, and findings from World Bank (2022a) that estimate, on average, a one-to-one correspondence between the duration of school closure and the extent of learning loss. Because of the complexity of long-term growth simulations, the analysis focuses on 61 economies that represent a range of regions and national income levels. Decerf et al. (forthcoming) provide more details on this approach.

Beyond the length of school closures, the size of the economic growth impacts in each country in the long-term growth model simulations depend on several parameters. The first is the quality of education: other things being equal, a year of school closure has less effect on human capital formation and economic growth in countries with poor-quality schools. On average, one year of schooling closure becomes two-thirds of learning-adjusted years of schooling lost (estimates of prepandemic school quality are taken from Kraay 2018). The second parameter is the size of the affected school-age cohorts in school in 2020–21 relative to the size of the working-age population in the future. By 2050, this ratio is about one-third, although it varies across countries and accumulates at different rates over time. As for the third parameter, the effects on growth depend on the return to years of learning-adjusted schooling, which are assumed to be 12 percent (and so the return to a year of raw schooling is 8 percent). In a typical country, the effect on the gross domestic product per capita in the *very* long run is the product of four numbers—school closure length × education quality adjustment × returns to quality-adjusted attainment × relative size of affected cohort—though by 2050 it is only 70 percent as large because of partial adjustment of the physical capital stock.

These estimates of *FPY* are conservative for two reasons. First, the analysis assumes that the future income of all students is affected to the same degree, even though disadvantaged individuals may have suffered heavier learning losses (Bundervoet, Davalos, and Garcia 2022). This finding suggests that future income of the poor and near-poor should be more than proportionally affected, pointing toward larger future impacts on poverty. Second, some alternative projections of the economic consequences of school closures typically yield larger losses in part because of the inclusion of losses in work experience, which are not addressed here (Samaniego et al. 2022).

directly capture this dimension. By contrast, the years of life associated with excess mortality and school closures capture the subsequent *consequences* of the impact of the pandemic on these dimensions. These consequences occur mainly in the future. For example, the consequence of the premature pandemic-induced death of a 60-year-old individual in 2020 is that she will lose the 15 years of her residual life expectancy over the period 2020–35. Similarly, even though the connection is less deterministic, the consequence of the learning loss a student experiences because of school closures in 2020–21 is that the student may spend additional years in poverty over the next decades. The objective of this analysis is not to investigate the impacts of the pandemic over different time horizons, but merely to compare the impacts (on three dimensions) that occurred over the period 2020–21 by expressing them in comparable units, even though some detriments may not appear until the future.[2]

Because the analysis presents the estimated impact on each dimension either through a number of years of life lost or through a number of additional years lived under the poverty line, this approach remains agnostic to the relative weight afforded to poverty years and years of life lost. It therefore allows policy makers to set their own weights and determine which dimension of loss is most consequential for well-being.

The approach here also enables policy makers to consider the total well-being loss that the pandemic generated from March 2020 to December 2021. The well-being loss is also a country-specific measure. When dealing with the pandemic, governments typically do not calibrate their responses as a function of a global standard such as the MPM. Instead, they make trade-offs between the dimensions (mortality, poverty, and education) in accordance with country-specific standards. For this reason, the analysis moves beyond the MPM and the international poverty line and adopts a country-specific absolute poverty line—the societal poverty line. The societal poverty line, anchored to its 2019 level, is closer in value to each country's national poverty line.

As for education detriments, the learning loss from school closures, if not addressed, will result in future losses in well-being when learning losses translate into reduced earnings during the working life of the affected student cohorts. Thus the weight that a government attributes to school closures depends on the size of the cumulated future earning losses, which, in turn, depend on the characteristics of a country's school system, the amount of schooling postponed over the pandemic period, and various characteristics of the economy today and in the future.

Summary of results

A comparison of the increase in years of poverty directly due to pandemic-related economic contraction and years of life lost can be obtained for 159 economies because more computationally intensive long-term growth projections are not needed for this comparison. Middle-income countries experience a higher current poverty shock than high-income ones, as shown in chapter 1, for at least two reasons: differences in the scope of social protection policies adopted in response to the pandemic outbreak and differences in initial poverty levels. HICs likely enacted stronger social protection measures in response to the pandemic, and they typically have a smaller proportion of their population near their societal poverty line. Poverty levels actually fell in some HICs, most likely the result of their social protection measures, which explains why the additional current poverty years are much smaller in HICs (see the third column of table 3.4). Middle-income countries also experienced a higher mortality shock. Interestingly, HICs did not suffer a more severe mortality shock than LICs, in spite of their older populations, who are more at risk for severe disease. Unequal vaccine rollouts and flatter COVID-19 age mortality curves in LICs are likely among the drivers of this pattern (Demombynes et al. 2021).

TABLE 3.4

Years lost to premature mortality exceed increase in years lived in poverty in about half of economies

Country income group	Coverage (number of economies)	Excess mortality (YLL, lost years per 100 persons)	Increase in current poverty years (CPY, years per 100 persons)	Fraction of economies for which CPY < YLL
Low-income	31	3.1	5.2	0.26
Lower-middle-income	33	4.6	5.4	0.42
Upper-middle-income	41	5.5	4.9	0.54
High-income	54	3.0	0.6	0.72
All economies	**159**	**4.0**	**3.6**	**0.52**

Sources: Original calculations based on poverty data from World Bank, Global Monitoring Database; excess mortality estimates from Wang et al. 2022; mortality estimates from Heuveline 2022.
Note: The table compares average excess mortality and increase in current poverty during 2020–21 by country income group for 159 economies. Average values for economies in the sample group are not weighted for population.

Fifty-two percent of countries experienced a greater number of years of life lost than an increase in years in poverty due to the current period shock, as shown in table 3.4. For these countries, if it is assumed that individuals would rather spend one year in poverty than lose this year of life to premature mortality, then this suggests that well-being losses from excess mortality may, in fact, dominate the well-being losses from additional poverty. Surprisingly, according to the estimates, 26 percent of LICs and 42 percent of LMICs suffer more lost years of life than an increase in poverty years. This finding applies to the majority of UMICs and HICs as well. These estimates stand in partial contrast with expectations early in the pandemic period that additional poverty would be a larger source of well-being losses than mortality, at least for 2020 (Decerf et al. 2021; Ferreira et al. 2021).

The analysis that combines information on life years lost and current poverty change with future poverty impacts associated with learning losses focuses on 61 economies. These simulations suggest that the reduction in the year-to-year economic growth due to school closure-related learning losses is small, leading typically to a reduction of 1–3 percent of gross domestic product (GDP) per capita in 2050. These results are largely consistent with those of other studies that project the economic consequences of learning loss (Psacharopoulos et al. 2021; Samaniego et al. 2022). However, this relatively small reduction still leads to a substantial number of future poverty years because the learning losses in 2020 and 2021 will carry a legacy over several decades. The long-term growth model exercise estimates an average cumulative GDP loss over the period 2020–50 of 53 percent of the 2020 GDP per capita.[3] The growth rates produced by the long-term growth model simulations produce a range of future poverty years across countries because of variations in the duration of school closures, the quality of learning in that country, and characteristics of the national economies. For example, resource-rich countries depend less on human capital for growth and thus their future growth is less affected by learning losses.

For the 61 economies in the simulations, all three sources of well-being losses are quite substantial. The average citizen of these countries (unweighted by population) will experience 15 lost days per person due to premature mortality, an additional 15 days of current poverty per person, and 42 additional future poverty days per person.[4] Figure 3.4 plots the three well-being loss measures in number of years per 100 persons for each economy. This figure captures the variation in the impacts of the three sources, and it suggests that countries experienced the pandemic period up to the end of 2021 very differently, in part because of the national policies they adopted.

Table 3.5 summarizes the magnitude of loss for each dimension by country income group. The summary indicates that, for a wide range of countries and a wide range of valuation of relative loss, the cumulative losses from premature mortality and learning deficits often exceed the immediate impacts of an increase in monetary poverty. According to the simulations, 80 percent of countries will experience greater total years of future poverty due to learning loss than current poverty years: 83 percent of LICs, 75 percent of LMICs, 72 percent of UMICs, and 93 percent of HICs. But interpretations of these findings should be made with care. Even though the future increase in total years in poverty due to the learning loss may be greater than the immediate increase due to the current poverty shock, the future increase is spread over a 30-year period, whereas the immediate increase spans only a two-year period. Therefore, the income losses in 2020–21 may still represent a shock deeper in severity than the future increase in poverty, even if the current increase in poverty appears lower in this exercise.

The fraction of countries that have more years of life lost to premature mortality than years spent in current poverty is 51 percent. Most of the countries in this category are HICs (80 percent) and UMICs (56 percent), whereas LICs account for 17 percent and LMICs for 44 percent. In many countries, both mortality and school closures may yield larger well-being losses than current poverty, even with conservative relative valuations of premature mortality.

FIGURE 3.4

The pandemic's impact on well-being through additional current and future poverty and excess mortality varies substantially across economies

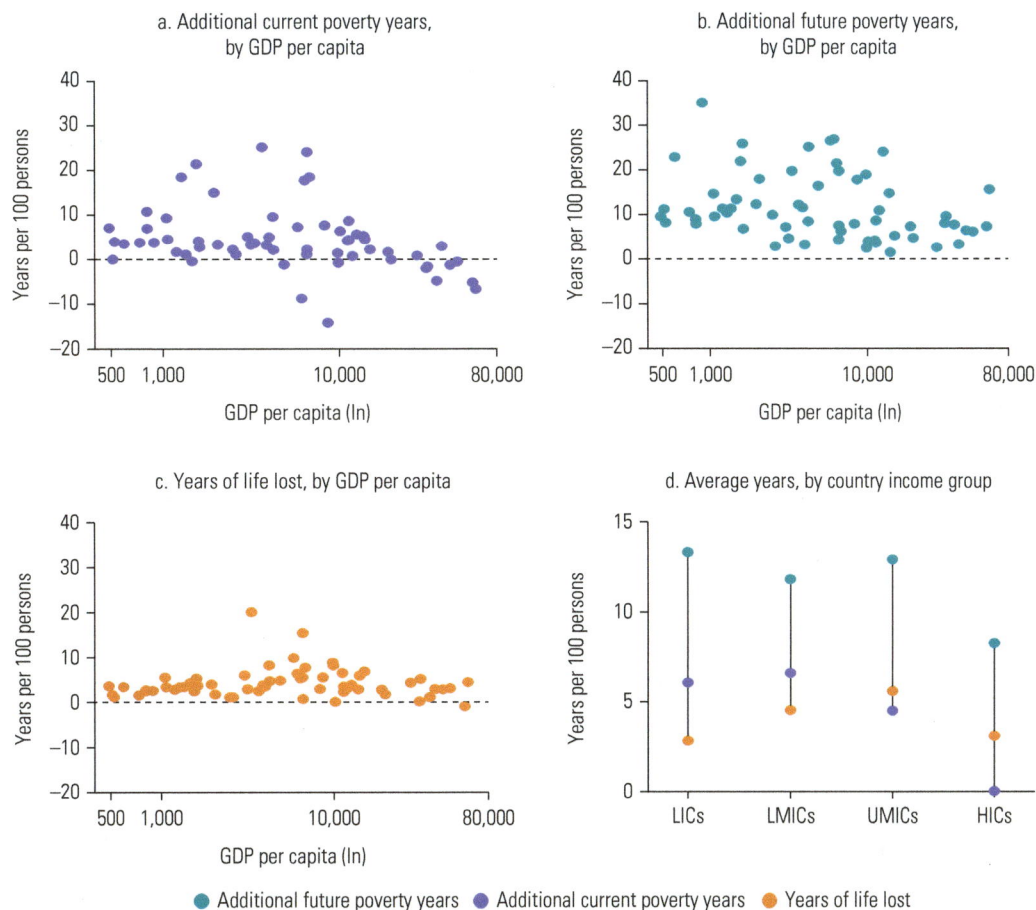

a. Additional current poverty years, by GDP per capita

b. Additional future poverty years, by GDP per capita

c. Years of life lost, by GDP per capita

d. Average years, by country income group

● Additional future poverty years   ● Additional current poverty years   ● Years of life lost

Sources: Original estimates based on poverty data from World Bank, Global Monitoring Database; excess mortality data from Wang et al. 2022; mortality data from Heuveline 2022.
Note: The figure shows the number of years per 100 persons, in each economy, of additional current poverty (panel a), additional future poverty due to school closures (panel b), and life lost due to excess mortality (panel c). Economies are sorted by GDP per capita on the horizontal axis using a logarithmic scale. Panel d shows the same metrics aggregated by income category using a simple average (not weighted by population). Each measure is calculated as the peak value occurring between 2020 and 2021, and the poverty line used is the societal poverty line anchored to its 2019 level. GDP per capita is for 2019 expressed in 2015 constant US dollars. GDP = gross domestic product; HICs = high-income countries; LICs = low-income countries; LMICs = lower-middle-income countries; ln = logarithm; UMICs = upper-middle-income countries.

These documented pandemic impacts across the dimensions of premature mortality, monetary poverty, and learning loss underscore the importance of monitoring well-being in a broader fashion than monitoring monetary poverty alone. The relative magnitude of losses across these dimensions and how these magnitudes vary by country highlight the potential trade-offs that policies aimed at addressing the impacts of the pandemic face. Remediating the recent learning losses is likely a key need for many countries, perhaps as important as the need to protect the poor and vulnerable from the income losses of this recent period. One important way to address these losses is through fiscal policy. Part 2 of this report turns to the role fiscal policy can play in promoting an inclusive and effective recovery.

107

TABLE 3.5

Years lost to premature mortality and the increase in years of future poverty exceed the increase in years of current poverty in most economies

Country income group	Excess mortality (YLL, years per 100 persons)	Current poverty (CPY, years per 100 persons)	Future poverty (FPY, years per 100 persons)	Fraction of economies for which largest additional well-being loss may not be due to current poverty		
				YLL > CPY	FPY > CPY	YLL > CPY and/or FPY > CPY
Low-income	2.8	6.1	13.3	0.17	0.83	0.83
Lower-middle-income	4.5	6.6	11.8	0.44	0.75	0.75
Upper-middle-income	5.6	4.5	12.9	0.56	0.72	0.78
High-income	3.1	0.0	8.3	0.80	0.93	1.00
All economies	**4.1**	**4.2**	**11.5**	**0.51**	**0.80**	**0.84**

Sources: Original calculations based on poverty data from the World Bank's Global Monitoring Database; excess mortality estimates from Wang et al. 2022; mortality estimates from Heuveline 2022.

Note: The table compares well-being losses due to excess mortality, current poverty, and future poverty (school closures) during the COVID-19 pandemic (2020–21), by country income group. Current poverty captures the increase in years spent in societal poverty over the period 2020–21. Future poverty captures the impact that the school closures over the period 2020–21 are estimated to have on years spent in societal poverty over 2020–50. In both cases, the societal poverty threshold is fixed at its 2019 value. Average values for "all economies" are not weighted for population. CPY is number of additional (current) poverty years spent in 2020 and 2021; FPY is number of additional (future) poverty years due to school closures in 2020 and 2021; YLL is number of years of life lost due to excess mortality in 2020 and 2021.

Notes

1. The Global Monitoring Database (GMD) is the World Bank's repository of multitopic income and expenditure household surveys used to monitor global poverty and shared prosperity. The household survey data are typically collected by national statistical offices in each country, and then compiled, processed, and harmonized. The process is coordinated by the Data for Goals (D4G) team and supported by the six regional statistics teams in the Poverty and Equity Global Practice. The Development Data Group contributes historical data (before the 1990s) and recent survey data from the Luxembourg Income Study (LIS) Database. Selected variables have been harmonized to the extent possible so that levels and trends in poverty and other key sociodemographic attributes can be reasonably compared across and within countries over time. The GMD's harmonized microdata are used in the global poverty measures reported in the World Bank's Poverty and Inequality Platform, the World Bank's multidimensional poverty measure, and the Global Database of Shared Prosperity. As of June 2022, the GMD contained more than 2,000 household surveys conducted in 170 economies. For a few economies, the welfare aggregate of the GMD spans up to 40 years, from 1971 to 2021, whereas for most other economies coverage is significantly less.

2. This exercise compares current monetary loss with future losses due to current nonmonetary impacts on learning and mortality. Although the conclusion of chapter 1 suggests that the direct poverty implications of the pandemic period will extend beyond 2021, this exercise looks just at the immediate effects on poverty in relation to the long-run effects of learning loss and premature mortality. It ignores the possibly longer-lived consequences of the immediate poverty increase on future poverty levels.

3. See table 3C.1 in online annex 3C for a list of economies included in this analysis.

4. When weighted by population, the average citizen of these countries will experience an additional 19 days of current poverty, 11 lost days due to premature mortality, and 37 additional future poverty days. These global numbers are heavily driven by the simulations for China and India, in which China has almost no reported excess mortality and India has a very large estimated increase in current poverty.

References

Alkire, Sabina, José Manuel Roche, Paola Ballon, James Foster, Maria Emma Santos, and Suman Seth. 2015. *Multidimensional Poverty Measurement and Analysis*. New York: Oxford University Press.

Ahmed, Tashrik, Timothy Roberton, Petra Vergeer, Peter M. Hansen, Michael A. Peters, Anthony Adofo Ofosu, Charles Mwansambo, et al. 2022. Healthcare utilization and maternal and child mortality during the COVID-19 pandemic in 18 low-and middle-income countries: An interrupted time-series analysis with mathematical modeling of administrative data. *PLoS Medicine*, 19(8), e1004070.

Azevedo, João Pedro, Amer Hasan, Diana Goldemberg, Syedah Aroob Iqbal, and Koen Geven. 2021. "Simulating the Potential Impacts of COVID-19 School Closures on Schooling and Learning Outcomes: A Set of Global Estimates." *World Bank Research Observer*, March 17, 2021. doi:10.1093/wbro/lkab003.

Baland, Jean-Marie, Guilhem Cassan, and Benoit Decerf. 2022. "Poverty-Adjusted Life Expectancy: A Consistent Index of the Quantity and the Quality of Life." Policy Research Working Paper 10133, World Bank, Washington, DC.

Bourguignon, François, and Satya R. Chakravarty. 1999. "A Family of Multidimensional Poverty Measures." In *Advances in Econometrics, Income Distribution and Scientific Methodology*, edited by Daniel J. Slottje, 331–44. Physica-Verlag HD.

Bundervoet, Tom, Maria E. Davalos, and Natalia Garcia. 2022. "The Short-Term Impacts of COVID-19 on Households in Developing Countries: An Overview Based on a Harmonized Dataset of High-Frequency Surveys." *World Development* 153 (May): 105844.

Decerf, Benoit, Francisco H. Ferreira, Daniel G. Mahler, and Olivier Sterck. 2021. "Lives and Livelihoods: Estimates of the Global Mortality and Poverty Effects of the Covid-19 Pandemic." *World Development* 146: 105561.

Decerf, Benoit, Jed Friedman, Arthur Galego, Steven Pennings, and Nishant Yonzan. Forthcoming. "Lives, Livelihoods, and Learning: Current and Future Wellbeing Impacts of the Covid-19 Pandemic."

Demombynes, Gabriel, Damien de Walque, Paul Gubbins, Beatriz Piedad Urdinola, and Jeremy Veillard. 2021. "COVID-19 Age-Mortality Curves for 2020 Are Flatter in Developing Countries Using Both Official Death Counts and Excess Deaths." Policy Research Working Paper 9313, World Bank, Washington, DC. https://open knowledge.worldbank.org/handle/10986/36425.

De Paz Nieves, Carmen, Isis Gaddis, and Miriam Muller. 2021. "Gender and COVID-19: What Have We Learnt, One Year Later?" Policy Research Working Paper 9709, World Bank, Washington, DC. https://openknowledge.worldbank.org/handle/10986/35829?locale-attribute=fr.

Éliás, Boglárka Anna, and Attila Jámbor. 2021. "Food Security and COVID-19: A Systematic Review of the First-Year Experience." *Sustainability 2021* 13 (9): 52–94. https://doi.org/10.3390/su13095294.

Ferreira, Francisco H. G., Olivier Sterck, Daniel G. Mahler, and Benoit Decerf. 2021. "Death and Destitution: The Global Distribution of Welfare Losses from the COVID-19 Pandemic." *LSE Public Policy Review* 1 (4).

Heuveline, Patrick. 2022. "Global and National Declines in Life Expectancy: An End-of-2021 Assessment." *Population and Development Review* 48 (1): 31–50.

Jain, Radhika, and Pascaline Dupas. 2022. "The Effects of India's COVID-19 Lockdown on Critical Non-COVID Health Care and Outcomes: Evidence from Dialysis Patients." *Social Science and Medicine* 296: 114762. https://doi.org/10.1016/j.socscimed.2022.114762.

Kraay, Aart. 2018. "Methodology for a World Bank Human Capital Index." Policy Research Working Paper 8593, World Bank, Washington, DC.

Lausi, Giulia, Alessandra Pizzo, Clarissa Cricenti, Michela Baldi, Rita Desiderio, Anna Maria Giannini, and Emanuela Mari. 2021. "Intimate Partner Violence during the COVID-19 Pandemic: A Review of the Phenomenon from Victims' and Help Professionals' Perspectives." *International Journal of Environmental Research and Public Health* 18 (12): 6204. doi:10.3390/ijerph18126204.

Loayza, Norman V., Arthur Galego Mendes, Fabian Mendez Ramos, and Steven Michael Pennings. 2022. "Assessing the Effects of Natural Resources on Long-Term Growth: An Extension of the World Bank Long Term Growth Model." Policy Research Working Paper 9965, World Bank, Washington, DC.

https://openknowledge.worldbank.org/handle/10986/37162?show=full.

Loayza, Norman V., and Steven Michael Pennings. Forthcoming. "Chapter 1: The Standard Long Term Growth Model." In *The Long Term Growth Model: Fundamentals, Extensions and Applications,* edited by Norman V. Loayza and Steve Michael Pennings. Washington, DC: World Bank.

Moscoviz, Laura, and David K. Evans. 2022. "Learning Loss and Student Dropouts during the COVID-19 Pandemic: A Review of the Evidence Two Years after Schools Shut Down." Working Paper 609, Center for Global Development, Washington, DC. https://www.cgdev.org/publication/learning-loss-and-student-dropouts-during-covid-19-pandemic-review-evidence-two-years.

Moynihan, Ray, Sharon Sanders, Zoe A. Michaleff, Anna Mae Scott, Justin Clark, Emma J. To, Mark Jones, et al. 2021. "Impact of COVID-19 Pandemic on Utilisation of Healthcare Services: A Systematic Review." *BMJ Open* 11: e045343. doi:10.1136/bmjopen-2020-045343.

Neidhöfer, Guido, Nora Lustig, and Mariano Tommasi. 2021. "Intergenerational Transmission of Lockdown Consequences: Prognosis of the Longer-Run Persistence of COVID-19 in Latin America." CEQ Working Paper 99, Commitment to Equity Institute, Tulane University, New Orleans.

Picchioni, Fiorelli, Luis F. Goulao, and Dominique Roberfroid. 2021. "The Impact of COVID-19 on Diet Quality, Food Security and Nutrition in Low and Middle Income Countries: A Systematic Review of the Evidence." *Clinical Nutrition.* doi:10.1016/j.clnu.2021.08.015.

Psacharopoulos, George, Victoria Collis, Harry Anthony Patrinos, and Emiliana Vegas. 2021. "The COVID-19 Cost of School Closures in Earnings and Income across the World." *Comparative Education Review* 65 (2).

Riumallo-Herl, Carlos, David Canning, and Joshua A. Salomon. 2018. "Measuring Health and Economic Wellbeing in the Sustainable Development Goals Era: Development of a Poverty-Free Life Expectancy Metric and Estimates for 90 Countries." *Lancet Global Health* 6 (8): e843–e858.

Samaniego, Robert, Remi Jedwab, Paul Romer, and Asif Islam. 2022. "Scars of Pandemics from Lost Schooling and Experience: Aggregate Implications and Gender Differences through the Lens of COVID-19." Policy Research Working Paper 9932, World Bank, Washington, DC.

Shapira, Gil, Tashrik Ahmed, Salomé Henriette Paulette Drouard, Pablo Amor Fernandez, Eeshani Kandpal, Charles Nzelu, Chea Sanford Wesseh, et al. 2021. "Disruptions in Maternal and Child Health Service Utilization during COVID-19: Analysis from Eight Sub-Saharan African Countries." *Health Policy Plan* 36 (7): 1140–51. doi:10.1093/heapol/czab064.

Wang, H., K. R. Paulson, S. A. Pease, S. Watson, H. Comfort, P. Zheng, A. Y. Aravkin, et al. 2022. "Estimating Excess Mortality Due to the COVID-19 Pandemic: A Systematic Analysis of COVID-19-Related Mortality, 2020–21." *The Lancet* 399 (10334): 1513–36.

WHO (World Health Organization). 2022a. *Third Round of the Global Pulse Survey on Continuity of Essential Health Services during the COVID-19 Pandemic: Interim Report November–December 2021.* Geneva: WHO. https://www.who.int/publications/i/item/WHO-2019-nCoV-EHS_continuity-survey-2022.1.

WHO (World Health Organization). 2022b. "14.9 Million Excess Deaths Associated with the COVID-19 Pandemic in 2020 and 2021." News release, May 5, 2022. WHO, Geneva. https://www.who.int/news/item/05-05-2022-14.9-million-excess-deaths-were-associated-with-the-covid-19-pandemic-in-2020-and-2021.

World Bank. 2018. *Poverty and Shared Prosperity 2018: Piecing Together the Poverty Puzzle.* Washington, DC: World Bank.

World Bank. 2020. *Poverty and Shared Prosperity 2020: Reversals of Fortune.* Washington, DC: World Bank.

World Bank. 2022a. *Collapse and Recovery: How the COVID-19 Pandemic Eroded Human Capital and What to Do About It.* Washington, DC: World Bank.

World Bank. 2022b. *The State of Global Learning Poverty: 2022 Update.* Washington, DC: World Bank.

World Bank and UNICEF (United Nations Children's Fund). 2022. *The Impact of COVID-19 on the Welfare of Households with Children.* Washington, DC: World Bank.

Part 2.
Fiscal Policy for an
Inclusive Recovery

Part 2. Fiscal Policy for an Inclusive Recovery

Part 1 of this report presented both new and updated evidence on the barriers to global progress on poverty and inequality in all of their dimensions. The impact of the COVID-19 pandemic on poverty was deep and widespread, and it will have long-run effects on the ability of children to live lives free of poverty and vulnerability. The Russian invasion of Ukraine is yet another shock for households that have not fully recovered lost income from the pandemic and were already facing the long-term challenges of the climate crisis. These compounding crises have the potential to alter the long-term development trajectory in many countries. Meanwhile, the ongoing trade disruptions, worsening macroeconomic imbalances, and record high debt are rendering efforts to return to reducing poverty even more challenging. Rising interest rates and a medium-term outlook of poor growth and high inflation are also constraining the policy options in low- and middle-income countries.

Policy plays a key role in altering welfare trajectories in times of crisis and recovery. During the COVID-19 crisis, various public health policies, such as stay-at-home directives, as well as new and existing monetary, financial, and fiscal policies, affected the dynamics of disease transmission and altered growth, poverty, and learning outcomes. The use of policy to affect critical outcomes in times of crisis is again on view during the unfolding food and energy price crisis. Governments are engaging in large food purchases and implementing export restrictions (USDA 2022) to try to manage food price impacts, and they are offering subsidies (or energy tax reductions) to deal with rising food prices. Food export bans risk exacerbating food price volatility, as in the 2006–08 food price crisis (Martin and Anderson 2011). Monetary, trade, and fiscal policies (such as lower food tariffs or cash transfers) tailored to specific country conditions could mitigate the impact, but some policies will be more effective than others (Benson et al. 2013).

Part 2 of this report focuses on fiscal policy—the decisions governments make on revenue raising and spending—and how it affects poverty and inequality. Indeed, many of the policy choices made during crisis and noncrisis times affect growth and welfare outcomes, and these choices span a range of monetary, financial, regulatory, and trade dimensions.

Although the second part of the report concentrates on the role of fiscal policy, it starts from the recognition that the same policy can have very different effects in different countries. Higher-income economies are more resilient in the face of shocks because their households and firms are better endowed with wealth, health, and education and thus are able to adapt to changing circumstances (World Bank 2013). By contrast, governments in low- and middle-income countries face policy options with more limited effectiveness during a crisis because of the structure of their economies (Loayza 2020). A stay-at-home order does little if people are too poor to stay at home. Financial sector policy is less effective when it cannot reach a large informal sector. Fiscal policy cannot achieve much if fiscal options are restricted. And the structure of an economy can limit the reach of standard fiscal policy instruments. Finally, various features of an economy can amplify the impact of any shock or limit the impact of policies to address the crisis.

Why focus on fiscal policy?

This report concentrates on fiscal policy for three reasons. First, fiscal policies have wide-ranging impacts on poverty and inequality. They affect growth, employment, and wages, as well as the services available, the prices people pay, and the income people have left after taxes are paid and transfers are received. Governments use fiscal policy to pursue a variety of policy goals, including promoting economic growth and providing access to basic services. Public investment in infrastructure, basic services, and research and development (R&D) is a key driver of inclusive growth. Fiscal policy is also one of the main vehicles for implementing the prevailing social contract and so has the potential to significantly influence the current and future distribution of income and opportunity. Furthermore, fiscal policy is a critical tool when it comes to fighting economic crises, protecting households and firms from the worst impacts of downturns, and reigniting growth.

Second, in many countries fiscal policy is currently under considerable pressure. The fiscal policy choices that governments make in these moments of crisis can act as a lifeline for poor and vulnerable households, or they can further impoverish the poor and increase inequality. Even as governments decide which fiscal policies are the most suitable for achieving an inclusive recovery and long-run growth, they must deal with rising fiscal deficits and debt burdens (a problem before the pandemic and one exacerbated by it), with little space for fiscal policy to support the recovery and prepare for ongoing and future crises. Low- and middle-income countries are significantly more in debt today than two years ago. In fact, in 2020 more emerging economies experienced country credit rating downgrades than over the entire 2010–19 period. Countries have simultaneously faced lower revenue stemming from the crisis and the need to pursue expansionary fiscal policy to mitigate the worst impacts of the downturn. As a result, many countries now need to raise revenue, reduce spending, or both to escape debt distress. Historically, fiscal policy decisions in moments of tight fiscal space and debt crises have often hurt the poor, both in the immediate term and in later years, limiting their opportunities. It is essential to navigate the current challenge in ways that do not further impoverish the poor today or reduce the opportunities they might enjoy tomorrow.

Third, new analysis in three areas provides important insights into the poverty and inequality impacts of good fiscal policy making in crisis and noncrisis times. Chapter 4 analyzes the welfare impact of the COVID-19 fiscal response. Chapter 5 presents a harmonized analysis of how taxes, transfers, and subsidies have affected poverty and inequality in 94 countries. And chapter 6 looks at the emerging insights from a new approach to valuing the impact of fiscal policies on welfare. The final chapter discusses the policy implications that emerge from these areas and examines the degree to which better fiscal policy can put poverty and inequality reduction back on track in the coming years.[1]

Fiscal policy is only part of the policy solution to addressing poverty and inequality. In fact, many other policy choices, such as labor market regulations, affect personal incomes and have a large impact on welfare. There is also a strong relationship between fiscal policy and instruments such as monetary policy. In the context of rising inflation across the world, governments may want to expand fiscal spending to support households. However, expansive fiscal policy may work at cross-purposes with monetary policy oriented to tame inflation. If inflation continues to rise and recovery continues to stall, this tension will increase.

What is in part 2?

Chapter 4 examines how fiscal policy was used during the pandemic and how it has been used to manage the 2022 food price crisis. The fiscal response to the pandemic matched its historic impact on poverty and inequality and protected many households from poverty. Countries in all income categories have used fiscal policy to effectively mitigate the impacts of the crisis.

Microsimulations in low- and middle-income countries suggest poverty would have been, on average, 2.4 percentage points higher without a fiscal response. Impact evaluations have consistently shown that, when received, transfers are highly effective in allaying food insecurity, increasing employment, and reducing poverty. However, the scale of the fiscal response was limited and less protective in low- and middle-income countries than in high-income countries. Microsimulations also suggest that nearly all losses were mitigated in high-income countries through fiscal policy, that about half of losses were reduced in upper-middle-income countries, and that just over a quarter of losses were mitigated in lower-middle-income and lower-income countries.

The chapter provides a first look at lessons learned from this global experience. It highlights not only the impressive achievements on the scale, speed, and targeting of the response but also what underpinned the vastly different abilities of fiscal policy to protect welfare in richer and poorer countries: access to finance, the structure of economies, and the existing reach of the tax and benefit system. These findings give insights into how to strengthen the protective role of fiscal policy during the continuing food price crisis and in an increasingly risky world (taken up in chapter 7).

Chapter 5 looks at the fiscal systems countries had going into the pandemic. It brings together fiscal incidence analysis for 94 countries to document where the tax burden falls across the income distribution and who benefits from spending on transfers and subsidies. This information highlights who will benefit and lose from the policy options governments currently face on how to raise taxes, reduce exemptions, and reorient spending to address fiscal constraints and provide continued support to poor and vulnerable households.

In bringing this work together, the chapter documents how taxes and transfers have an immediate impact on inequality and poverty across countries. All countries reduce inequality through taxation, subsidies, and transfers, but in each income category there are countries that successfully reduce poverty through these measures, whereas many other countries see poverty increase. The chapter considers how taxes and benefits contribute to this pattern and points to the types of policies that can raise revenue and reverse this trend to ensure that poor households are not out of pocket in a pandemic recovery.

Fiscal policy for poverty reduction requires not only considering who benefits from a given policy but also assessing the impact of a fiscal policy on growth. Historically, growth in the labor incomes of poor households has driven poverty reduction (Azevedo et al. 2013), and it is the low growth rates of recent years that make returning to a path of poverty reduction so challenging. Prioritizing fiscal policies that bring growth and revenue-raising strategies that have as little negative impact on growth as possible is essential.

One way of measuring the impact of fiscal policy on growth is by valuing a fiscal policy in terms of the long-run growth it brings intended beneficiaries and any growth impacts it has on nonbeneficiaries. Chapter 6 looks at how to assess the value of fiscal policies. It considers what a measure of value should include and provides examples of how fiscal policy has been valued in the recent literature.

The chapter highlights that some of the highest-value fiscal decisions made by governments support the long-run income growth of households. Examples include investments in health and the education of children, roads, electricity, and R&D, especially investments that the private sector cannot or would not make—that is, investments that address market failure or provide public goods. For example, spending that invests early in a child's life can be transformative and set the stage for a lifetime of higher earnings. When these policies benefit households at the bottom of the income distribution, the impact on poverty and inequality can be very large. However, beneficial policies can be hard to prioritize precisely because their benefits accrue over the long term and are not realized today. For politicians, this time frame does not align with political realities that require immediate results, and long-run benefits may also be less valuable to some households that find it difficult to look beyond the present. The chapter points to what can help governments prioritize the long run in decision-making, noting the key role of improving governance and access to low-interest finance. The chapter concludes with a look at how to increase the efficiency of spending, which is particularly important in times of tightening fiscal budgets.

Chapter 7 concludes the report by taking a broad look at the policy options available to strengthen the ability of fiscal policy to support and protect poverty reduction and inequality, especially those options likely to be the most beneficial in the current climate of constrained fiscal space and continuing crises. It includes some back-of-the-envelope calculations to show how choosing good policies can help countries recover some of the losses of the past two years and get back on track in reducing poverty and inequality. Technical feasibility is a key lens through which policies are discussed in the report. However, the true feasibility of sustained and effective reform relies on ensuring political support. Although this report does not focus on what makes a reform politically feasible (something that has to be determined on a country-by-country basis), it highlights some of the key dimensions of political economy constraints in making these changes, and the analysis and tools discussed allow one to clearly identify the winners and losers from any reform. Chapter 7 ends by considering the degree to which better fiscal policy making can get countries back on track to reduce poverty and inequality. The need for global action is underscored.

Note

1. The focus is on above-the-line fiscal measures, which affect revenue and spending today rather than the acquisition of assets or promises to pay in the future. A recent International Monetary Fund publication discusses the distinction between above-the-line and below-the-line measures: "'Above-the-line' measures involve revenue raising and government expenditure, which affects the overall fiscal balance and government debt. . . . 'Below-the-line' measures generally involve the creation of assets or liabilities without affecting fiscal revenues and spending today. Examples include government provision of loans or equity injection in firms" (IMF 2020, 77). Below-the-line measures are discussed in *World Development Report 2022: Finance for an Equitable Recovery* (World Bank 2022).

References

Azevedo, Joao Pedro, Gabriela Inchauste, Jaime Saavedra, and Hernan Winkler. 2013. "Is Labor Income Responsible for Poverty Reduction? A Decomposition Approach." Policy Research Working Paper 6414, World Bank, Washington, DC.

Benson, Todd, Nicholas Minot, John Pender, Miguel Robles, and Joachim von Braun. 2013. "Information to Guide Policy Responses to Higher Global Food Prices: The Data and Analyses Required." *Food Policy* 38: 47–58.

IMF (International Monetary Fund). 2020. *Fiscal Monitor*. April, IMF, Washington, DC.

Loayza, Norman V. 2020. "Costs and Trade-Offs in the Fight against the COVID-19 Pandemic: A Developing Country Perspective." Research and Policy Briefs 35, World Bank, Washington, DC.

Martin, Will, and Kym Anderson. 2011. "Export Restrictions and Price Insulation during Commodity Price Booms." Policy Research Working Paper 5645, World Bank, Washington, DC.

USDA (United States Department of Agriculture). 2022. "The Ukraine Conflict and Other Factors Contributing to High Commodity Prices and Food Insecurity." USDA, Washington, DC. https://www.fas.usda.gov/data/ukraine-conflict-and-other-factors-contributing-high-commodity-prices-and-food-insecurity.

World Bank. 2013. *World Development Report 2014: Risk and Opportunity—Managing Risk for Development*. Washington, DC: World Bank.

World Bank. 2022. *World Development Report 2022: Finance for an Equitable Recovery*. Washington, DC: World Bank.

Protecting Households with Fiscal Policy: Learning from COVID-19

Summary

The COVID-19 pandemic has acted as a global stress test of the ability of fiscal systems to protect household welfare in a crisis. The fiscal response has been unprecedented in scale, with nearly all countries implementing some measures designed to mitigate the impact of the crisis. Microsimulations in low- and middle-income countries suggest that poverty would have been 2.4 percent higher, on average, without this support.

This chapter is a first look at the lessons learned from this global experience to date. It examines not only the new fiscal policies implemented during the crisis—and highlights impressive achievements in the magnitude, speed, and targeting of the response—but also the vastly different abilities of fiscal policy to protect welfare in richer and poorer countries. Indeed, richer countries were able to protect welfare, and often jobs, from the contraction in global demand and the impacts of local lockdowns, whereas poorer countries were less able to do so. Many low- and middle-income countries found themselves constrained by lack of finance, low levels of formalization, and weak systems for delivering timely social support to households in need. On average, low-income countries, using fiscal measures, reduced the increase in poverty by about a quarter; lower-middle-income countries reduced the increase in poverty by about a third; and upper-middle-income countries halved the poverty increase. Meanwhile, there were notable exceptions in each income group where countries were able to innovate to overcome constraints (such as Togo) or even overcompensate so that poverty fell (such as Brazil and South Africa).

What lessons emerged from this global stress test? There are at least three: the importance of a country's ability to borrow to finance a fiscal response; the challenges of reaching households and protecting jobs in informal economies; and the need for delivery systems that can identify vulnerable people (not just the chronically poor) and provide support quickly. These lessons have implications for how to better prepare fiscally for a crisis by addressing debt, preparing contingent financing, and developing delivery systems that can meet the challenges of a crisis—all will increase the protective power of fiscal policy. The world is in the throes of compounding crises, and these lessons remain valid for future crises, whether climate, conflict, or health in nature. An initial

---

Chapter 4 online annex available at http://hdl.handle.net/10986/37739:

4A. Microsimulations of the Impact of COVID-19 and the Fiscal Policy Response on Poverty.

assessment of the response to the food and energy price crisis that emerged in 2022 highlights the need to heed these lessons as many governments (93 percent of those that implemented an early fiscal response) turn to inefficient subsidies rather than well-targeted support to manage the crisis.

Finally, this chapter delivers a reality check on the limits of the protection afforded by fiscal policy for many poor households in the near term. Support is needed for other instruments to build the capacity of poor households to protect their welfare in a crisis.

The nature of the fiscal response to the COVID-19 crisis

Globally, the fiscal response to the COVID-19 crisis has been unprecedented in scale, matching its historic impact on growth, poverty, and inequality, as discussed in part 1 of this report. The pandemic prompted an increase in spending around the world: as of September 2021, over US$17 trillion or 20 percent of the 2020 global gross domestic product (GDP) had been committed to the pandemic fiscal response.[1] More than US$10 trillion consisted of forgone tax revenue or additional spending in the health and nonhealth sectors (above-the-line measures), and about US$6 trillion went toward equity injections, loans (below-the-line measures), and guarantees.[2]

The extraordinary fiscal response worldwide to counteract the social and economic impacts of the pandemic has been widely documented in the literature (IMF 2020a, 2020b, 2021; World Bank 2021c and other World Bank regional economic updates; World Bank 2022d). Romer (2021) suggests that spending in advanced economies was four times as large during the pandemic as during the 2007–09 global financial crisis. Meanwhile, the Economic Commission for Latin America and the Caribbean found that the fiscal response in Latin American countries in 2020 amounted to the highest-ever public spending since fiscal data were first published in 1950 (ECLAC 2021). Most of the growth in primary spending took the form of cash transfers and subsidies.

Although the size of the fiscal response to the pandemic has been historic, this chapter does not document the response per se. Instead, it asks, what has been the impact of the fiscal response on household welfare? The data that answer this question are only just emerging and so will, at best, provide an incomplete answer. Other assessments will be needed at a future point when more data and evidence are available.

This section begins by summarizing some key differences in the size and nature of the response across countries. In what has been dubbed "the great financing divide," the size of the COVID-19 fiscal response varied tremendously (figure 4.1; also see World Bank 2022d). Lower-income countries spent significantly less than higher-income countries, whether measured in percentage of GDP or per capita GDP. Once spending on automatic stabilizers is taken into account, the gap in crisis-induced spending between lower- and higher-income countries could further widen.[3] The Fiscal Monitor database maintained by the International Monetary Fund (IMF) includes ad hoc fiscal measures announced by governments in response to the pandemic, but it does not capture expenditure on automatic stabilizers, such as unemployment insurance, which are more prevalent in higher-income countries.[4]

Health spending was ramped up significantly in upper-middle-income countries (UMICs) and high-income countries (HICs) during the first year of the pandemic. Although there were large differences in the per capita allocation across countries, health spending as a share of GDP was comparatively uniform. On average, it accounted for about a quarter of above-the-line spending.[5] Most COVID-19–related health spending was for treatments, followed by testing and contact tracing and purchases of medical goods (WHO 2021a). Despite increased spending, the health expenditure as a share of the total general government expenditure did not increase in 2020 in the majority of countries for which there are data, mainly because their total expenditure grew just as fast as or faster than health spending.[6] Their education expenditure also fell from its share in previous years (figure 4.2; also see Al-Samarrai et al. 2021).

Spending on the nonhealth sector response—most of which consisted of policies to support households and firms—accounted for most of the disparities between countries. Across regions,

FIGURE 4.1

COVID-19 elicited an unprecedented, but highly unequal, fiscal response

a. By income group

b. By region

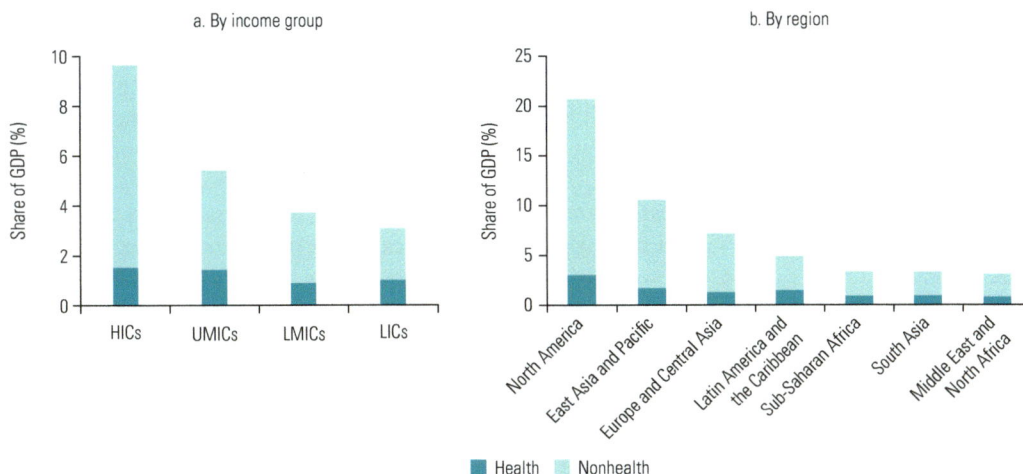

Health   Nonhealth

Source: Original estimates based on data from International Monetary Fund, Database of Fiscal Policy Responses to COVID-19, https://www.imf.org/en/Topics/imf-and-covid19/Fiscal-Policies-Database-in-Response-to-COVID-19.
Note: The figure shows the above-the-line additional spending/forgone revenue in response to COVID-19, as a share of 2020 GDP, in each income group (panel a) and region (panel b). The response includes measures for implementation in 2020, 2021, and beyond. GDP = gross domestic product; HICs = high-income countries; LICs = low-income countries; LMICs = lower-middle-income countries; UMICs = upper-middle-income countries.

FIGURE 4.2

Health spending increased, but the share of spending on education fell in many countries

a. HICs

b. UMICs

c. Total

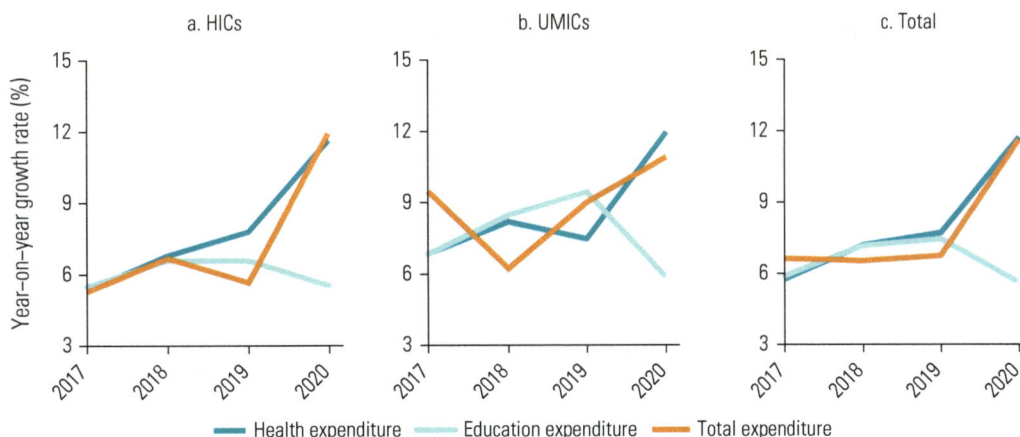

Health expenditure   Education expenditure   Total expenditure

Sources: Original estimates based on data from International Monetary Fund, Government Finance Statistics database, Classification of the Functions of Government (COFOG), https://data.imf.org/gfs; United Nations Educational, Scientific and Cultural Organization, Institute for Statistics (UIS) database, http://uis.unesco.org/.
Note: The figure shows the year-on-year growth rate of health, education, and total government expenditure from 2017 to 2020 in HICs (panel a), UMICs (panel b), and combined (panel c). The sample includes 13 UMICs and 33 HICs for health expenditure (COFOG), 15 UMICs and 34 HICs for education expenditure (COFOG and UIS), and 16 UMICs and 33 HICs for total expenditure (COFOG). HICs = high-income countries; UMICs = upper-middle-income countries.

per capita spending was especially low in South Asia and Sub-Saharan Africa. Not only were poorer countries limited in the scale of the fiscal measures they could afford, but, as described in what follows, the nature of the response they could implement during the fast-moving crisis was also different.

Richer countries directed a larger share of their spending toward measures to support firms and save jobs, such as wage subsidies and providing firms with liquidity, which likely helped mitigate the impact of the pandemic and facilitated recovery efforts. This pattern is confirmed in several data sources. Benmelech and Tzur-Ilan (2020), using data through May 2020 from the IMF's Database of Fiscal Policy Responses to COVID-19, find that higher-income countries directed 3.5 percent of GDP toward businesses, compared with 1.2 percent in lower-income countries.[7] Analysis of expenditure data for job-related policies also reveals large disparities in fiscal expenditure targeted at firms, with low-income countries (LICs) spending the least, about 1.5 percent, and HICs spending the most, about 5.4 percent (Kamran et al. 2022). Wage subsidies were reported less in lower-middle-income countries (LMICs) and LICs, and LICs were also less able to provide firms with liquidity, something that was almost universally implemented. Labor market activation measures were also adopted more in richer countries (figure 4.3). Common revenue measures included deferral of corporate or individual tax payments, each adopted by at least 60 countries; reductions or deferrals of social security payments; tax relief to firms and households; and the lowering of indirect taxes such as the value added tax (VAT)—see IMF (2020b).

A large number of programs supported households in the form of transfers and subsidies—a response popular in lower-income countries (figure 4.3). Among the types of social assistance programs, poorer countries focused disproportionately on utility subsidies and food or other in-kind transfers. Almost all countries implemented cash transfers.

FIGURE 4.3

Nearly all countries provided support to households and firms, but the type of support varied by income group

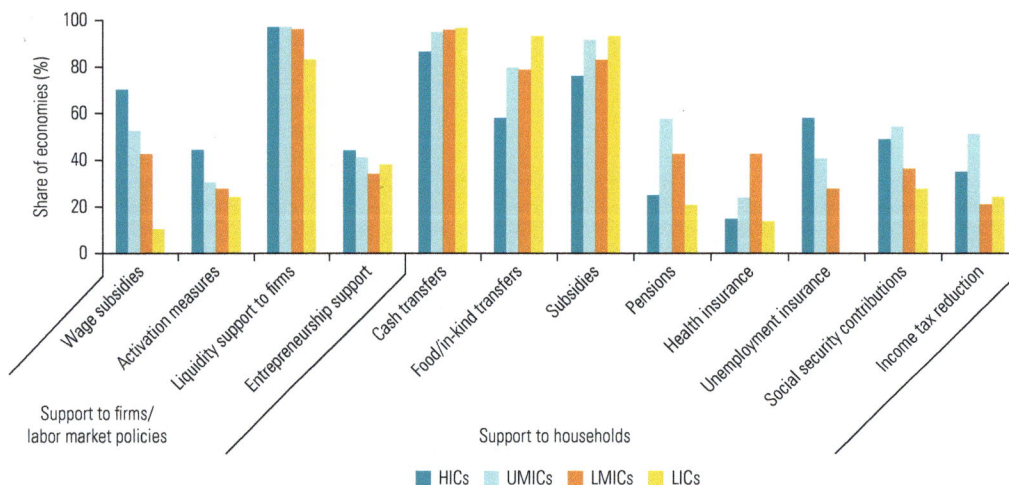

Sources: Original estimates based on Gentilini et al. 2022a and Kamran et al. 2022.
Note: The figure shows the share of economies in each income group that adopted at least one measure for each category of support to firms and households in response to COVID-19. Data on liquidity support to firms, entrepreneurship support, and income tax reduction from Kamran et al. 2022. HICs = high-income countries; LICs = low-income countries; LMICs = lower-middle-income countries; UMICs = upper-middle-income countries.

The impact of the fiscal response on household welfare

To truly assess impact, one must consider a counterfactual: What would have happened in each country had fiscal support not been provided? In the absence of such a counterfactual, three sets of questions are posed to assess whether the fiscal responses possessed the characteristics needed to be effective:

1. Was the fiscal response *adequate*? Was support large enough and broad enough to cover all those who had experienced losses, or at least those who had experienced losses and needed support to meet their immediate needs? Were those who received support better able to meet their basic needs?

2. Was the fiscal response *timely*? Did the support arrive when people needed it—that is, before households experiencing losses could no longer meet their basic needs or before they engaged in costly coping strategies such as selling assets? And did the support last long enough?

3. Was the fiscal support *well targeted*—that is, did it reach those who were experiencing losses, or the poorest who would find it the most challenging to cope with the losses experienced?

In seeking answers to these questions, this chapter considers both the support provided directly to households and the support provided to workers via support to firms. Firm and household outcomes tend to be correlated. For example, food insecurity was higher in countries that experienced more severe labor adjustments, and a larger share of households reported income losses in countries where firms experienced greater sales losses (figure 4.4). This finding confirms the importance of considering both firms and households in assessing the impact of a fiscal response on household welfare.

FIGURE 4.4

Household and firm outcomes are strongly correlated in low- and middle-income countries

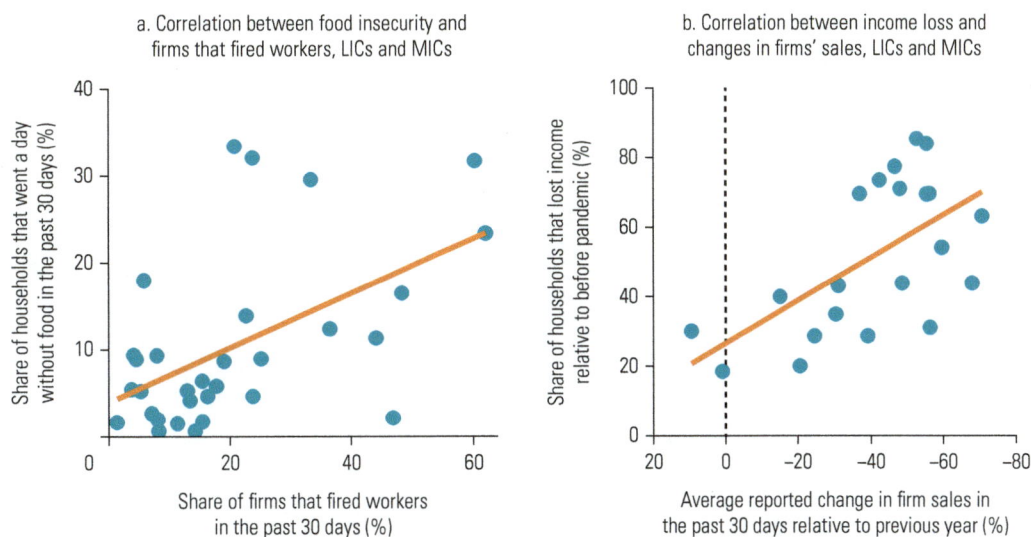

a. Correlation between food insecurity and firms that fired workers, LICs and MICs

b. Correlation between income loss and changes in firms' sales, LICs and MICs

Sources: Original estimates based on data from World Bank COVID-19 high-frequency phone surveys and COVID-19 Business Pulse Surveys.
Note: The figure shows the relationship between food insecurity and firm layoffs (panel a), and household income loss and change in firm sales (panel b). Each dot indicates economy averages from a pair of firm and household surveys conducted within two months of each other. The sample includes 25 low- and middle-income economies in panel a and 15 in panel b. LICs = low-income countries; MICs = middle-income countries.

Adequacy

Coverage of support was smaller than needed, particularly in poorer countries

The previous section documented large differences in the fiscal responses across countries. However, the impacts of the crisis also varied across country income groups, which could have influenced the size of the response. As a first assessment of the adequacy of support, data from the World Bank's high-frequency phone surveys, or HFPS (see box 2.2 in chapter 2 for details) and similar data from the World Bank's COVID-19 Business Pulse Surveys (BPS) are used to compare the shares of households and firms reporting losses with the shares of households and firms reporting receiving support.[8]

Although the data come with several important limitations for assessing coverage,[9] there is a very strong correlation between the share of the population receiving support, as reported by the HFPS, and the share of the population receiving social assistance, as reported by administrative data collected by Gentilini et al. (2022a) and the IMF data on nonhealth response spending per capita,[10] suggesting that the data do include aspects of the response. Similarly, the share of firms that report receiving support is also well correlated with the IMF data on the nonhealth fiscal response.

The survey data confirm what is expected from the results presented in the previous section—fiscal support was more far-reaching in UMICs than in LMICs and LICs. In UMICs, 47 percent of respondents in the household survey reported receiving support, compared

FIGURE 4.5

Fiscal support received by households and firms was lower in poorer economies

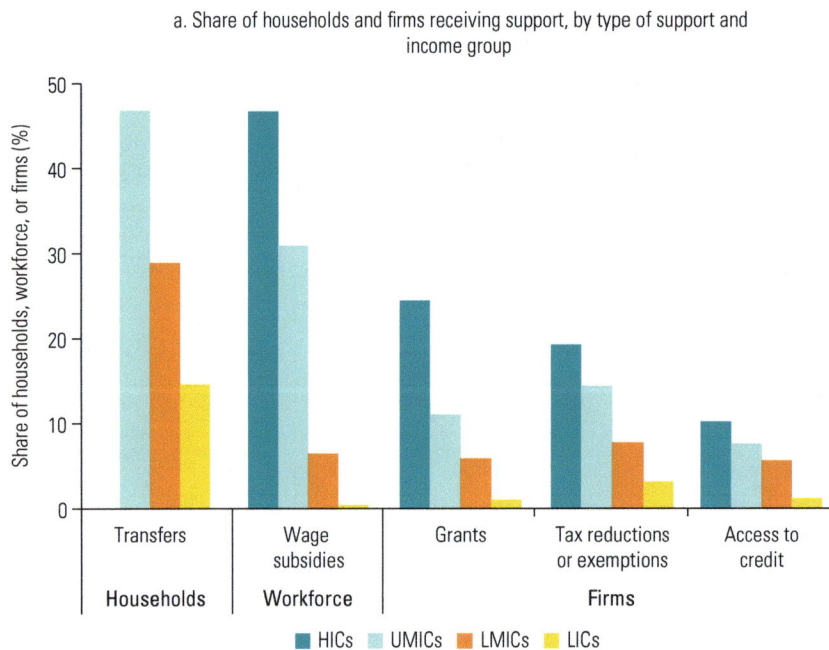

a. Share of households and firms receiving support, by type of support and income group

Sources: Original estimates based on data from World Bank COVID-19 high-frequency phone surveys (HFPS) and COVID-19 Business Pulse Surveys (BPS).
Note: The figure shows the share of households or firms in each income group reporting receipt of each type of public support, using the average of economy averages. In economies with multiple surveys, the survey with the highest share of households/firms reporting receipt of support is used. The share of the workforce receiving wage subsidies is shown, calculated using firm labor share weights (when available). The share of firms receiving support is shown for other categories of firm support. The sample includes 65 low- and middle-income economies for support to households (HFPS) and 83 economies for support to firms (BPS). Economies are weighted equally. HICs = high-income countries; LICs = low-income countries; LMICs = lower-middle-income countries; UMICs = upper-middle-income countries.

(continued)

FIGURE 4.5

Fiscal support received by households and firms was lower in poorer economies *(continued)*

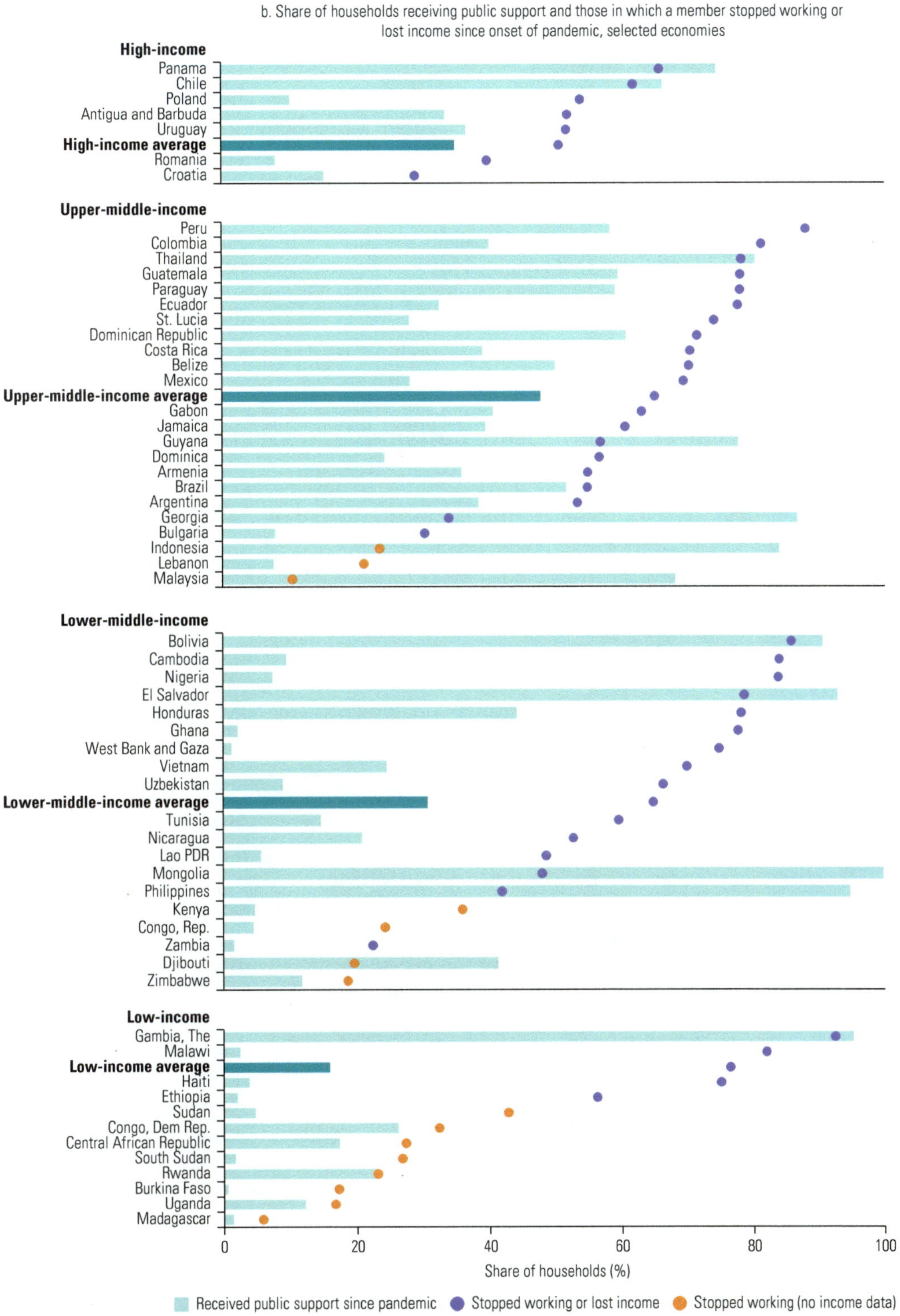
b. Share of households receiving public support and those in which a member stopped working or lost income since onset of pandemic, selected economies
High-income
Panama
Chile
Poland
Antigua and Barbuda
Uruguay
High-income average
Romania
Croatia
Upper-middle-income
Peru
Colombia
Thailand
Guatemala
Paraguay
Ecuador
St. Lucia
Dominican Republic
Costa Rica
Belize
Mexico
Upper-middle-income average
Gabon
Jamaica
Guyana
Dominica
Armenia
Brazil
Argentina
Georgia
Bulgaria
Indonesia
Lebanon
Malaysia
Lower-middle-income
Bolivia
Cambodia
Nigeria
El Salvador
Honduras
Ghana
West Bank and Gaza
Vietnam
Uzbekistan
Lower-middle-income average
Tunisia
Nicaragua
Lao PDR
Mongolia
Philippines
Kenya
Congo, Rep.
Zambia
Djibouti
Zimbabwe
Low-income
Gambia, The
Malawi
Low-income average
Haiti
Ethiopia
Sudan
Congo, Dem Rep.
Central African Republic
South Sudan
Rwanda
Burkina Faso
Uganda
Madagascar
0
20
40
60
80
100
Share of households (%)
Received public support since pandemic
Stopped working or lost income
Stopped working (no income data)

Source: Original estimates based on data from World Bank COVID-19 high-frequency phone surveys.

Note: The figure shows the maximum share of households reporting public support and job or income loss compared to before the pandemic from any survey conducted in an economy between April 2020 and August 2021. Where surveys did not collect data on income loss, the figure shows only the share of households with a respondent who stopped working. In this figure, economies are categorized using the 2020–21 income categorization.

with 29 percent in LMICs and 15 percent in LICs (figure 4.5, panel a). Likewise, 43 percent of firms in UMICs reported receiving support in the form of wage subsidies, grants, fiscal exemptions, or access to credit, compared with 20 percent in LMICs and 6 percent in LICs (figure 4.5, panel a). This discrepancy was particularly pronounced for the share of the labor force employed in firms receiving wage subsidies, presumably due to differences in the size of the informal sector in these countries.

The poverty impacts presented in chapter 1 for 2020 suggest, however, that needs were not necessarily lower in LMICs and LICs. Chapter 1 highlights that increases in poverty in 2020 were prevalent in countries in all income groups (figure 1.11). Thus lower rates of coverage imply that many affected households and firms in LMICs and LICs were without support. The household and firm survey data suggest this prevalency was not necessarily driven by smaller impacts of the crisis in LMICs and LICs (at least not as reflected in the share of households and firms that reported losses). Figure 4.5, panel b, shows that the share of households that reported receiving support was often less than the share of households reporting income losses.

Because of lack of data, it is not possible to determine whether the size of transfers was large enough to fully cover losses among the most vulnerable groups.

Those who received support were better able to meet their basic needs

To assess whether support, when provided, was appropriate in meeting household needs, the emerging body of literature on the impacts of social assistance provided as part of the COVID-19 response was reviewed. Published papers and working papers using data collected after assistance and a plausible identification strategy for determining impact were included in the review. About half of the 11 papers reviewed evaluated government programs; the others evaluated transfers provided by nongovernmental organizations, but gave insight into the impact of receiving a transfer during the pandemic. The papers consistently reveal that assistance had an impact, improving consumption, food security, labor market outcomes, and health services use (figure 4.6). These findings are consistent with evaluations in HICs as well (see, for example, Chetty et al. 2020).

Cross-country analysis shows that transfers encouraged people to stay at home, particularly in poorer places, with corresponding health benefits (Aminjonov, Bargain, and Bernard 2021). This effect was also observed in a randomized controlled trial setting in Kenya (Banerjee et al. 2020), where transfers reduced both reported hunger and the number of people in a household who were infected. By way of comparison, Brooks et al. (2020) find that cash transfers to female entrepreneurs made their business more likely to be operating.

Household survey data also underscore the effectiveness of transfers provided. In Brazil, data show a 7.5 percent decline in poverty measured against the US$5.50 poverty line during 2020, despite widespread labor income losses (World Bank 2022a). This decline highlights the exceptional generosity of the emergency transfers provided. In Colombia, transfers reduced the increase in poverty from 9.0 percentage points to 6.8 percentage points (DANE 2021), and in the Dominican Republic transfers reduced the increase in poverty from 8.1 percentage points to just 2.4 percentage points (CTP 2021). In Costa Rica, although transfers reduced poverty by 4 percentage points, the income losses during the pandemic were severe. As a result, overall poverty increased significantly, by 6 percentage points (World Bank, forthcoming b). In Indonesia, the 2020 official poverty data suggest that fiscal policy protected people against the worst of the crisis, with poverty increasing to 10.2 percent rather than the 11.6 percent projected by simulations with no compensation (Ali and Tiwari 2020).

Support to firms also appears to have had a strong impact on job retention. According to BPS data,[11] firms that were financially constrained presented worse labor market impacts (reduced

FIGURE 4.6

Support provided to households had significant impact

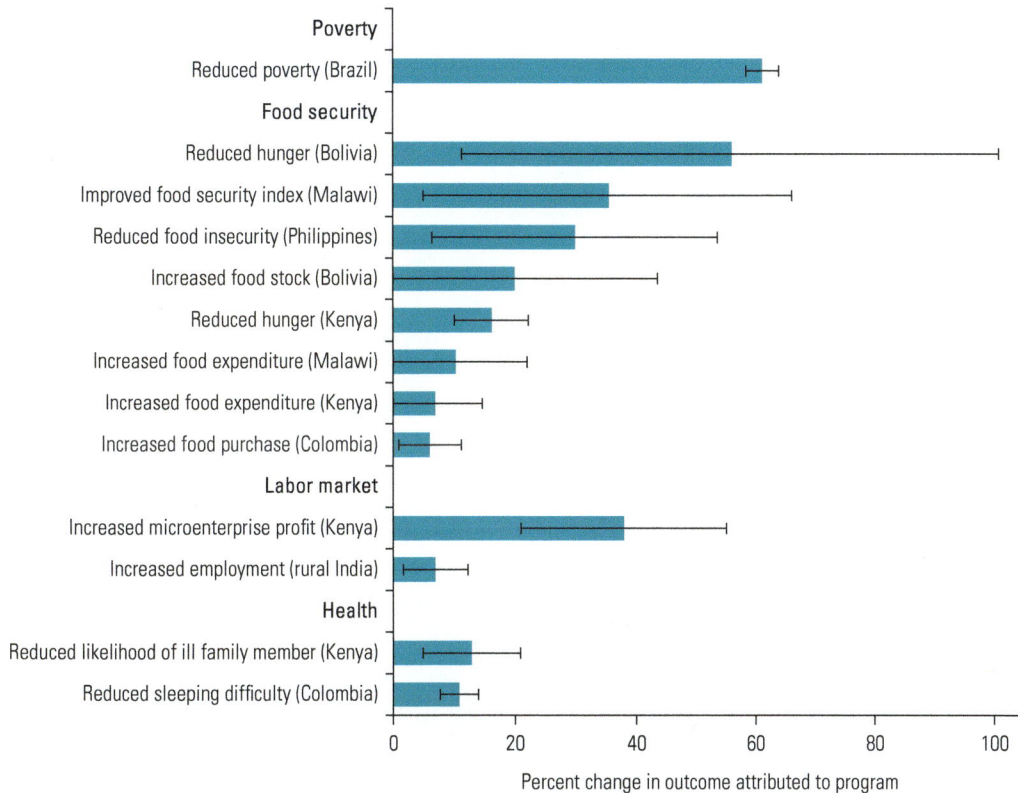

Sources: Original estimates based on Bottan, Hoffmann, and Vera-Cossio 2021 (Bolivia); Menezes-Filho, Komatsu, and Rosa 2021 (Brazil); Londoño-Vélez and Pablo Querubin 2022 (Colombia); Afridi, Mahajan, and Sangwan 2022 (India); Banerjee et al. 2020 and Brooks et al. 2020 (Kenya); Aggarwal et al. 2020 (Malawi); Cho et al. 2021 (Philippines).
Note: The figure shows the estimated impact of fiscal support—most often cash transfers, but sometimes public works programs—on different outcomes, as a percentage change, based on ex post evaluations in selected economies. Ninety-five percent confidence intervals are shown.

working hours and wages, higher layoffs, fewer hirings) and an increased likelihood of falling into arrears (Farazi and Lopez-Cordova 2022). Cirera et al. (2021) use the BPS data to show that credit, cash transfers, and tax support during the COVID-19 pandemic were positively associated with expected sales growth. The authors also find that receiving wage subsidies is associated with a lower probability of firing workers. Gourinchas et al. (2021), using data from 27 European countries, estimate that, in the absence of government support, the small and medium enterprise failure rate would have been about 5.5 percentage points higher. In Chile, Albagli, Fernández, and Huneeus (2021) find that firms that received a new loan or entered into a refinancing operation increased employment relative to firms that did not.

These findings are consistent with the literature on fiscal response in other crises. At the country level, Cerra, Fatás, and Saxena (2020) show that the size of a fiscal policy response during a crisis is correlated with the ability to recover economic output. Rigorous evidence on the impact of cash transfers provided in response to a disaster is limited, but what is available shows significant short- and long-run welfare benefits (Del Carpio and Macours 2010;

Ivaschenko et al. 2020; Macours, Schady, and Vakis 2012; Mansur, Doyle, and Ivaschenko 2017; Pople et al. 2021). Earlier, Aker et al. (2016) found that cash transfers delivered by mobile phone to women in Niger after a drought provided sustained benefits for food security and diet diversity, compared with cash transfers delivered in person. This outcome arose because women spent less time traveling to receive the transfer. This finding is consistent with emerging literature that shows that the impact of noncrisis cash transfers is affected by who in the household receives the transfer.

Regular cash transfers to households, provided as part of regular fiscal policy, not emergency support, also helped protect household welfare during the early stage of the pandemic. The additional regular income from cash transfers protects a household's standard of living when risks materialize, protecting consumption and assets. Two papers highlight that households receiving regular transfer income were better able to protect their food security than households that did not receive transfers (Abay et al., forthcoming; Bottan, Hoffmann, and Vera-Cossio 2021). This finding is consistent with the existing evidence that evaluates the impact of regular cash transfers in a crisis (de Janvry et al. 2006; Knippenberg and Hoddinot 2019; Pega et al. 2017).

Timeliness

Support was announced quickly, but it took time to arrive

The impact of the pandemic was felt most acutely during its first three to four months, from March to June 2020, when many countries implemented nationwide lockdowns in the face of uncertainties about the pandemic. According to the HFPS and BPS, employment and income losses were widespread from April to June. Households tried to cope by using their assets and savings, but food insecurity was disturbingly high during this period of many lockdowns (figure 4.7). A result of this use of assets and savings is that the financial position of many households is now weaker. This pattern of widespread losses experienced immediately at the start of the crisis is borne out in data collected in national surveys at the country level (such as World Bank, forthcoming a, c). The HFPS data reveal improvements in late 2020 but that food insecurity increased again in 2021 without the same levels of job loss. This finding may reflect food price inflation in 2021 (see box 1.4 in chapter 1), poorer job quality in the immediate period of recovery (as documented in chapter 2), households reaching their coping capacity, or the premature withdrawal of government support.

At the outset of the pandemic, countries quickly announced that households and businesses would receive support to keep them afloat. By June 2020, 52 percent of the total spending on the pandemic fiscal response had been announced, including 1,145 social protection measures in LICs and middle-income countries (MICs) and many measures supporting firms (figure 4.8). This support was in part financed by US$125 billion from multilaterals (IMF, World Bank Group, regional development banks, and the United Nations system), 70 percent of which was committed by July and 40 percent disbursed by then (Yang et al. 2021). By many accounts, this response was historically quick and compares well with the speed of response in other crises (Yang et al. 2021), although there was variation across countries, with LICs slower to announce support.

Although some countries were able to implement these measures quickly, often against the odds, in many countries implementation proceeded more slowly, as indicated by the financing data. Financial transfers from the multilateral system directly to government budgets were disbursed quickly, but other financial transfers that were financing specific projects were disbursed much more slowly. Only 13 percent of funds committed to projects by the multilateral system was disbursed by July 2020 (Yang et al. 2021). On average, countries began implementation

FIGURE 4.7

Households quickly employed coping strategies in response to lower labor incomes

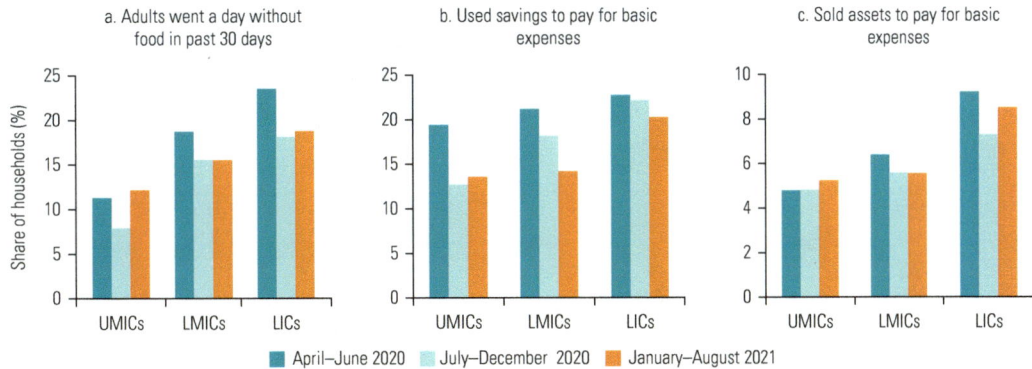

a. Adults went a day without food in past 30 days

b. Used savings to pay for basic expenses

c. Sold assets to pay for basic expenses

■ April–June 2020 ■ July–December 2020 ■ January–August 2021

Source: Original estimates based on data from World Bank COVID-19 high-frequency phone surveys.
Note: The figure shows the share of households in each income group experiencing food insecurity (panel a), using savings (panel b), and selling assets (panel c) for three periods during the pandemic. To account for the fact that the sample of economies with observations changes for each period, the numbers presented are the predicted values from a regression with time dummies and country-fixed effects (taking the average of the country-fixed effects for each income category within each period). The sample includes 37 countries in panel a, 34 in panel b, and 35 in panel c, Economies are weighted equally. LICs = low-income countries; LMICs = lower-middle-income countries; UMICs = upper-middle-income countries.

FIGURE 4.8

Countries announced fiscal support quickly at the outset of pandemic

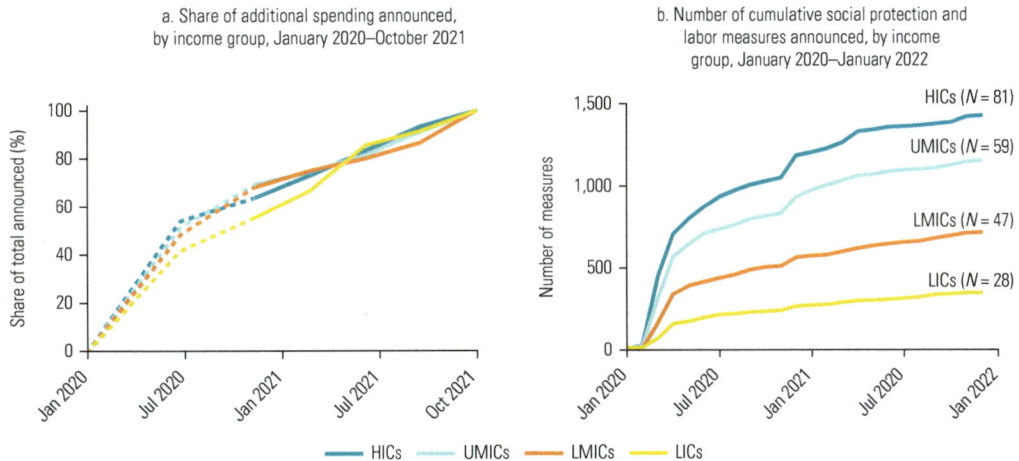

a. Share of additional spending announced, by income group, January 2020–October 2021

b. Number of cumulative social protection and labor measures announced, by income group, January 2020–January 2022

HICs (*N* = 81)
UMICs (*N* = 59)
LMICs (*N* = 47)
LICs (*N* = 28)

— HICs — UMICs — LMICs — LICs

Sources: Original estimates based on data from International Monetary Fund, Database of Fiscal Policy Responses to COVID-19, https://www.imf.org/en/Topics/imf-and-covid19/Fiscal-Policies-Database-in-Response-to-COVID-19; and Gentilini et al. 2022a.
Note: Panel a shows announced additional spending or forgone revenue as a share of total spending announced up to October 2021 in each income group. The dotted lines reflect that data for June 2020 are available for fewer economies. The sample includes a 175-economy panel from October 2020 to October 2021. Panel b shows the cumulative number of social protection and labor measures planned or implemented in each income group. The sample includes 215 economies. HICs = high-income countries; LICs = low-income countries; LMICs = lower-middle-income countries; UMICs = upper-middle-income countries.

of a support measure about a month after announcing it (Gentilini et al. 2022a), but there is a large variation across countries and measures. In an analysis of cash transfer programs in 53 LICs and MICs, Beazley, Marzi, and Steller (2021) find that beneficiaries received payment 83 days, on average, after the first day of stay-at-home orders (which prompted many of the income losses). This payment period, however, varied by region. The East Asia and Pacific and the Middle East and North Africa regions were the quickest to disburse (on average, 25 and 28 days, respectively), followed by Latin America and the Caribbean and South Asia (60 and 65 days, respectively). The average for Sub-Saharan Africa was 132 days.

FIGURE 4.9

Fiscal support often arrived after needs emerged

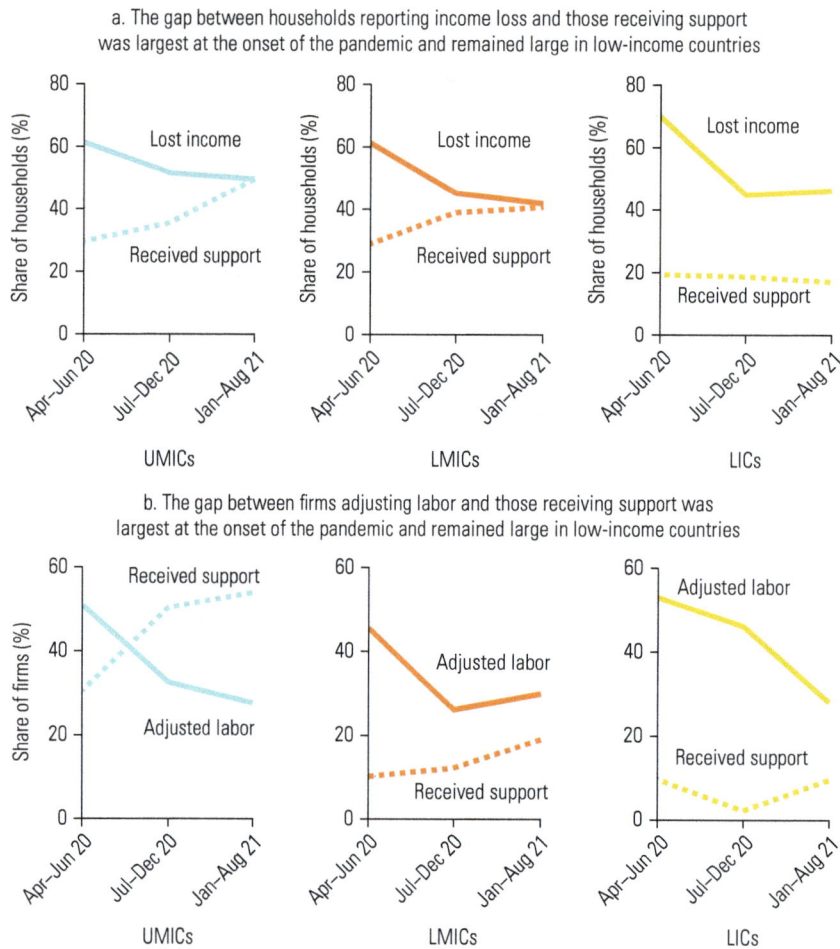

a. The gap between households reporting income loss and those receiving support was largest at the onset of the pandemic and remained large in low-income countries

b. The gap between firms adjusting labor and those receiving support was largest at the onset of the pandemic and remained large in low-income countries

Sources: Original estimates based on data from World Bank COVID-19 high-frequency phone surveys and COVID-19 Business Pulse Surveys.
Note: Panel a shows the share of households in each income group that lost income and the share of households that received support across three periods during the pandemic. Lost income = total income decreased relative to before the pandemic. Panel b shows the share of firms in each income group that adjusted labor and the share of firms that received support across three periods during the pandemic. Adjusted labor = firm fired workers, reduced hours, or cut wages in the past 30 days. To account for the fact that the sample of economies with observations changes for each period, the numbers presented are the predicted values from a regression with time dummies and economy-fixed effects (taking the average of the economy-fixed effects for each income category within each period). The sample includes 21 economies in panel a and 34 economies in panel b. Economies are weighted equally. LICs = low-income countries; LMICs = lower-middle-income countries; UMICs = upper-middle-income countries.

The result was that many households and firms did not receive support during the period they needed it most—at the start of the pandemic (figure 4.9). Twenty-nine percent of households in UMICs and LMICs reported receiving support before July 2020, but only 19 percent of households did so in LICs. This amount increased to 36 percent in UMICs and 39 percent in LMICs in the period July–December 2020. The pattern for firms is similar (figure 4.9, panel b), with support increasing over time, particularly in UMICs.

COVID-19 fiscal support was withdrawn prematurely in some countries, followed by a weak response to the ensuing food and energy price crisis

In view of the length of the crisis, the weak recovery of the labor market (documented in chapter 2), and the compounding effects of higher food and energy prices, it appears that fiscal support was withdrawn prematurely in some countries. The average duration of announced social assistance programs was 4.5 months, but again there is wide variation across countries. The majority of programs lasted for less than three months, and nearly half of new programs were one-off transfers. Gentilini et al. (2022a) estimate that 21 percent were still active as of February 2022. As of July 2022, most programs had been discontinued. Only 16 percent of programs were extended over the period 2020–21, although there was an additional surge of social protection measures announced in the first half of 2021 (figure 4.8, panel b).

In Brazil, the incomes of the poorest 40 percent fell by about 9 percent from August to October 2020, when the amounts of emergency transfers were cut in half. From 2020 to 2021, further reductions in the coverage and benefits of the emergency programs, combined with a labor market that had not yet fully recovered, resulted in an increase in poverty of almost 6 percentage points, although still below 2019 levels (World Bank 2022a). In Indonesia, although a second round of fiscal support measures was introduced in 2021, reaching more households than the support provided in 2020, the size of the transfers in most programs was less generous, and so the impact on poverty was more muted than if the 2020 transfer levels had been maintained (World Bank, forthcoming d).

In 2022, governments began implementing new measures to help households manage the impact of the food price shock. Many of the same households—the urban poor and vulnerable—that were affected most by the COVID-19 crisis were also those hit the hardest by higher food and energy prices (see chapters 1 and 2). Governments often turned to unorthodox policy measures, such as large food purchases and export restrictions (USDA 2022), to try to manage food price impacts, while also adopting fiscal policy measures largely used to protect household welfare.

The impacts of these measures on household welfare will have to be assessed in due course, but many observers suggest that these fiscal responses are significantly more productive than protectionist trade policies (Glauber and Laborde 2022). However, the data on policy trackers point to two clear patterns in the type of support provided that cause concern: (1) the number of countries implementing measures targeting households and the number of measures implemented are much lower than during the early part of the COVID-19 pandemic; and (2) cash or in-kind transfers are much less likely to be implemented than early on in the pandemic (figure 4.10). Lessons from the pandemic and analysis of cash transfers and subsidies (see chapters 5 and 6) suggest this support method may result in quicker delivery of support, but that support will have less impact and be less well targeted to poor and vulnerable households.

In 2022, the fiscal response to rising food and energy prices was much smaller and focused on subsidies

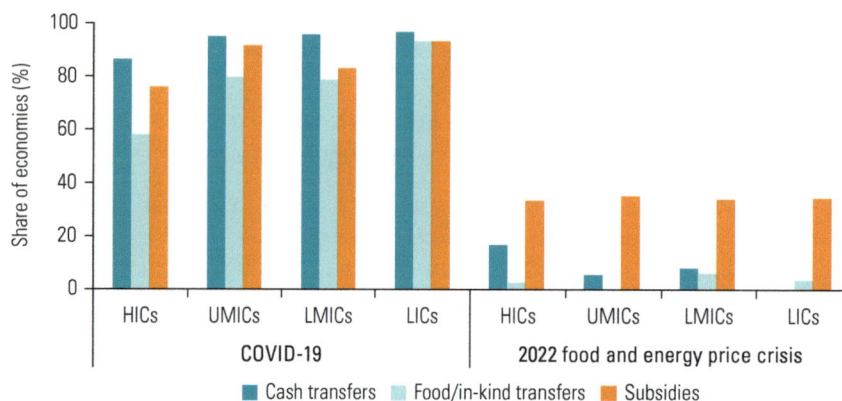

Sources: Original estimates based on Gentilini et al. 2022a and Gentilini et al. 2022b.
Note: The figure shows the share of economies in each income group that provided each type of support in response to COVID-19 or the 2022 food and energy price crisis. Estimates for the 2022 price crisis are based on the first version of Gentilini et al. 2022b (April 2022) and thus only include measures implemented before then. HICs = high-income countries; LICs = low-income countries; LMICs = lower-middle-income countries; UMICs = upper-middle-income countries.

Targeting

Many countries provided universal support during the pandemic, but often using inefficient means

Great uncertainty surrounded how the pandemic would evolve and affect households and firms. This uncertainty may have encouraged broad coverage of support rather than attempts to anticipate losses and target those who were vulnerable. Strong political considerations encourage the provision of broad support as well: it can be hard to secure enough political support for narrowly targeted programs, even during a crisis. Perhaps for that reason, many countries chose to provide support to all households through universal transfers or subsidies instead of directing support by means of categorical or means-tested targeting (figure 4.11).

When countries provided universal support to households, subsidies were favored over universal transfers (figure 4.11). Subsidies were used across all country income groups, but more so in LICs (93 percent) than in HICs (76 percent), with UMICs and LMICs falling in between. Universal transfers were implemented in almost half of HICs and UMICs, but in only a quarter of LMICs and a tenth of LICs. Because support had to be delivered quickly at a time when social interactions were limited, governments tended to use existing delivery systems to support households. This meant using suspensions of tax and utility payments and subsidies in countries with limited social assistance delivery systems whose small programs target the chronically poor. However, other countries such as Togo (box 4.1) and South Africa (box 7.3 in chapter 7) that had very limited social transfers before the crisis innovated to rapidly expand the coverage of targeted cash transfers.

A cost is incurred in providing support to more people than needed, but, because of the widespread work and income losses arising from the pandemic and the challenge of targeting beneficiaries accurately, the cost may have been worthwhile. However, because universal support largely took the form of subsidies, the cost of covering more people than necessary was

FIGURE 4.11

Countries implemented more broad-based support than targeted support during COVID-19

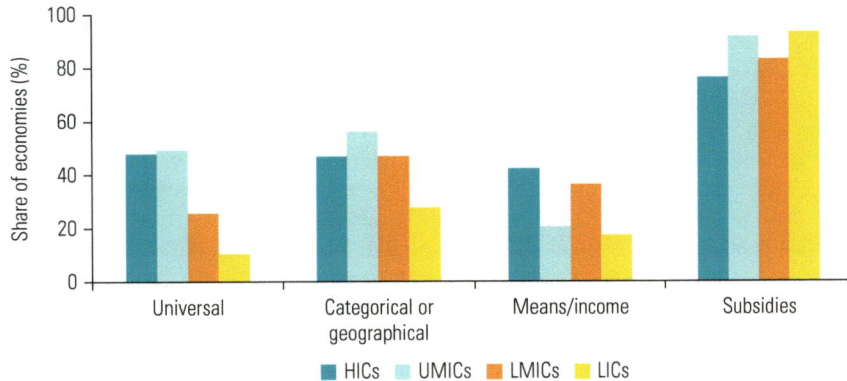

Source: Gentilini et al. 2022a.
Note: The figure shows the share of economies in each income group that adopted at least one measure in response to the COVID-19 crisis using the targeting method indicated. HICs = high-income countries; LICs = low-income countries; LMICs = lower-middle-income countries; UMICs = upper-middle-income countries.

BOX 4.1

COVID-19 cash transfers in Togo

Togo's Novissi cash transfer program used a digital platform to quickly register people, target beneficiaries, and deliver support during the COVID-19 pandemic. Before the crisis, all social protection and labor programs covered only 3 percent of the population of Togo, based on the latest survey.[a] By the end of April 2020, the Novissi enrollment and payment system, developed by the government within weeks of the onset of the crisis, had delivered mobile money to 12 percent of the adult population (450,000 people). By mid-2021, transfers had reached almost a quarter of the adult population (Lawson 2022).

Digital identification was possible thanks to the population registry from the February 2020 election. Because of recently updated voter information and mandatory voting, approximately 93 percent of adults were included in the electoral database (Lawson, Bakari, and Vasconcellos 2021). Voter information included name, address, occupation, and a stamped security code (NSF number). These could be cross-checked during enrollment and used to identify informal workers in specific locations.

Voters could register on basic mobile phones with 2G network coverage using Unstructured Supplementary Service Data (USSD) codes, an offline technology already widely used for mobile payments in Togo. To register, applicants dialed *855# and entered the information on their voter card. The first payment was made immediately if they met the eligibility criteria, and a mobile money account was automatically created if none existed. A radio campaign and in-person post office agents helped to reduce program exclusion by assisting those who did not have a mobile phone or needed help registering.

Targeting by the Novissi program evolved over the pandemic. Initially, cash transfers were rolled out to informal workers in districts experiencing strict lockdowns. In mid-2020, curfew measures began to be implemented in smaller geographic areas (cantons), and the eligibility for Novissi transfers was updated accordingly and expanded to include some formal workers (Debenedetti 2021).

In October 2020, the government expanded Novissi to the poorest cantons of the country. Without a detailed social registry, it relied on machine learning methods to target the poorest beneficiaries, partnering with GiveDirectly and academia (University of California at Berkeley,

(continued)

131

COVID-19 cash transfers in Togo *(continued)*

Innovations for Poverty Action, and Northwestern University). It began by identifying the poorest cantons from satellite data (and other big data) using algorithms trained on household surveys (Chi et al. 2022). Information collected in a representative phone survey in September 2020 was then matched to mobile phone call detail records and used as a ground truth to train algorithms to estimate consumption for all 5.7 million active mobile numbers in Togo from patterns of phone use (Aiken et al. 2022). The poorest individuals based on these consumption estimates (subject to a budget constraint) in the poorest 200 cantons were eligible for transfers.

In an ex post evaluation, Aiken et al. (2022) found that the phone-based targeting method reduced exclusion errors by 4–21 percent relative to the geographic targeting options available to the government for the rural expansion of Novissi. In addition, the authors simulated a hypothetical nationwide transfer program to the poorest. The phone-based targeting method again excluded fewer eligible beneficiaries than the most feasible alternatives (50 percent exclusion errors), except for assigning transfers to the poorest occupation category (48 percent). Hypothetical targeting methods that require an up-to-date comprehensive social registry such as an asset index or perfectly calibrated proxy means test resulted in better targeting in this simulation (46 and 37 percent exclusion errors, respectively), but no such registry existed in Togo. Among mobile phone subscribers, the machine learning approach did not systematically exclude women or specific ethnic groups, religions, age groups, or types of households. Novissi highlights how innovative methods and data could complement traditional social protection systems, particularly in a crisis when existing social registries are insufficient or outdated.

a. World Bank, Atlas of Social Protection: Indicators of Resilience and Equity (ASPIRE) database, https://www .worldbank.org/en/data/datatopics/aspire.

particularly high. Subsidies are costly because better-off households receive the largest share of the benefits of subsidies, and they are likely neither poor nor vulnerable to falling into poverty (chapter 5). The extent to which this is true depends on the nature of the subsidy. More than three-quarters of countries implemented subsidies or waivers related to housing rents, water, electricity, heating, and telecommunications; and more than half of countries implemented waivers on mortgage and loan repayments—see Gentilini et al. (2022a) on the types of subsidies implemented. Subsidies for food—something consumed more equally across the income distribution—were much less common. There is evidence that much of the benefit of these types of subsidies went to nonpoor households. For example, Berkouwer et al. (2021) find that during the pandemic in Ghana electricity subsidies benefited richer households more than poor households.

Subsidies are also more costly because they do not have the long-run growth benefits of transfers (see chapter 6 for a fuller discussion). If universal support must be provided for political reasons, it is much less costly to provide it in the form of universal transfers than costlier universal subsidies.

Targeting the new poor for support was challenging

Assessing whether targeted fiscal support went to the right people and firms is challenging. One reason is that support distributed during the crisis was multipurpose. For households, support was sometimes intended to meet the needs of those affected the most, to protect the poor and vulnerable, or to provide the financial support people needed to stay home. For firms, support may have been intended to aid viable, productive firms that needed to be kept afloat to avoid economic scarring—or firms in sectors experiencing large losses or those employing many workers.

Significant data challenges further complicate the task of assessing the quality of targeting. The HFPS and BPS highlight which households and firms were experiencing losses, but not the size of losses or whether the losses made it difficult for households to meet basic needs or for firms to stay afloat. The data on support received likely capture social assistance and insurance, but not necessarily subsidies, exemptions, or wage supports provided to their employers.

Given these constraints, this section does not offer a comprehensive assessment of the quality of targeting during the crisis. Instead, it looks at the extent to which countries used targeted instruments and the degree to which countries reached people who reported income or employment losses or reached firms that reported cutting back on workers or wages.

Programs that have built-in automatic stabilizers, such as unemployment insurance or self-targeting employment guarantee schemes, automatically target those affected or in need through self-selection. However, unemployment insurance formed a very small part of the response across countries. In Brazil, it contributed just 7 percent of the overall poverty impact of the fiscal response (Cereda, Rubiao, and Sousa 2020). In Ecuador, unemployment insurance payments increased income by less than 1 percent in the lowest decile, compared with COVID-19–related benefits, which increased income by 13 percent (Jara, Montesdeoca, and Tasseva 2021). Analyses of a range of countries in Africa found that automatic stabilizers had negligible effects (Lastunen et al. 2021). Public works were used by households in need, but often at later stages of the crisis, when social distancing restrictions had eased and aversion behavior had abated. For example, in one survey of poorer households in India, 16 percent reported working on the Mahatma Gandhi National Rural Employment Guarantee Act (MG-NREGA) program in May 2020, compared with 54 percent in September 2020 (Gelb et al. 2022). Supply constraints also limited the degree to which employment guarantee schemes were able to act as an automatic stabilizer.

Lower-income countries were most likely to implement programs targeted to specific categories of people (such as those living in a certain place or working in a specific profession), whereas higher-income countries were more likely to use means-tested programs (figure 4.11). Although some targeted social assistance programs increased support to existing beneficiaries, most were new or were existing programs expanding to include additional beneficiaries.

The HFPS data indicate the types of households that received support. Figure 4.12, panels a and b, depict how much more likely households were to receive support if they had characteristics that are typically highly correlated with being structurally poor (having a higher dependency ratio and having lower education). Each dot represents a country. Households receiving support were generally more likely to have characteristics associated with being poor: they had higher dependency ratios, were less educated, and were more rural (results for rural not shown). In many countries, existing social assistance programs are targeted to households that were structurally poor before the crisis—often rural, agricultural households.

Poor households were not necessarily those affected most by the COVID-19 crisis. The most affected were more likely to be urban than rural and to work in services or manufacturing than in agriculture (see chapter 2)—that is, those who would have been considered vulnerable, but not poor, before the crisis. Figure 4.12, panels c and d, show how much more likely all households and low-educated households that experienced income or job losses were to receive support. In most but not all countries, households were more likely to receive support if they reported income or job losses, but few countries saw a difference in the share of households receiving support larger than 10 percentage points. Bigger differences are documented for higher-income countries, suggesting they were better able than lower-income countries to target support to those experiencing losses.[12] This finding may reflect the increased use of automatic stabilizers in these countries or better data systems that allow targeting based on need. The challenge of

FIGURE 4.12

A breakdown by country income group reveals it was challenging to direct support to need

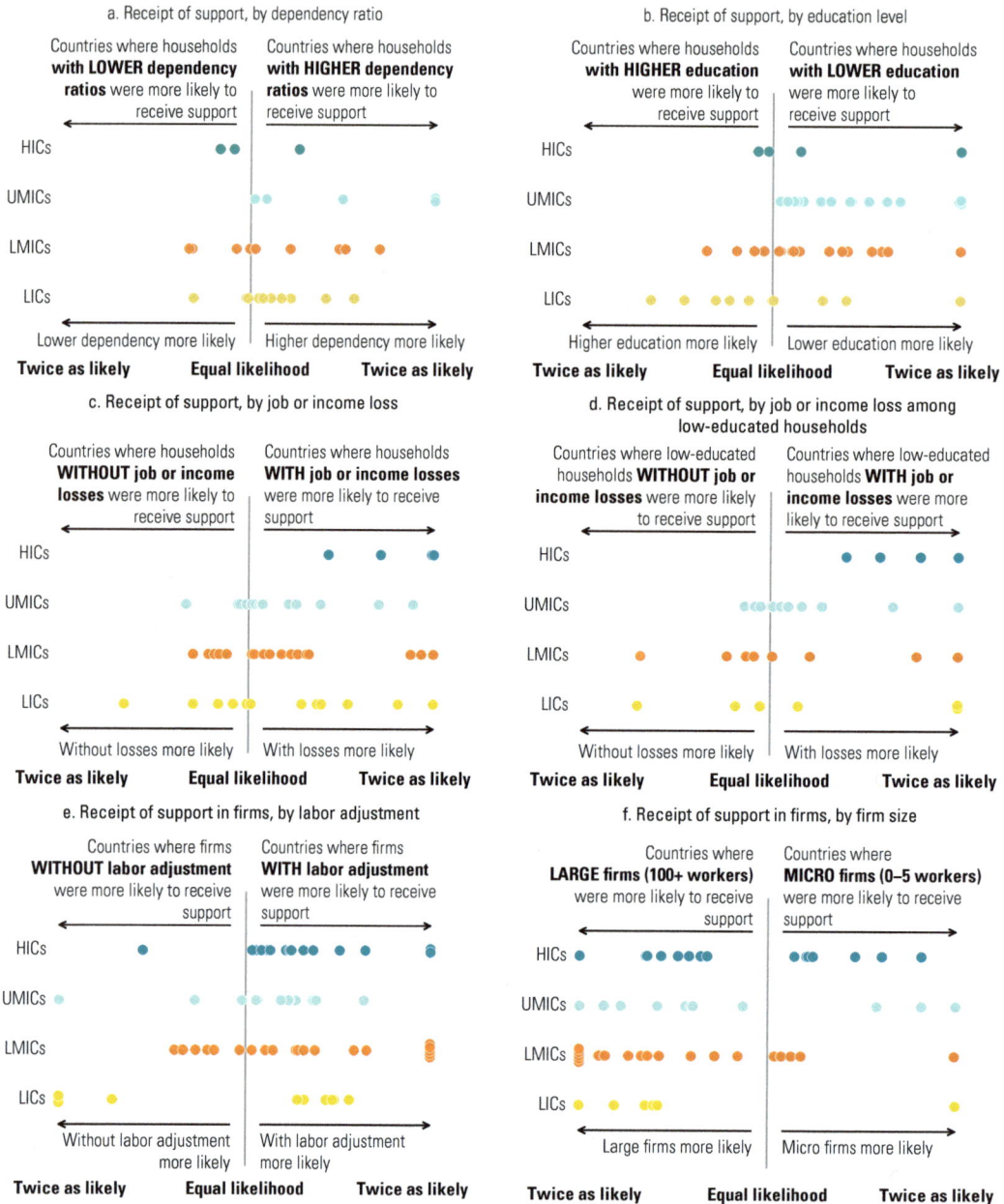

a. Receipt of support, by dependency ratio

Countries where households **with LOWER dependency ratios** were more likely to receive support

Countries where households **with HIGHER dependency ratios** were more likely to receive support

HICs / UMICs / LMICs / LICs

Lower dependency more likely | Higher dependency more likely

Twice as likely — Equal likelihood — Twice as likely

b. Receipt of support, by education level

Countries where households **with HIGHER education** were more likely to receive support

Countries where households **with LOWER education** were more likely to receive support

HICs / UMICs / LMICs / LICs

Higher education more likely | Lower education more likely

Twice as likely — Equal likelihood — Twice as likely

c. Receipt of support, by job or income loss

Countries where households **WITHOUT job or income losses** were more likely to receive support

Countries where households **WITH job or income losses** were more likely to receive support

HICs / UMICs / LMICs / LICs

Without losses more likely | With losses more likely

Twice as likely — Equal likelihood — Twice as likely

d. Receipt of support, by job or income loss among low-educated households

Countries where low-educated households **WITHOUT job or income losses** were more likely to receive support

Countries where low-educated households **WITH job or income losses** were more likely to receive support

HICs / UMICs / LMICs / LICs

Without losses more likely | With losses more likely

Twice as likely — Equal likelihood — Twice as likely

e. Receipt of support in firms, by labor adjustment

Countries where firms **WITHOUT labor adjustment** were more likely to receive support

Countries where firms **WITH labor adjustment** were more likely to receive support

HICs / UMICs / LMICs / LICs

Without labor adjustment more likely | With labor adjustment more likely

Twice as likely — Equal likelihood — Twice as likely

f. Receipt of support in firms, by firm size

Countries where **LARGE firms (100+ workers)** were more likely to receive support

Countries where **MICRO firms (0–5 workers)** were more likely to receive support

HICs / UMICs / LMICs / LICs

Large firms more likely | Micro firms more likely

Twice as likely — Equal likelihood — Twice as likely

Sources: Original estimates based on data from World Bank COVID-19 high-frequency phone surveys (HFPS) and COVID-19 Business Pulse Surveys (BPS).
Note: The figures show the difference in the share of households (or firms) receiving support between two groups. Each dot represents one economy. Panel a shows the difference between the share of households with high dependency ratios that received support and the share of households with low dependency ratios that received support. High dependency ratios are defined as higher than the country median, and low dependency ratios are lower than the country median. The x-axis scale ranges from 0 percent at the center line, indicating equal likelihood, to 100 percent at the limit on both sides, indicating twice the number of households received support relative to the other group. Values are truncated at 100 so that countries where one group was more than twice as likely to receive support are shown using vertically stacked dots at the limits of the x-axis. Panel b shows the difference between those with higher or lower education. Lower education is defined as primary or less in LICs and LMICs, and secondary or less in UMICs and HICs. Panel c shows the difference between those that lost a job or income and those that did not. Panel d shows the same difference as panel c, but restricts the sample to low-educated households using the same definition as panel b. Panels e and f show the same measure for firms with labor adjustment and large firms, respectively. In panel e, firms with labor adjustment either fired workers, reduced hours, or cut wages in the past 30 days. In panel f, large firms have more than 100 workers and micro firms have 0 to 5 workers. Mid-size firms are excluded from the sample. HICs = high-income countries; LICs = low-income countries; LMICs = lower-middle-income countries; UMICs = upper-middle-income countries.

targeting need in a crisis is not unique to COVID-19. Few studies examine the quality of targeting of disaster response, but one study does show that it can be challenging in a crisis to target the neediest using objective criteria (Broussard, Dercon, and Somanathan 2014).

Country analyses highlight the challenge in reaching the new poor through delivery systems designed to reach the existing poor. For example, Battacharya and Sinha Roy (2021) investigate how India's social protection response was able to reach a large share of households by using existing systems—nearly 85 percent of rural households and 69 percent of urban households received food or cash support—and the challenges it faced in providing cash transfers to urban poor who were not in existing programs. A third of the urban poor were able to access cash transfers, compared with more than half of the rural poor. The authors also highlight that the broad reach of food and cash assistance resulted in the adequacy of the transfers being limited relative to the size of consumption losses (about 5 percent for each of the food and cash transfers, compared with the 45 percent losses in consumption being recorded). In this report, the case studies for Togo and South Africa detail how challenging it was to provide transfers to a group of households quite vulnerable during the crisis, but never before recipients of direct government support, and how these countries overcame these challenges (see boxes 4.1 and 7.3). Regional analyses highlight the same challenge. For example, two studies of the fiscal response in the East Asia and Pacific region show that support to households in the region has, in general, been pro-poor, but it has been difficult to reach informal workers and middle-class households facing large losses and vulnerable to falling into poverty (Mason et al. 2020; World Bank 2022c).

At the firm level, support received correlated well with the losses reported, but larger firms were much more likely to receive support in the majority of countries with data. According to figure 4.12, panel e, firms reporting cuts in employment were more likely to receive support, suggesting that the means of targeting to losses worked well.[13] However, larger firms were more likely to receive support than smaller firms, and in LICs there was a bigger gap in receiving support between smaller and larger firms (figure 4.12, panel f). These findings correspond to those from the literature: government support often went to firms that did not need it to survive (Gourinchas et al. 2021). Moreover, less productive and larger firms, regardless of their precrisis innovation, received government support during the crisis, thereby reducing competition and productivity growth (Bruhn, Demirgüç-Kunt, and Singer 2021).

Summary: An unprecedented response was more limited in poorer countries

The overall finding in this section is that fiscal support for firms and households has made a difference during the COVID-19 crisis, and some countries have indeed been able to stave off the worst effects of the pandemic by using fiscal measures. However, in most cases the fiscal response probably was not adequate because it did not reach many households and firms when they needed it, given the scale and speed of the losses experienced.

The question of overall impact can be assessed by reviewing microsimulations of the impact of the crisis and the degree to which the fiscal response mitigated this impact. These studies have been collated, concentrating on those of low- and middle-income countries, but also including studies conducted by the World Bank in HICs.[14] Results from reviewed microsimulations (those published or produced by World Bank teams) are summarized in figure 4.13 using the national poverty line for each country or, if not available, the international poverty line relevant to the country based on its income class. Microsimulations of the impacts of the crisis and fiscal response on poverty reveal that the estimated impacts of the crisis on poverty increased with country income level. Households in UMICs were

FIGURE 4.13

In simulations, fiscal policy reduced the impact of the COVID-19 crisis on poverty but less so in poorer economies

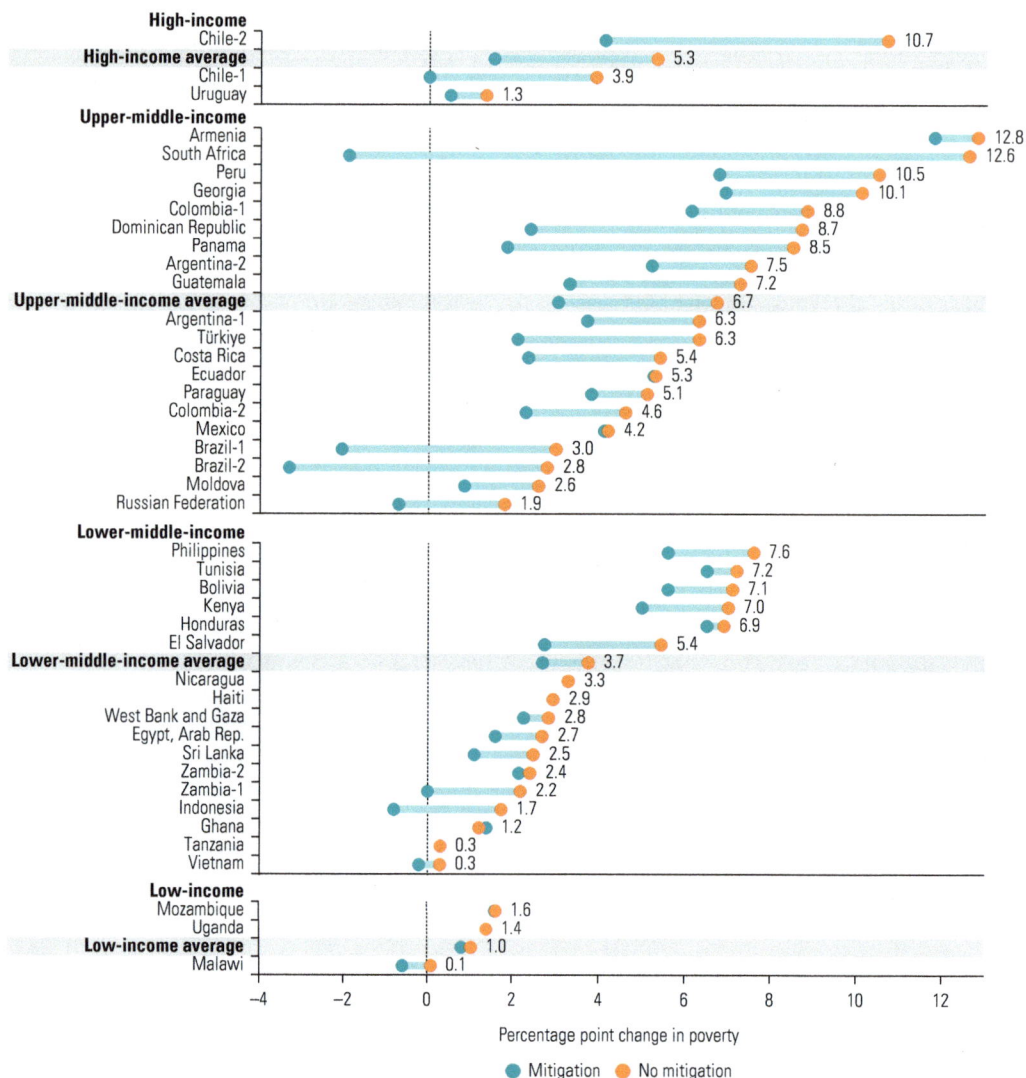

Sources: *High-income:* World Bank 2021b (Chile-1, Uruguay); Ricci et al. 2021 (Chile-2). *Upper-middle-income:* World Bank 2021b (Argentina-1, Costa Rica, Ecuador, Guatemala, Mexico, Panama, Peru); Lustig et al. 2021 (Argentina-2, Brazil-2, Colombia-1, Colombia-2); World Bank 2020 (Russian Federation); Cereda, Rubiao, and Sousa 2020 (Brazil-1); World Bank 2021d (Moldova); Canavire and Granados Ibarra 2021 (Paraguay); Nebiler, Celik, and Baez 2021 (Türkiye); CTP 2021 (Dominican Republic); Davalos, Juliet, and Manuel 2021 (Colombia-1); Fuchs 2020 (Georgia); Barnes et al. 2021 (South Africa); Fuchs et al. 2020 (Armenia); *Lower-middle-income:* World Bank 2021b (Bolivia, El Salvador, Haiti, Honduras, Nicaragua); Ali and Tiwari 2020 (Indonesia); Gansey, Genoni, and Helmy 2022 (Arab Republic of Egypt); Hoogeveen and Lopez-Acevedo 2021 (Tunisia, West Bank and Gaza); Pape and Delius 2021 (Kenya); Belghith, Fernandez, and David, forthcoming (Philippines); Lastunen et al. 2021 (Ghana, Tanzania, Zambia-2); World Bank 2021a (Vietnam); Kim and de Silva 2021 (Sri Lanka); Boban Varghese et al. 2021 (Zambia-1). *Low-income:* Magalasi 2021 (Malawi); Lastunen et al. 2021 (Mozambique, Uganda).

Note: The figure shows the results of two simulations from each economy study: one showing the increase in poverty that would have occurred had no fiscal response been present (no mitigation), and one showing the increase in poverty taking into account the fiscal response (mitigation). The increase in poverty is measured against the national poverty line or the global poverty line appropriate to the economy income category. For some economies, more than one study is available, as indicated by the use of "1" or "2" after the economy name in the figure. Full details of the data used are in online annex 4A, table 4A.1.

expected to fare much worse than households in LMICs and LICs, with much larger antici-pated impacts on poverty.

Microsimulations find that in many countries the fiscal response successfully mitigated the impact of the crisis on poverty. Some notable examples are Brazil, Chile, Indonesia, South Africa, Uruguay, and Zambia—all countries expected to ameliorate nearly all of the impact of the COVID-19 shock on poverty (in at least one set of simulations available). Many other countries halved the expected impact of a large shock through fiscal measures. Examples are Guatemala, Paraguay, Sri Lanka, and Türkiye.

However, fiscal policy was anticipated to be more effective in mitigating the impact in higher-income countries. The fiscal response offset three quarters of the impact of the crisis on poverty in the two HICs included in the review,[15] which is consistent with the broader litera-ture. Stantcheva (2022) reviews microsimulations for HICs and finds that the fiscal response was able to offset the rising inequality caused by the pandemic in most HICs, resulting in significant inequality reductions in 2020. A Eurostat analysis finds that, although the poorest quintile experienced earned income losses of about 10 percent, disposable income increased by 2 percent (Eurostat 2020). In the United States, the early fiscal response reduced poverty (Han, Meyer, and Sullivan 2020).

In UMICs, although there was still a sizable increase in poverty—7 percentage points, on average—fiscal policy was able to reduce the impact by about half. Fiscal policy was less effec-tive in LMICs and LICs. In LMICs, although the poverty impact of the crisis was estimated to be, on average, 4 percentage points, fiscal policy was able to bring that down to 3 percentage points. The impact of the fiscal policy response was estimated to be negligible for two of the three LICs included in the review and fully mitigated for the third (Malawi), but the impact of the crisis was also estimated to be much smaller, increasing poverty by, on average, 1 percent-age point.

Factors that influenced the impact of fiscal policy

Three broad factors determined the scale and effectiveness of a country's fiscal response to the pandemic: its ability to borrow, the structure of the economy, and the nature of the existing fiscal benefit system. Although less quantifiable, case studies also bring out the importance of leadership and communication around transfer eligibility and amounts (Beazley, Marzi, and Steller 2021; Gentilini 2022).

The scale of the response, largely driven by access to external finance, determined impact

The scale of the response was a large determinant of the size of the mitigated poverty impact. Sixteen of the microsimulation reports provided data on the cost of the fiscal response simu-lated. The reduction in poverty resulting from this spending and the amount spent as a share of GDP are plotted in figure 4.14 and show a strong correlation between the size of the impact and amount spent (correlation, 0.70).

An emerging literature has assessed what drove the scale of fiscal responses and highlights the importance of a country's ability to take on new debt. According to this literature, countries with cheaper access to financing, reflected in a higher sovereign credit rating, achieved a larger fiscal response. Figure 4.15 shows the unconditional correlation between sovereign credit rating and (1) the COVID-19 fiscal response and (2) the growth in external borrowing from 2019 to 2020 for low- and middle-income countries. The correlation between spending and a country's sovereign credit rating holds for different time periods, country groups, and controls (Apeti et al. 2021; Benmelech and Tzur-Ilan 2020). Table 4.1 reports the results of these regressions, and also shows that this correlation holds when considering updated IMF data on above-the-line spend-ing as a share of GDP for LICs and MICs only.

FIGURE 4.14

Fiscal policy reduced poverty more when more was spent

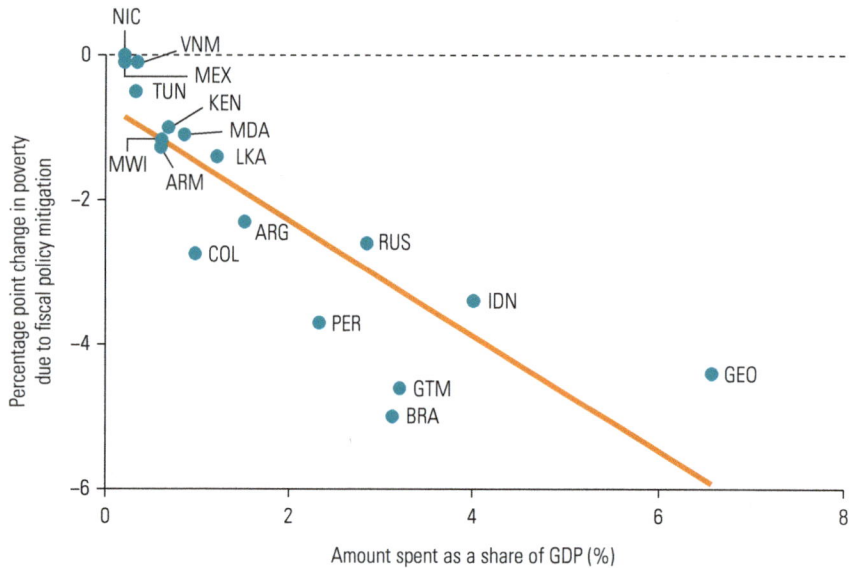

Sources: Percentage point change in poverty and cost estimates are based on the same reports used as sources in figure 4.13.
Note: The figure shows the correlation between the percentage point change in poverty due to fiscal policy mitigation and share of GDP spent on mitigation, based on the same microsimulation studies as figure 4.13 (see online annex 4A, table 4A.1).

FIGURE 4.15

A higher credit rating was correlated with a larger fiscal response and increased external borrowing

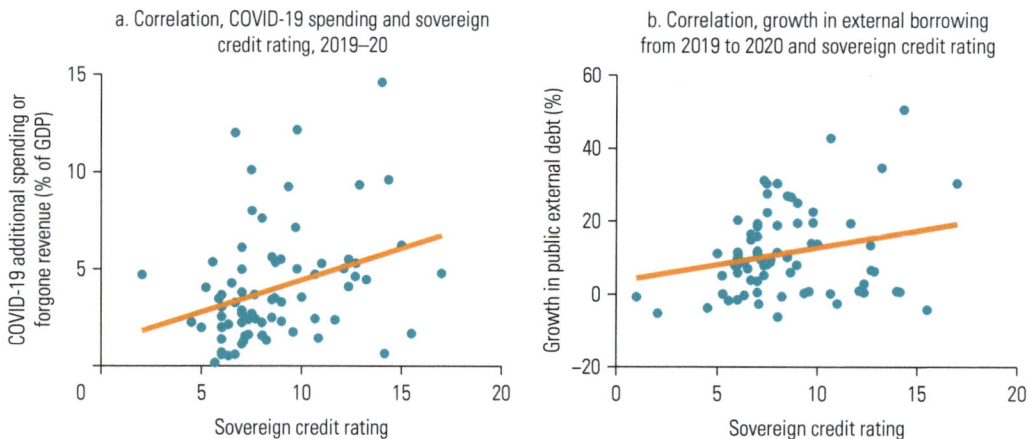

Sources: Original estimates based on data from International Monetary Fund, Database of Fiscal Policy Responses to COVID-19, https://www.imf.org/en/Topics/imf-and-covid19/Fiscal-Policies-Database-in-Response-to-COVID-19; Kose et al. 2022; World Bank, International Debt Statistics, https://www.worldbank.org/en/programs/debt-statistics/ids.
Note: The figure shows cross-country correlations between 2019 sovereign credit ratings (Kose et al. 2022) and COVID-19 fiscal response (panel a) and external borrowing (panel b). Sovereign credit rating is the 2019 average of foreign currency long-term sovereign debt ratings by Moody's, Standard & Poor's, and Fitch Ratings converted to a numerical index from 1 (worst) to 21 (best). External borrowing is measured using the percentage growth in public and publicly guaranteed external debt stocks from 2019 to 2020, based on World Bank, International Debt Statistics. The sample includes low- and middle-income economies.

TABLE 4.1

Cross-country correlations highlight the importance of access to external borrowing

Covariate	Benmelech and Tzur-Ilan (2020)	Apeti et al. (2021)			World Bank estimates
Credit rating	0.267*** (0.090)	0.5871*** (0.1235)			0.5479*** (0.1903)
Debt to GDP (log)	0.015 (0.012)		0.1054 (0.8621)		0.3996 (0.7473)
Government expenditure to GDP	−0.079** (0.038)				0.0707 (0.0532)
Debt-to-tax ratio (log)				−1.6920** (0.6765)	
GDP per capita (log)	1.262** (0.490)	−0.1547 (0.5246)	1.6153*** (0.5409)	1.6661*** (0.5286)	−0.8260 (0.6082)
Countries	79 (few LICs and LMICs)	107			66 (LICs and MICs)
Time period	April–June 2020	April–September 2020			April 2020–October 2021
Dependent variable	Fiscal spending (excluding guarantees) as a share of GDP	Fiscal stimuli as a share of GDP (above-the-line measures and liquidity support)			Fiscal spending (above-the-line measures) as a share of GDP
Other covariates	Population, COVID-19 cases	Infection fatality rate,[a] democratization index,[a] population density, inflation			Infection fatality rate[a]

Sources: Apeti et al. 2021; Benmelech and Tzur-Ilan 2020. World Bank estimates based on data from the International Monetary Fund's Database of Fiscal Policy Responses to COVID-19, October 2021, https://www.imf.org/en/Topics/imf-and-covid19/Fiscal-Policies-Database-in-Response-to-COVID-19.
Note: In the World Bank estimates, measures of government effectiveness were added, but none was significant. These results show specifications without these measures included. GDP = gross domestic product; LICs = low-income countries; LMICs = lower-middle-income countries; MICs = middle-income countries.
a. These other covariates are significant.
*p < .05 **p < .01 *** p < .001.

Other evidence also points to the importance of access to external finance in the crisis response. Although these cross-country regressions alone do not provide causal evidence that access to external finance was an important determinant of the scale of the response—and there are indeed many other dimensions of fiscal space (Kose et al. 2022)—it is consistent with a pattern found in other crises historically. An existing literature points out that fiscal procyclicality stems in part from an inability to access external financing during downturns (see, for example, Frankel, Vegh, and Vuletin 2013; Gavin and Perotti 1997; Kraay and Serven 2013). Moreover, in a survey of country governments reported in *World Development Report 2022* (World Bank 2022d), access to external financing was cited as a constraint, particularly by countries in income groups that had the smallest fiscal response—LICs and LMICs. Policy makers in these countries were most concerned about access to foreign aid (94 percent and 84 percent, respectively) and access to external borrowing and debt sustainability (83 percent and 61–65 percent, respectively). UMICs were more concerned about access to domestic borrowing and debt sustainability than access to external borrowing or foreign aid.

Many LICs had limited access to external borrowing and relied on donor aid and concessional lending. The median ratio of multilateral funds (grants and loans) committed as part of the COVID-19 response relative to the announced fiscal response of governments was 50 percent for UMICs, 73 percent for LMICs, and 95 percent for LICs. This finding suggests that for LICs little fiscal response was provided beyond what was funded by the IMF, development banks (the World Bank Group and regional banks), and the United Nations.[16] Moreover, going into the crisis, more than half of the low- and lower-middle-income International Development Association (IDA) countries (38) were in debt distress and so could not borrow much. Their main source of external finance was highly-concessional flows from multilateral development banks.

The type of financing available is a factor in the speed of the response. Access to domestic financing, if available, can facilitate quick disbursement because it is often quick to operationalize and is directly under the government's control. For example, in Albania budget reallocations were used to quickly finance an early response in 2020.[17] An analysis of implementation of cash transfers highlights the importance of access to domestic financing in allowing countries to respond more quickly. This finding could reflect other factors that are correlated with access to domestic financing (such as capacity to implement). However, the case studies in Beazley, Marzi, and Steller (2021) often identify access to domestic financing as an important aspect of quick implementation.

The type and impact of support depended on the structure of the economy

During the pandemic, the type and impact of the fiscal support provided depended on the structure of the economy—that is, the nature of consumption, employment, and production. Countries with large informal sectors found it difficult to protect firms and jobs. The share of workers in firms in both LICs and MICs receiving wage subsidy support was larger in countries with a greater share of formal workers in the economy before the crisis (figure 4.16), even when controlling for the overall level of spending and GDP per capita. This finding is worrisome because of emerging evidence suggesting that spending to protect jobs may have had more impact in hastening economic recovery, increasing employment, and reducing

FIGURE 4.16

Support reached more households in formal economies and in countries with high prepandemic rates of social assistance

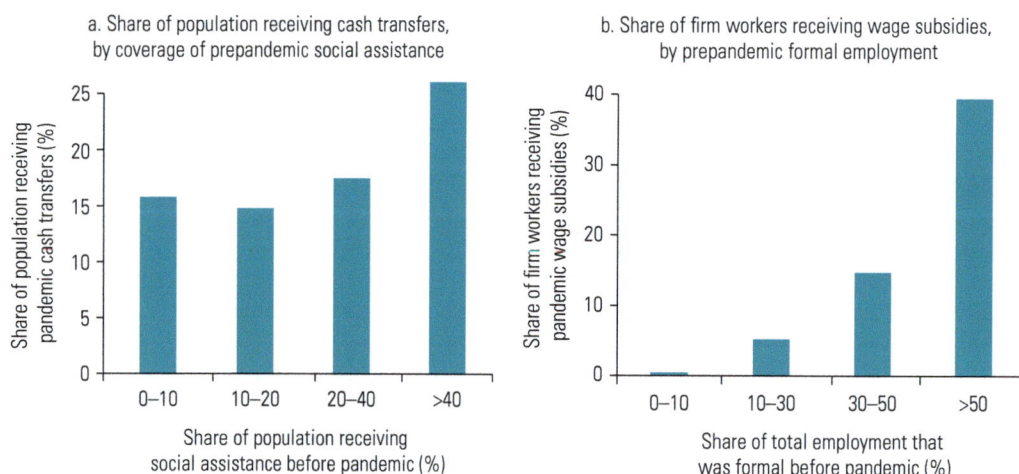

a. Share of population receiving cash transfers, by coverage of prepandemic social assistance

b. Share of firm workers receiving wage subsidies, by prepandemic formal employment

Sources: Original estimates based on data from World Bank, Atlas of Social Protection Indicators of Resilience and Equity (ASPIRE), https://www.worldbank.org/en/data/datatopics/aspire; Gentilini et al. 2022a; International Labour Organization, ILOSTAT database, https://ilostat.ilo.org/data/; and World Bank COVID-19 Business Pulse Surveys.
Note: Panel a shows the average coverage of the largest COVID-19 cash transfer program for different levels of prepandemic social assistance coverage. The sample includes 77 low- and middle-income economies. Panel b shows the average share of firm labor reporting the receipt of support in surveys for different levels of prepandemic formal employment. The sample includes 45 low- and middle-income economies. Economies are weighted equally.

poverty than income support measures (see Demirgüç-Kunt, Lokshin, and Torre, forthcoming; World Bank forthcoming c).

The type of response provided to households was also influenced by the degree of formalization of the labor market. Few LICs and MICs have widespread automatic stabilizers in place, and the share of workers covered by unemployment insurance is low (Asenjo and Pignatti 2019). Contreras-Gonzalez et al. (2022) find that countries that had limited use of unemployment insurance before the crisis were less likely to use that insurance to support households during the crisis. As a result, unemployment insurance benefits were only a small part of the fiscal response in most countries. Instead, countries targeted informal sector workers not covered by insurance or wage subsidies in new social assistance programs (Kamran et al. 2022).

The impact of transfers also depended on the structure of the economy. This interplay of shocks, policy impact, and poverty is well illustrated by Aminjonov, Bargain, and Bernard (2021). They consider worker mobility (based on smartphone data) in both higher- and lower-poverty regions in a sample of 43 low- and middle-income countries. A combination of lockdowns and private aversion behavior drove a dramatic reduction in mobility to and from workplaces at the start of the pandemic. However, the reductions in mobility were larger in the lower-poverty regions (region- and date-fixed effects are included in the analysis). These were areas better able to accommodate a stay-at-home order in part because of the prevailing nature of work and so a higher prevalence of households better able to afford to stay at home. Regions that received income support also saw lower rates of workplace mobility because these transfers allowed more households to afford to stay at home. As a result of this dynamic, income support policies had a larger impact on mobility in areas with higher poverty rates than in those with lower poverty rates.

Detailed analysis of the United States confirms the importance of economic structure in determining the impact of the fiscal policy response. Chetty et al. (2020) compile and analyze a unique set of data to assess the impacts of the pandemic and the policy response on rich and poor neighborhoods in the United States. They find that the fiscal stimulus received by households increased spending more in poorer neighborhoods than in rich ones. As a result, there was an increase in small business revenue in low-rent neighborhoods at the time stimulus payments were made, whereas stimulus payments had no impact in high-rent neighborhoods. This finding corresponds with those in the broader economic literature on local and fiscal multipliers. Economies in which spending is liquidity-constrained (as a result of chronic poverty or temporary crisis conditions) have a higher local multiplier from fiscal transfers.[18]

Speed and targeting were easier where benefit systems were well developed

The crisis highlighted the importance of the foundational elements of a social protection system in facilitating a fast response. The number of beneficiaries in newly announced social assistance programs was strongly correlated with the size of the existing social protection system before the crisis (figure 4.16). The speed of response was also influenced by the nature of the precrisis benefit system (see, for example, World Bank 2022c). Scaling up to existing recipients of government transfers (vertical expansion) happened quickly (54 days from stay-at-home order), but establishing a new system or expanding an existing system to new households took much longer (83 days for setting up a new scheme or 128 days for adapting an existing scheme to new beneficiaries)—see Beazley, Marzi, and Steller (2021). However, considerable variation in the speed of implementation cannot be explained by this factor (Gentilini et al. 2022a).

Gentilini (2022) provides a detailed analysis of what lessons can be learned from the COVID-19 response for investing in crisis delivery. A couple of key points are noted here. Countries in which existing social registries or databases were used to identify beneficiaries were able to implement horizontal scale-ups and new programs more quickly (Beazley, Marzi, and Steller 2021). In the five cases in which social registries were used to identify new beneficiaries, scaling up was faster than in cases in which other databases or forms of enrollment were used (Gentilini et al. 2022a). However, more detailed case studies underscore the importance of complementing the use of existing databases with on-demand registration and programs with alternate targeting approaches because existing databases inevitably leave out some newly poor people. As described in box 4.1, Togo used voter registration data to identify beneficiaries. Countries with larger formal economies and an ability to link multiple databases were able to use multiple sources of data (for example, personal income tax databases) to identify beneficiaries (Gentilini 2022 and box 7.3 in chapter 7).

Finally, during the crisis, when transfers were made using a digital payment system, implementation was quicker—51 days, compared with 84 days from stay-at-home orders to first payment (Gentilini 2022). This method of transfer was also highlighted in case studies that examined speed of implementation (Beazley, Marzi, and Steller 2021). Togo demonstrated that focusing on digital systems, even in a setting in which the social protection system was limited going into the crisis, allowed quick targeting and payments (box 4.1).[19]

Conclusion

Fiscal support to firms and households protected welfare during the COVID-19 crisis. Some countries were able to stave off the worst effects of the pandemic by using fiscal measures, but in many countries the response did not reach many households and firms when they needed it because of the scale and speed of the losses experienced. Among the lessons from this global stress test on fiscal crisis response systems are recognizing the importance of a country's ability to borrow for a fiscal response; overcoming the challenges of reaching households and protecting jobs in informal economies; and providing delivery systems that can identify the needs of vulnerable people (not just the chronically poor) and provide support quickly. Without systems that can identify need and reach households quickly, a crisis response has to rely on blunt instruments such as transfers targeting the chronically poor, who may not be those most affected by the crisis, or untargeted support measures such as subsidies. Subsidies were used frequently in response to the COVID-19 crisis and even more as countries turn to food and energy subsidies, which are often not well targeted to those most in need. Although HICs have financing available to provide more generous crisis support, this approach is hard to sustain in most LICs and MICs.

These lessons have implications for how to prepare fiscal systems for a crisis response. Addressing debt, preparing contingent financing, and developing delivery systems to deliver in a crisis will increase the protective power of fiscal policy. Chapter 7 lays out policy priorities based on the findings in this chapter. The chapter also includes a reality check on the limits of the protection afforded by fiscal policy for many poor households in the near term. For that reason, as described in chapter 7, there is a need to support other instruments to build the capacity of poor households to protect their welfare in a crisis.

Notes

1. The response includes measures for implementation in 2020, 2021, and beyond.
2. International Monetary Fund, Database of Fiscal Policy Responses to COVID-19, October 2021, https://www.imf.org/en/Topics /imf-and-covid19/Fiscal-Policies-Database-in -Response-to-COVID-19.
3. Automatic stabilizers are components of the tax and benefit system that adjust automatically to cyclical changes in the economy without discretionary government action. Stabilizers include unemployment insurance (on the expenditure side), social security, and income taxation (on the revenue side). Because the size of automatic stabilizers tends to be correlated with the size of an economy, they are larger in

high-income countries. But they are smaller in the United States than in Europe, where generous unemployment insurance played a key role in absorbing household income shocks during the global financial crisis (Dolls, Fuest, and Peichl 2012).

4. International Monetary Fund, Database of Fiscal Policy Responses to COVID-19, October 2021, https://www.imf.org/en/Topics/imf-and-covid19/Fiscal-Policies-Database-in-Response-to-COVID-19.

5. Although detailed information on health expenditure for most low- and middle-income countries is yet to be published, there is some indication that the COVID-19 health sector response reflects at least some repurposing of other funds. For example, 20 percent of countries that participated in a May 2020 World Health Organization (WHO) country survey reported that government funds had been reallocated from noncommunicable diseases (NCDs) to non-NCD services. About a third of countries did not know whether such a reallocation had occurred at the time of the survey. About 94 percent of countries reported that all or some NCD health staff had been reallocated to support COVID-19 efforts, which led to widespread disruptions in health care during the pandemic (WHO 2020, 2021b). In the Democratic Republic of Congo, the share of reprogrammed funding had risen from 6 percent in April 2020 to 33 percent by October 2020 (WHO 2021b).

6. The share of health expenditure fell in 15 of 22 countries considered by WHO (2021a) and in 33 of 56 countries for which government expenditure data for 2020 were available in the IMF's Expenditure by Functions of Government (COFOG) database at the time of writing (https://data.imf.org/?sk=ca012d95-6151-4a84-a89b-3914d718b878&hide_uv=1).

7. International Monetary Fund, Database of Fiscal Policy Responses to COVID-19, October 2021, https://www.imf.org/en/Topics/imf-and-covid19/Fiscal-Policies-Database-in-Response-to-COVID-19.

8. World Bank, COVID-19 High-Frequency Monitoring Dashboard, https://www.worldbank.org/en/data/interactive/2020/11/11/covid-19-high-frequency-monitoring-dashboard; World Bank, COVID-19 Business Pulse Survey Dashboard,

https://www.worldbank.org/en/data/interactive/2021/01/19/covid-19-business-pulse-survey-dashboard.

9. Answers to "loss of income or employment" for households, for example, are collected only from a "yes" or "no" response providing no information on the size of the losses or the degree to which those losses push a household into poverty. Similarly for firms, "loss of sales or reductions in employment" is only collected as a "yes" or "no" response. In the household survey, "support received from the government" does not distinguish between regular support that would have been received regardless of the crisis and additional support received as part of the government's fiscal response. The wording of the questions may also make it unlikely for data to include support received through subsidies and tax or payment exemptions. The Business Pulse Survey collects information about "support received" from national or local governments, although firms may also be reporting access to new credit or loans that may not be necessarily the result of explicit fiscal measures. This challenge is addressed by focusing on those categories of support that could only be provided by governments (for example, wage subsidies).

10. International Monetary Fund, Database of Fiscal Policy Responses to COVID-19, October 2021, https://www.imf.org/en/Topics/imf-and-covid19/Fiscal-Policies-Database-in-Response-to-COVID-19.

11. World Bank, COVID-19 Business Pulse Survey Dashboard, https://www.worldbank.org/en/data/interactive/2021/01/19/covid-19-business-pulse-survey-dashboard.

12. This is also true when examining percentage differences and when looking only at employment losses or at food insecurity as a measure of those affected.

13. Targeting was often sectoral. See, for example, Köhler and Hill (2022) for South Africa.

14. Microsimulations of the likely impact of the crisis and the impact of the fiscal response were conducted for other countries by World Bank country poverty teams and researchers outside of the World Bank in the early months of the crisis. These microsimulations use macroeconomics data on sectoral losses to model which households would lose

income and by how much (based on the sectors in which they worked). Multiple studies for a single country may be reported if studies were both undertaken by the World Bank and published by external researchers. For some countries, World Bank estimates were available as part of country-level projections and regional projections. Because regional projections may make some assumptions requiring harmonizing data across the region, regional estimates are presented only when there is no country study. The microsimulations also use policy announcements of fiscal support to identify what the likely benefits of the fiscal response would be across households based on which support they are modeled to receive. The fiscal simulations included cash transfers but sometimes other support such as in-kind transfers and unemployment benefits. For studies where various estimates are provided, the summary captures the worst scenario for a country. Survey data from Colombia and the Dominican Republic suggest that the microsimulation models are accurate in predicting both the impact of labor income losses—which would have increased poverty by 9.0 percentage points and 8.1 percentage points, respectively, at the national poverty line—and the effectiveness of transfers in reducing the increase. Comparisons of the Brazil and Costa Rica results also show that the models perform quite well (although the impact of transfers was larger than simulated in Brazil and the labor income losses larger than simulated in Costa Rica). In Indonesia, microsimulation results also correspond quite well to official survey data, although official survey data show a more modest rise in poverty than projected.

15. Although this is true in only one set of the microsimulation results for Chile.

16. Calculated using multilateral funds committed (as recorded by the Centre for Disaster Protection) and announced fiscal response from the IMF.

17. Total spending comprises spending by line ministries, debt repayment, and transfers to local government. These reallocations were not costless, because they represented cuts to other spending. In fact, the estimated value forgone

due to the budget reallocations was US$113 million, or 0.76 percent of GDP. Preparation of the eurobond was already under way, which helped the government borrow quickly and prevent larger budget cuts.

18. See, for example, Egger et al. (2019); Gechert and Rannenberg (2018); Pennings (2021); also see chapter 6 for a fuller discussion on the multiplier effects of cash transfers.

19. Although less quantifiable, case studies bring out the importance of leadership and communication around transfer eligibility and amounts (Beazley, Marzi, and Steller 2021; World Bank 2022b).

References

Abay, Kibrom, Guush Berhane, John Hoddinott, and Kibrom Tafere. Forthcoming. "COVID-19 and Food Security in Ethiopia: Do Social Protection Programs Protect?" *Economic Development and Cultural Change.*

Afridi, Farzana, Kanika Mahajan, and Nikita Sangwan. 2022. "Employment Guaranteed? Social Protection during a Pandemic." *Oxford Open Economics* 1 (1): 1–15.

Aggarwal, Shilpa, Dahyeon Jeong, Naresh Kumar, David Sungho Park, Jonathan Robinson, and Alan Spearot. 2020. "Did COVID-19 Market Disruptions Disrupt Food Security? Evidence from Households in Rural Liberia and Malawi." Working Paper 27932, National Bureau of Economic Research, Cambridge, MA.

Aiken, Emily, Suzanne Bellue, Dean Karlan, Chris Udry, and Joshua E. Blumenstock. 2022. "Machine Learning and Phone Data Can Improve Targeting of Humanitarian Aid." *Nature* 603: 864–70.

Aker, Jenny C., Rachid Boumnijel, Amanda McClelland, and Niall Tierney. 2016. "Payment Mechanisms and Antipoverty Programs: Evidence from a Mobile Money Cash Transfer Experiment in Niger." *Economic Development and Cultural Change* 65 (1): 1–37.

Albagli, Elías, Andrés Fernández, and Federico Huneeus. "Firms' Margins of Adjustment in the Wake of COVID: Microevidence from Chile." Presentation at the Central Bank of Chile, Santiago, Chile, January 12, 2021.

Ali, Rabia, and Sailesh Tiwari. 2020. "Ex-Ante Poverty and Distributional Impacts of COVID–19 in

Indonesia." Indonesia COVID-19 Observatory Brief 1, World Bank, Washington, DC.

Al-Samarrai, Samer, Pedro Cerdan-Infantes, Aliya Bigarinova, Juanita Bodmer, Marianne Joy Anacleto Vital, Manos Antoninis, Bilal Fouad Barakat, et al. 2021. *Education Finance Watch 2021* (English). Washington, DC: World Bank.

Aminjonov, Ulugbek, Olivier Bargain, and Tanguy Bernard. 2021. "Gimme Shelter: Social Distancing and Income Support in Times of Pandemic." Discussion Paper 02042, International Food Policy Research Institute, Washington, DC.

Apeti, Ablam Estel, Jean-Louis Combes, Xavier Debrun, and Alexandru Minea. 2021. "Did Fiscal Space Foster Covid-19's Fiscal Stimuli?" *Covid Economics* 74: 71–93.

Asenjo, Antonia, and Clemente Pignatti. 2019. "Unemployment Insurance Schemes around the World: Evidence and Policy Options." ILO Working Paper 49, International Labour Organisation, Geneva.

Banerjee, Abhijit, Michael Faye, Alan Krueger, Paul Niehaus, and Tavneet Suri. 2020. "Effects of a Universal Basic Income during the Pandemic." Working paper, University of California San Diego.

Barnes, Helen, Gabriel Espi-Sanchis, Murray Leibbrandt, David McLennan, Michael Noble, Jukka Pirttilä, Wynnona Steyn, et al. 2021. "Analysis of the Distributional Effects of COVID-19 and State-Led Remedial Measures in South Africa." Working Paper 2021/68, United Nations University World Institute for Development Economics Research, Helsinki.

Battacharya, Shrayana, and Sutirtha Sinha Roy. 2021. "Intent to Implementation: Tracking India's Social Protection Response to COVID-19." Social Protection and Jobs Discussion Paper 2107, World Bank, Washington, DC.

Beazley, Rodolfo, Marta Marzi, and Rachael Steller. 2021. *Drivers of Timely and Large-Scale Cash Responses to COVID-19: What Does the Data Say?* Social Protection Approaches to COVID-19 Expert Advice Service (SPACE), DAI Global UK Ltd., United Kingdom.

Belghith, Nadia Belhaj Hassine, Francine Claire Fernandez, and Clarissa Crisostomo David. Forthcoming. "Inequality in the Philippines: Past, Present, and Prospects for the Future." World Bank, Washington, DC.

Benmelech, Efraim, and Nitzan Tzur-Ilan. 2020. "The Determinants of Fiscal and Monetary Policies during the COVID-19 Crisis." Working Paper 27461, National Bureau of Economic Research, Cambridge, MA.

Berkouwer, Susanna B., Pierre E. Biscaye, Eric Hsu, Oliver W. Kim, Kenneth Lee, Edward Miguel, and Catherine Wolfram. 2021. "Money or Power? Financial Infrastructure and Optimal Policy." Working Paper 29086, National Bureau of Economic Research, Cambridge, MA.

Boban Varghese, Paul, Arden Finn, Sarang Chaudhary, Renata Mayer Gukovas, and Ramya Sundaram. 2021. "COVID-19, Poverty, and Social Safety Net Response in Zambia." Policy Research Working Paper 9571, World Bank, Washington, DC.

Bottan, Nicolas, Bridget Hoffmann, and Diego A. Vera-Cossio. 2021. "Stepping Up during a Crisis: The Unintended Effects of a Noncontributory Pension Program during the COVID-19 Pandemic." *Journal of Development Economics* 150: 102635.

Brooks, Wyatt, Kevin Donovan, Terence Johnson, and Jackline Oluoch-Aridi. 2020. "Cash Transfers as a Response to COVID-19: A Randomized Experiment in Kenya." Discussion Paper 1082, Yale University, New Haven, CT.

Broussard, Nzinga, Stefan Dercon, and Rohini Somanathan. 2014. "Aid and Agency in Africa: Explaining Food Disbursements across Ethiopian Households, 1994–2004." *Journal of Development Economics* 108 (C): 128–137.

Bruhn, Miriam, Asli Demirgüç-Kunt, and Dorothe Singer. 2021. "Competition and Firm Recovery Post-COVID-19." Policy Research Working Paper 9851, World Bank, Washington, DC.

Canavire, Gustavo Javier, and Silvia Juliana Granados Ibarra. 2021. "Paraguay Poverty and Equity Update." Working paper, World Bank, Washington, DC.

Cereda, Fabio, Rafael M. Rubiao, and Liliana D. Sousa. 2020. "COVID-19, Labor Market Shocks, Poverty in Brazil: A Microsimulation Analysis." World Bank, Washington, DC.

Cerra, Valerie, Antonio Fatás, and Sweta C. Saxena. 2020. "Hysteresis and Business Cycles." Working Paper WP/20/73, International Monetary Fund, Washington, DC.

Chetty, Raj, John N. Friedman, Nathaniel Hendren, Michael Stepner, and Opportunity Insights Team. 2020. "The Economic Impacts of COVID-19: Evidence from a New Public Database Built Using Private Sector Data." Working Paper 27431, National Bureau of Economic Research, Cambridge, MA.

Chi, Guanghua, Han Fang, Sourav Chatterjee, and Joshua E. Blumenstock. 2022. "Microestimates of Wealth for All Low- and Middle-Income Countries." *Proceedings of the National Academy of Sciences* 119 (3).

Cho, Yoonyoung, Jorge Avalos, Yasuhiro Kawasoe, Doug Johnson, and Ruth Rodriguez. 2021. "Mitigating the Impact of COVID-19 on the Welfare of Low Income Households in the Philippines: The Role of Social Protection." COVID-19 Low Income HOPE Survey Note 1, World Bank, Washington, DC.

Cirera, Xavier, Marcio Cruz, Elwyn Davies, Arti Grover, Leonardo Iacovone, Jose Ernesto Lopez Cordova, et al. 2021."Policies to Support Businesses through the COVID-19 Shock: A Firm-Level Perspective." *World Bank Research Observer* 36 (1): 41–66.

Contreras-Gonzalez, Ivette, Melanie Khamis, David Newhouse, and Michael Weber. 2022. "How Did Countries Respond to the COVID-19 Crisis? Emerging Patterns on Labor Market Policies." *Jobs Watch Brief.*

CTP (Comité Técnico Interinstitucional de Pobreza). 2021. "Boletín de Estadisticas Oficiales de Pobreza Monetaria en la República Dominicana año 6, no. 8." Ministry of Economics, Planning and Development, Government of the Dominican Republic, Santo Domingo.

DANE (National Administrative Department of Statistics). 2021. "Pobreza Monetaria en Colombia Resultados 2020." DANE, Government of Colombia, Bogatá. https://www .dane.gov.co/files/investigaciones/condiciones_vida /pobreza/2020/Presentacion-pobreza-monetaria _2020.pdf.

Davalos, María Eugenia, Pico Julieth, and Monroy Juan Manuel. 2021. "COVID-19: Micro simulaciones para evaluar el impacto en pobreza y desigualdad en Colombia." Unpublished manuscript, Poverty and Equity Global Practice, World Bank, Washington, DC.

Debenedetti, Luciana. 2021. "Togo's Novissi Cash Transfer: Designing and Implementing a Fully Digital Social Assistance Program during COVID-19." Innovations for Poverty Action, Washington, DC.

de Janvry, Alain, Elisabeth Sadoulet, Pantelis Solomon, and Renos Vakis. 2006. "Uninsured Risk and Asset Protection: Can Conditional Cash Transfer Programs Serve as Safety Nets?" Social Protection Discussion Paper 604, World Bank, Washington, DC.

Del Carpio, Ximena V., and Karen Macours. 2010. "Leveling the Intra-Household Playing Field: Compensation and Specialization in Child Labor Allocation." In *Child Labor and the Transition between School and Work.* United Kingdom: Emerald Group Publishing Limited.

Demirgüç-Kunt, Asli, Michael Lokshin, and Iván Torre. Forthcoming. "Protect Incomes or Protect Jobs? The Role of Social Policies in Postpandemic Recovery." Background paper prepared for Europe and Central Asia Economic Update, World Bank, Washington, DC.

Dolls, Mathias, Clemens Fuest, and Andreas Peichl. 2012. "Automatic Stabilizers and Economic Crisis: US vs. Europe." *Journal of Public Economics* 96 (3–4): 279–94.

ECLAC (Economic Commission for Latin America and the Caribbean). 2021. *Fiscal Panorama of Latin America and the Caribbean, 2021.* LC/ PUB.2021/5-P. Santiago, Chile: ECLAC.

Egger, Dennis, Johannes Haushofer, Edward Miguel, Paul Niehaus, and Michael W. Walker. 2019. "General Equilibrium Effects of Cash Transfers: Experimental Evidence from Kenya." Working Paper 26600, National Bureau of Economic Research, Cambridge, MA.

Eurostat. 2020. "Impact of COVID-19 on Employment Income—Advanced Estimates." https://ec.europa .eu/eurostat/statistics-explained/index.php?title =Impact_of_COVID-19_on_employment_income _-_advanced_estimates&stable=1.

Farazi, Subika, and Jose Ernesto Lopez-Cordova. 2022. "Financial Constraints, Firm Performance, and Policy Support during the COVID-19 Pandemic." Unpublished manuscript, World Bank, Washington, DC.

Frankel, Jeffrey, Carlos Vegh, and Guillermo Vuletin. 2013. "On Graduation from Fiscal Procyclicality." *Journal of Development Economics* 100: 32–47.

Fuchs, Alan. 2020. *Poverty and Welfare Impacts of COVID-19 and Mitigation Policies in Georgia* (English). Washington, DC: World Bank.

Fuchs, Alan, Gonzalez Icaza, Maria Fernanda, and Natsuko Kiso Nozaki. 2020. *Poverty and Welfare Impacts of COVID-19 and Mitigation*

Policies in Armenia (English). Washington, DC: World Bank.

Gansey R., M. E. Genoni, and I. Helmy. 2022. "The Role of Cash Transfers in Smoothing the Income Shock of COVID-19 in Egypt." Background paper prepared for Egypt Poverty Assessment, World Bank, Washington, DC.

Gavin, Michael, and Roberto Perotti. 1997. "Fiscal Policy in Latin America." *NBER Macroeconomics Annual* 12: 11–61.

Gechert, Sebastian, and Ansgar Rannenberg. 2018. "Which Fiscal Multipliers Are Regime-Dependent? A Meta-Regression Analysis." *Journal of Economic Surveys* 32 (4): 1160–82.

Gelb, Alan, Anurodh Giri, Anit Mukherjee, Ritesh Rautela, Mitul Thapliya, and Brian Webster. 2022. "Beyond India's Lockdown: PMGKY Benefits during the COVID-19 Crisis and State of Digital Payments." Policy Paper 257, Centre for Global Development, Washington, DC.

Gentilini, Ugo. 2022. "Cash Transfers in Pandemic Times: Evidence, Practices, and Implications from the Largest Scale Up in History." World Bank, Washington, DC.

Gentilini, Ugo, Mohamed Almenfi, Hrishikesh T. M. M. Iyengar, Yuko Okamura, John Austin Downes, Pamela Dale, Michael Weber, et al. 2022a. "Social Protection and Jobs Responses to COVID-19: A Real-Time Review of Country Measures (Living Paper, Version 16)." World Bank, Washington, DC.

Gentilini, Ugo, Mohamed Almenfi, Hrishikesh T. M. M. Iyengar, Yuko Okamura, Emilio Raul Urteaga, Giorgia Valleriani, Jimmy Vulembera Muhindo, et al. 2022b. "Tracking Global Social Protection Responses to Price Shocks: Version 1." Discussion Paper 2208, World Bank, Washington, DC.

Glauber, Joseph, and David Laborde. 2022. "Do No Harm: Measured Policy Responses Are Key to Addressing Food Security Impacts of the Ukraine Crisis." *IFPRI Blog*, April 12, 2022. https://www.ifpri.org/blog/do-no-harm-measured-policy-responses-are-key-addressing-food-security-impacts-ukraine-crisis.

Gourinchas, Pierre-Olivier, Sebnem Kalemli-Özcan, Veronika Penciakova, and Nick Sander. 2021. "Fiscal Policy in the Age of COVID: Does It Get in All of the Cracks?" Working Paper 29293, National Bureau of Economic Research, Cambridge, MA. doi:10.3386/w29293.

Han, J., B. D. Meyer, and J. X. Sullivan. 2020. "Income and Poverty in the COVID-19 Pandemic." *Brookings Papers on Economic Activity* 2020 (2): 85–118. doi:10.1353/eca.2020.0007.

Hoogeveen, Johannes G., and Gladys Lopez-Acevedo, eds. 2021. *Distributional Impacts of COVID-19 in the Middle East and North Africa Region 2021*. MENA Development Report. Washington, DC: World Bank.

IMF (International Monetary Fund). 2020a. "Policies for the Recovery." *Fiscal Monitor,* October, IMF, Washington, DC.

IMF (International Monetary Fund). 2020b. "Policies to Support People during the Pandemic." *Fiscal Monitor*, April, IMF, Washington, DC.

IMF (International Monetary Fund). 2021. "Strengthening the Credibility of Public Finances." *Fiscal Monitor,* October, IMF, Washington, DC.

Ivaschenko, Oleksiy, Jesse Doyle, Jaekyun Kim, Jonathan Sibley, and Zaineb Majoka. 2020. "Does 'Manna from Heaven' Help? The Role of Cash Transfers in Disaster Recovery—Lessons from Fiji after Tropical Cyclone Winston." *Disasters* 44 (3): 455–76.

Jara, H. Xavier, Lourdes Montesdeoca, and Iva Tasseva. 2021. "The Role of Automatic Stabilizers and Emergency Tax–Benefit Policies during the COVID-19 Pandemic in Ecuador." Working Paper 2021/4, United Nations University World Institute for Development Economics Research, Helsinki.

Kamran, Mareeha, Ingrid Mujica, María Belén Fonteñez, David Newhouse, Claudia Rodriguez Alas, and Michael Weber. 2022. "Exploring Two Years of Labor Market Policy Responses to COVID-19: A Global Effort to Protect Workers and Jobs." *Jobs Watch COVID-19 Brief*, World Bank, Washington, DC.

Kim, Yeon Soo, and Tiloka de Silva. 2021. "The COVID-19 Impact on Livelihoods and Poverty in Sri Lanka." Background note to *Sri Lanka Poverty Assessment*, World Bank, Washington, DC.

Knippenberg, Erwin, and John Hoddinott. 2019. "Shocks, Social Protection, and Resilience: Evidence from Ethiopia." Gates Open Research 3-702. https://gatesopenresearch.org/documents/3-702.

Köhler, Timothy, and Robert Hill. 2022. "Wage Subsidies and COVID-19: The Distribution and Dynamics of South Africa's TERS Policy." *Development Southern Africa*. https://doi.org/10.1080/0376835X.2022.2057927.

Kose, M. Ayhan, Sergio Kurlat, Franziska Ohnsorge, and Naotaka Sugawara. 2022. "A Cross-Country Database of Fiscal Space." *Journal of International Money and Finance* 102682.

Kraay, Aart, and Luis Serven. 2013. *Fiscal Policy as a Tool for Stabilization in Developing Countries.* Washington, DC: World Bank.

Lastunen, Jesse, Pia Rattenhuber, Kwabena Adu-Ababio, Katrin Gasior, H. Xavier Jara, Maria Jouste, David McLennan, et al. 2021. "The Mitigating Role of Tax and Benefit Rescue Packages for Poverty and Inequality in Africa amid the COVID-19 Pandemic." Working Paper 2021/148, United Nations University World Institute for Development Economics Research, Helsinki, Finland.

Lawson, Cina. 2022. "In the Trenches: Technology-Driven Development." *Finance and Development* 59 (001).

Lawson, Cina, Shegun Adjadi Bakari, and Beatriz Vasconcellos. 2021. "Togo's Digital Response to COVID-19." In *2020 State of Digital Transformation*, edited by David Eaves and Lauren Lombardo. Ash Center for Democratic Governance and Innovation, Harvard University, Cambridge, MA.

Londoño-Vélez, Juliana, and Pablo Querubin. 2022. "The Impact of Emergency Cash Assistance in a Pandemic: Experimental Evidence from Colombia." *Review of Economics and Statistics* 104 (1): 157–65.

Lustig, Nora, Valentina Martinez Pabon, Federico Sanz, and Stephen N. Younger. 2021. "The Impact of COVID-19 and Expanded Social Assistance on Inequality and Poverty in Argentina, Brazil, Colombia and Mexico." Working Paper 92, Council on Environmental Quality, Washington, DC.

Macours, Karen, Norbert Schady, and Renos Vakis. 2012. "Cash Transfers, Behavioral Changes, and Cognitive Development in Early Childhood: Evidence from a Randomized Experiment." *American Economic Journal: Applied Economics* 4 (2): 247–73.

Magalasi, Chimwemwe. 2021. "The Short-Term Distributional Impact of COVID-19 in Malawi."

Euromod Working Paper EM 07/21, University of Essex, Essex, UK.

Mansur, Aisha, Jesse Doyle, and Oleksiy Ivaschenko. 2017. "Social Protection and Humanitarian Assistance Nexus for Disaster Response: Lessons Learnt from Fiji's Tropical Cyclone Winston." Social Protection and Labor Discussion Paper 1701, World Bank, Washington, DC.

Mason, Andrew D., Maria Ana Lugo, Ugo Gentilini, Lydia Kim, Mohamed Almenfi, and Ikuko Uochi. 2020. "The Socioeconomic Impacts of COVID-19 in East Asia and the Pacific." Background paper B.4 for the October 2020 EAP Economic Update, Office of the East Asia and Pacific Chief Economist, World Bank, Washington, DC.

Menezes-Filho, Naercio, Bruno K. Komatsu, and João Pedro Rosa. 2021. "Reducing Poverty and Inequality during the Coronavirus Outbreak: The Emergency Aid Transfers in Brazil." Policy Paper 54, Institute of Education and Research (Insper), Brazil.

Nebiler, Metin, Cigdem Celik, and Javier Baez 2021. "Containment Measures and Effects on Mobility and Economic Activity." Poverty and Equity presentation: "Monitoring COVID-19 Household Welfare Effects in Turkey," World Bank, Washington, DC.

Pape, Utz, and Antonia Delius. 2021. "How COVID-19 Continues to Affect Livelihoods in Kenya: Rapid Response Phone Survey Rounds 1 to 5." Policy Note, World Bank, Washington, DC.

Pega, F., S. Z. Liu, S. Walter, R. Pabayo, R. Saith, and S. K. Lhachimi. 2017. "Unconditional Cash Transfers for Reducing Poverty and Vulnerabilities: Effect on Use of Health Services and Health Outcomes in Low- and Middle-Income Countries." *Cochrane Database of Systematic Reviews* 11 (11). doi: 10.1002/14651858.CD011135.pub2.

Pennings, Steven. 2021. "Cross-Region Transfer Multipliers in a Monetary Union: Evidence from Social Security and Stimulus Payments." *American Economic Review* 111 (5): 1689–1719.

Pople, Ashley, Ruth Hill, Stefan Dercon, and Ben Brunckhorst. 2021. "Anticipatory Cash Transfers in Climate Disaster Response." Working Paper 6, Centre for Disaster Protection, London.

Ricci, Luca Antonio, Metodij Hadzi-Vaskov, Samuel Pienknagura Loor, Jose Torres, Christopher

Evans, Chiara Fratto, Ivan Burgara, Roberto Schatan, Shakill Hassan, Romain Veyrune, Junghwan Mok, Trinidad Saavedra, and Jacobus de Hoop. 2021. "Chile: Selected Issues." Country Report No 21/84, International Monetary Fund, Washington, DC.

Romer, Christina. 2021. "The Fiscal Policy Response to the Pandemic." Brookings Paper on Economic Activity, Spring 2021, Brookings Institution, Washington, DC.

Stantcheva, Stefanie. 2022. "Inequalities in the Times of a Pandemic." Working Paper 29657, National Bureau of Economic Research, Cambridge, MA.

USDA (US Department of Agriculture). 2022. "The Ukraine Conflict and Other Factors Contributing to High Commodity Prices and Food Insecurity." https://www.fas.usda.gov/data/ukraine-conflict-and-other-factors-contributing-high-commodity-prices-and-food-insecurity.

WHO (World Health Organization). 2020. *The Impact of the COVID-19 Pandemic on Noncommunicable Disease Resources and Services: Results of a Rapid Assessment.* Geneva, Switzerland: WHO.

WHO (World Health Organization). 2021a. *Global Expenditure on Health: Public Spending on the Rise?* Geneva, Switzerland: WHO.

WHO (World Health Organization). 2021b. *Second Round of the National Pulse Survey on Continuity of Essential Health Services during the COVID-19 Pandemic, January–March 2021.* Geneva, Switzerland: WHO.

World Bank. 2020. "Russia's Economy Loses Momentum amidst COVID-19 Resurgence; Awaits Relief from Vaccine." Russia Economic Report 44, World Bank, Washington, DC. https://openknowledge.worldbank.org/handle/10986/34950.

World Bank. 2021a. *A Year Deferred—Early Experiences and Lessons from COVID-19 in Vietnam* (English). Washington, DC: World Bank.

World Bank. 2021b. "The Gradual Rise and Rapid Decline of the Middle Class in Latin America and the Caribbean." World Bank, Washington, DC. https://openknowledge.worldbank.org/handle/10986/35834.

World Bank. 2021c. "Uneven Recovery." East Asia and Pacific Economic Update (April), World Bank, Washington, DC.

World Bank. 2021d. "Welfare Impacts of the COVID-19 Pandemic in Moldova: Main Channels and Impact of Mitigation Measures." Summary Note, World Bank, Washington, DC.

World Bank. 2022a. *Brazil Poverty and Equity Assessment: Looking Ahead of Two Crises.* Washington, DC: World Bank.

World Bank. 2022b. *Collapse and Recovery: How the COVID-19 Pandemic Eroded Human Capital and What to Do about It.* Washington, DC: World Bank.

World Bank. 2022c. *Impacts of COVID-19 on Households and Firms in Six East Asian Countries.* Washington, DC: World Bank.

World Bank. 2022d. *World Development Report 2022: Finance for an Equitable Recovery.* Washington, DC: World Bank.

World Bank. Forthcoming a. *A Global Pandemic and Then a War: Effects on the Poor and Vulnerable in Latin America and the Caribbean.* Washington, DC: World Bank.

World Bank. Forthcoming b. *Costa Rica Poverty and Inclusion Assessment.* Washington, DC: World Bank.

World Bank. Forthcoming c. *Europe and Central Asia Economic Update, Fall 2022: Social Protection for Recovery.* Europe and Central Asia Economic Update 14. Washington, DC: World Bank.

World Bank. Forthcoming d. *Indonesia Poverty Assessment.* Washington, DC: World Bank.

Yang, Yi, Dillan Patel, Ruth Vargas Hill, and Michèle Plichta. 2021. "Funding COVID-19 Response: Tracking Global Humanitarian and Development Funding to Meet Crisis Needs." Working Paper 5, Centre for Disaster Protection and Development Initiatives, London.

Taxes, Transfers, and Subsidies: Improving Progressivity and Reducing the Cost to the Poor

Summary

Taxes, transfers, and subsidies are core components of fiscal policy, and their potential effect on household welfare is considerable. This chapter considers their immediate impact on the amount of money households have and the prices they face. These potential impacts are even more important during this time of fiscal consolidation, when revenues need to be raised and spending needs to be cut or redirected.

Only in recent years has the immediate impact on households of taxes, transfers, subsidies, and spending on human capital been analyzed in a consistent and relatively comprehensive manner across low- and middle-income economies, thanks to the widespread use of the Commitment to Equity tool for fiscal incidence analysis. This chapter brings together this analysis of 94 economies for the most comprehensive exploration across all regions and income levels of what has been learned.

Taken together, taxes, transfers, and subsidies reduce inequality in all economies and finance spending on security, health, education, and investments for growth and poverty reduction. However, although high-income economies effectively ensure that taxes, transfers, and subsidies do not reduce the income of poor households while they finance long-run spending, this is not the case in low- and middle-income economies. In two-thirds of low- and middle-income economies, the income of poor households is lower by the time they have paid taxes and received transfers and subsidies. This drop occurs because taxes are predominantly collected through indirect taxes, and transfers are too low to compensate. Subsidies often take up much more fiscal space than targeted transfers, but they are poorly targeted to poor households.

In each income group, some economies did more to reduce both inequality and poverty even before COVID-19; however, the pattern across income categories highlights that, although good and bad policy choices exist, it is a challenge to raise revenues without lowering the incomes of poor households when an economy has a large informal sector and limited safety net coverage. More revenues can be raised from progressive forms of taxation, even in an informal economy, but in many economies a combination of nonprogressive taxation with generous and well-targeted transfers can

Chapter 5 online annexes available at http://hdl.handle.net/10986/37739:
5A. Redistributive Impact of Old-Age Contributory Pensions; 5B. Progressivity and Regressivity of Taxes and Transfers; 5C. Tax Expenditure Assessments; and 5D. Economy-Level Results on Indirect Taxes, Direct Transfers, and Net Impacts, by Market Income Decile.

also be effective. Regardless of the tax mix, spending needs to transition from poorly targeted subsidies and tax expenditures to better-targeted transfers, although subsidies are popular and hard to remove once in place. Finally, poorer economies can take advantage of new data and technology to make both revenue generation and transfers more progressive, achieving through fiscal policy the degree of inequality and poverty reduction that today's rich economies took decades to achieve.

Introduction

Fiscal policy has many roles: generating revenues to finance the core business of government, providing public goods and services, achieving macroeconomic stabilization, helping to dampen the impact of adverse shocks, stimulating economic growth, and helping to reduce poverty and inequality.[1] The optimal balance will depend on the country context and society's preferences. This chapter focuses on the potential of one part of fiscal policy—taxes, transfers, and subsidies— to reduce poverty and inequality in the short run.

Taxes, transfers, and subsidies are key government instruments for addressing poverty and inequality. Typically ranging from 10 percent to 25 percent of gross domestic product (GDP) in developing economies, the potential effect on household welfare is considerable. In addition to long-run impacts (see chapter 6), they also have an immediate effect on the money that households have and on the prices they face. That is the focus of this chapter. However, the distributional impact of taxes and transfers varies significantly across economies. Understanding the extent to which taxes and transfers are redistributive in different regions and across income levels can help individual economies benchmark their current fiscal system and learn how it could become more progressive. Fiscal incidence analysis indicates who benefits from fiscal policy in the short run and by how much, allowing an assessment of how equalizing it is.

As countries navigate the COVID-19 crisis and seek renewed economic growth, mostly from positions of increased fiscal pressure, questions about how they can generate greater revenues without imposing a heavy burden on the poor and vulnerable, and how they should spend and invest revenues to benefit the poor, are more relevant than ever. In particular, many countries are assessing how to better provide income support in the short run in a well-targeted manner. The lessons of this chapter, although developed from an analysis of fiscal policies from before 2020, identify the options available to countries with the types of fiscal systems and economic structure they have, and will hopefully help guide policy makers toward an inclusive recovery.

It is only recently that fiscal incidence analysis has been conducted in enough low- and middle-income countries in a comparable manner so as to allow a comparative cross-country picture of the impact of taxes, transfers, and subsidies on inequality and welfare. This progress is a result of the wide use in recent years of the Commitment to Equity (CEQ) approach to fiscal incidence analysis.[2] CEQ is a diagnostic tool that helps identify how fiscal policy affects equity (see box 5.1).[3] The methodology is described in Lustig (2018) and has now been implemented in more than 80 economies, largely by the CEQ Institute and the World Bank (this chapter complements the CEQ data with separate Organisation for Economic Co-operation and Development [OECD] data to reach 94 economies in total). In March 2020, one of the main CEQ indicators, which measure how much fiscal policy reduces inequality, was adopted as Sustainable Development Goal 10.4.2, establishing a new global standard for assessing government effectiveness in tackling inequality (see Lustig, Mariotti, and Sánchez-Páramo 2020). This chapter draws on the data resulting from the implementation of the CEQ tool, allowing the most comprehensive assessment of the impact of taxes and transfers on inequality and poverty across low- and middle-income economies, building on the 29-economy study in Lustig (2018).

Data on the distributive impacts of taxes, transfers, and subsidies come from the CEQ Institute, OECD, and World Bank databases, which collectively cover 94 economies over the past decade across all income groups and regions, to varying degrees.[4] In general, the databases focus on direct household taxes and indirect taxes on consumption as well as direct transfers to households, spending on health and education, and energy and food subsidies. Agriculture subsidies are sometimes

BOX 5.1

The CEQ framework: An integrated approach to fiscal incidence analysis

The Commitment to Equity (CEQ) approach addresses how taxes and spending affect different households and how various fiscal objectives and reforms might be achieved in a progressive manner. The CEQ approach assesses household welfare before the payment of any taxes or receipt of any public spending benefits. It then applies each tax and transfer systematically to build a picture of how each fiscal instrument and the system as a whole affect monetary poverty and inequality, using the same nationally representative household surveys underpinning part 1 of this report. The framework is outlined in figure B5.1.1 (simplified from Lustig 2018; see online annex 5A for a more complete diagram including different treatments of pensions and their contributions), which shows how fiscal policy affects household income through different taxes and transfers.

Prefiscal household welfare is based on households' market income—how much they earn and receive from private transfers and remittances, as well as social security pensions. At this starting point, standard measures of welfare—such as the poverty headcount rate and the Gini index of inequality—can be estimated, serving as the baseline distributional measures before households interact with fiscal policy. Each household then receives direct transfers and pays income taxes. Households may also benefit indirectly by buying some goods or services at subsidized prices and paying taxes indirectly, because most goods and services have value added tax or goods and services tax added. Finally, they can receive in-kind benefits by sending their children to school or using public health services, for which they might pay a fee as well. The CEQ approach reassesses household welfare, because each tax or transfer is modeled to understand how poverty and inequality change with each fiscal instrument and to measure the overall impact of the fiscal system.

FIGURE B5.1.1

CEQ framework: Fiscal policy impacts on household income through taxes and transfers

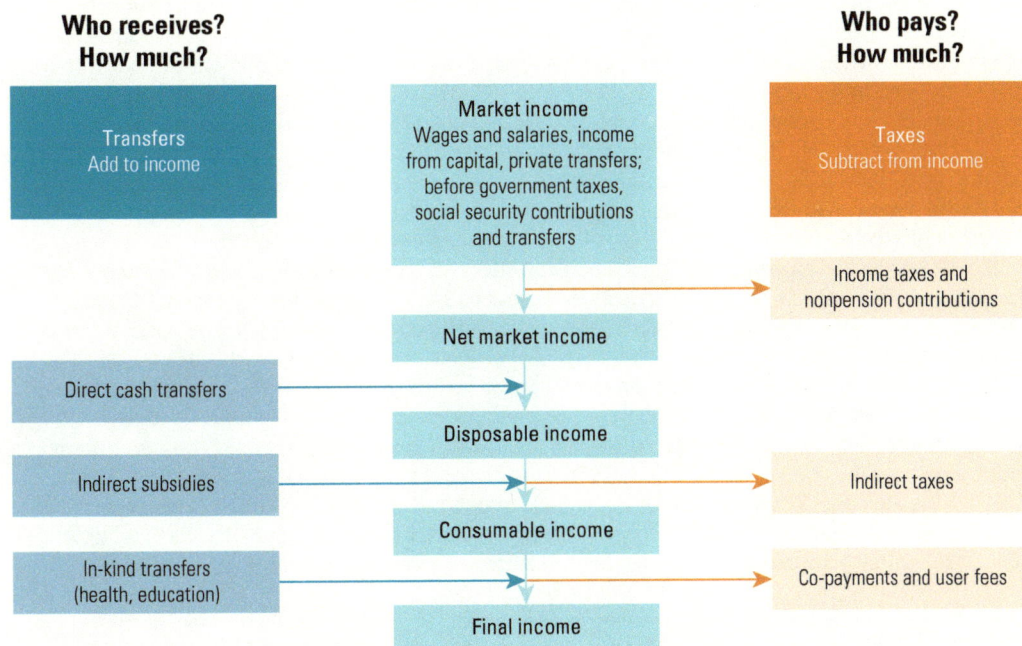

Source: World Bank, simplified from Lustig 2018.

(continued)

BOX 5.1

The CEQ framework: An integrated approach to fiscal incidence analysis *(continued)*

In economies where the household survey measures income, market income is constructed directly and is in fact the same welfare measure as that used in part 1 of this report to measure poverty. In most economies, however, surveys instead measure consumption, which is used to estimate official poverty and inequality. In this case, household consumption from the survey is equated with disposable income in figure B5.1.1. Lustig (2018) discusses how the CEQ approach varies with income and consumption surveys.

As described previously, pension income is considered part of prefiscal market income. In this approach pension contributions are treated as compulsory savings and not a direct tax. However, pensions can be treated as a government transfer instead of deferred income from previous savings. In this case a household's market income is only that from nonpension sources, and pension contributions are treated as a tax. All data in this chapter largely treat pensions as outside of the fiscal redistribution system. The difference in approach makes little difference in low-income economies but becomes particularly important for upper-middle-income economies. Online annex 5A gives a more complete account, along with a fuller discussion of why the preferred set of results treats pensions as deferred income.

The CEQ framework has two important advantages. First, it assesses both tax and expenditure policies, and examines their joint rather than individual effect. Second, it uses a standardized methodology, making it comparable across economies and time and allowing international benchmarking. However, it is also important to note what the CEQ framework does not do. It does not include behavioral effects (such as consumer substitution and labor market decisions, although it does model tax evasion and non-take-up of social benefits), general equilibrium effects (such as the multiplier effect of cash transfers on the economy and the second-round tax effects it may create), or intertemporal effects (such as the long-run benefits of public education). Nor does it cover all taxes and spending or all people. In particular, it does not generally include corporate income tax or infrastructure spending and can suffer from low coverage of the richest people, who are often underrepresented in household surveys. Typically, CEQ analyses include personal income, value added, and excise taxes—which average about 63 percent of tax revenue collected—and transfers, subsidies, and health and education spending—which average about 38 percent of expenditure (based on data from 19 CEQ analyses that report these shares).

The chapter focuses on changes between market income, disposable income, and consumable income, when the CEQ data are reasonably comprehensive. Even then, the value of revenue included is greater than the value of spending included. This difference does not reflect missing data or methodological shortcomings but rather reflects the nature of the income concepts used in the CEQ, which focuses on understanding the short-run changes in monetary measures of poverty and inequality. It does so because spending on in-kind services such as health and education (included in the CEQ) or security (not included in the CEQ), despite having an immediate impact on nonmonetary poverty, does not have an immediate impact on monetary welfare measures used in this chapter. As chapter 6 discusses, these investments have impacts on income measures in the long run, but they do not have an immediate income effect that can offset the reduction in income brought about by taxes. As a result, consumable income—used often in this chapter—includes personal income, value added, and excise taxes (9–12 percent of GDP) and spending on subsidies and transfers (typically 3–8 percent of GDP).[a] Consumable income should be on average about 4–6 percent lower than market income. The analysis examines whether changes in income are overall equalizing (reducing the Gini) and whether the poorest households are experiencing reductions in income (increasing poverty).

a. These ranges reflect the range from low-income economies to non-OECD (Organisation for Economic Co-operation and Development) high-income economies. Specifically, the revenue included as a share of GDP is 9 percent in low-income economies, 10 percent in lower-middle-income economies, 11 percent in upper-middle-income economies, and 12 percent in non-OECD high-income economies. The spending included as a share of GDP is 3 percent in low-income economies, 4 percent in lower-middle-income economies, 5 percent in upper-middle-income economies, and 8 percent in non-OECD high-income economies.

TABLE 5.1

Number of fiscal incidence studies, by region and income category

	OECD	HICs	LICs	LMICs	UMICs	Total
Advanced economies	31	—	—	—	—	**31**
East Asia and Pacific	—	—	—	2	2	**4**
South Asia	—	—	—	2	—	**2**
Europe and Central Asia	2	2	1	3	7	**15**
Latin America and the Caribbean	1	2	—	4	11	**18**
Middle East and North Africa	—	—	—	2	2	**4**
Sub-Saharan Africa	—	1	8	8	3	**20**
Total	**34**	**5**	**9**	**21**	**25**	**94**

Sources: CEQ Data Center on Fiscal Redistribution, https://commitmentoequity.org/datacenter; OECD; World Bank.
Note: OECD studies include direct taxes and transfers but not indirect taxes and subsidies or in-kind health and education spending. All other columns are CEQ studies, which represent all regions and income categories. Where both OECD and CEQ fiscal incidence data are available, OECD data are used; see endnote 6. HICs column includes all high-income countries that are not part of the OECD; HICs = high-income countries; LICs = low-income countries; LMICs = lower-middle-income countries; OECD = Organisation for Economic Co-operation and Development; UMICs = upper-middle-income countries; — = not available.

included, as are employer-paid health insurance, and individual economy reports may include childcare investments or subsidies. However, active labor market policies are excluded,[5] as are corporate income tax (CIT), infrastructure spending, and many tax incentives. Importantly, data for OECD economies include only direct taxes and transfers, not indirect taxes or subsidies. Data for the 94 economies (table 5.1) include 9 low-income countries (LICs), 21 lower-middle-income countries (LMICs), 25 upper-middle-income countries (UMICs), 5 non-OECD high-income countries (HICs), and 34 OECD HICs (for the 5 economies for which both CEQ and OECD data are available, OECD data are used[6]). In terms of regional coverage, the data include 20 Sub-Saharan Africa economies, 18 from Latin America and the Caribbean, 15 from Europe and Central Asia, 4 from East Asia and Pacific, 4 from the Middle East and North Africa, and 2 from South Asia.[7] The earliest included study is from 2009, with 40 up until 2015 and 54 since.

Tax and spending levels for a broader set of economies than for which CEQ data are available are drawn from international databases.[8] The International Centre for Tax and Development database contains tax revenues as a percentage of GDP for most economies (beyond the 94 for which there are fiscal incidence data), both in aggregate and by tax instrument. No similarly comprehensive database exists for fiscal expenditures; this chapter has constructed new data aggregates from the World Bank BOOST database and the International Monetary Fund Government Finance Statistics database (which cover 129 economies between them). Additional data on agriculture subsidy spending come from the IO Consortium Database (79 economies), on energy subsidy spending from the International Institute for Sustainable Development (154 economies), and on tax expenditures from the Global Tax Expenditures Database.[9]

The impact of taxes and transfers on short-term poverty and inequality

Taxes and spending reduce inequality in all economies but less in low-income than in high-income economies

This section looks at how household welfare changes across economies when different taxes and transfers (including subsidies) are accounted for. In particular, inequality has been estimated for three different concepts of income: market income (before any fiscal policy), disposable income (after direct taxes and transfers), and consumable income (disposable income after indirect taxes and subsidies as well). The change in inequality between these different income concepts quantifies the distributional impact of taxes and transfers, both in aggregate and by different instrument types. A similar exercise was conducted for poverty. This section also looks at how the inequality picture changes once spending on education and health is included, but the incidence of education and health spending is addressed more fully in chapter 6.

Before turning to the findings, there are two important points to bear in mind about the focus of the analysis. First, this chapter focuses on the short-run impact of taxes, transfers, and subsidies on inequality and poverty. It does not explore the role of fiscal policy and other policies in addressing the factors that cause inequality, such as active labor market policies, directed technological change, competition, and corporate governance policies (see, for example, Atkinson 2016). Second, the degree to which taxes, transfers, and subsidies reduce inequality will in part be a function of prefiscal income inequality. For example, the analysis presented in this chapter shows that South Africa achieves the greatest absolute reduction in inequality through taxes and transfers, but it also has the highest levels of inequality before taxes and transfers. Taxes and transfers do a lot to reduce inequality there, but inequality remains high. Taxes and transfers in the Kyrgyz Republic do relatively little to reduce inequality, but the level of inequality before taxes and transfers is lower than in many other economies analyzed.

All economies achieve at least some redistribution through taxes and transfers, but the extent varies significantly, both between different income levels and particularly within them. Figure 5.1, panel a, provides a comprehensive international snapshot of the distributional effects of taxes, transfers, and subsidies.[10] Whereas the rest of the chapter presents patterns aggregated to income levels (LIC, LMIC, UMIC, HIC, and OECD), this figure highlights the variation of outcomes across economies. A key feature to note is that, in addition to obvious differences between country income categories, considerable variation also occurs within income categories: they have different starting levels of inequality, they achieve different levels of fiscal redistribution, and they end up at different postfiscal levels of inequality. For example, prefiscal (market) inequality spans 17 points for LICs, from 32 to 49; 36 points for LMICs (23 to 59); 45 points for UMICs (29 to 74); and 18 points for HICs (38 to 56). Similar within-income category ranges occur in final income inequality: 15 points for LICs (32 to 47), 28 points for LMICs (22 to 51), 32 points for UMICs (23 to 55), and 14 points for HICs (29 to 43). The consequent degree of fiscal redistribution varies by income group, ranging from 0 points to 4 points in LICs, from 1 point to 14 points in LMICs, from 3 points to 19 points in UMICs, and from 7 points to 13 points in HICs.

Nonetheless, key patterns emerge across income groups. First, taxes, transfers, and subsidies in richer economies reduce inequality to a greater extent than in poorer ones. Despite the wide variation in both starting inequality and degree of fiscal redistribution that exists within each income category, there are some important regularities (figure 5.1, panel b):

- *Prefiscal inequality is relatively low for LICs, higher for LMICs and UMICs, then lower for HICs.* The average Gini before taxes and transfers in LICs is relatively low (36 points), increases for LMICs (42) and UMICs (48), and falls back for HICs (40 in non-OECD and 41 in OECD). This result resembles the famous Kuznets curve, in which inequality has an inverse U-shaped relationship with income, rising and then falling as economies get richer.

- *Average redistribution increases with income.* OECD economies do the most redistribution through taxes and transfers (12 points);[11] HICs redistribute more in through taxes and transfers (4.5 points) and through health and education spending noncash (4.8 points) than UMICs (3.9 points and 4.4 points), which do more than LMICs (3.3 points and 2.4 points), and LICs (0.7 point and 2.4 points).

- *Direct taxes and transfers always reduce inequality.* Direct taxes and transfers are the main channel for redistribution in HICs and OECD economies.

- *Health and education spending also reduce inequality in all economies.* In-kind spending is the most important source of redistribution in developing economies (data are not available for OECD economies).

- *Indirect taxes and subsidies have a more mixed redistributive impact.* Taken together, they are modestly redistributive in UMICs (0.5-point decrease) and LMICs (0.8-point decrease), neutral in LICs, and regressive in HICs (1.1-point increase).

FIGURE 5.1

Taxes, transfers, and subsidies reduce inequality in all economies, but in different ways, from different starting positions, and to different degrees

a. By economy

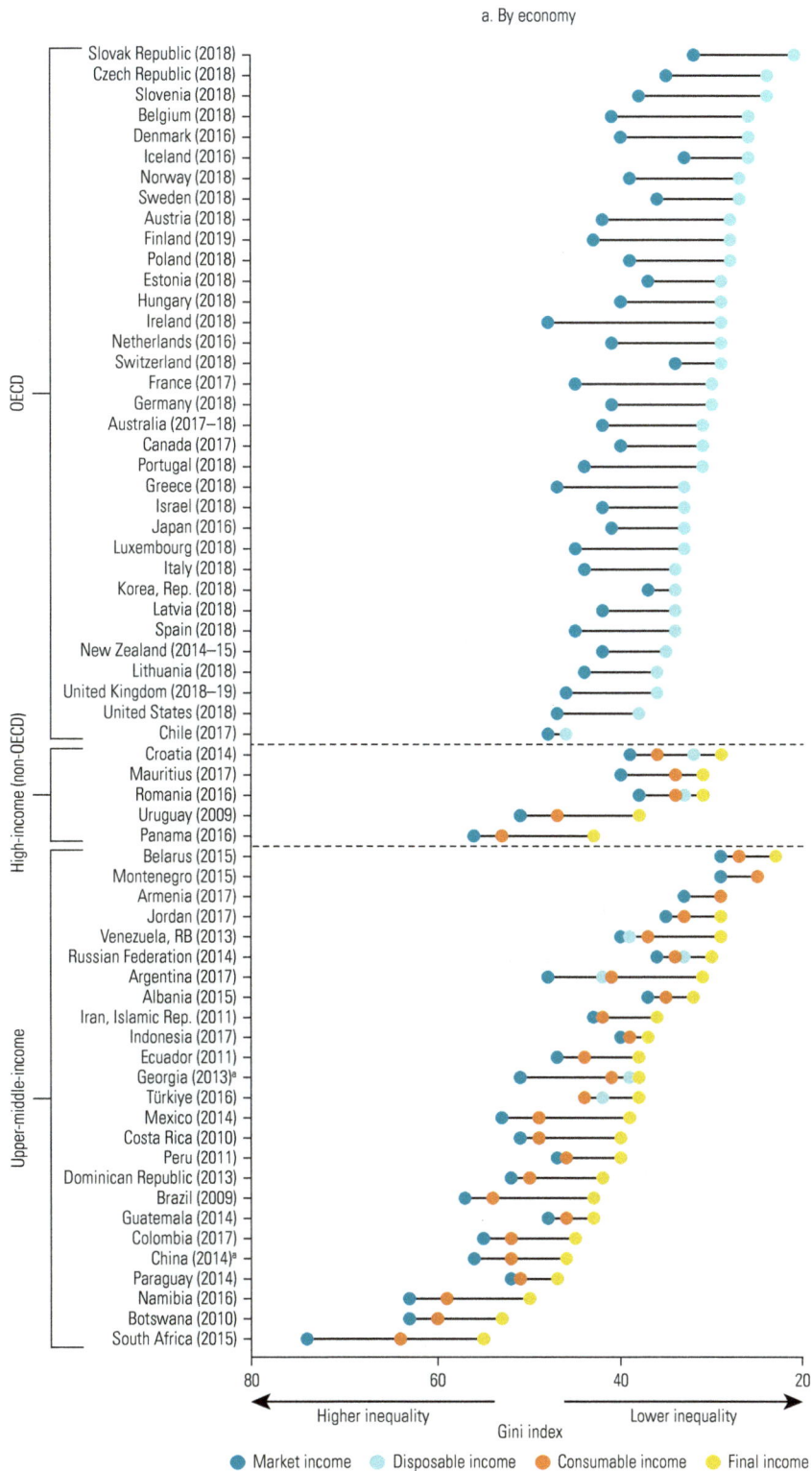

Market income   Disposable income   Consumable income   Final income

(continued)

157

FIGURE 5.1

Taxes, transfers, and subsidies reduce inequality in all economies, but in different ways, from different starting positions, and to different degrees *(continued)*

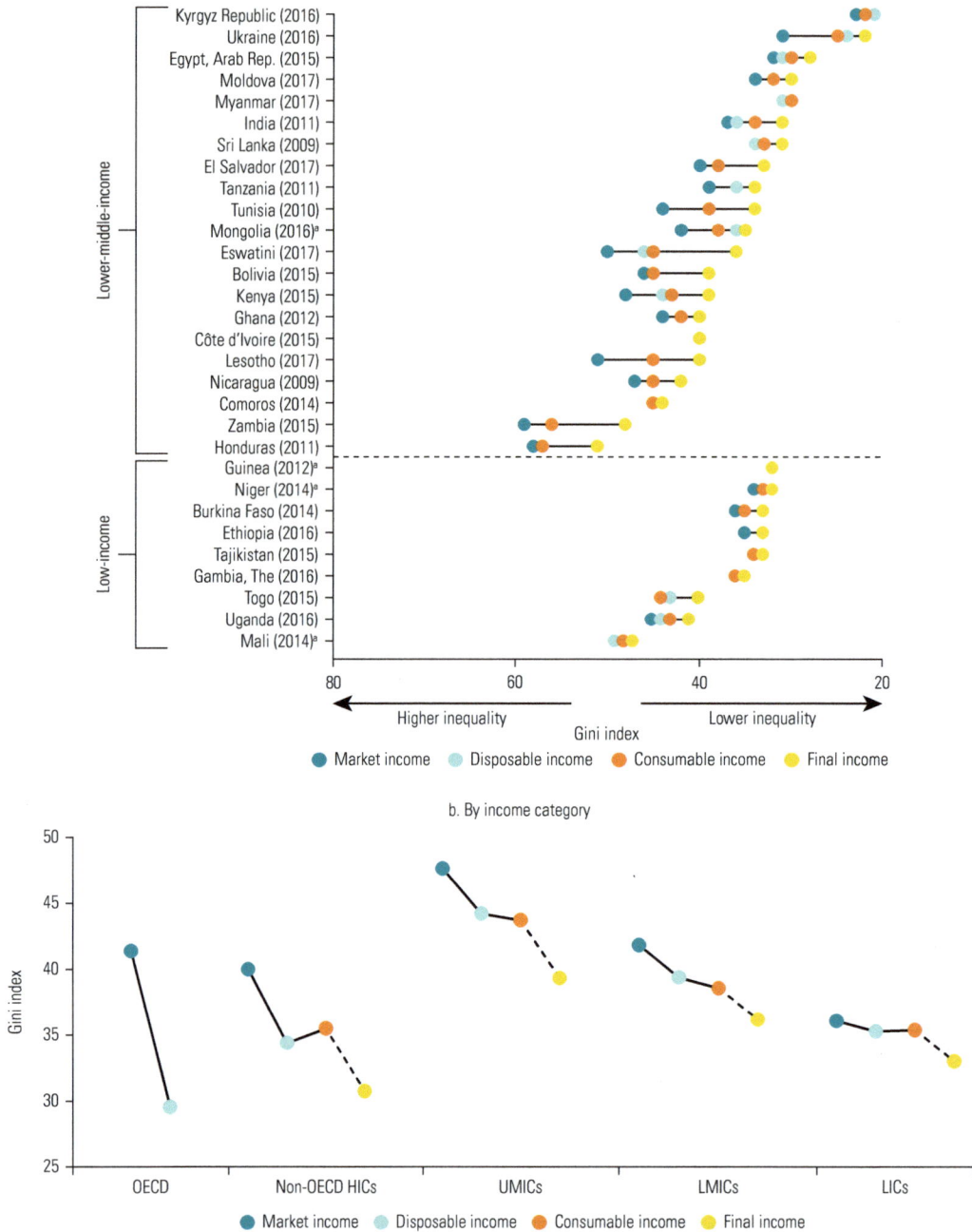

Sources: Original estimates based on data from CEQ Institute, CEQ Data Center on Fiscal Redistribution, https://commitmentoequity.org /datacenter; OECD data; World Bank data.

Note: Panel a shows the Gini index in each economy at market income, disposable income (with direct taxes and transfers), consumable income (with indirect taxes and subsidies), and final income (with health and education spending). Panel b shows the same measures aggregated by income group. OECD countries form a separate group and have data for market and disposable income only. HICs = high-income countries; LICs = low-income countries; LMICs = lower-middle-income countries; OECD = Organisation for Economic Co-operation and Development; UMICs = upper-middle-income countries. In this figure, economies are categorized using the 2020-21 income categorization.

a. Pensions treated as government transfers.

Taken together, taxes, transfers, and subsidies reduce the income of poor households in most low- and lower-middle-income economies

The second key pattern is that fiscal policy can leave poor households with lower incomes in the short term, even though revenues might be used to finance goods and services that reduce the poverty of these households in the long term—such as through spending on education and infrastructure. In the short term, households pay taxes and benefit in cash terms from direct transfers and subsidized goods and services. They also benefit from in-kind benefits from spending on health, education, and infrastructure (panel b of figure 5.1 shows health and education spending often benefits poorer households). However, because households do not receive health, education, infrastructure, and other services in cash, they do not increase their monetary incomes today. Consequently, it is possible for fiscal policy to reduce poverty in the long run through investments in human capital accumulation and from the benefits of infrastructure spending while leaving households poorer today. That is, households can have lower real incomes in the short term after paying taxes, and receiving transfers and subsidies. Even when such payments to and from the state do reduce the incomes of poor households, they may still reduce inequality. Inequality decreases if richer households pay proportionally more tax than poorer households relative to what they receive in cash benefits.

Indeed, although taxes, transfers, and subsidies reduce inequality in all economies to some extent, they lower incomes for the poor in the short term in most developing economies.[12] HICs reduce short-term poverty by 2 points on average (figure 5.2, panel b), mostly through direct transfers; indirect taxes reverse some of the gains and, in the case of Romania, increase poverty (figure 5.2, panel a). For all other income categories, poorer households are worse off on average in cash terms after taxes, transfers, and subsidies, and consequently poverty increases in the short-term. Moreover, even in countries where poverty is reduced, some households still are poorer because of payments to and from the state.[13]

What drives this result? In the majority of UMICs (14 of 23) and LMICs (14 of 17), the burden of indirect taxes generally offsets the benefit of direct transfers and subsidies in low-income deciles, and poverty increases slightly (by 0.1 point in UMICs and 1.6 points in LMICs).[14] In LICs, direct transfers are so small that the combined effect is to increase short-term poverty in almost all economies, by 1.2 points on average (although the extent of the impact will depend on how informal consumption is treated; see later discussion).

Thus, taxes, transfers, and subsidies can both reduce inequality today and finance spending while also placing a short-term burden on currently poorer households. This effect can be seen by comparing consumable income (income after taxes, transfers, and subsidies) to market income for each decile. Figure 5.3 shows the median of this ratio by decile for HICs, UMICs, LMICs, and LICs. On average, HICs and UMICs leave the poorest three deciles with more cash in hand than before taxes and cash benefits. Similarly, the poorest decile in LMICs ends up with more cash than its prefiscal income, but the second decile and above have less income after paying taxes and receiving transfers and subsidies. All deciles in LICs have less consumable income than market income. Although figure 5.3 shows a stark contrast across income categories, in most income categories some economies leave the poorest deciles with more consumable income than market income through the design of their tax, transfer, and subsidy systems. Uruguay (HIC) and Bolivia (LMIC) do so, and Ethiopia (LIC) finances long-term public investments while minimizing the impact on poverty; these countries are discussed further below.[15] The next section looks at the role that individual taxes and transfers play in shaping these outcomes.

FIGURE 5.2

Taxes, transfers, and subsidies increase short-term poverty in a majority of non-HICs

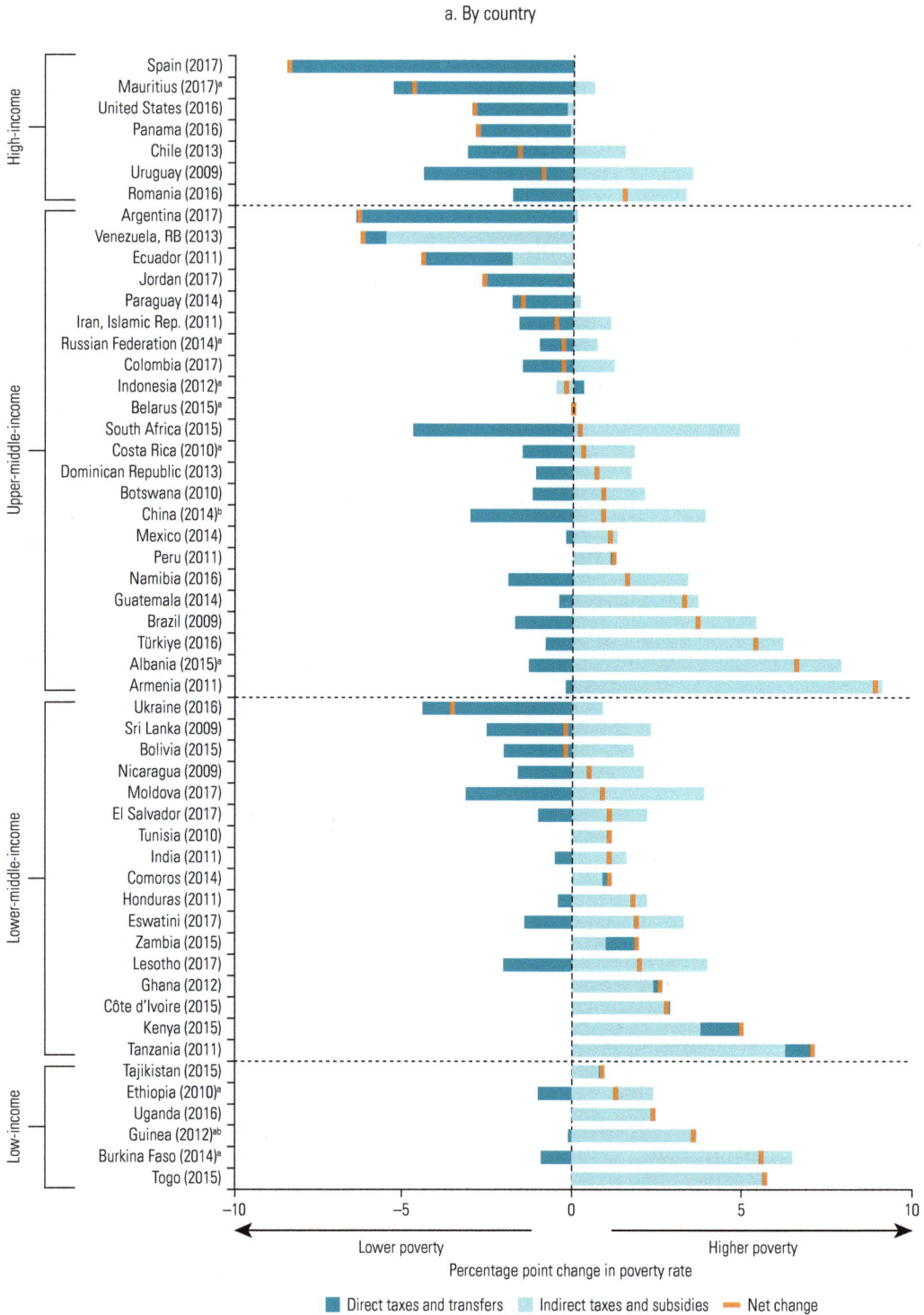

a. By country

High-income
- Spain (2017)
- Mauritius (2017)[a]
- United States (2016)
- Panama (2016)
- Chile (2013)
- Uruguay (2009)
- Romania (2016)

Upper-middle-income
- Argentina (2017)
- Venezuela, RB (2013)
- Ecuador (2011)
- Jordan (2017)
- Paraguay (2014)
- Iran, Islamic Rep. (2011)
- Russian Federation (2014)[a]
- Colombia (2017)
- Indonesia (2012)[a]
- Belarus (2015)[a]
- South Africa (2015)
- Costa Rica (2010)[a]
- Dominican Republic (2013)
- Botswana (2010)
- China (2014)[b]
- Mexico (2014)
- Peru (2011)
- Namibia (2016)
- Guatemala (2014)
- Brazil (2009)
- Türkiye (2016)
- Albania (2015)[a]
- Armenia (2011)

Lower-middle-income
- Ukraine (2016)
- Sri Lanka (2009)
- Bolivia (2015)
- Nicaragua (2009)
- Moldova (2017)
- El Salvador (2017)
- Tunisia (2010)
- India (2011)
- Comoros (2014)
- Honduras (2011)
- Eswatini (2017)
- Zambia (2015)
- Lesotho (2017)
- Ghana (2012)
- Côte d'Ivoire (2015)
- Kenya (2015)
- Tanzania (2011)

Low-income
- Tajikistan (2015)
- Ethiopia (2010)[a]
- Uganda (2016)
- Guinea (2012)[ab]
- Burkina Faso (2014)[a]
- Togo (2015)

x-axis: −10, −5, 0, 5, 10

← Lower poverty   Higher poverty →

Percentage point change in poverty rate

Legend:
- Direct taxes and transfers
- Indirect taxes and subsidies
- Net change

(continued)

160

FIGURE 5.2

Taxes, transfers, and subsidies increase short-term poverty in a majority of non-HICs
(continued)

b. By income category

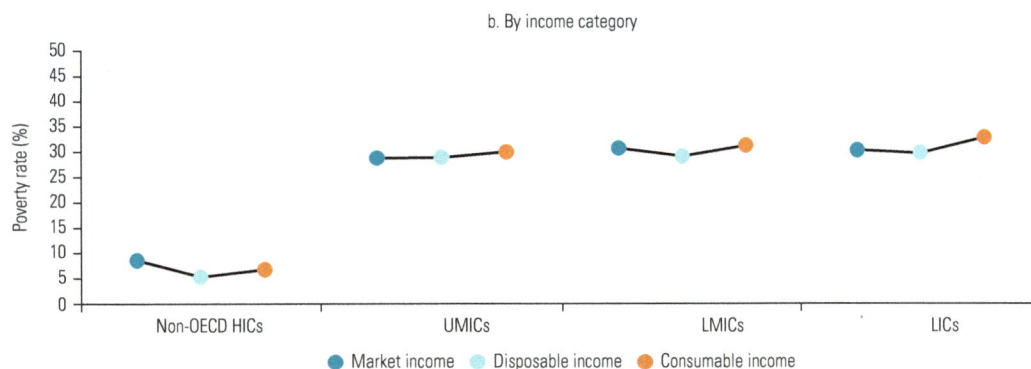

● Market income   ● Disposable income   ● Consumable income

Sources: Original estimates based on data from CEQ Institute, CEQ Data Center on Fiscal Redistribution, https://commitmentoequity.org /datacenter; OECD data; World Bank data.
Note: Panel a shows the percentage point change in poverty rate in each economy due to direct taxes on income and transfers to households, indirect taxes (such as value added tax) and subsidies that change the prices people face, and the net change due to both. Panel b shows the poverty rate at (prefiscal) market income, disposable income (adding direct taxes and transfers), and consumable income (adding indirect taxes and subsidies), aggregated by income group using the median. The income group's relevant international poverty line is used (in 2011 PPP, US$1.90 a day for LICs, US$3.20 a day for LMICs, US$5.50 a day for UMICs and non-OECD HICs). HICs = high-income countries; LICs = low-income countries; LMICs = lower-middle-income countries; OECD = Organisation for Economic Co-operation and Development; PPP = purchasing power parity; UMICs = upper-middle-income countries. In this figure, economies are categorized using the 2020-21 income categorization.
a. Poverty measured with 2005 PPP poverty lines.
b. Pensions treated as government transfers.

FIGURE 5.3

Taxes, transfers, and subsidies increase consumable income for the poorest households at all income levels except LICs

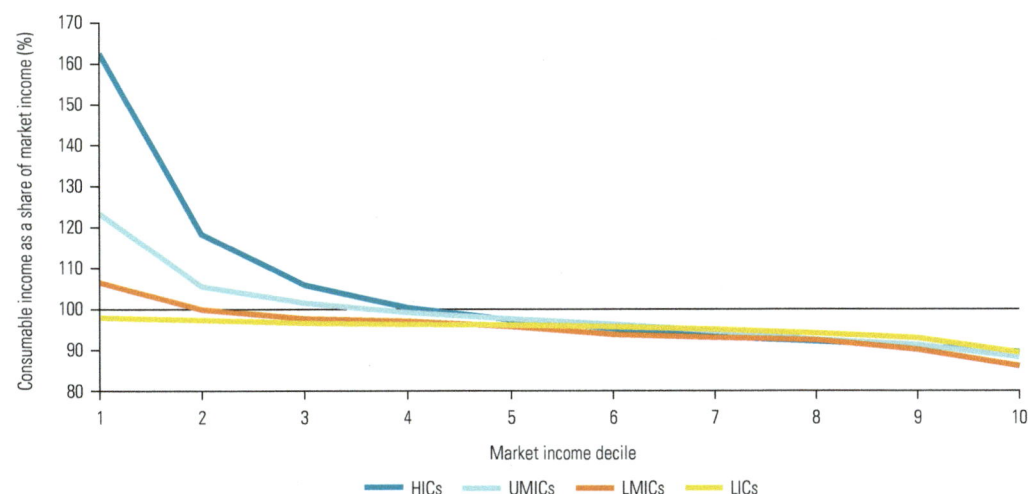

━━ HICs   ━━ UMICs   ━━ LMICs   ━━ LICs

Sources: Original estimates based on data from CEQ Institute, CEQ Data Center on Fiscal Redistribution, https://commitmentoequity.org /datacenter; Organisation for Economic Co-operation and Development data; World Bank data.
Note: The figure shows consumable income (income after direct and indirect taxes have been paid and cash transfers and subsidies have been received) as a percentage of market income (income before any taxes have been paid or transfers or subsidies received) by market income decile, aggregated by income group using the median. The sample includes 5 HICs, 19 UMICs, 16 LMICs, and 3 LICs. HICs = high-income countries; LICs = low-income countries; LMICs = lower-middle-income countries; UMICs = upper-middle-income countries.

Taxation and distribution

Richer economies collect most revenue from direct taxes; poorer economies rely on indirect taxes

As countries get richer, they collect more in tax revenues and the tax mix changes to include a greater share of direct taxation, such as personal income tax (PIT). On average UMICs and HICs collect 20 percent of GDP in taxes, and LICs just 12 percent, compared with 33 percent for OECD economies. Which specific taxes drive this gap in revenue collection? Figure 5.4 breaks down total revenue by type of tax (see box 5.2); it also shows nontax revenues and grants although they are excluded from CEQ analyses. Indirect taxes collect similar amounts across development stages, about 7–10 percent of GDP. Poorer economies rely a little more on international trade taxes and a little less on value added tax (VAT) and excise taxes. The key difference in tax revenues arises from direct taxation, equivalent to 5–7 percent of GDP in LICs and LMICs and 10–11 percent in UMICs and HICs, compared with 23 percent in OECD economies. Within direct taxes, CIT is relatively constant, at 2–3 percent of GDP, with the main increase in direct taxation for OECD economies coming from PIT, payroll taxes, and social security contributions, which represent 7.5 percent or less of GDP in non-OECD economies but 19 percent in OECD economies. Property taxes are salient only in OECD economies but, even there, are still relatively small.

Low- and middle-income economies rely relatively more on indirect taxation and, as a consequence, have a lower redistributive impact from taxes than OECD economies do (pre- and posttax incomes are more even). Direct taxes, generally paid more by richer households, play a limited distributional role in non-OECD economies; they represent less revenue, are constrained by high degrees of informality and self-employment, exclude many households in the upper half of the income distribution because of high tax exemption thresholds, and are constrained by

---

FIGURE 5.4

Developing economies rely on indirect taxes for a majority of revenues; as economies get richer, they collect more through direct taxes, the main source of OECD revenues

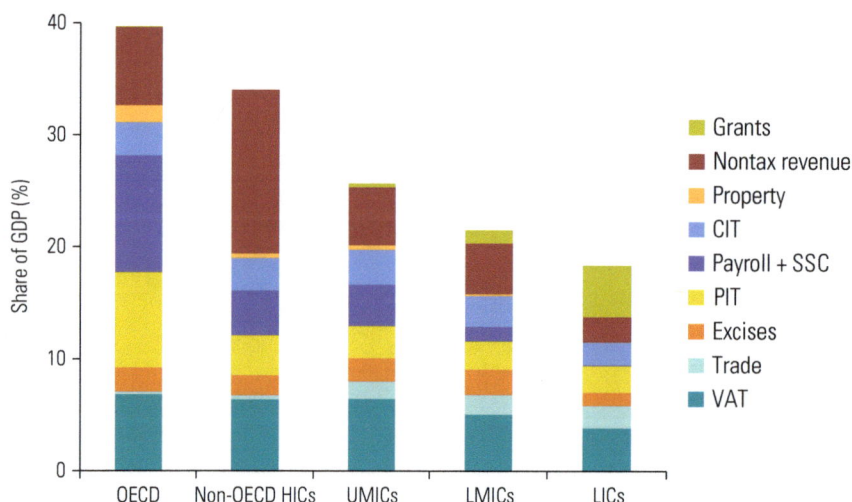

Source: International Centre for Tax and Development.

Note: The figure shows the composition of government revenue as a percentage of GDP, aggregated by income group. OECD countries form a separate group. Data by revenue type are from 2020 when available or the most recent available year back to 2015. The sample includes 155 economies. CIT = corporate income tax; GDP = gross domestic product; HICs = high-income countries; LICs = low-income countries; LMICs = lower-middle-income countries; OECD = Organisation for Economic Co-operation and Development; PIT = personal income tax; SSC = social security contribution; UMICs = upper-middle-income countries; VAT = value added tax.

BOX 5.2

Different types of tax instruments

Tax instruments are typically separated into two main categories: *direct taxes*—imposed on income, profits, and wealth—and *indirect taxes*—levied on the purchase of goods and services.

Direct taxes are paid straight to the government by economic agents (individuals and firms). The main direct taxes are personal income tax, corporate income tax, and property tax. These taxes are levied on individual income (salary, capital income such as dividends or rental income, and capital gains), the profits of corporations, the estimated value of property, and, in a few countries, total wealth. Social security contributions and payroll taxes are often considered direct taxes because they are also proportional to income, but typically their revenue serves a different purpose: it funds social insurance programs, such as unemployment benefits, health insurance, and, in some countries, pensions. As such, social security contributions often more resemble insurance premium payments or deferred income savings.

Indirect taxes are collected by a third party during a transaction. The main indirect taxes are sales tax and value added tax (VAT), excise tax on the production of specific goods (for example, alcohol or tobacco), and trade tax on imports and exports. Indirect taxes are considered easier to administer than direct taxes because they are remitted at limited points of collection and by fewer economic agents (for example, main ports for trade tax and large retailers for sales tax or VAT). The main indirect tax in most countries is VAT. Unlike sales tax, which only the firm selling to the final consumer remits to the government, VAT is levied at each stage of the supply chain, from initial production of inputs to final point of sale. Each agent in the value chain remits the VAT on its sales, but only after netting off the VAT it has paid on its own inputs, meaning that one party to each transaction has an incentive to report it, improving compliance.

tax administrative capacity. The more prevalent indirect taxes are also paid by poorer households (potentially at lower effective rates because of informality, as discussed later), for which they can represent a significant share of income. To alleviate the tax burden of indirect taxes on poor households, many economies apply exemptions and reduced rates to food and other staples commonly consumed by the poor; however, these exemptions tend to benefit richer households even more in absolute terms and to reduce tax collection. Thus, reliance on indirect taxation to raise revenues in developing economies can be a significant burden on poorer households unless the revenue is recycled back into progressive spending.

Direct taxes are progressive

Direct taxes are progressive—that is, for richer households payments represent more of their income than for poorer households. Figure 5.5, panel a, looks at direct taxes paid by each decile as a percentage of its market income (that is, an incidence curve), whereas panel c looks at them as a percentage of total taxes paid (that is, concentration shares). These two charts and concepts, explained in box 5.3, are referenced throughout this chapter. For example, in OECD economies, households in decile 1 (the poorest 10 percent of people) pay 6 percent of their market income in direct taxes, whereas households in decile 10 (the richest 10 percent of people) pay 28 percent. The steep incidence curve here indicates that direct taxes in OECD economies are progressive, because richer households pay a greater proportion of their income. As the concentration shares show, decile 10 pays about 41 percent of all direct taxes in OECD economies, and decile 1 pays less than 1 percent.

As economies become richer, the direct tax base expands, allowing for greater revenue collection from progressive tax instruments. The incidence curve slopes upward for all income levels—richer households pay a greater share of their income in direct taxes in all economies (figure 5.5, panel a). The breadth and depth of direct taxes change, however, as economies grow wealthier. In LICs, usually only the richest decile pays direct taxes and, even then, only an average of 5 percent of income. As income grows in an economy, more household deciles start paying direct taxes and the average taxes paid as a share of income rise, indicating a broadening of the tax base (a greater number of people from across the distribution are paying some income tax rather than revenues' relying on just a few). The largest difference is for OECD economies, where the poorest decile pays about 6 percent of income in direct taxes—a higher level than all but the richest decile in UMICs—whereas the rest of the distribution pays significantly more in direct taxes than anyone in non-HIC countries. The height of the incidence curve above the horizontal axis shows that much more revenue is collected in direct taxation compared with developing economies. This broad direct tax base is also reflected in the concentration curves (figure 5.5, panel c). Again, all curves slope upward, indicating progressivity with respect to share of total tax—that is, richer households pay more. With the tax base broadening as economies get richer, however, poorer deciles start to pay some tax and the burden does not rest as heavily on the

---

FIGURE 5.5

Direct taxes collect a higher percentage of income from richer households, but indirect taxes collect more relative to incomes from poorer households

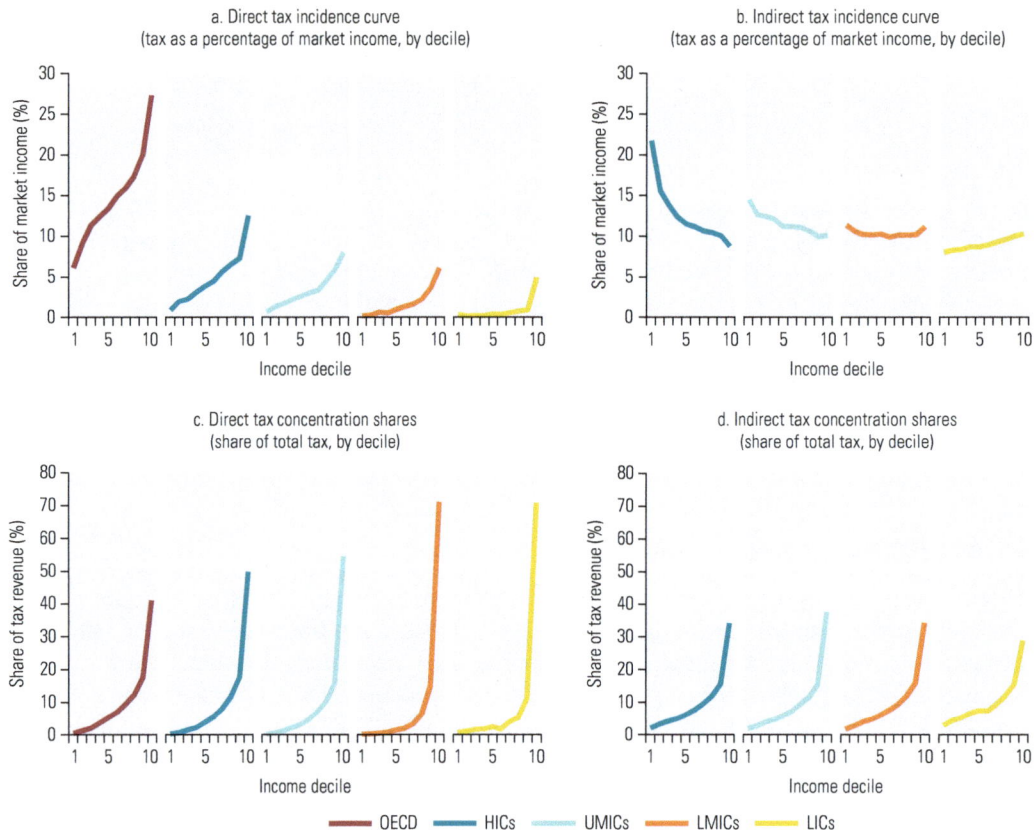

a. Direct tax incidence curve
(tax as a percentage of market income, by decile)

b. Indirect tax incidence curve
(tax as a percentage of market income, by decile)

c. Direct tax concentration shares
(share of total tax, by decile)

d. Indirect tax concentration shares
(share of total tax, by decile)

OECD   HICs   UMICs   LMICs   LICs

Sources: Sosa and Wai-Poi, forthcoming, based on data from CEQ Institute, CEQ Data Center on Fiscal Redistribution, https://commitmentoequity.org/datacenter; OECD data; World Bank data.

Note: The figure shows direct and indirect tax incidence curves and concentration shares, aggregated by income group. Incidence curves show tax as a percentage of market income by market income decile. Concentration shares show tax as a percentage of total tax revenue by market income decile. Indirect tax incidence is not available for OECD countries. HICs = high-income countries; LICs = low-income countries; LMICs = lower-middle-income countries; OECD = Organisation for Economic Co-operation and Development; UMICs = upper-middle-income countries.

richest households. In these economies, direct taxation is still progressive, but the broader base can finance higher levels of public goods and transfers.

Direct taxes are paid only by formal workers, further reducing the progressivity of income taxes in LICs. The de jure level of PIT liable on income above the exemption thresholds is not always paid in developing economies, especially by self-employed individuals, for whom income is difficult to observe and is not withheld at the source as is done by larger corporations (Kleven et al. 2011). The difficulties in taxing self-employment income have led economies to set the tax eligibility threshold such that the share of self-employed above it is low, with salaried workers representing at least 80 percent of the workforce above this level (Jensen 2022). As income grows in an economy, structural change moves workers out of agriculture and informal employment, and into larger manufacturing or service firms; such movement increases the share of salaried workers, which in turn allows countries to reduce their PIT thresholds and cover a broader share of the population. This pattern is observed consistently across time and economies. Thus, although PIT covers at least half of HIC populations, it covers 20 percent or less in UMICs and often less than 10 percent in LMICs and LICs, partly explaining why PIT collects so little revenue in these economies (and thus is much less equalizing than in HICs and OECD economies). Most CEQ studies assume that self-employed individuals do not pay PIT, so in effect noncollection from the 15–20 percent of the self-employed with income higher than the exemption threshold is included in progressivity estimates. However, capital income from rents or interest is also often not declared, nor is income from professional partnerships. These sources of income are often

BOX 5.3

Incidence curves, concentration shares, and fiscal progressivity

The *incidence* of a particular tax or transfer is its share of a household's market income. A transfer that represents a greater percent of income for poorer households than for richer households (or a tax that represents a greater percent of income for richer households) is progressive *with respect to income*. Figure B5.3.1 shows stylized examples of progressive, neutral, and regressive incidence curves—first for a transfer, subsidy, or other benefit received by households and second for a tax paid.

The *concentration share* of a particular tax or transfer is how much of the total tax is paid or how much of the total benefit is received by a household. A transfer in which more goes to poorer households in absolute terms (that is, of the total budget) than to richer households is progressive *with respect to the share of benefits*. Any transfer in which poorer households receive a share that is higher than their share of pretransfer incomes will be equalizing. That is, the posttransfer income distribution will be more equal than the pretransfer income distribution (even if the share of the transfer to the poor is less than the share to the rich). If the poor receive a greater share of benefits than the rich, such a transfer will be not only equalizing but also pro-poor: the per capita transfer falls with income. For a tax to reduce inequality, not only must the rich pay a greater share of it but they must also pay a greater share than they already enjoy of total household income. This condition may seem counterintuitive, but consider an example in which A earns $10 and B earns $90. A pays $5 in tax, whereas B pays $10. B is paying a greater share of total tax revenue collected (67 percent); however, because she has an even greater share of income (90 percent), the tax increases inequality: the posttax incomes are $5 and $80, and B now has 94 percent of total income!

Figure B5.3.2 shows two examples of taxes of which richer households pay a greater share: one tax reduces inequality because the share paid by the rich is greater than their share of total income, and the other increases inequality because, even though the rich pay a greater share of the tax, it is less than their share of income, meaning their posttax income share goes up. Note that the concentration shares add up to 100 percent.

(continued)

Incidence curves, concentration shares, and fiscal progressivity *(continued)*

Progressive, neutral, and regressive incidence curves

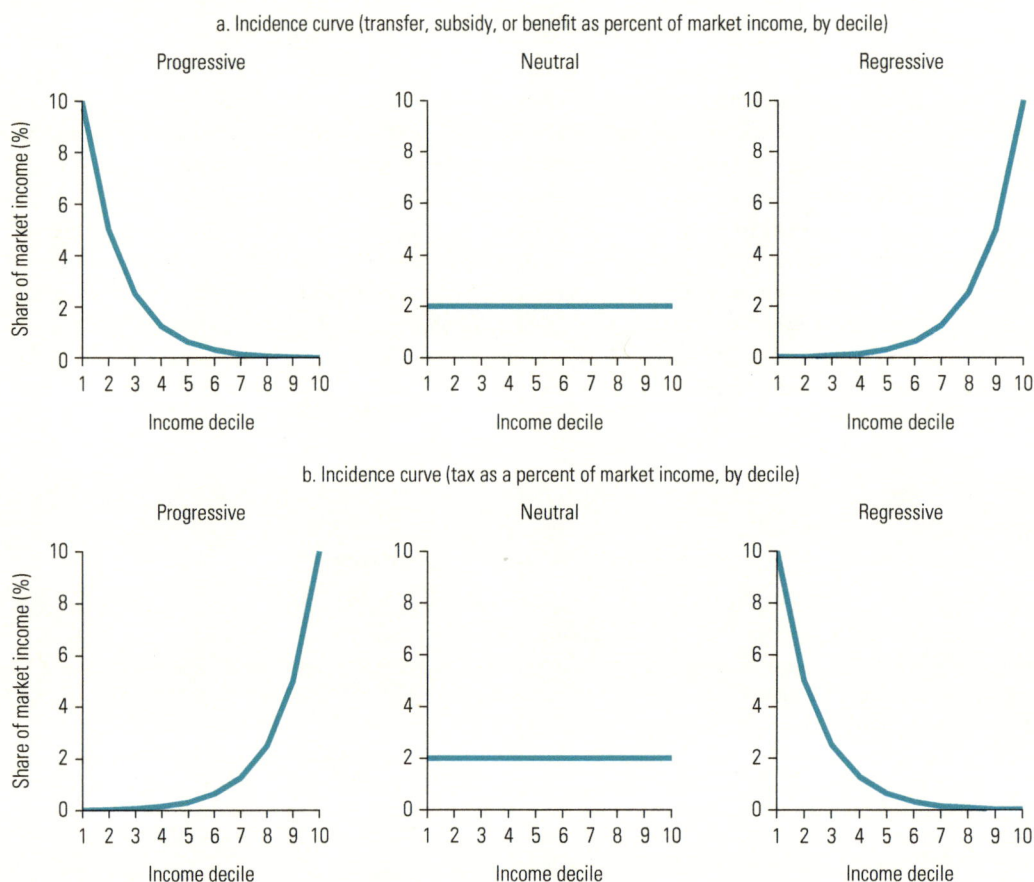

a. Incidence curve (transfer, subsidy, or benefit as percent of market income, by decile)

b. Incidence curve (tax as a percent of market income, by decile)

Source: World Bank.

It is possible for an instrument to have a regressive concentration but progressive incidence, as is often the case with fuel subsidies. Richer households consume much more fuel (and therefore a greater share of the total subsidy) than poorer households, but the meager benefits to the poor represent a greater share of their even more meager incomes. It is also possible for an instrument to have a progressive concentration but regressive incidence, as is often the case with indirect taxes such as value added tax. Richer households pay a greater share of the total tax because they consume more, but poorer households pay more relative to their income (and poor incomes are closer to consumption than rich incomes). In fact, indirect taxes and subsidies can be seen as mirror images of each other.

A more exact way to both represent progressivity/regressivity and quantify it is with Lorenz curves of income and concentration curves (not shares) of a tax or transfer (see online annex 5B).

(continued)

BOX 5.3

Incidence curves, concentration shares, and fiscal progressivity *(continued)*

FIGURE B5.3.2

Inequality-reducing and inequality-increasing concentration shares

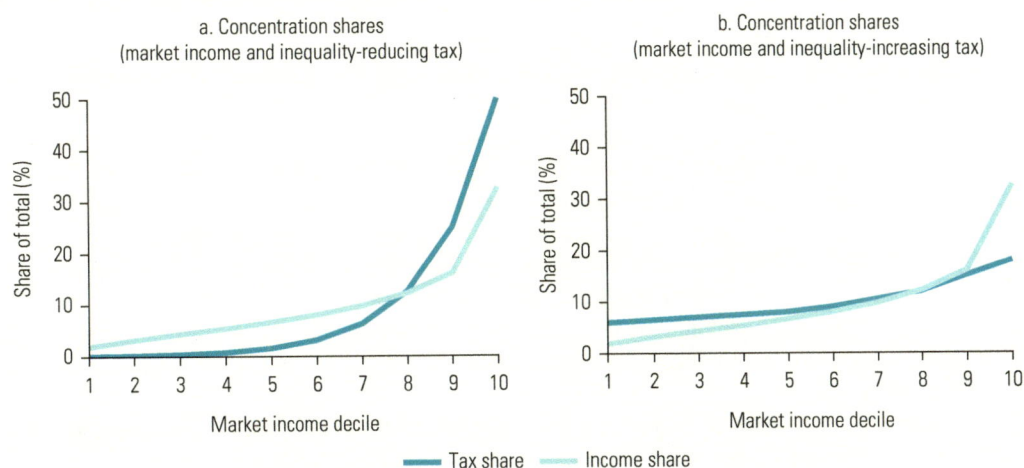

a. Concentration shares
(market income and inequality-reducing tax)

b. Concentration shares
(market income and inequality-increasing tax)

—— Tax share —— Income share

Source: World Bank.

counted as taxed in CEQ analysis; because this income is earned by richer households, CEQ data may overstate PIT progressivity.

Given that household surveys often miss the richest households, however, what are the implications for the incidence of PIT if surveys could better capture the top of the income distribution?[16] Our best guess is that, if the richest households were accurately represented in household surveys,[17] PIT incidence would be measured as more progressive than currently estimated. In all countries, PIT tends to be quite concentrated, with a small number of rich taxpayers paying a large share of total taxes; to the extent that these households are not included, the PIT incidence and concentration curves can be underestimated at the top. A few studies have tried to evaluate the extent of missed income by merging survey data with administrative data from tax returns.[18] Using one of the available methods to correct misreporting of top incomes, Blanchet, Flores, and Morgan (2022) discuss how these two types of data sets can be merged and illustrate this method with data from a few economies. For example, the share of pre-tax national income going to the richest 1 percent of households in Chile increases 3 percentage points from the share reported in the survey data once tax administrative data are included; this adjustment increases the Gini index by 5 points. In Brazil, the top 1 percent's share increases from 10 percent to 24 percent and the Gini index from 51 points to 62 points. Missing top incomes is not an issue specific to the CEQ and OECD data on fiscal redistribution but affects any inequality measure relying on survey data. Among the important consequences is that, if the share of missing income from survey data that CEQ and OECD studies rely on is large, so too is a large share of PIT. Not accounting for these tax revenues could affect fiscal redistribution indicators, but the order of magnitude of this effect is unclear. Complete data could lead to both a higher Gini index and larger equalizing effects of PIT, if a reasonable share of the income of the missing rich households is observable and taxable, as would be the case for salaried income and other types of income withheld at the source (for example, dividends from large corporations). Hence, the omission of some rich individuals likely dominates tax evasion by rich self-employed professionals and the difficulty of taxing some capital income common at the top of the distribution. On balance, direct taxes are likely more progressive than currently estimated in CEQ (and other household survey–based) data.

Indirect taxes are generally regressive or neutral to incomes

Indirect taxes are generally neutral or regressive with respect to income: richer households pay a share of total tax that is equal to or lower than their share of pretax income. The incidence curve and concentration shares for indirect taxes are shown in figure 5.5, panels b and d. The shares do not change much across income levels, with the richest decile paying 30–40 percent of all indirect taxes and the bottom half paying 20–25 percent. Unlike for direct taxes, however, the incidence curves for indirect taxes are flat and even slope downward for richer economies. This result indicates that indirect taxes are not progressive: they are neutral in most poorer economies[19] and regressive in richer ones, in that poorer households pay at least as high a share of their income in indirect taxes as richer households do.[20] Unlike direct tax incidence curves, those for indirect taxes are above 5 percent for all deciles at all income levels, illustrating the breadth of the indirect tax base in developing economies (covering more people) and their reliance on these taxes as a revenue source.

Why are indirect taxes often less regressive in poorer economies? VAT exemptions and preferential rates for specific products—often foods and staples making up a larger share of poorer households' consumption baskets—play a significant role in developing economies. These exemptions make the effective tax rate on consumption lower for poorer households, although these tax expenditures—the tax revenue forgone due to exemptions—are also enjoyed by richer households. Yet, even with tax exemptions on necessities, poorer households pay indirect taxes in all countries, which reduces their purchasing power and can increase short-term poverty in the absence of offsetting transfers.

Poor households are more likely to buy from informal stores, which do not remit taxes. Figure 5.6 shows how the share of total consumption from home production and small store purchases changes with household expenditure in three example economies at different income

FIGURE 5.6

Poorer households buy more from informal vendors, reducing their effective indirect tax rates

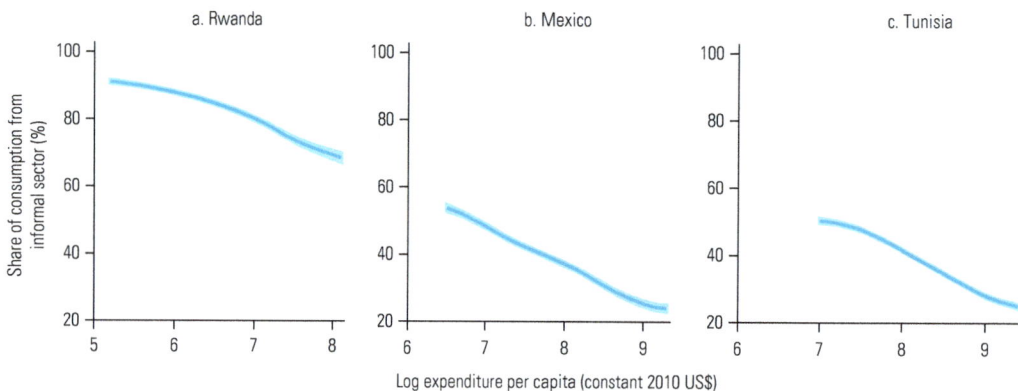

Source: Bachas, Gadenne, and Jensen 2020.
Note: The figure shows a polynomial fit of consumption from the informal sector as a percentage of total expenditure, across the expenditure distribution, in Rwanda, Mexico, and Tunisia based on household-level data. Countries are ordered by median per capita expenditure from left (panel a) to right (panel c); 95 percent confidence intervals are shown.

levels. In all three, poorer households consume a much larger share from the informal sector than richer households do. These patterns apply broadly to more than 32 economies for which data are available (Bachas, Gadenne, and Jensen 2020). Purchases from the informal sector still bear some indirect tax if informal vendors buy goods and services from formal suppliers (including rent and utilities as well as inventory), but there will be no tax on the informal vendor's value added (including labor) so the effective tax rate will be lower than the same good sold at a formal location. For example, a haircut at an informal location may not have VAT charged on its price, but the electricity used at the shop likely does include VAT, which in turn is incorporated into the final price. In effect, poorer households will face a lower effective indirect tax rate because of their higher likelihood of purchasing from the informal sector. This outcome makes indirect taxes less regressive than usually estimated when informality is not accounted for. Depending on the assumptions, accounting for informality implies that indirect taxation reduces inequality by 1–2 points instead of the close-to-zero effect currently observed (Bachas, Gadenne, and Jensen 2020). The exact calibration of the effect of the informal sector on the distributional incidence of indirect taxes requires price incidence analysis following changes to VAT rates in both formal and informal stores, which is demanding in terms of data, and the results are likely to depend on the context. At the same time, although informality may make taxes on consumption more progressive, it also means that these taxes collect less revenue, which in turn reduces the fiscal space for (more efficient) redistribution through cash transfers and in-kind expenditures.

Thus, informality undermines the already weak rationale for using indirect tax exemptions and preferential rates to reduce the burden on the poor. Many economies tax food and staples at lower rates than other goods and services because these items represent a larger share of poor households' consumption. However, poor households in developing economies commonly shop at small, unregistered stores and markets, if not consuming directly from home production, whereas richer household shopping occurs predominantly in large chain stores and supermarkets. Consequently, when informal consumption is considered, VAT exemptions meant to reduce the burden of indirect taxes accrue disproportionately to richer households, diminishing their rationale. Further, these tax exemptions reduce total revenue collection, and the complexity in administering multiple tax rates creates additional opportunities for tax avoidance and evasion.

Additional important taxes are missing from the fiscal incidence studies used as a basis for this chapter, which affects both how much revenue is collected and from whom. OECD data capture only PIT and leave out consumption tax; and, although the CEQ analysis captures the two main tax instruments in most economies (consumption and personal income taxes), it does not consider taxes on corporate profits, and usually not on property or on international trade (tariffs). Although assessing their distributional implications is challenging, the incidence is likely to be progressive, implying that the results reported here may underestimate the degree of progressivity of the tax system.

CIT collects between 2 percent and 3 percent of GDP, and incidence is likely to be progressive. The exact incidence is subject to debate, but studies in OECD economies show that shareholders tend to bear more than half of the burden, the rest borne by workers or consumers.[21] That shareholders often belong to the top of the income distribution suggests that CIT is progressive, especially in poorer economies where the workers of large firms are themselves well-off. CIT also acts as a backstop, ensuring that some tax is paid by business owners who otherwise might not pay income tax. CIT is not included in the CEQ framework because survey data do not capture household capital ownership well. In Chile, a unique CEQ study used rare administrative data on taxpayers' accrued corporate income to allocate a share of corporate income to households (Candia and Engel 2018). Direct taxes were estimated to be responsible for 16 percent of the fiscal reduction in inequality; this reduction increased to 20 percent after including CIT, indicating that CIT is progressive in Chile, at least.

Although property taxes collect little revenue in developing economies, they are usually progressive. This progressivity is because they increase with the value of land and property owned, which is highly correlated with income (although the progressivity of any property tax in practice will depend on its design as well as the nature of local property ownership and rental markets).[22] However, property taxes do not raise much revenue in non-OECD economies because of various challenges. Administratively, land cadasters and valuations are often outdated, and property rights for both urban homeowners and rural landowners are often not widely documented. In addition, property taxes are often raised by local governments with even more limited capacity and sometimes conflicting objectives. Finally, political economy issues on this sensitive tax limit the effective taxes collected; these issues and potential solutions are discussed further in chapter 7. Although incidence data on property taxes are hard to come by, simple assumptions suggest that they are progressive given the concentration of real estate wealth. In OECD economies, more than 50 percent of real estate wealth is concentrated in the richest decile, higher than for income. However, property taxes often apply flat rates (and fewer exemptions), and homeownership rates can be high in developing economies. Further, some economies apply land taxes, which are likely to be less progressive and can fall on poorer agricultural workers and landowners, especially if a flat rate is applied on an area basis.

Taxes on trade (tariffs) are an important revenue source in LICs, but their incidence is likely neutral. Tariff revenues are often about 1–2 percent of GDP in many economies, or one-sixth of tax revenues in LICs and one-eighth to one-ninth in LMICs and UMICs. Their incidence depends on several factors, such as consumption patterns, income portfolios, and initial tariffs. Artuc, Porto, and Rijkers (2021) estimate that the removal of agricultural tariffs would increase total income by 2–3 percent; in half of the economies studied, their incidence would be regressive and in the other half progressive.

In the case of Chile, including some of the missing elements in the CEQ analysis suggests that it would further reduce inequality by roughly 2 points. The back-of-the-envelope analysis in box 5.4 quantifies the impact of informal consumption, missing top incomes, and corporate

---

BOX 5.4

Chile: The distributional impact of commonly missing CEQ fiscal instruments

The 2013 Commitment to Equity (CEQ) analysis for Chile starts with a baseline market income Gini index of 49.4. After accounting for all the fiscal policies commonly included in a CEQ study (including in-kind health and education spending), the final income Gini index is 42.0. Several adjustments are then made to this estimate to try to account for fiscal policies not commonly included. First, using the model-based estimation of Bachas, Gadenne, and Jensen (2020), accounting for patterns of informal consumption implies that fiscal policy would reduce inequality by an additional point. Second, Blanchet, Flores, and Morgan (2022) find that using administrative tax microdata increases the concentration of income among the richest 1 percent of households by 25 percent compared with using only survey data. Conservatively, this extends the marginal effect of direct income taxes from the baseline CEQ analysis by 25 percent, reducing the Gini index by an additional 0.3 point. Modeling missing corporate income and property taxes is even more challenging; however, the inclusion of corporate income taxes using a unique tax microdata source in Chile finds that direct taxes account for 20 percent of the fiscal system's reduction in inequality (compared with 16 percent without corporate income taxes; Candia and Engel 2018). This change is equivalent to a further 0.3-point reduction in the Gini index. Finally, in Chile, the property tax is likely to further reduce the Gini coefficient for several reasons: real estate wealth is concentrated at the top, the property tax has an exemption threshold for low-value properties, and it charges a nontrivial rate (1.2 percent in urban areas, 1.0 percent in rural areas). Thus, a complete picture of fiscal policy in Chile could further reduce the Gini index by about an additional 2 points, a 25 percent increase in the overall redistributive gain compared with the baseline assessment. In addition, the inclusion of top incomes and accrued corporate income means that the market-income level of inequality is higher compared with the baseline estimate.

income and property taxes. In doing so, inequality at the market income stage is reduced by close to 9.5 points by the final-income stage, 2.0 points more than the baseline 7.5 points estimated for Chile (Martínez-Aguilar et al. 2017).

Transfers and distribution

All economies spend on subsidies; richer economies spend more on direct transfers

With taxes playing a limited role in redistribution in developing economies, spending choices become paramount for equity. Direct transfers play a critical role in developing economies because they are the best option for offsetting the burden of indirect tax for poorer households. Even at low levels of income, when spending on direct transfers is low, spending on indirect subsidies represents close to 3 percent of GDP, is not well targeted, and crowds out more progressive spending.

Richer economies raise more revenue and so can spend more than poorer economies, increasing discretionary and progressive social spending (figure 5.7, panel a). Moreover, there appears to be a fixed cost of governance (basic public administration and security). The average "other" spending across economy income levels is relatively constant (panel b), so lower levels of total spending mean lower levels of such nonfixed spending. The majority of "other" is categorized as general public services, economic affairs, and public order. Other studies have estimated infrastructure spending for low- and middle-income economies at 3.5–5.0 percent of GDP, 90 percent of which is spent by the public sector (Fay et al. 2019).

FIGURE 5.7

Richer economies spend more on education, health, and social protection

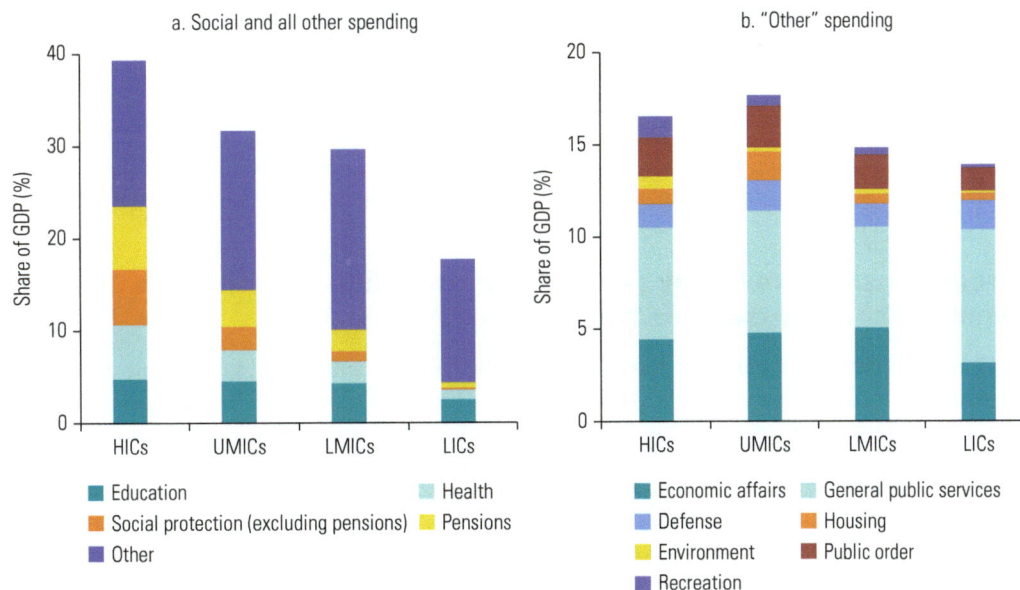

a. Social and all other spending

b. "Other" spending

Legend panel a: Education; Health; Social protection (excluding pensions); Pensions; Other

Legend panel b: Economic affairs; General public services; Defense; Housing; Environment; Public order; Recreation

Sources: Sosa and Wai-Poi, forthcoming, based on data from World Bank, BOOST Open Budget Portal, https://www.worldbank.org/en /programs/boost-portal; International Monetary Fund, Government Finance Statistics database, https://data.imf.org/gfs.
Note: The figure shows each category of public expenditure as a percentage of GDP, aggregated by income group. "Other" in panel a is defined residually as the difference between total spending and social spending. Panel b shows "Other" categories. For LMICs, there is a gap between the sum of explicit "Other" categories and the implied "Other" in panel a. GDP = gross domestic product; HICs = high-income countries; LICs = low-income countries; LMICs = lower-middle-income countries; UMICs = upper-middle-income countries.

As total spending increases, greater space is available for spending on education, health, social protection, subsidies, and pensions, among other things. The choices economies make on average at each income level are apparent in figure 5.7, except for subsidies, which are not easily identified in the main spending database; major subsidies are quantified from separate data sources next. Within these social spending categories, poorer economies tend to invest first in education, which makes up 14 percent of total spending in LICs, a greater share than in other income groups, or about 2.5 percent of GDP. LIC spending in the other discretionary categories is much lower, except for subsidies (figure 5.8), which are a similar size to education, and more than health and social protection spending combined. As economies get richer, they tend to spend a higher share on health and social protection. Health spending averages 6 percent of total spending in LICs, 8 percent in LMICs, 11 percent in UMICs, and 15 percent in HICs; social protection (excluding pensions) averages 1 percent, 4 percent, 8 percent, and 15 percent, respectively; and pensions average 3 percent, 8 percent, 13 percent, and 17 percent, respectively.[23] However, subsidy spending remains higher than social protection spending (excluding pensions) in LMICs and about the same size in UMICs, indicating that in many economies choosing to spend on subsidies can crowd out other spending. Meanwhile, "other" spending as a share of total spending falls from 75 percent to 66 percent to 54 percent to 40 percent, respectively. How economies might evaluate the merits of different spending choices is taken up further in chapter 6.

Available data on subsidy spending likely underestimate total spending on subsidies, yet still show that subsidy spending is high at all income levels, with budgets often much higher than for social protection (figure 5.8, panel e). Global databases on agricultural and energy subsidies provide an idea of how much economies of different income levels spend on these two common and largest subsidies. Energy subsidies alone—mostly petrol, natural gas, and electricity—average over 2 percent of GDP at all non-OECD income levels (figure 5.8, panel a). Although this average is driven by nearly 7 percent of GDP levels in the energy-rich Middle East and Central Asia region, energy subsidies still account for about 1 percent of GDP in all other developing regions (panel b).

Agricultural subsidies are also significant in some economies. Panels c and d of figure 5.8 show the magnitude of agricultural support by income class and region. This support includes direct fiscal support to producers: input subsidies (for example, fertilizers and seeds), output subsidies (for example, based on production), and decoupled transfers (payments to farmers regardless of type and volume of production). Although smaller than energy subsidies, direct agricultural subsidies cost 0.30–0.45 percent of GDP on average (and are considerably larger in some economies), a significant fiscal burden when potentially more progressive direct transfers often lack adequate budget to have an impact. As discussed next, however, once in place, subsidies are difficult to remove.

Direct transfers are highly progressive; spending on subsidies benefits richer households more

CEQ analysis covers spending on direct transfers, indirect subsidies, and health and education. This section focuses on the spending on direct transfers and subsidies. Health and education spending, as well as other spending not included in the CEQ methodology, such as infrastructure spending, is discussed in chapter 6, albeit with a different objective not directly related to the distributional implications of fiscal policy.

Well-targeted direct transfers go mostly to poorer households and often represent a significant boost to their low incomes. As is the case with taxes, the value of direct transfers relative to market incomes for richer and poorer households can be assessed (figure 5.9, panel a); the CEQ and OECD data are based on actual social assistance take-up and reflect the errors that will arise when benefits are targeted, an issue taken up later in this chapter. The incidence curve for direct transfers slopes downward at all income levels, indicating that average direct transfers for poorer households represent a greater share of their income. In fact, in practically all economies, cash transfers are pro-poor in the sense that the per capita transfer (and not just the ratio of the transfer to the pretransfer income) declines with income. However, the benefits are very small in LICs and LMICs for all households (because of the low level of direct transfer spending), becoming more valuable to poorer households only in UMICs and HICs. Like direct taxes, direct transfers are also progressive: poorer households receive a greater share of total direct transfers than richer households (figure 5.9, panel c). Unlike direct taxes, the progressivity increases as economies get richer; benefits become even more concentrated on the poorest, reflecting better data and administrative capacity to assess household welfare and eligibility for targeted transfers.[24] Smaller and less-well-targeted direct transfer spending means that the direct transfers play a more limited role in LICs than elsewhere, with implications for how much they can offset short-term increases in poverty due to indirect taxes.

FIGURE 5.8

Subsidies are expensive in many developing economies, often exceeding social protection budgets

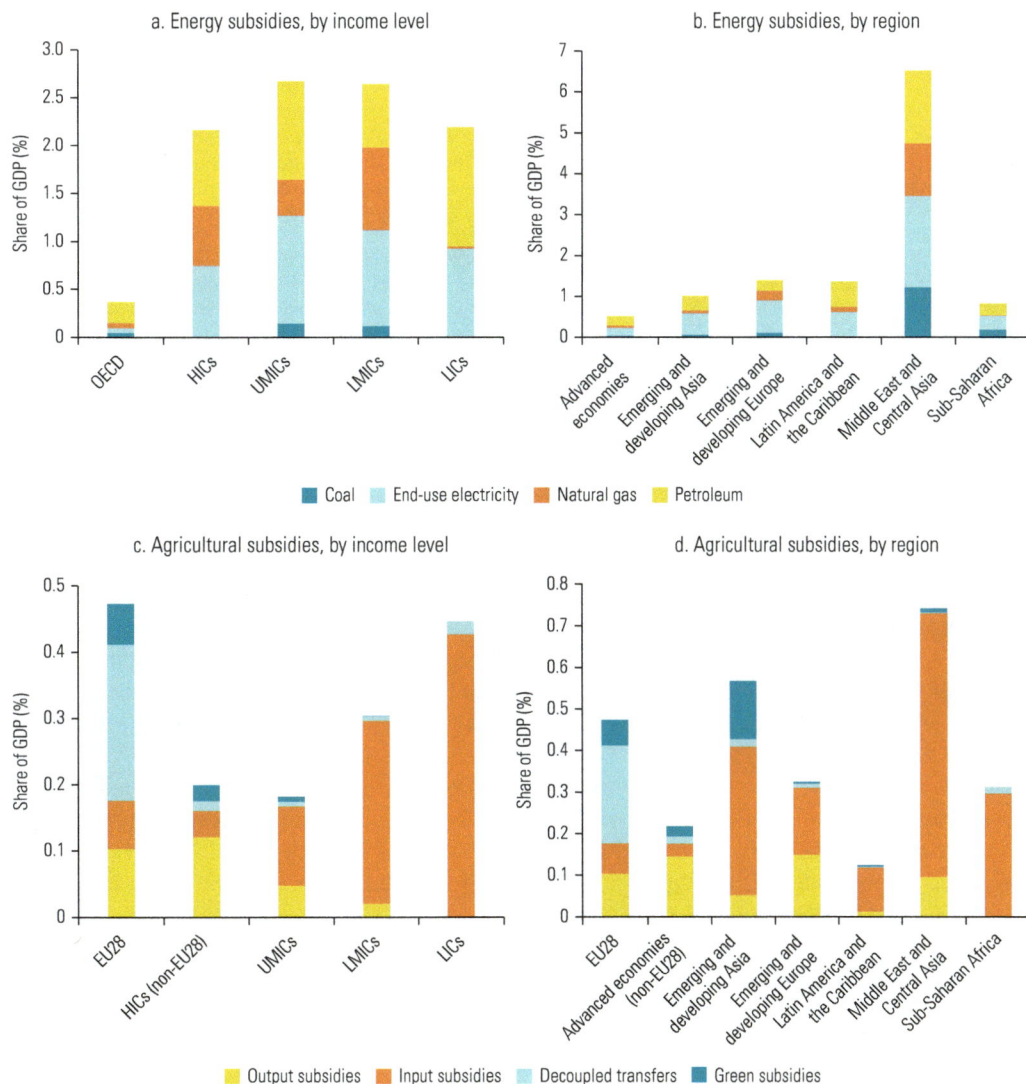

(continued)

FIGURE 5.8

Subsidies are expensive in many developing economies, often exceeding social protection budgets *(continued)*

e. Energy and agricultural subsidies compared to
social protection spending, by income level

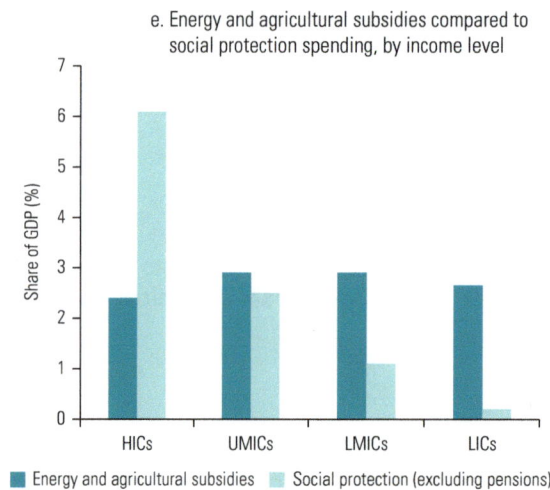

Sources: Agricultural subsidies: International Organisations Consortium for Measuring the Policy Environment for Agriculture database, http://www.ag-incentives.org/; energy subsidies: International Institute for Sustainable Development, https://www.iisd. org/; social protection: World Bank, BOOST Open Budget Portal, https://www.worldbank.org/en/programs/boost-portal, and International Monetary Fund, Government Finance Statistics database, https://data.imf.org/gfs.
Note: The figure shows spending on different types of energy and agricultural subsidies as a percentage of GDP, aggregated by income group and region. Agricultural subsidies calculated as averages for the period 2016–18. Energy subsidies calculated as average subsidies for the period 2017–19. Panel e compares total spending on energy and agricultural subsidies with spending on social protection (excluding pensions), aggregated by income group. EU28 = European Union group of 28 countries; GDP = gross domestic product; HICs = high-income countries; LICs = low-income countries; LMICs = lower-middle-income countries; OECD = Organisation for Economic Co-operation and Development; UMICs = upper-middle-income countries.

Indirect subsidies provide relatively little support to poorer households, and a large share of these subsidies often goes to richer households. The subsidies may increase or decrease inequality, but even when reducing inequality they are always less efficient at doing so than cash transfers: the share of subsidies benefiting each decile is similar in HICs, but at lower income levels the share accruing to richer households grows larger and larger (figure 5.9, panel d). In the poorest economies, more than half of all benefits go to the richest 20 percent. Moreover, although the benefits represent a greater percentage of market income for poorer households than they do for richer ones (and thus reduce inequality, albeit in an inefficient manner), these benefits are never more than 3–4 percent of income, meaning they provide relatively little support anyway (figure 5.9, panel b).

The broad benefits that subsidies provide can make them popular, but more broadly based direct transfers would in most cases be a better policy choice. In addition to being regressive, subsidies are also often distortionary, difficult to remove, and not well-suited for their intended purposes. Energy subsidies encourage wasteful energy consumption, exacerbating climate change. Commercial and agricultural water subsidies can also have negative environmental impacts (see chapter 6 for a fuller discussion). Once in place, subsidies can be very difficult to remove. People become accustomed to cheap prices, and removing a subsidy can seem psychologically equivalent to a tax increase or a new tax. At the same time, households can face genuine hardship if subsidies are removed without mitigating measures (the poor may receive a smaller share of benefits, but, as panel c of figure 5.9 shows, the benefits are usually a larger share of their income than for the rich); redirecting some of the subsidy savings to targeted cash transfers can offset the impact of higher prices for the poor.[25] Finally, subsidies are frequently

Most transfers go to poorer households and provide strong income support; most subsidies go to richer households and provide little support to poorer ones

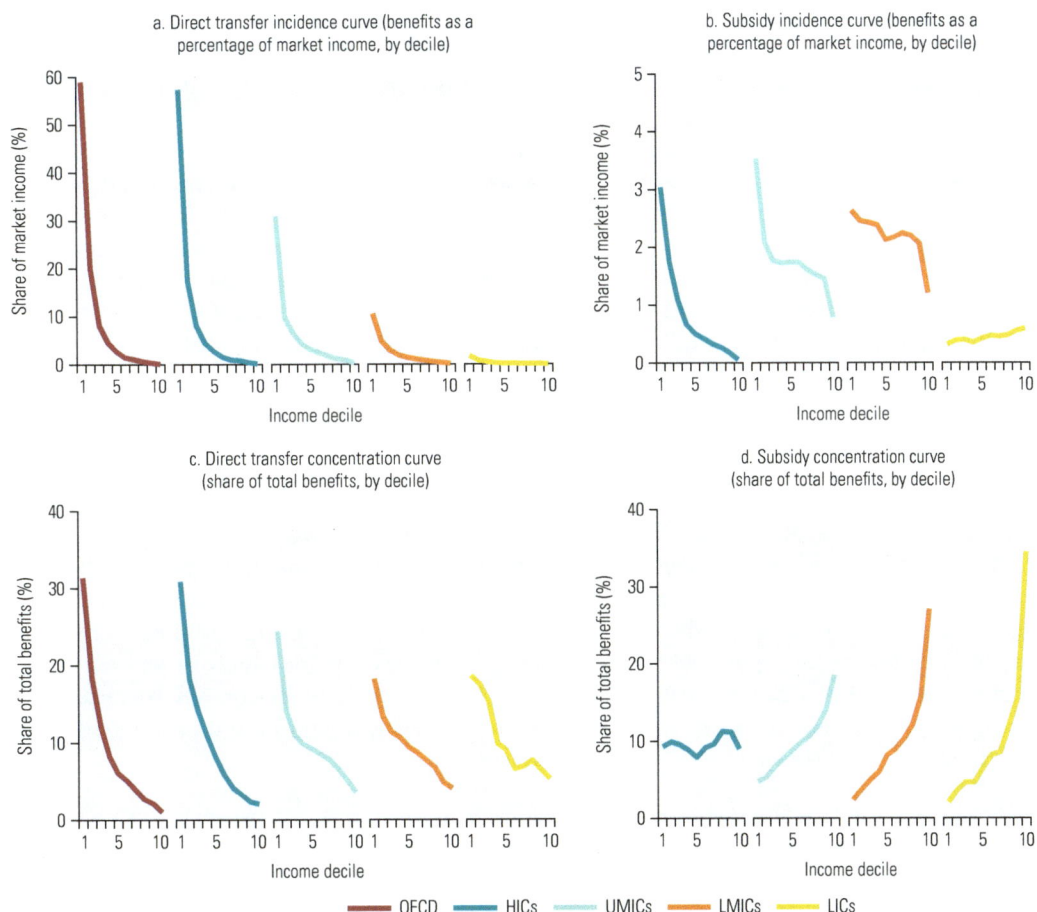

a. Direct transfer incidence curve (benefits as a percentage of market income, by decile)

b. Subsidy incidence curve (benefits as a percentage of market income, by decile)

c. Direct transfer concentration curve (share of total benefits, by decile)

d. Subsidy concentration curve (share of total benefits, by decile)

OECD — HICs — UMICs — LMICs — LICs

Sources: Sosa and Wai-Poi, forthcoming, based on data from CEQ Institute, CEQ Data Center on Fiscal Redistribution, https://commitmentoequity.org/datacenter; OECD data; World Bank data.
Note: The figure shows direct transfer and subsidy incidence curves and concentration shares, aggregated by income group. Incidence curves show transfers/subsidies as a percentage of market income by market income decile. Concentration shares show transfers/subsidies as a percentage of total benefits by market income decile. Subsidy incidence is not available for OECD countries. HICs = high-income countries; LICs = low-income countries; LMICs = lower-middle-income countries; OECD = Organisation for Economic Co-operation and Development; UMICs = upper-middle-income countries.

not fit for their intended purposes; there are often better policy alternatives for a given policy objective. For example, targeted direct cash transfers (social assistance) are more progressive, less costly, and less distortionary. Even in a crisis, there can be other options (see chapter 4).

Many types of subsidies may appeal to policy makers, however. Common subsidies include food, fuel, utilities (electricity and water), agricultural (seeds, fertilizer), housing, credit, and wages; and they are used for a number of reasons. For example, they may be easier to administer (that is, they do not require assessing which households are poor) or quicker to provide support in a crisis (that is, they do not require establishing household eligibility, extracting beneficiaries from a social registry, or paying transfers). As noted, subsidies may also be popular (and therefore politically unpopular to remove) or may support vested political and business interests. Evaluating the desirability of subsidies thus requires considering not only their incidence but also their adequacy (degree of income support provided), their cost, and how they distort incentives or create externalities. Fuel subsidies score poorly on all accounts: they cost a lot, mostly benefit richer households, and encourage wasteful and environmentally damaging energy consumption (although their removal will hurt the poor without accompanying compensation measures; such measures can cost far less than the savings from subsidy removal). Other subsidies may have more merit, at least in particular circumstances.

Another reason subsidies may be used (and a drawback to targeted cash transfers) is the targeting errors that will arise when benefits are focused on a particular subgroup. Poverty-targeted programs will inevitably exclude some poor households and include some nonpoor households, because household income or consumption is not directly observed (as it is in richer economies with highly formalized employment and incomes) but is instead inferred. The process of determining who is eligible for targeted assistance can introduce inaccuracies at all points of the delivery chain: poor households may not know they are eligible or how to apply; the data used to infer eligibility may not be available or may be costly to collect or out-of-date, especially during a shock; and the way eligibility is inferred (the targeting method, such as by statistical model—proxy means test—or community agreement) will be imperfect and errors can be large. Subsidized goods and services avoid such errors by being available to all. Despite these reasons for using subsidies, targeted transfers still provide support much more efficiently than subsidies, as the incidence curves and concentration shares—which include targeting errors—indicate; and significant international experience exists on how to minimize targeting errors in any economy context (see Grosh et al. 2022 for a recent and comprehensive review).

Nonetheless, whether a subsidy is the best way to help poorer households needs to be considered carefully. This concern is particularly salient at the time of writing when the Russian invasion of Ukraine has led to sharply higher food and fuel prices. A number of economies are considering (or are) implementing subsidies in response (see chapter 4). Long experience shows that this response may not be the best approach, not only because of the cost and inefficiency of subsidies (highlighted further in chapter 6)[26] but also because of how hard they are to unwind. For example, Inchauste and Victor (2017, 1) observe:

> Subsidies that begin small with noble, well-focused purposes to ensure price stability can become entrenched. The presence of a subsidy attracts supportive interest groups that mobilize politically to press for larger, more permanent subsidies. As a result, removal or redirection of the subsidy becomes harder. Indeed, the problem of energy subsidies isn't one of expert knowledge about their perverse effects. It is, rather, a problem of political economy.

Another form of subsidy is tax expenditures—that is, taxes not collected because of exemptions or reduced rates—which are, on average, as high as 4 percent of GDP. CEQ studies model exemptions for indirect taxes, which simply means taxes are not applied to consumption of those items. The studies do not capture the size of the tax forgone or the incidence of these tax expenditures. A new data set assembles tax expenditure assessments from more than 100 economies at all income levels (Redonda, von Haldenwang, and Aliu 2022). On average, tax expenditures represent approximately 20 percent of forgone revenue. As a share of revenue collection, tax expenditures tend to be slightly higher in low-income and middle-income economies than in OECD economies (and tax expenditures might be underestimated in poorer economies). Half of all tax expenditures are geared toward indirect taxes, whereas tax expenditures for CIT and PIT each account for about 15 percent; see online annex 5C for a full set of results. Although some indirect tax exemptions on necessities help reduce poverty and inequality, they are a coarse redistribution instrument, especially if poor households purchase frequently from the informal sector; targeted transfers are better suited for redistributive objectives. Other indirect tax exemptions, such as on utilities and fuel, are often regressive (Harris et al. 2018). Assessing the distributional effects of CIT and PIT expenditures is more challenging, although it is probable that they are not generally progressive (for example, mortgage deductions for PIT are regressive). Thus, tax expenditures are large, not transparent, and unlikely to be progressive; and their impact is insufficiently assessed. Rationalizing tax expenditures and narrowing their objectives could open fiscal space; a key first step is making information on them more readily available.

Economies of all income levels and capacities can achieve progressive fiscal policy

HICs offset significant indirect revenue collection with well-targeted and adequate direct transfers for the poor. Indirect taxes can collect more revenue if regressive and costly exemptions are not used, and if their impact on the poorest households is offset cost-effectively through targeted direct transfers—both of which HICs generally do well. For example, although HICs collect a median 18 percent of market income from decile 1 in indirect taxes, these households also receive direct transfers representing an average of 70 percent of market income, so the combined impact is a net 53 percent gain (figure 5.10, panel a). The well-targeted nature of direct transfers in HICs means this net gain tapers quickly; decile 2 receives 8 percent net benefits, decile 3 is unchanged, and all other deciles are net contributors. Box 5.5 profiles the example of how Uruguay uses indirect taxes and direct transfers.

FIGURE 5.10

The indirect tax burden usually exceeds the benefit of direct transfers for the poor in all but HICs

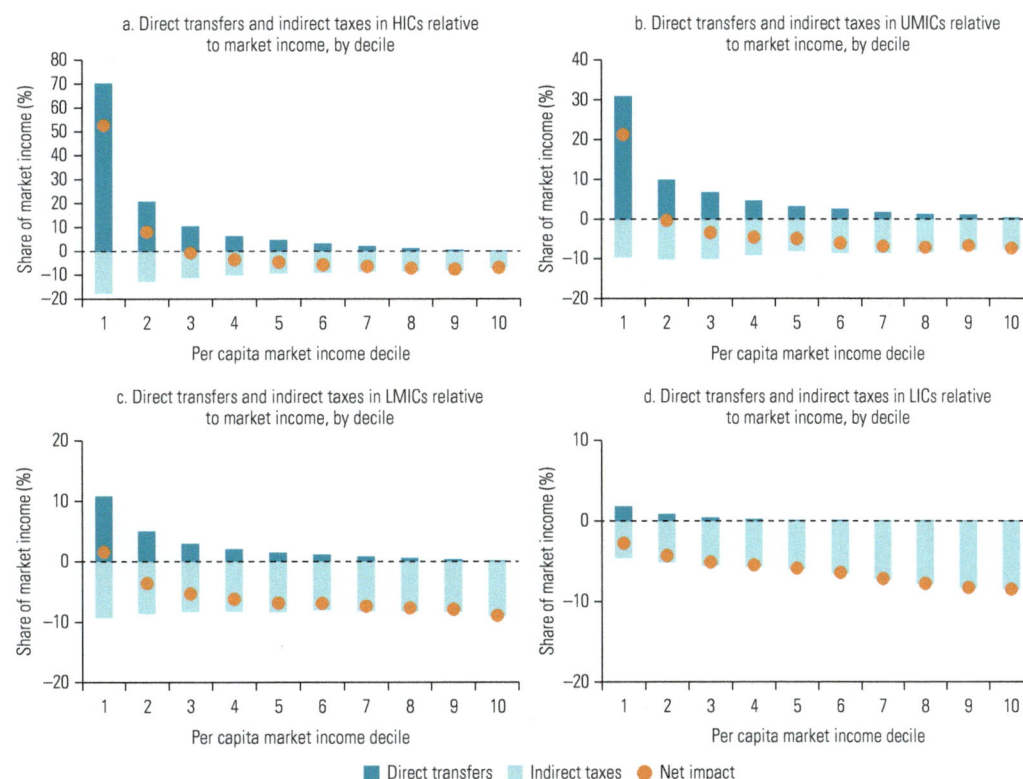

a. Direct transfers and indirect taxes in HICs relative to market income, by decile

b. Direct transfers and indirect taxes in UMICs relative to market income, by decile

c. Direct transfers and indirect taxes in LMICs relative to market income, by decile

d. Direct transfers and indirect taxes in LICs relative to market income, by decile

Direct transfers   Indirect taxes   Net impact

Sources: Sosa and Wai-Poi, forthcoming, based on data from CEQ Institute, CEQ Data Center on Fiscal Redistribution, https://commitmentoequity.org/datacenter; OECD data; World Bank data.
Note: The figure shows direct transfers, indirect taxes, and the net impact of both as a percentage of market income at each income decile, aggregated by income group using median decile results. Indirect tax incidence is not available for OECD economies. The net incidence is calculated at income level as the residual of the median incidence of taxes and transfers, which does not match the median of the net incidence at the economy level. HICs = high-income countries; LICs = low-income countries; LMICs = lower-middle-income countries; OECD = Organisation for Economic Co-operation and Development; UMICs = upper-middle-income countries.

In many UMICs and LMICs and most LICs, however, the combination of indirect taxes and direct transfers has a negative impact on the poor. The median impact on decile 1 in UMICs is 21 percent and about zero for decile 2 (figure 5.10, panel b); in LMICs, decile 1 benefits are less than 2 percent of market income and negative elsewhere in the distribution (panel c), as they are for all LIC deciles (panel d). Moreover, in many countries, the net impact is negative even for the poorest decile (see online annex 5D for a complete list of countries). However, there are good examples among both UMICs and LMICs where strong indirect tax revenues are combined with well-targeted and generous direct transfers to raise net revenues and reduce poverty and inequality, including Bolivia (box 5.6). Limited fiscal space constrains LICs more in terms of direct transfers, but Ethiopia (also box 5.6) provides an example of how indirect tax burdens can be mitigated for the poorest.

BOX 5.5

Uruguay: The impact of indirect taxes and direct transfers

Uruguay's high indirect taxes (12.5 percent of GDP in 2009 Commitment to Equity year) are offset by generous direct transfers (2.2 percent of GDP), with short-term poverty falling by 0.9 point (figure B5.5.1). The combination of indirect taxes and direct transfers does well to support the poorest 20 percent, who pay 14.2 percent of market income in tax but receive 40.5 percent of market income in benefits. Moreover, the system tapers so that (1) the net impact on the poorest 40 percent is mildly positive (12.3 percent of market income paid in taxes and 18.2 percent of market income received in transfers) and (2) all deciles in the top 60 percent pay more in indirect taxes than they receive in transfers.

In addition, Uruguay raised 2.5 percent of GDP in personal income taxes, 2.7 percent in corporate income taxes, and 1.3 percent in property taxes while spending 6.6 percent on health and 4.8 percent on education. Taxes, transfers, and subsidies reduced inequality by 3.7 points, and inequality fell by 12.8 points when health and education spending are also included.

FIGURE B5.5.1

Net incidence of transfers and indirect taxes in Uruguay

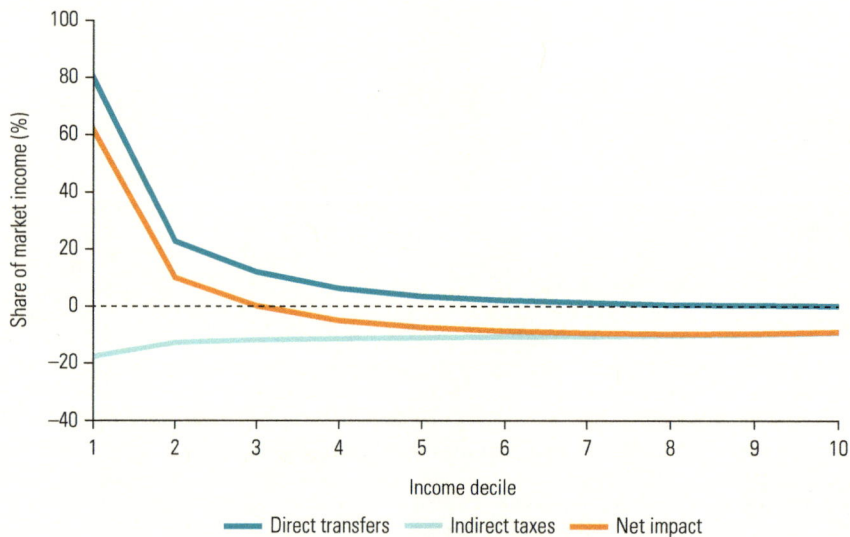

Sources: CEQ Institute, CEQ Data Center on Fiscal Redistribution, https://commitmentoequity.org/datacenter; World Bank data.
Note: The figure shows direct transfers, indirect taxes, and the net impact as a percentage of market income, by market income decile, for Uruguay.

BOX 5.6

Bolivia and Ethiopia: Fiscal system impact on poverty and inequality

In its 2015 Commitment to Equity year, Bolivia collected 13.7 percent in indirect taxes (costing 15 percent of market income for the bottom 10 percent) but spent 1.8 percent on direct transfers (the benefits were worth 40 percent relative to the bottom 10 percent's market income), resulting in a 24 percent of market income net gain to the poorest 10 percent and neutral impact for the second-poorest 10 percent (figure B5.6.1). Overall, Bolivia's fiscal policy reduces poverty slightly, by 0.3 point. Moreover, taxes, transfers, and subsidies reduced the Gini index by 1.2 points, and including the 13 percent of GDP spent on education and health reduced the Gini index by 6.7 points. Bolivia collected 5.6 percent of GDP in progressive personal income taxes to help finance its social expenditures.

Ethiopia collected 3.7 percent of GDP in indirect taxes in its 2016 Commitment to Equity year, but they represented only 1.6 percent of market income for the bottom 20 percent and 1.7 percent for the bottom 40 percent because of the high informality of consumption in rural areas (figure B5.6.2). This low incidence of indirect taxes combined with a modest 0.4 percent of GDP in direct transfers meant inequality was reduced by 2.0 points in cash terms. Despite the positive net impact of indirect taxes and direct transfers on the poorest three deciles, with poverty at market incomes above 30 percent and decile 4 paying more on average in indirect taxes than it received in direct transfers, short-term poverty increased by 1.3 points. Thus, direct transfers were progressive and equalizing, and almost completely offset the poverty-inducing burden of indirect taxes. Moreover, part of the small poverty increase is due to a low personal income tax eligibility threshold and a regressive land use fee, whereas electricity subsidies did not benefit poor households—who often do not use electricity. That is, with changes to personal income and land taxes as well as subsidies, Ethiopia likely could achieve a similar fiscal balance while reducing poverty.

FIGURE B5.6.1

Net incidence of transfers and indirect taxes in Bolivia

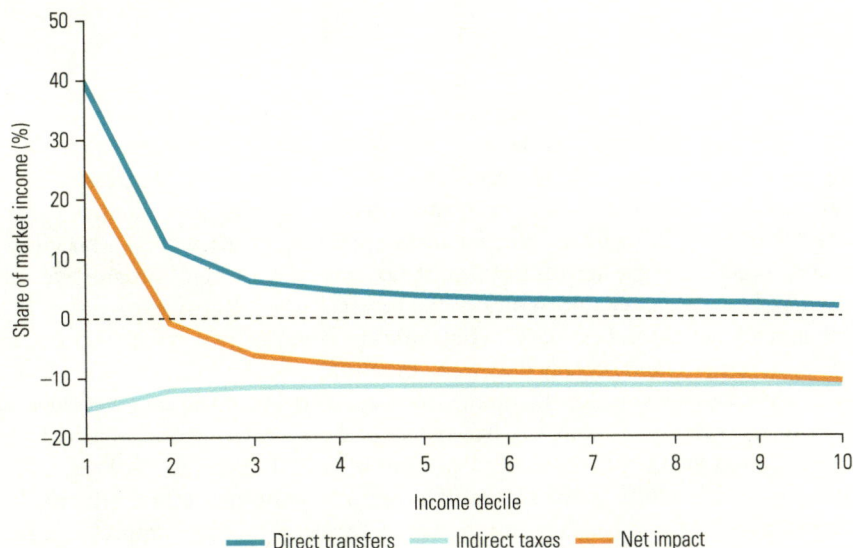

Sources: CEQ Institute, CEQ Data Center on Fiscal Redistribution, https://commitmentoequity.org/datacenter; World Bank data.
Note: The figure shows direct transfers, indirect taxes, and the net impact as a percentage of market income, by market income decile, for Bolivia.

(continued)

Bolivia and Ethiopia: Fiscal system impact on poverty and inequality *(continued)*

Net incidence of transfers and indirect taxes in Ethiopia

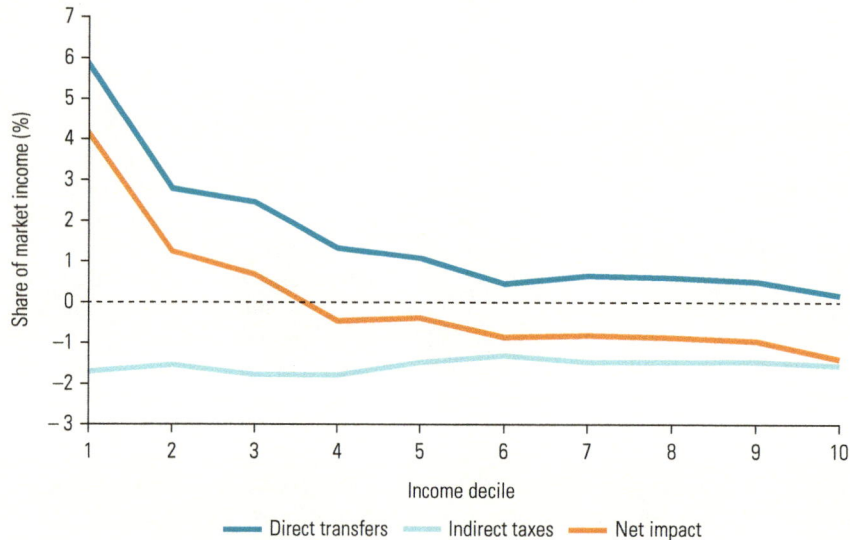

Sources: CEQ Institute, CEQ Data Center on Fiscal Redistribution, https://commitmentoequity.org/datacenter; World Bank data.
Note: The figure shows direct transfers, indirect taxes, and the net impact as a percentage of market income, by market income decile, for Ethiopia.

Conclusion

Taxes, transfers, and subsidies can have an immediate and significant impact on inequality and poverty in the short term. Richer economies tend to have more progressive impacts with taxes, transfers, and subsidies than poorer ones because the richer economies (1) raise more revenue and thus create more fiscal space for social spending, (2) have greater tax administrative capacity and so collect a greater proportion of tax revenues through progressive direct taxes such as PIT, and (3) are better able to means-test targeted direct transfers to poorer households. Nonetheless, at all income and capacity levels, there are examples of economies that pursue more progressive tax, transfer, and subsidy policies than others.

Importantly, when today's high-income economies were at similar stages of development to today's developing economies, their tax systems looked very different and collected much lower revenue: the United States collected only 7 percent of GDP in taxes in 1900 versus 37 percent a century later (Wallis 2000). In the nineteenth century, economies relied principally on trade tariffs, complemented by excise and property taxes. Taxation could be progressive, although its efficiency cost was arguably high: indirect taxes were akin to luxury taxes on specific products, and direct taxes on property relied upon simple heuristics to determine tax liabilities. In the case of the general property tax in the United States, for example, state and local governments levied high rates on both financial and real estate property, akin to an annual wealth tax (Dray, Landais, and Stantcheva 2022). Major changes in taxation occurred in the period between the two world wars, and shortly after, with the introduction and expansion of PIT and the creation of payroll taxes to fund broader social insurance (Wallis 2000). These new instruments accompanied a substantial increase in government size, which continued at a slower pace in the 1960s and 1970s, with the expansion of payroll taxes and social contributions and the adoption of VAT.

A current of the literature argues that major progressive tax reforms, such as the expansion of PIT (or the adoption of wealth taxes), occurred only under exceptional circumstances: in the wake of warfare and following the economic collapse brought by the Great Depression (Scheve and Stasavage 2010, 2012). The COVID-19 pandemic also represents a unique shock calling for governmental response. Even if this view is historically correct, developing economies do not need to follow the circuitous route to progressive revenue mobilization of western economies. They can learn from this history and benefit from the increased efficiency and lower administrative cost of raising revenue, brought by better access to information, technology, and administrative know-how. Indeed, certain policy lessons emerge from the review of this chapter. Investments in tax capacity combined with the potential of new data and innovative technologies mean that developing economies may be able to collect a greater share of progressive direct taxation at earlier stages of development than in the past. A more progressive tax mix with greater fiscal equity can be achieved directly through revenue generation. Nonetheless, the majority of developing economy revenues will continue to come from indirect taxation in the medium term, which means the currently widespread use of VAT preferential rates and exemptions not only results in expensive expenditures that often benefit the rich but also reduces needed fiscal space for both investments in growth and social spending. The reliance on indirect taxes also means that the burden of progressivity falls more heavily on public spending, which will largely determine the net distributional impact of fiscal policy.

In turn, economies need to consider not only the long-term returns on different spending (as chapter 6 explores) but also who benefits in the short term. Subsidies are generally expensive, regressive, and distortionary; a transition away from subsidies to a broader and more targeted social safety net will likely reduce inequality and poverty but also create more fiscal space for needed investments to restart growth as economies try to recover from the shock of COVID-19. However, the need to finance an inclusive recovery in the face of limited fiscal space means the efficiency of redistributive spending beyond the use of subsidies also needs to be examined. For example, in 2015, Indonesia redirected substantial spending away from fuel subsidies to greater infrastructure investment and higher spending on health and social protection. Revisiting its social assistance spending mix, it moved away from subsidized food transfers that were costly but had relatively little redistributive impact. In addition, Indonesia massively expanded its conditional cash transfer program, which had the highest redistributive effect per dollar spent but little aggregate impact because of low budgets (see Indonesia, Ministry of Finance and World Bank 2015, 2020). It also invested significantly in improving its targeting of social assistance and the entire delivery chain over a number of years (Holmemo et al. 2020).

This brief snapshot of Indonesia's relative success in moving from heavy fuel subsidy spending to a more targeted but broad social assistance framework belies the complicated political economy of subsidy reform. Beaton, Lontoh, and Wai-Poi (2017) provide an in-depth review of six major subsidy reform attempts in Indonesia between 2000 and 2015, some successful and some not. In particular, they highlight the importance of coalition building, analysis and preparation, coordinated messaging, and timing and opportunism. Of particular relevance to the current chapter is

> the importance of social assistance in mitigating the impact of reforms over time and the virtuous circle that can take place between subsidy reforms and investments in social assistance capacity. As countries develop more sophisticated tools to assist businesses and households, it becomes easier for them to manage some of the negative impacts of higher energy prices through more effective, more-efficient policy tools. At the same time, subsidy reforms can liberate funding that allows for investments in social assistance capacity. Most of Indonesia's fuel price increases have

been coupled with some form of support targeted at the needy, and as this support has improved over time, so too has the likelihood of successful price increases. (Beaton, Lontoh, and Wai-Poi 2017, 134)

Inchauste and Victor (2017, 33–34) synthesize the experience of Indonesia as well as that of the Dominican Republic, Ghana, and Jordan, concluding that "the most successful reforms nearly always involve a large amount of political engineering" and that

> energy subsidies often follow a life cycle. They begin with noble goals, such as helping to smooth out price fluctuations to protect the poor, but evolve in ways that inflate their cost and make reform politically difficult. One pattern evident across each of these cases is that breaking that life cycle has required the creation of alternative mechanisms for delivering benefits to the poor—notably cash transfers. Policy makers have, in most cases, created these programs in response to pressures and opportunities unrelated to the problem of energy subsidy. But once in place, the opportunity to adopt much more efficient social policy has made other reforms, including energy-related reforms, possible.

Chapter 7 explores these and other issues in more depth, such as the different progressive tax and transfer strategies available in different economy contexts and how new green and digital tax instruments could increase fiscal space. It also asks why subsidies remain such popular fiscal instruments and briefly considers the political economy of fiscal reform.

Notes

1. For a primer, see Horton and El-Ganainy (2020).
2. This chapter builds on Fuchs, Sosa, and Wai-Poi (2021), and is being extended to a global review of CEQ studies (Sosa and Wai-Poi, forthcoming). It also adds significant new material on taxation, original to this chapter.
3. The CEQ approach was developed by the Commitment to Equity Institute (CEQ Institute) at Tulane University. For information on the methodology, implementation guidelines, applications, and software of the CEQ approach, see Lustig (2018).
4. See CEQ Institute (https://commitmento-equity.org/datacenter/) for data from all CEQ Institute studies and many World Bank ones. OECD and additional World Bank data from individual country studies have been compiled for this report. The compiled database used in this chapter and in Sosa and Wai-Poi (forthcoming) are being publicly released.
5. The global ASPIRE data indicate that active labor market policies represent a small share of spending compared with that on social assistance, social insurance, and pensions as of January 2022 (see World Bank, forthcoming).
6. OECD compiles fiscal incidence data from each member, usually estimated by the national statistical agency, and in all cases representing the official incidence data for that economy. In five economies there are both OECD and CEQ data: Chile, Croatia, Poland, Spain, and the United States. In each case OECD data are used, despite not including the indirect tax and subsidy results from the CEQ data set, because OECD data are based on official economy estimates and are more recent than CEQ data—fiscal years 2011 (United States), 2013 (Chile), 2014 (Poland), 2016 (Spain), and 2017 (Croatia).
7. Based on the World Bank's country income and regional classifications (https://datahelpdesk.worldbank.org/knowledgebase/articles/906519-world-bank-country-and-lending-groups).
8. The tax and spending levels and compositions from these databases as discussed in this chapter differ from the tax and spending components included in individual CEQ economy studies, which do not include all taxes and spending. This chapter uses the more comprehensive databases for a discussion of levels and compositions of taxes and spending, and the CEQ data for a discussion of incidence.
9. See International Centre for Tax and Development (https://www.ictd.ac/dataset/grd/); World Bank, BOOST (https://www.worldbank.org/en/programs/boost-portal);

International Monetary Fund Government Finance Statistics (https://data.imf.org/?sk =a0867067-d23c-4ebc-ad23-d3b015045405); IO Consortium Database, http://www.ag -incentives.org/); and Global Tax Expenditures Database (https://gted.net/data-download/).

10. Some of the analyses in this chapter present data aggregated by income group. Medians were used to aggregate results from CEQ fiscal incidence analyses. Figure 5.1, panel b, and figure 5.2, panel b, depict a synthetic category for each income group constructed using the median value (Gini index or poverty rate) at each income definition. Similarly, a synthetic income category is built using the median values per decile in figure 5.3, figure 5.5, figure 5.9, and figure 5.10. Consequently, each synthetic income category is not the median economy but the median results for each decile, and as such does not represent any single economy. Last, averages of observations at the economy level per income group were used to aggregate indicators depicted in figure 5.4, figure 5.7, and figure 5.8.

11. This redistribution is the effect only of direct taxes and transfers.

12. The empirical findings of this chapter are broadly consistent with the earlier findings of the 29-economy study in chapter 10 of Lustig (2018). The main difference is that this chapter finds a majority of developing economies increase short-term poverty through fiscal policy whereas the earlier study found this increase occurs less commonly. The earlier study used the extreme international poverty line (US$1.25 at the time, and now US$2.15) for all economies, whereas this chapter uses the international poverty line most appropriate to each economy's income level. The earlier study notes that at higher poverty lines the number of countries in which the headcount for consumable income is higher than that for market income rises (Lustig 2018).

13. If more poor individuals are lifted out of poverty by fiscal policy than moved into it, the poverty rate falls. Nonetheless, for a number of individuals, the taxes paid can be greater than the benefits received; these individuals can fall below the poverty line as a result (or fall further below if already there). See the discussion of "fiscal impoverishment" in Higgins and Lustig (2016).

14. In Ecuador and República Bolivariana de Venezuela, however, at the time of the CEQ study, indirect subsidies more than offset indirect taxes and further reduced poverty.

15. Poverty decreases (slightly) after fiscal policy in Bolivia in 2015 at the US$3.20-a-day international poverty line (2011 PPP) because many households in the poorest deciles are net fiscal beneficiaries. At the higher US$5.50-a-day line (2011 PPP), poverty increases (by 2 points) because many households in the higher deciles are net contributors.

16. This issue is reflected in the usually large gap between both total income/consumption in household surveys and the national accounts, and between the total PIT revenue estimated in surveys and the total revenue collected in administrative data. See Lustig (2019) for a discussion of reasons for missing top incomes in survey data.

17. Missing top incomes in household survey data are a common phenomenon in most countries (see, for example, Lustig 2019; Ravallion 2022).

18. Piketty (2003) and Piketty and Saez (2003) are the key reference works, and Atkinson and Piketty (2007, 2010) represent the main cross-country studies.

19. The indirect tax curve for LICs actually slopes mildly upward, indicating that richer households pay more as a percentage of income than poorer ones. This difference likely depends on the particular economy being studied, but a possible explanation is that VAT exemptions on foods and other staples are common in poor economies but that these items make up such a large share of the consumption basket that the effective indirect tax rate for poorer households ends up being less than that of richer households for whom nonexempt goods represent a greater share of their consumption basket. In some LICs, data on purchases in informal markets were available and explicitly modeled, which also contributes to an upward-sloping indirect tax curve.

20. The incidence of indirect taxes and subsidies, as well as in-kind spending, is not available for OECD economies.

21. Studies in Germany and the United States estimate that workers bear less than 40 percent of the incidence of corporate income taxes, the rest being borne by shareholders and

landowners (Fuest, Peichl, and Siegloch 2018; Suárez Serrato and Zidar 2016).

22. Inequality in land and property ownership is always larger than that of income, reflecting the even greater concentration of wealth than of income.

23. These differences reflect in part an older population profile in richer economies, but also the fiscal space to finance pensions.

24. Nonetheless, targeting transfers to poorer households is possible for economies of all income levels. See Grosh et al. (2022) for a comprehensive review.

25. Successful examples exist of subsidies being removed and temporary mitigation measures put in place, such as subsidy reform with temporary unconditional cash transfers in Indonesia (see World Bank 2012), as well as fuel and bread subsidies being removed first for richer households and then later for all households in Jordan (see Rodriguez and Wai-Poi 2021).

26. Not all energy subsidies are as regressive as blanket subsidies or price deduction for all consumers. For example, the electricity sector in a number of economies targets support to poorer customers, often in a timebound manner with clear eligibility criteria. Commonly such subsidies are by way of either lifeline tariffs or tariffs that step up with consumption volume. Lifeline tariffs provide very cheap electricity for a small level of initial consumption to ensure all can afford a basic amount of electricity. Stepped tariffs increase prices with each consumption block, initially being priced below cost recovery (a subsidy) and then reaching or even exceeding cost recovery for later blocks. The idea is that poorer households consume less and so benefit from the cheaper tariffs. Issues arise with the lifeline or stepped tariff approaches. Poor households are often quite large and the lifeline block usually quite small, so it does not help them very much in an energy crisis. Moreover, some poor households consume in large quantities through grouped apartment purchases, and others pay their landlord part of the metered amount; both of these groups are not well-served by lifelines. And poor households without meters don't benefit either. Moreover, with stepped tariffs, large poor households can cross-subsidize rich small households. Targeting based on

utility consumption can be inefficient because the consumption gradient slopes only mildly upward with income and depends where one lives (in terms of cooling and heating), how big one's household is, and so on. An alternative is to target utility subsidies not through tariffs but through a rebate on the bill, using the same mechanism as a cash transfer to determine who is eligible. This method may not help the poor who do not have a bill in their name (they get it through their landlord, get it off the black market, and so on).

References

Artuc, Erhan, Guido Porto, and Bob Rijkers. 2021. "Household Impacts of Tariffs: Data and Results from Agricultural Trade Protection." *World Bank Economic Review* 35 (3): 563–85.

Atkinson, A. B. 2016. *Inequality: What Can Be Done?* Cambridge, MA: Harvard University Press.

Atkinson, A. B., and Thomas Piketty. 2007. *Top Incomes over the Twentieth Century: A Contrast between Continental European and English-Speaking Countries.* Oxford, UK: Oxford University Press.

Atkinson, A. B., and Thomas Piketty. 2010. *Top Incomes: A Global Perspective.* Oxford, UK: Oxford University Press.

Bachas, Pierre, Lucie Gadenne, and Anders Jensen. 2020. "Informality, Consumption Taxes, and Redistribution." Working Paper 27429, National Bureau of Economic Research, Cambridge, MA.

Beaton, Chris, Lucky Lontoh, and Matthew Wai-Poi. 2017. "Indonesia: Pricing Reforms, Social Assistance, and the Importance of Perceptions." In *The Political Economy of Energy Subsidy Reform,* edited by Gabriela Inchauste and David Victor. Washington, DC: World Bank.

Blanchet, Thomas, Ignacio Flores, and Marc Morgan. 2022. "The Weight of the Rich: Improving Surveys Using Tax Data." *Journal of Economic Inequality* 20: 119–50.

Candia, Bernardo, and Eduardo Engel. 2018. "Taxes, Transfers, and Income Distribution in Chile: Incorporating Undistributed Profits." Working Paper 82, Commitment to Equity Institute, Tulane University, New Orleans, LA.

Dray, Sacha, Camille Landais, and Stefanie Stantcheva. 2022. "Wealth and Property

Taxation in the United States." Unpublished manuscript, Harvard University.

Fay, Marianne, Hyoung Il Lee, Massimo Mastruzzi, Sungmin Han, and Moonkyoung Cho. 2019. "A Look at How Much Countries Are Spending on Infrastructure." Policy Research Working Paper 8730, World Bank, Washington, DC.

Fuchs, Alan, Mariano Sosa, and Matthew Wai-Poi. 2021. "Progressive Domestic Resource Mobilization for a COVID-19 Recovery." Policy Note, World Bank, Washington, DC.

Fuest, Clemens, Andreas Peichl, and Sebastian Siegloch. 2018. "Do Higher Corporate Taxes Reduce Wages? Micro Evidence from Germany." *American Economic Review* 108 (2): 393–418.

Grosh, Margaret, Phillippe Leite, Matthew Wai-Poi, and Emil Tesliuc. 2022. *Revisiting Targeting in Social Assistance: A New Look at Old Dilemmas.* Washington, DC: World Bank.

Harris, Tom, David Phillips, Ross Warwick, Maya Goldman, Jon Jellema, Karolina Goraus, and Gabriela Inchauste. 2018. "Redistribution via VAT and Cash Transfers: An Assessment in Four Low- and Middle-Income Countries." Working Paper W18/11, Institute for Fiscal Studies, London.

Higgins, Dean, and Nora Lustig. 2016. "Can a Poverty-Reducing and Progressive Tax and Transfer System Hurt the Poor?" *Journal of Development Economics* 122 (C): 63–75.

Holmemo, Camilla, Pablo Acosta, Tina George, Robert Palacios, Juul Pinxten, Shonali Sen, and Sailesh Tiwari. 2020. "Investing in People: Social Protection for Indonesia's 2045 Vision." World Bank, Washington, DC.

Horton, Mark, and Asmaa El-Ganainy. 2020. "Fiscal Policy: Taking and Giving Away." *Finance & Development*, February 24, 2020. https://www .imf.org/external/pubs/ft/fandd/basics/fiscpol .htm.

Inchauste, Gabriela, and David Victor. 2017. *The Political Economy of Energy Reform.* Washington, DC: World Bank.

Indonesia, Ministry of Finance and World Bank. 2015. "Taxes and Public Spending in Indonesia: Who Pays and Who Benefits?" World Bank, Jakarta. https://openknowledge.worldbank.org /handle/10986/23600.

Indonesia, Ministry of Finance and World Bank. 2020. "Revisiting the Impact of Government Spending and Taxes on Poverty and Inequality in Indonesia." World Bank, Jakarta. https://documents1 .worldbank.org/curated/en/108171597378171969 /Revisiting-the-Impact-of-Government-Spending -and-Taxes-on-Poverty-and-Inequality-in-Indo nesia.pdf.

Jensen, Anders. 2022. "Employment Structure and the Rise of the Modern Tax System." *American Economic Review* 112 (1): 213–34.

Kleven, Henrik Jacobsen, Martin B. Knudsen, Claus Thustrup Kreiner, Søren Pedersen, and Emmanuel Saez. 2011. "Unwilling or Unable to Cheat? Evidence from a Tax Audit Experiment in Denmark." *Econometrica* 79 (3): 651–92.

Lustig, Nora, ed. 2018. *Commitment to Equity Handbook: Estimating the Impact of Fiscal Policy on Inequality and Poverty.* Washington, DC: Brookings Institution Press.

Lustig, Nora. 2019. "The 'Missing Rich' in Household Surveys: Causes and Correction Approaches." Working Paper Series 75, Commitment to Equity Institute, Tulane University, New Orleans, LA.

Lustig, Nora, Chiara Mariotti, and Carolina Sánchez-Páramo. 2020. "The Redistributive Impact of Fiscal Policy Indicator: A New Global Standard for Assessing Government Effectiveness in Tackling Inequality within the SDG Framework." *Data Blog*, June 11, 2020. https://blogs .worldbank.org/opendata/redistributive-impact -fiscal-policy-indicator-new-global-standard -assessing-government.

Martínez-Aguilar, Sandra, Alan Fuchs, Eduardo Ortiz-Juarez, and Giselle Del Carmen. 2017. "The Impact of Fiscal Policy on Inequality and Poverty in Chile." Working Paper Series 46, Commitment to Equity Institute, Tulane University, New Orleans, LA.

Piketty, Thomas. 2003. "Income Inequality in France, 1901–1998." *Journal of Political Economy* 111 (5): 1004–42.

Piketty, Thomas, and Emmanuel Saez. 2003. "Income Inequality in the United States, 1913–1998." *Quarterly Journal of Economics* 18 (1):1–39.

Ravallion, Martin. 2022. "Missing Top Income Recipients." *Journal of Economic Inequality* 20: 205–22.

Redonda, Agustin, Christian von Haldenwang, and Flurim Aliu. 2022. Global Tax Expenditures Database, Version 1.1.3. https://doi.org/10.5281 /zenodo.6334212.

Rodriguez, Laura, and Matthew Wai-Poi. 2021. *Fiscal Policy, Poverty, and Inequality in Jordan: The Role of Taxes and Public Spending.* Washington, DC: World Bank.

Scheve, Kenneth, and David Stasavage. 2010. "The Conscription of Wealth: Mass Warfare and the Demand for Progressive Taxation." *International Organization* 64 (4): 529–61.

Scheve, Kenneth, and David Stasavage. 2012. "Democracy, War, and Wealth: Evidence from Two Centuries of Inheritance Taxation." *American Political Science Review* 106 (1): 81–102.

Sosa, Mariano, and Matthew Wai-Poi. Forthcoming. "Fiscal Policy and Equity in Developing Countries: A Survey of International Patterns and Lessons." Background paper for *Poverty and Shared Prosperity 2022,* World Bank, Washington, DC.

Suárez Serrato, Juan Carlos, and Owen Zidar. 2016. "Who Benefits from State Corporate Tax Cuts? A Local Labor Markets Approach with Heterogeneous Firms." *American Economic Review* 106 (9): 2582–2624.

Wallis, John Joseph. 2000. "American Government Finance in the Long Run: 1790 to 1990." *Journal of Economic Perspectives* 14 (1): 61–82.

World Bank. 2012. *Protecting the Poor and Vulnerable in Indonesia.* Washington, DC: World Bank.

World Bank. Forthcoming. *Charting a Course Towards Universal Social Protection: Equity, Resilience, and Opportunity for All.* Washington, DC: World Bank.

Fiscal Policy for Growth: Identifying High-Value Fiscal Policies

Summary

The impact of fiscal policies on poverty and inequality depends not only on who receives what but also on the degree to which these policies support growth in the short and long run. The comprehensive valuation of a tax or spending policy considers the full impact of the policy on both direct and indirect beneficiaries, and will depend on the characteristics of the local economy.

This chapter considers the key elements of valuing fiscal policies and how information on the full value of policies can inform policy challenges of the current moment—challenges such as fiscal consolidation that minimizes impacts on poverty and inequality, and whether to respond to rising food prices with cash transfers or subsidies.

Drawing on recent evidence, the chapter discusses the knowledge about high-value policy choices. Three broad findings come out of this discussion: (1) policies that improve early life outcomes are generally of high value, across many contexts; (2) policies that bring transformative growth tend to be of high value; and (3) spending to address market failures is often of higher value than subsidizing behavior in the absence of positive externalities.

Despite the evidence, high-value policies can be hard to prioritize precisely because their benefits are not realized today but accrue over the long term. For politicians, this time frame does not align with political realities that require immediate results, and long-run benefits may also have less value to some households that are more present biased or governments that face high costs of borrowing. As a result, fiscal decision-making can often overlook long-run growth benefits.

The chapter concludes with a discussion on how improving the efficiency of spending can increase the value of spending.

Introduction

All government policies are made under tight resource constraints. This is particularly true in developing economies, where raising tax revenue is challenging, borrowing is costly, and government aid is limited. The trade-offs are particularly apparent today; even as governments decide which fiscal policies are most suitable for achieving an inclusive recovery and long-run growth, they must deal with inflationary pressures and rising fiscal deficits and debt burdens, with little space for fiscal

---

Chapter 6 online annex available at http://hdl.handle.net/10986/37739:
6A. Additional Material on the Marginal Value of Public Funds.

policy to support the recovery and prepare for ongoing and future crises. Many countries now confront the need to raise revenue, reduce spending, or both to escape debt distress.

Thus, governments face difficult fiscal trade-offs: Which policies should they spend scarce resources on? Should they reduce spending on cash transfers in order to finance spending on schools, or should they finance such spending by raising taxes, or by taking on more debt? Furthermore, which tax policies raise revenue most efficiently?

Historically, fiscal policy decisions in moments of tight fiscal space and debt crises have often hurt the poor, both in the immediate term and in limiting the opportunities later available to them. It is essential to navigate the current challenge in ways that do not further impoverish the poor today or reduce the opportunities they might enjoy tomorrow.

Making these difficult policy choices in a way that reduces poverty requires assessing both who benefits from a policy and the value of a policy in terms of its impact on growth or of the other outcomes it brings. The incidence analysis presented in chapter 5 explored who benefits from different policies and by how much, and gives a good indication of short-term impact. Often, a discussion of the impact of fiscal policies on poverty and inequality focuses only on those factors, but a full assessment also requires assessing the value of a policy. This chapter explores how to assess the value of tax and spending decisions in a way that counts both their immediate impact and their long-run impact on the growth of household incomes and subsequent government revenue. The value of a given policy needs to consider its full impact on beneficiaries, both the intended direct beneficiaries and indirect beneficiaries not directly targeted by the policy. The value will depend on the characteristics of beneficiaries and the nature of the local economy—see, for example, chapter 4's discussion on the impacts of transfers during the pandemic—so an approach to policy valuation needs to consider these differences in context.

This information helps governments choose policies. For example, how can governments raise taxes or reduce spending in a way that minimizes impacts on poor people, or should they choose cash transfers or subsidies to address rising food prices? Choosing policies requires a welfare judgment as well: How much does a society value an additional dollar in the hands of the beneficiaries of one policy versus the beneficiaries of another? Choices will also reflect the challenge of incorporating long-run benefits into policy decisions or the specific political economy of a given country.

The chapter discusses current knowledge about *high-value policy choices*—that is, policy choices that achieve lasting benefits relative to their cost. It highlights three broad findings: (1) policies that improve early life outcomes are typically of high value, across contexts; (2) policies that bring transformative growth tend to be of high value; and (3) spending to address market failures is often of a higher value than subsidizing behavior in the absence of positive externalities (the presence of a positive externality, however, may justify a subsidy). The reality of fiscal decision-making is that it can be hard to prioritize these high-value investments, and the chapter also presents a brief summary of these constraints.

Because increasing the efficiency of spending likely also increases the value of spending, by freeing resources for other uses, the chapter concludes with a discussion of some aspects of how to increase efficiency.

Measuring the value of fiscal policies

A measure of a policy's value needs to be comprehensive, measuring the extent to which a policy improves the lives of all those affected. The total benefits of a policy include benefits accruing to intended beneficiaries of the policy and to those who are not necessarily intended beneficiaries but are nevertheless affected by it. Ensuring the measure includes all those affected is important because, for some policies, impacts on nontargeted households can be large. These benefits include both short-term benefits and long-term benefits discounted back to today, which is key, because it can take many years for returns to public spending to materialize.

The value of a policy also needs to take into account government costs to implement it. The net cost to government includes direct spending on the policy (or revenue received, in the case of tax policies) plus any indirect impacts from this policy on the government's budget—in both the short and long run. The indirect impacts of a policy on the government budget are referred to as the *fiscal externalities* of the policy. For example, if a policy increases worker wages, income tax revenues will increase, which will help offset the government's initial up-front costs of the policy.[1] Accounting for fiscal externalities when calculating net costs can be critical.

In order for it to inform policy prioritization, the measure of a policy's value is most useful if that measure has the following features:

- It is *comparable* across different types of policies. Different policy categories often have different measures to assess policy value (Hendren and Sprung-Keyser 2020). Health interventions may report the policy cost per life saved; education policies, the cost per student enrolled; and studies of tax policy changes, the implied marginal excess burden, or the marginal cost of funds. These varying measures of welfare make it very difficult for governments and policy makers to compare policies across sectors and, thus, to make informed fiscal trade-offs. It is also important that governments can compare the value of additional spending versus raising taxes.

- It is *context specific*. The private benefits from a fiscal policy will depend greatly on local context; for example, the private benefit to schooling will depend on the returns to schooling in a given country or for a given person in that country (depending on gender and ethnicity, for example). The degree to which a government benefits from implementing a given policy will depend on how much of that private return it subsequently taxes.

- It allows the possibility of *combining* the valuation of the policy for beneficiaries with social welfare weights applied to those beneficiaries. The purpose of calculating the value of a policy is to help make fiscal policy choices. The informed policy choice will also depend on identifying the beneficiaries of a policy and the value that society places on benefiting those people versus others. Doing so requires a valuation measure that can be combined with social welfare weights that capture the value to a society of benefiting one group over another (see the following discussion).

A number of different measures can capture the value of a policy in this way. The concept of the marginal value of public funds (MVPF), a systematic way of determining this value, has resurfaced in recent years and is being applied to a vast range of policies in the United States (Hendren and Sprung-Keyser 2020). It is now also being used more broadly, and this chapter applies it to selected interventions in low- and middle-income settings. The MVPF can be constructed, in principle, for any tax policy and any form of government expenditure.[2] The MVPF provides a measure of a policy's "bang for the buck," the total benefits accruing to all those affected by the policy relative to the net cost of the policy to the government. The MVPF takes into account all the benefits of a policy outlined earlier (namely, the long- and short-run benefits of the policy for intended beneficiaries and others affected by the policy) as well as the full costs of the policy (the direct costs and fiscal externalities). All benefits are measured in monetary units, allowing policy makers to compare policies across a wide variety of sectors that deliver different goods and services.[3] The higher the MVPF, the higher the benefits generated for the marginal dollar of spending. An MVPF of 2 indicates that $1 dollar of policy costs generates $2 of total benefits. Box 6.1 provides further details, and online annex 6A provides an example of how to calculate the MVPF for a cash transfer in a low- or middle-income country.

Online annex 6A also discusses similar policy valuation measures and how the MVPF differs from them. The MVPF can be applied across a range of tax and spending instruments and has other nice features outlined in box 6.1. At various points in this chapter, the discussion of policy value provides examples using the MVPF.

BOX 6.1

Calculating the value of a policy using the MVPF

Calculating the MVPF
One calculates the marginal value of public funds (MVPF) using evidence on policies' impacts and costs, using the calculation

$$MVPF = \frac{Total\ benefits}{Net\ cost\ to\ government}.$$

Predominantly applied in the United States, the concept can have arduous data requirements, especially in the context of developing economies, but it is being increasingly used (for example, Bergstrom, Dodd, and Rios 2022). Even in the absence of the full range of data and evidence needed to accurately construct the MVPF, calculating it with the best available data and evidence can still provide clarity on what drives the value of different policies and the range of likely values for some relevant policies in a given context. At the bare minimum, it provides policy makers with a much-needed unifying framework to help guide the fiscal decision-making process. Online annex 6A provides a more detailed description of calculating the MVPF for a cash transfer. In some cases, the long-term impacts on future government revenue, discounted back to today, fully offset initial up-front costs. In these situations, a policy is said to pay for itself and thus to have an infinite MVPF.[a]

One can calculate the MVPF for tax reforms as well as fiscal spending, which Hendren and Sprung-Keyser (2020) do for reforms to top personal income tax rates in the United States. Interestingly, the MVPFs of these reforms depend crucially on the pre-reform tax rate. For example, those authors find that a 1981 reform that lowered the top tax rate from 70 percent to 50 percent had an infinite MVPF because, in response to this large tax reduction, top earners substantially increased their reported income, leading to an increase in tax revenue. Thus, the tax reform paid for itself, generating an infinite MVPF. Conversely, they show that starting from a top tax rate of 39.6 percent and reducing it to 31.0 percent results in a much lower MVPF (1.85). When starting from a lower tax rate, the increase in earnings of top earners cannot fully compensate the government for its lost tax revenue. Thus, the MVPF is no longer infinite.

Because it focuses solely on the ratio of total benefits to net cost, the MVPF abstracts from how a policy's total cost will be financed. A particularly nice feature of the MVPF, it allows policy makers to explore different options to finance a particular expenditure, in direct contrast with other commonly used measures of policy value (see online annex 6A for further discussion). To account for the overall constraint in spending, one can compare the MVPF of spending on a particular policy with the MVPF associated with raising taxes or the MVPF of spending on an alternative policy.

Making fiscal policy choices using the MVPF
Consider a government deciding whether to spend an additional dollar on policy A. Suppose that, in order to fund this additional dollar, the government must reduce spending on policy B by $1. Should the government spend this dollar on policy A at the expense of policy B? When the two policies affect the same group of individuals, it becomes much easier to answer this question. If the value of policy A is higher than that of policy B (that is, policy A generates more benefits per dollar spent), the government should spend the dollar on policy A at the expense of policy B. Rarely, however, do two policies affect the exact same group of individuals.

In a more realistic scenario (that is, policy A and policy B affect different groups of people), policy makers must decide how much they value a dollar in the hands of those affected by policy A relative to those affected by policy B. For example, consider the case where the value of policy B is twice that of policy A. If the government values giving $2 to policy B beneficiaries

(continued)

BOX 6.1

Calculating the value of a policy using the MVPF *(continued)*

less than it values giving $1 to policy A beneficiaries, then redirecting money from policy B to policy A is worthwhile. Alternatively, if the government values giving $2 to policy B beneficiaries *more than* giving $1 to policy A beneficiaries, then it should not redirect money from policy B to policy A.

Because policies A and B can represent any two policies the government spends money on or receives money from, policy makers can compare spending across vastly different policies and consider various alternatives to finance spending on a particular policy. For example, if policy A represents spending on a cash transfer program and policy B on road construction, policy makers could then decide if they should increase spending on cash transfers or on roads. Alternatively, policy makers could consider alternative sources of financing for the cash transfer. For example, policy B could represent raising taxes on top earners (or reducing tax cuts on top earners) or increasing debt (that is, reducing spending on a future government program). A lower MVPF is better for raising revenue because it indicates a lower cost to households relative to the gain for governments.

a. When a policy has a negative net cost to the government and positive benefits accruing to those affected, it is said to "pay for itself." In these special cases, the policy has an infinite MVPF and it is always beneficial for the government to fund such policies. As seen in Hendren and Sprung-Keyser (2020), in the United States, policies that invest in the health and education of low-income children often have infinite MVPFs because, as adults, beneficiary children pay back more than the initial cost of the policies through additional tax revenue and reduced transfer payments. A later section of the chapter conjectures that policies with large long-run benefits in developing economies will also likely have infinite MVPFs despite the reduced ability of developing economies to recoup costs via taxing increased earnings.

Using information on the value of policies to inform policy choices

The incidence and value of a policy can inform prioritization

Combining information on the value of a policy with information on who benefits can inform policy choices. Figure 6.1 shows how information on value and beneficiaries can be combined. The vertical axis shows the value of a policy, and the horizontal axis shows the share of a policy's benefits accruing to rich households. If governments place a higher weight on giving to the poor relative to the rich, governments will opt for policies that fall in the top left quadrant of the figure (that is, high-value policies that predominantly benefit the poor) at the expense of policies in the lower right quadrant (that is, low-value policies that predominantly benefit the rich).

Figure 6.1 highlights where some stylized policies would likely fall. Investments in early childhood development targeted to low-income households can have very high value because they can bring income growth benefits to beneficiaries for all their adult learning years; thus, such policies would likely fall in the top left quadrant. Targeted unconditional cash transfers, although predominantly benefiting the poor, will likely generate less "bang for the buck" and could fall in the bottom left quadrant. As discussed later, energy subsidies—likely low-value policies with a larger share of benefits accruing to the rich—would fall in the bottom right quadrant. Finally, reducing the top labor income tax rate, despite benefiting only wealthy households, can result in a high-value policy if the starting top tax rate is high or a low-value policy if the starting top tax rate is low (Hendren and Sprung-Keyser 2020).

FIGURE 6.1

Fiscal policy trade-offs

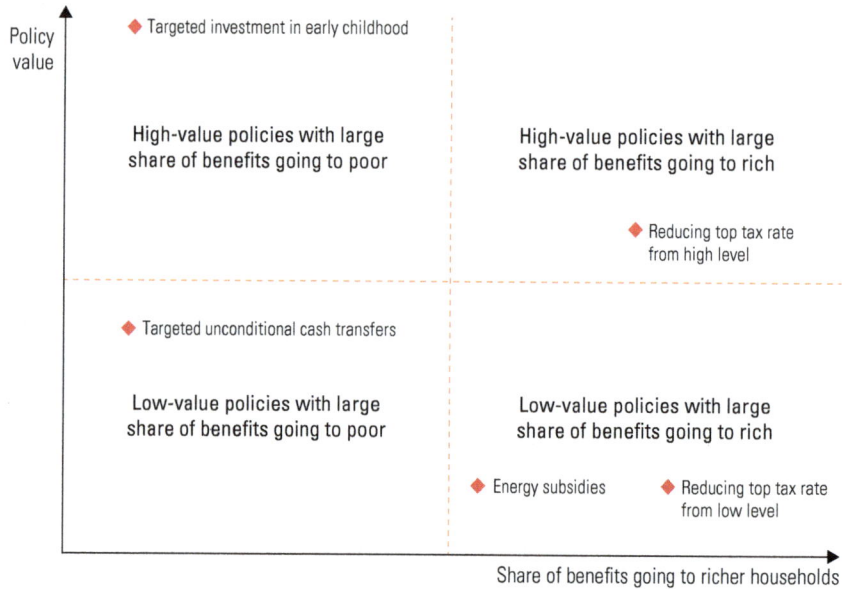

Source: World Bank.

Although highly informative, this type of analysis is not enough for policy prioritization. When two policies affect different groups of people, policy makers must determine how much they value a dollar in the hands of the beneficiaries of one policy versus those of another. This setup also lacks some important factors. Governments often choose not between two policies but on a package of policies. And policies can have complementary effects. For example, as detailed in the example of cash transfers in online annex 6A, the value of cash transfers depends on the returns to education, which are influenced by many additional policy choices. Finally, a high value on its own does not provide the rationale for government financing. The decision will also depend on the ability to meet the same objective through purely private provision. Although it does not provide all the information needed for policy prioritization, the information contained in figure 6.1 provides key inputs to these decisions and allows for greater transparency about the choice of one policy over another.

Addressing rising prices: Cash transfers are of higher value and more targeted than subsidies

Chapter 4 points out that income support has been withdrawn too quickly for some vulnerable groups of people who still have much lower employment and earnings than before the COVID-19 crisis. Higher food and energy prices are hurting many of these same groups (for example, the urban poor). Some groups will likely need continued income support until growth recovers. Chapter 4 also documents that, despite the slower overall fiscal response in 2022 than in 2020, governments have tended to use subsidies more to combat increasing prices. This section considers the evidence on the value of specific commodity subsidies that are being considered as part of the fiscal response.

Given the current challenge of higher food and energy prices facing consumers, especially the poor, it may seem at first glance that subsidizing food and energy prices is a good option. As highlighted in chapter 5, a larger share of spending on subsidies goes to better-off households.

Thus, in figure 6.1, a subsidy policy would end up further to the right than a cash transfer. However, it is also important to consider the value of the two policies. The following paragraphs examine what is known about the value of subsidies relative to the value of cash transfers.

A relatively large and growing evidence base concerns the effectiveness of cash transfers, which allows the value of a cash transfer to be measured. In online annex 6A, this evidence is used to calculate the MVPF for a typical targeted unconditional cash transfer program in a low-income country (LIC) or middle-income country (MIC) setting. Beyond the value of the cash transfer itself, cash transfers have value when beneficiaries can increase their income as a result of the transfer, either because the transfer relieves liquidity constraints to income generation or because it enables increased investments in the education of children in the household (with benefits for their future earnings). This value is lowered if the transfer disincentivizes labor force participation. Using systematic reviews of likely impacts as well as estimates of the likely value of future earnings increases for children in the household, the benefit to beneficiaries of US$1 of transfer is estimated to be US$1.11–US$1.61 in LICs and US$1.65–US$2.69 in MICs. The range of benefits and differences between LICs and MICs indicates the importance of context and other complementary policies that can increase or decrease the size of different channels of impact. Benefits to beneficiaries are larger in MICs, for example, in large part because MICs have a greater ability to tax the future gains in earnings of beneficiary children (which, in turn, lowers the overall net cost of the cash transfer program in MICs relative to LICs).

Increasingly, cash transfers are shown to have an impact also on nonbeneficiaries because beneficiaries spend (or in some cases share) transfer income in the local community or market. As discussed in online annex 6A, the initial literature suggests a likely positive impact but with a wide range of possible estimates. On the basis of this evidence, it is estimated that US$1 of transfers to beneficiaries has an impact of US$0 to US$0.18 on nonbeneficiaries.

The cost of providing cash transfers is not negligible. Online annex 6A reports estimates from Kondylis and Loeser (2021), who review cash transfer programs primarily in Sub-Saharan Africa and indicate that the cost of providing a transfer is US$0.18 for each US$1 transferred. Some positive fiscal externalities, however, can reduce the net cost: governments receive value added tax paid on transfer income that is spent, and they receive taxes paid on additional earnings and the spending that results from those additional earnings. The ability of a government to tax earnings and spending determines the size of such revenues. LICs have lower tax rates (see chapter 5), so the positive externality is estimated to be US$0.03–US$0.05 for every US$1 transferred compared to US$0.12–US$0.22 in MICs. Putting these estimates together implies that a typical cash transfer in a typical LIC setting has an MVPF of 1.0–1.6, and an MVPF of 1.6–3.0 in a typical MIC setting.

The value of a subsidy will vary with the type of subsidy. Take first a food subsidy. A key question to consider is whether the channels of impact present for a cash transfer will also be present for a transfer made to households in the form of a lower price on food. That is, would a food subsidy have the same impacts on short-run consumption growth and educational attainment of children in beneficiary households, and would a food subsidy have a similar impact on nonbeneficiaries through stimulating local economic activity as a cash transfer? There is little evidence on the impact of food price subsidies, but the literature on in-kind food transfers versus cash transfers offers some insights. Evidence in the United States suggests that food transfers reduce labor earnings, even though they can increase earnings in adulthood for children in households receiving food transfers (Hendren and Sprung-Keyser 2020). The literature for LICs and MICs is less clear. It shows that the modality of the transfer often has small or negligible impacts on the share of food in overall consumption, although in some instances in-kind food transfers increase food consumption more than cash (Gentilini 2016; Hidrobo et al. 2014). Similar to the in-kind transfer, food subsidies will likely have a greater effect on food consumption than cash transfers, because the only way to receive them is to spend on food (and often on specific foods).

To the extent that nonfood spending drives the income growth observed, a subsidy that induces a smaller increase in nonfood spending than a cash transfer will have a lower income growth impact. To the extent that nonfood spending goes to goods produced in the local economy (for example, informal services), lower nonfood spending will reduce the local multiplier effect in relation to cash transfers. However, the size of this difference will depend on the nature of local food markets and how food subsidies are provided. Nevertheless, the main concerns with the long-run value of food subsidies on food consumers are twofold: (1) they distort food spending decisions, discouraging substitution even when beneficial; and (2) they can partially benefit food suppliers instead of the poorer consumers they are intended to benefit. For example, one of the reasons the South African government chose to provide cash transfers rather than food vouchers during the pandemic is because the main beneficiaries of food vouchers were typically large multinational supermarket chains and not the smaller shops in local neighborhoods. These smaller shops needed support during the pandemic, and spending there would more likely contribute to a local multiplier effect.

Providing food subsidies may be administratively cheaper than delivering cash, but any reduction in the growth impact reduces revenues and increases net costs. In sum, providing food subsidies is likely to be of lower value than providing cash transfers, although perhaps not by much. The more important distinction is the poor targeting of food subsidies in relation to a targeted cash transfer, as discussed in chapter 5.

There is a larger literature base to draw on to assess the likely value of energy subsidies. The literature on energy taxes can be used to inform the likely impact of energy subsidies. This literature suggests that higher energy prices have no negative impact on gross domestic product (GDP) or employment growth, which in turn suggests that subsidies would have no beneficial impact. Very little evidence exists to suggest that the energy taxes or carbon pricing policies introduced in the European Union and North American countries affect GDP (Bernard, Kichian, and Islam 2018 and Metcalf 2019 for British Columbia; Metcalf and Stock 2020 for the European Union) or total employment (Azevedo, Wolff, and Yamazaki 2019 and Yamazaki 2017 for British Columbia; Metcalf and Stock 2020 for the European Union; Dussaux 2020 for France; Martin, de Preux, and Wagner 2014 for the United Kingdom). Schoder (2021) and Wingender and Misch (2021) consider a broader range of countries. Wingender and Misch (2021) find that, in 38 economies, carbon prices have strong impacts on emissions but no impact on sectoral value added or employment. Schoder (2021) finds that, across 75 economies, environmental taxes have no impact on employment and no negative output effects when implemented during years of economic expansion or when GDP is above its potential, but otherwise such taxes can have negative growth impacts.

What is clear from this literature is that energy taxes reduce emissions with long-run environmental gains, particularly in high-emitting countries, as shown in many of the papers cited in the previous paragraph as well as other papers covering a range of countries and empirical methods. The positive effect on emissions, the resulting health and long-run productivity effects (especially when implemented in high-emitting countries), and the null effects on employment and GDP suggest that energy taxes will have an MVPF lower than 1 because the long-run cost is less than the revenue gained, a good thing when considering taxation. It also means, however, that the MVPF of energy subsidies is below 1, which means that spending on this policy is low value.

Table 6.1 summarizes the key features of cash transfers and energy subsidies using these calculations and the calculations in chapter 5. Because energy subsidies likely have low value with larger benefits going to the rich, it is hard to justify using them over cash transfers, which have higher value and are better targeted to those in need. The broad base of beneficiaries for subsidies can make them more politically popular, but a more broadly targeted transfer program could prove to be equally popular without being regressive and could have potentially higher value. In the current crisis, cash transfers are likely a better policy instrument than energy subsidies.

Beyond choosing spending on cash transfers over energy subsidies, increasing spending on cash transfers could also be valuable if it can be financed by choosing a form of financing with a low marginal cost. For example, it may be worth choosing to increase spending on cash transfers over spending on a tax reduction if the tax reduction has an MVPF below 0.9–1.6 in a LIC and 1.6–3.0 in a MIC. As the next section shows using data from the United States, spending on tax

TABLE 6.1

Cash transfers are higher value and better targeted than subsidies

	MVPF	Incidence	
		Share of spending to bottom 40 (%)	Share of spending to top 20 (%)
LICs			
Cash transfer	0.9–1.6	64	9
Energy subsidy	<1	13	57
MICs			
Cash transfer	1.6–3.0	57	11
Energy subsidy	<1	24	37

Source: Original calculations as explained in online annex 6A.
Note: LICs = low-income countries; MICs = middle-income countries; MVPF = marginal value of public funds.

reforms can be of higher value than this range (when tax rates are very high), but spending on tax reforms will be of lower value when tax rates are already low. It is also worth noting that valuing transfers at their MVPF rather than their face value would increase the progressivity of fiscal policy and reduce the degree to which fiscal policy was estimated to increase poverty in chapter 5.

Nonetheless, countries tend to use subsidies over transfers. The fact that subsidies benefit all households increases their popularity relative to targeted transfers, which may point to the need for less narrowly targeted transfer programs. Such programs would be more politically feasible while also preventing the types of distortions that reduce the value of social spending made via price subsidies. Subsidies are also much easier to implement quickly, as discussed in chapter 4, which can make them a preferred policy tool in a crisis when transfer systems are underdeveloped. This limitation then points to the need to invest in developing delivery systems in noncrisis times, discussed further in chapter 7.

High-value policies that support growth

The recent literature on policy evaluation and the application of the MVPF framework points to three broad findings on likely characteristics of high-value policies: (1) policies that improve child outcomes are of high value, across contexts; (2) policies that bring transformative growth tend to be of high value; and (3) spending to address market failures is often of higher value than subsidizing private behavior (in the absence of a positive externality).

Policies that improve child outcomes are often of high value, across contexts

Chapter 3 highlights the cost of the pandemic on the life chances of the following generation. Reversing this cost is a priority for today, even though the benefits will primarily be realized in the long run. Using the fiscal incidence analysis presented in chapter 5, box 6.2 shows that spending on health and education can be pro-poor. This section presents evidence showing that investment in child education and health will likely have high value, especially if it can reach poorer households. World Bank (2022) discusses in detail the types of policies that could represent this extra spending in the context of recovery from the pandemic shock.

Spending that invests early in a child's life can be transformative (if effectively implemented) and position the child for a lifetime of higher earnings. Most applications of the MVPF framework have been in high-income countries (HICs) and to policies typically in one of four domains: social insurance (health, unemployment, and disability insurance), education (from preschool to job and vocational training), taxes and cash transfers, and in-kind transfers. Despite very different fiscal trade-offs in the HIC setting than in LIC and MIC settings, the results from these

BOX 6.2

The progressivity of spending on education and health

Spending on child education and health likely has high value in low- and middle-income countries, but to what extent do those countries direct general spending on education and health to poorer households (that is, is it in the top left or right quadrant of figure 6.1)? The direction of spending can be assessed using the fiscal incidence analysis methods introduced in chapter 5. Figure B6.2.1 presents data on the average share of spending on education and health going to each decile of the income distribution (concentration shares) using Commitment to Equity data from chapter 5.[a] The Commitment to Equity framework allocates education and health spending to households on the basis of the cost of services delivery and the use of services.

A larger share of education spending goes to poorer households in richer countries than in poorer ones. Although poorer households (typically with more children) enjoy a much larger share of education spending in high-income and upper-middle-income countries, the share is about even in lower-middle-income countries and heavily favors the rich in low-income countries (figure B6.2.1, panel a). This discrepancy results because enrollment is lower in the poorest deciles in poorer countries, particularly at the secondary and tertiary levels, which are also more expensive to provide per student. Although not shown, a larger share of spending on primary education is progressive across all income categories, whereas spending on secondary and tertiary education is less regressive. Nevertheless, in the case of education spending, spending more may increase progressivity at these levels, especially if well targeted. For example, many low- and lower-middle-income countries still require fees for secondary education. Increasing spending by removing those fees will increase enrollment among poorer deciles, thus making this form of spending more progressive. Similarly, other education spending that reduces access barriers can increase the progressivity of spending.

Health spending is not disaggregated between spending on child health and adult health (where child health spending is expected to have a higher marginal value of public funds than adult spending). Figure B6.2.1, panel b, shows that only in high-income countries do poorer households have a larger share of total public health spending; the share is equal for upper-middle-income

FIGURE B6.2.1

Education and health concentration shares, by income category and decile

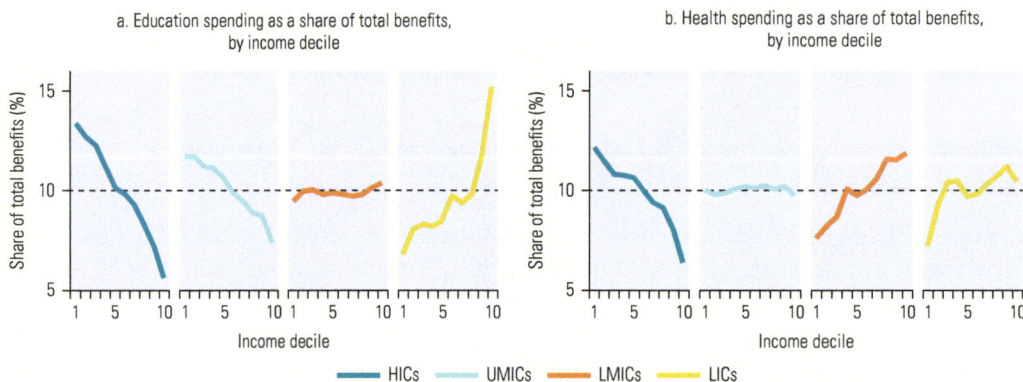

a. Education spending as a share of total benefits, by income decile

b. Health spending as a share of total benefits, by income decile

HICs   UMICs   LMICs   LICs

Sources: Sosa and Wai-Poi, forthcoming, based on data from CEQ Data Center on Fiscal Redistribution, https://commitmentoequity.org/data center; World Bank.
Note: The figure shows education spending (panel a) and health spending (panel b) as a share of total benefits by market income decile, aggregated at income level using median decile results. Education and health incidence are not available for Organisation for Economic Co-operation and Development countries. HICs = high-income countries; LICs = low-income countries; LMICs = lower-middle-income countries; UMICs = upper-middle-income countries.

(continued)

BOX 6.2

The progressivity of spending on education and health *(continued)*

countries and lower for low- and lower-middle-income countries. In many countries, the higher share of health spending for richer households is due to the availability of more expensive hospital care only in richer and urban areas that is at least partially provided through public spending, whereas basic primary health care may not even be available in some poorer and rural areas.

Understanding the progressivity of spending may also provide some indication as to its value, given that Hendren and Sprung-Keyser (2020) find that spending directed to low-income children has the highest marginal value of public funds. In general, health or education spending targeted to subpopulations in the greatest need may have greater returns.

a. CEQ Data Center on Fiscal Redistribution, https://commitmentoequity.org/datacenter.

applications may still offer important insights. Hendren and Sprung-Keyser (2020) conduct a welfare analysis of 133 policy changes in the United States over the past 50 years and find that spending on programs that improve low-income children's health and educational outcomes typically provide higher value compared with spending on programs focused on improving outcomes for adults (figure 6.2). The MVPF for programs targeted toward children is generally greater than 5.0, whereas that for programs targeted toward adults is typically between 0.5 and 2.0.

FIGURE 6.2

Average MVPF of policies in the United States, and of two policies targeted to children in low- and middle-income countries

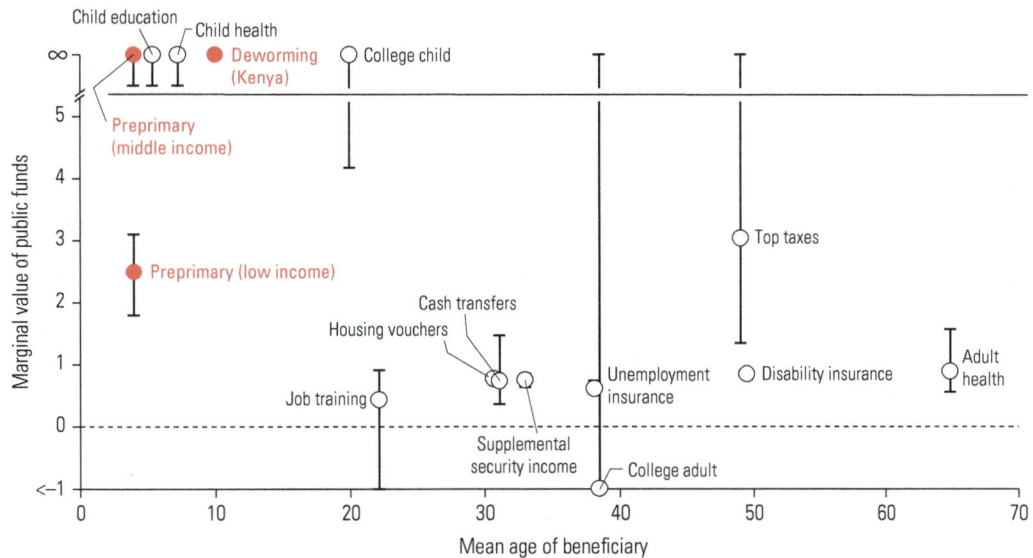

Sources: Hendren and Sprung-Keyser 2020 for US policies; Finkelstein and Hendren 2020 for deworming in Kenya; World Bank estimates using Holla et al. 2021 for preprimary education in low- and middle-income countries.
Note: The figure shows the estimated marginal value of public funds (MVPF) for different policy categories sorted by the mean age of beneficiaries on the x-axis. The data and methodology for policies in the United States are described in Hendren and Sprung-Keyser (2020) and online at https://www.policyinsights.org/. ∞ = infinity.

The evidence presented in the worked cash transfer example in online annex 6A highlights that this finding may hold true for LICs and MICs also. The impact of cash transfers on the schooling of children represented a large part of the value of the cash transfer program. A recent review of more than 50 studies on preprimary education in a wide variety of LICs and MICs provides some of the information necessary to generate an estimate of the likely MVPF of preprimary education investments (Holla et al. 2021). The studies demonstrate that investments in preprimary education often lead to substantial increases in children's cognitive and noncognitive skills (an increase in cognitive skills by 0.086 standard deviation on average). Using a similar method to calculate the MVPF from this spending as used in the cash transfer example shows that preprimary spending is likely to have an MVPF ranging from 1.8 to 3.1 in low-income settings and 35.1 to infinity in middle-income settings.[4] Additionally, using the results from Baird et al. (2016) who show that the estimated long-term revenue gain of deworming policy in Kenya is greater than the cost of deworming, Finkelstein and Hendren (2020) posit that deworming targeted to school-age children in Kenya has an infinite MVPF.

However, the limited applications to date of the MVPF approach in low- and middle-income settings generate only a partial picture. Ultimately, the similarity of results in LICs and MICs to child investments in HICs will depend on four factors: (1) whether policies targeting children's health and education can improve these outcomes at relatively low cost, (2) whether improving children's health and education in these settings leads to large earning gains, (3) the extent to which LICs and MICs can partially tax-back long-term benefits, and (4) whether LICs and MICs can borrow to fund investments with long-term gains at the same interest rate as HICs. This latter point helps determine how future gains are discounted to the present.

Evidence from recent cost-effectiveness evaluations highlights that some programs investing in the health and education of poor children in LICs and MICs can generate large impacts relative to up-front costs. Cost-effectiveness analysis conducted by the Abdul Latif Jameel Poverty Action Lab shows that a deworming program in Kenya, an iron and vitamin A supplement program in India, and the construction of village-based schools in Afghanistan all generate large gains in educational attainment relative to cost (see Bhula, Mahoney, and Murphy 2020).[5] Similarly, evaluations of preprimary investments also generate sizable learning gains relative to cost (Holla et al. 2021), as do some structured pedagogical investments (Evans and Yuan 2019). As in the United States, however, not all investments in child health and education have large returns relative to cost; for example, textbook provision in Kenya and computer-assisted learning in an Indian city led to student learning gains but only at a relatively high cost (Bhula, Mahoney, and Murphy 2020; McEwan, 2012).

To what extent can these short-term gains translate into long-term benefits in LICs and MICs? Montenegro and Patrinos (2021) find larger returns to schooling in developing economy settings, suggesting that gains in schooling generate relatively larger long-run returns, on average, in LICs and MICs than in HICs. This finding would suggest that programs that increase educational attainment in LICs and MICs create higher private benefits than do similar policies in HICs. Context, however, almost certainly matters; for example, Duflo, Dupas, and Kremer (2021) find that gains in earnings associated with secondary school completion in Ghana came primarily in the form of better access to rationed jobs in the public sector—that is, any gain to beneficiaries came at the expense of others. In such settings, rapidly expanding education without concomitant reforms or investments may result in a cohort of overeducated young people, perhaps frustrated in their aspirations. Therefore, investments in children's education may need to be accompanied by investments improving labor market opportunities so that long-term benefits can be realized from the short-term education gains. Policies that generate large, long-run gains will have lower MVPFs when interest rates are higher, because it is more costly for governments to finance investments by borrowing against future gains. Interest rates tend to be higher in LICs and MICs than in HICs.

The worked cash transfer example clearly shows that the lower a country's tax capacity, the less a government stands to gain in increased tax revenue from policies that generate large, long-term gains, thereby leading to lower MVPFs. Chapter 5 documents that LICs and MICs have substantially lower tax capacity than do HICs and so will have less to gain from what otherwise may be high-value policy choices. At the same time, as a country develops, so does its tax capacity (Jensen 2022).

Policies that bring transformative growth tend to be of high value

Beyond investments in child education and health, the impacts of other forms of transformative spending—spending that puts individuals and economies onto a higher growth path—are often realized in the long run. These policies are almost certainly high- (if not infinite-) MVPF policies. Such policies can include investments in research and development (R&D) and infrastructure as well as policies that bring long-run climate benefits.

Evidence from the Green Revolution indicates that spending on agricultural R&D can have large impacts for technology adopters on agricultural growth, investments in schooling, capital accumulation, and reductions in fertility and migration (both locational and sectoral). The same spending can bring benefits to nonadopters through lower food prices, environmental benefits from lower land use, and an increased pace of structural transformation. Delaying the Green Revolution for 10 years would have reduced GDP per capita in 2010 by 17 percent and resulted in a cumulative loss equivalent to one year of global GDP (Gollin, Hansen, and Wingender 2021). If the full cost of investments made by the agricultural research systems in developing the seeds that spurred the Green Revolution is less than the tax revenue earned from this additional GDP, the MVPF is infinite. In 2010, average tax revenue was 13.4 percent of GDP, so the present value of the investments in developing the new seeds would need to be less than 2.3 percent of GDP, which is highly likely.[6]

Infrastructure investments can have similarly high impacts on agricultural growth and stimulate structural transformation. Donaldson (2018) finds that connecting a district to the Indian railroad network increased agricultural income growth by 16 percent. Similarly, an infrastructure project that seeks to improve commuting in urban settings can also have a high MVPF. Direct beneficiaries, those who make use of expanded or improved public transit lines, will experience reduced travel times, which translates into monetary benefits (for example, by multiplying the reduction in travel time by a person's hourly wage). In addition, such an expansion likely has many indirect beneficiaries. For example, congestion may decrease, leading to a reduction in air pollution and a reduction in travel time for those who do not use public transit. Moreover, this type of transformation may lead to improvements in the allocation of workers to more productive jobs. For example, Zárate (2022) points out that the subway line expansion in Mexico City led to a reduction in informal sector employment and an increase in formal sector employment. Although fully measuring who a policy affects, and in what way and by how much, is difficult, understanding the impact on some aggregate measure—such as average per capita income or average per capita income for different groups of the population—is useful for gauging the overall size of the benefits from infrastructure investments. Both Tsivanidis (2019) and Zárate (2022) find that the public transit expansion in Bogotá and Mexico City (respectively) led to large gains in GDP; Tsivanidis (2019) shows that high-skilled workers and low-skilled workers benefit about the same.

The direct costs of such infrastructure projects include initial construction and future maintenance, operations, and overhead (discounted back to today). If such projects lead to increased GDP (from, say, workers reallocating to more-productive formal sector jobs), the government will likely experience gains in future tax revenue. For example, with more workers moving to formal jobs, the government will reap gains in future tax revenue because more workers in the formal sector mean more workers subject to labor income taxation.

Discounted gains in future tax revenue constitute the fiscal externalities of such projects. Notably, Tsivanidis (2019) and Zárate (2022) find that the gains in GDP outweigh the direct costs of public transit expansions in Colombia and Mexico, which suggests that such projects have a high MVPF (even potentially infinite, if the government recoups enough in tax revenue to cover the direct costs).

Not all policies within these categories are high-MVPF policies, and it is important to carefully consider the balance of sometimes-countervailing evidence. For example, Asher and Novosad (2020) find that rural roads in India have a very small impact on income, agricultural output, or asset accumulation for the period they measure, which could imply a low MVPF. However, Shamdasani (2021) finds increased diversification and commercialization in more remote villages connected by the same rural road building program, pointing to a higher MVPF for the same investment, particularly for more remote villages.

Spending to address market failures is often of higher value than subsidies

Often, fiscal spending to support income in the short run comes in the form of subsidies to production. However, spending that directly addresses market failures is often more cost-effective in the long run, and therefore of higher value, than subsidizing private behavior (in the absence of a positive externality, which is the typical justification for a subsidy). Two examples relevant for the current moment illustrate this difference.

First, a key question many countries currently face is how to increase agricultural production given the global reduction in food trade and the rising prices of inputs. Input subsidies (most famously, fertilizer subsidies, but also the underpricing of surface and groundwater) increase agricultural production in the short run. They also, however, can carry long-run costs to the natural resource base, distort incentives, and dissuade farmers from making long-run investments in productivity. Particularly in MICs, subsidies are large, amounting to about 5 percent of the value of agricultural production (FAO, UNDP, and UNEP 2021).

What other actions may support agricultural production and even increase agricultural productivity? A farmer's investment to increase productivity is based not only on current and forecasted input prices but also on current and forecasted output prices, knowledge on how best to invest, and access to credit, insurance, and labor markets (Duflo, Kremer, and Robinson 2008; Rosenzweig and Udry 2020). Subsidizing input prices may maintain production in the short run, but it does not address the root causes of market inefficiencies or a lack of knowledge.[7] Addressing these constraints on production should bring larger gains in the long run, and some interventions will also have immediate payoffs on production and productivity. Jones et al. (2022) provide an example of the benefits of addressing factor market frictions over subsidizing input costs, showing that, even when provided free water use, farmers limit their use of irrigation as a result of local labor market failures.

An Agricultural Technology Adoption Initiative review of lessons from 10 years of evaluating experiments on how to increase productivity among poorer farmers (smallholders in South Asia and Sub-Saharan Africa) points to the potential for well-designed policies in extension and marketing support (Bridle et al. 2019). The returns, and therefore the MVPF of business-as-usual extension (one of the main components of agricultural expenditure outside of subsidies), can be low; however, a large body of evidence shows that, when information is provided about a new technique that truly brings positive returns, and when that information is tailored (delivered by the right person at the right time and in an actionable, easy-to-use way), productivity gains can be large. Sometimes this information will even result in reducing the use of inputs for further productivity gains. For example, providing Bangladeshi farmers with color leaf charts and training resulted in a reduction in the use of urea fertilizer of 8 percent without compromising yields (Islam and Beg 2021). The intervention has a return of 2.8 percent as a result of reducing production costs and increasing environmental benefits.

Improving output market conditions for farmers is not just about increasing the spot price but about improving the functioning of markets, including market mechanisms that reduce risk and uncertainty. Public investments to provide price information have small impacts but, if delivered cost-effectively, can be worthwhile. Other market support policies can have a greater impact on providing incentives for farmers to invest in greater crop quantity or quality. Impact evaluations have shown that the certainty provided by sales contracts between farmers and buyers implemented at the beginning of the season can have sizeable productivity impacts without any additional support (Arouna, Michler, and Lokossou 2021). Investments in scales and third-party quality certification have also been shown to incentivize productivity investments with net income increases for farmers (Bernard et al. 2017; Saenger, Torero, and Qaim 2014).

A second urgent priority facing governments is increasing employment in urban areas. Chapter 2 highlights that, even at the end of 2021, employment was still below prepandemic levels, particularly for less educated households in urban areas. Supporting firms is a key priority, particularly for urban small and medium enterprises that are likely to provide needed employment opportunities.

Firms in LICs and MICs currently benefit from 40 percent of total tax expenditures, but little evidence exists to suggest that this spending affects growth or employment. There is, however, an increasing body of evidence on the types of public investments that can help firm growth. McKenzie (2021), McKenzie et al. (2021), and Quinn and Woodruff (2019) review this evidence and highlight that increasing capital has immediate and sustained impacts on small and medium enterprises. Less clear, however, is the role that public spending plays in increasing access to capital. Instead, these reviews highlight the need to increase access to capital through innovation in access to finance and hire-purchase agreements (Bari et al. 2021; Battaglia, Gulesci, and Madestam 2018; Field et al. 2013).

Similar to the evidence reported in the agricultural space, considerable experimentation on how to provide business training highlights that business-as-usual training for firms has a limited average impact on firms' productivity or growth. In contrast, customized management training can have a high immediate and sustained return when implemented well. Evidence on the provision of customized business services as a way of increasing overall growth is also encouraging (McKenzie 2021; McKenzie et al. 2021; Quinn and Woodruff 2019).

Constraints on investing in high-value policies

Because of the data gaps that prevent a comprehensive assessment of spending policies across countries (chapter 5), there are no systematic data with which to assess the share of public spending going to predominantly high-return policies. As discussed in the previous section, however, the evidence available points to underinvestment in high-MVPF policies with long-run benefits and a bias toward spending on policies that have more immediate impacts (such as tax exemptions and subsidies).

The choice to spend on low-value policies over high-value policies may just reveal the true social welfare weights that govern decision-making rather than reflect systemic constraints on investing in high-value policies. For example, the need to benefit a broad base of people rather than a narrowly targeted group of poor households (as discussed in the case of subsidies) may result in a policy choice with many direct beneficiaries even if it is of lower value. The choice to spend on low-value policies can also reflect effective lobbying by special interest groups that shift the weight in favor of policies benefiting those households. Better data and evidence on the beneficiaries and value of fiscal policy choices can help bring transparency to the choices being made. Chapter 7 discusses the need for better data and evidence, identified across the chapters in this report.

High-value policies are often those with benefits in the future; therefore, the discount rate or interest rate becomes important in determining the value of these policies. These key parameters determine how benefits in the future are valued today. Long-run benefits will be lower today when interest rates are high and in moments of crisis or fiscal consolidation when there are immediate pressing needs. This may also help explain the finding that countries, particularly LICs and MICs, cut spending on health and education—two areas where returns on spending tend to be realized in the long run—in the aftermath of financial crises, when interest rates tend to increase (Knowles, Pernia, and Racelis 1999; Mohseni-Cheraghlou 2016).

If individuals or governments actually value future benefits less than assumed in the MVPF calculations, then the MVPFs for policies that generate large, long-term gains will be lower than calculated. Governments making these types of policy decisions may discount benefits at higher rates than commonly used in MVPF calculations for three reasons:

1. There is an inherent present bias toward policy decisions driven by delivering results within electoral cycles rather than across generations (for example, Healey and Malhotra 2009 in the case of showing support for crisis response rather than risk reduction).

2. The discount rates held by poorer households tend to be higher, reflecting the present bias that comes with poverty and the need to meet immediate welfare needs (Mullainathan and Shafir 2013).

3. The interest rates faced by LIC and MIC governments tend to be higher than market interest rates as a result of constraints on borrowing.

Under these conditions, policies that carry clear short-run benefits while increasing opportunities for long-run growth will be needed. Alternatively, addressing the factors that cause discount or interest rates to be high will help governments reap the long-run returns to their investments.

Addressing the first challenge requires increasing commitment to long-term development objectives in the political arena. Doing so will often require increasing participation and contestability in the political process as discussed in *World Development Report 2017: Governance and the Law* (World Bank 2017). That report also underscores that greater transparency and information around decision-making can increase incentives for policy making that supports longer-term development objectives. Collecting data and generating evidence that renders more transparent the choices is an important part of this process, and chapter 7 discusses some of the priorities in this regard. In addition, chapter 7 discusses options to incentivize long-term decision-making in regard to crisis preparation.

The general process of income growth may ultimately reduce present bias for lower income, but it will take time for those gains to manifest and thus address the second challenge. On the third challenge, addressing debt and increasing access to low-cost financing should encourage investments in high-value policies.

Finally, some of the policies highlighted as particularly high value can be risky, yet the MVPF does not account for risk. For example, although the MVPF of spending on agricultural R&D was calculated as very high for the Green Revolution, spending on R&D can often result in technologies with a much lower return. Sharing this risk across a large number of countries is one justification for global public investment in agricultural and health R&D, which benefits many countries and can have particular impact in LICs and MICs. Examples include investments in the Consultative Group on International Agricultural Research and in the International AIDS Vaccine Initiative.

Increasing the value of policies through increased efficiency of spending

While making the right fiscal policy choices is key, increasing the efficiency of spending choices is also essential to maximize the value of spending. A high-value policy can quickly become low-value if implemented poorly. Examples of well-directed investments costing many times more than initial estimates or having underwhelming impacts are too common. For example, Baum, Mogues, and Verdier (2020) estimate that, on average, 35 percent of public investment in infrastructure is lost in the process of managing public funds, with even higher efficiency gaps in LICs. This estimate implies that a policy spending $1 to generate $1 of benefits will have an MVPF of only 1/1.35 = 0.74. Inefficiencies come in many forms, so there is no easy fix. A large literature explores causes of public sector inefficiencies, and it would be difficult to comprehensively summarize the findings here. Sources of such inefficiencies include political economy issues (which, for example, may direct scarce spending to well-off areas) and corruption.

Inefficiency can also originate in the behavior of bureaucrats and other public agents in relation to the incentives they face. Bureaucrats responsible for implementing policies or workers delivering services are subject to principal agent problems that can manifest in costly procurement, delayed projects, and underperforming or low-quality services. Emerging literature suggests that giving public servants more autonomy in their assigned tasks, perhaps coupled with constructive supervision, can improve public sector efficiency. Conversely, introducing stronger financial incentives linked to performance, and concomitant enhanced monitoring, may generate little gain. In Ghana and Nigeria, allowing bureaucrats to have input in policy formation and flexibility to manage budgets substantially increased project completion rates (Rasul and Rogger 2018; Rasul, Rogger, and Williams 2018). In contrast, management practices involving monitoring and incentive provision lowered completion rates. One study in Pakistan found that greater autonomy, in the form of bypassing procurement steps for generic goods, led to significant savings and was more effective than providing incentives (Bandiera et al. 2021). Evidence from Chile suggests that too much focus on audits can lead to less efficient procurement because audits incentivize simpler, lower-risk, and higher-cost procurement practices (Gerardino, Litschig, and Pomeranz 2020).

The performance of individual public servants can be just as influential as the right organizational structure for the overall efficiency of the public sector. Analysis of public procurement in the Russian Federation from 2011 to 2016 suggests the government would save US$13 billion annually if the bottom quartile of bureaucrats operated as effectively as the top quartile (Best, Hjort, and Szakonyi 2019). Experimental evidence from Indonesia finds that pay-for-performance (PFP) programs increased effort among those joining the civil service, but only if they had lower-than-average pro-social motivation (Banuri and Keefer 2015). If the public sector tends to attract applicants with pro-social motivation, it would suggest that performance pay, a widespread reform intended to promote efficiency of spending, is a weak instrument to improve efficiency.

An organizational structure that provides managerial autonomy and accountability also appears to influence spending efficiency in key sectors such as education and health. Better management practices in schools can improve the effectiveness of public spending on education. Cross-country evidence shows that higher-quality management in high schools is associated with better educational outcomes (Bloom et al. 2015). More autonomous government schools had higher management scores, and accountability for student performance was a key factor. An intervention to improve management in Indian schools by introducing detailed school ratings and improvement plans, but without changing accountability or incentives, was found to have no impact on student outcomes (Muralidharan and Singh 2020). Despite high compliance and expansion to 600,000 schools nationally, the program continued to appear ineffective at improving educational outcomes.

Teacher PFP programs can be effective in the right conditions, but they more often generate little gain. In Pakistan and Rwanda, PFP contracts attracted high-performance teachers and increased teacher effort (Brown and Andrabi 2021; Leaver et al. 2021). Evidence from rural primary schools in China and India suggests that linking teacher pay to student performance improves education outcomes (Loyalka et al. 2019; Muralidharan and Sundararaman 2011).

In rural Uganda, PFP increased attendance rates but improved test scores only in schools that also provided textbooks, suggesting that instructional resources are critical (Gilligan et al. 2022). Linking teacher promotions to performance in China was also associated with higher effort, but only when promotions were on the horizon (Karachiwalla and Park 2017). A review of 15 PFP evaluations in LICs and MICs finds that most failed to improve student test scores (Breeding, Béteille, and Evans 2019). Some programs had adverse effects, such as cheating to secure incentives, and only one-third of the programs were sustained beyond the evaluation period. For programs that did work, political will, teacher buy-in, and the technical capacity to comprehensively assess teacher performance appear to be key factors. Overall, evidence suggests that strengthening school management and teacher accountability for student outcomes could generate greater efficiencies in education spending and that PFP programs offer no inevitable payoff.

In parallel findings for the health sector, the literature suggests that providing flexible financing and decision-making power to health facilities can increase the value per dollar spent on primary health services. A review of financial incentives in health service delivery finds that performance-based financing can improve coverage in low-income settings with centralized health systems (de Walque et al. 2022). It finds, however, that PFP had limited impacts, especially relative to direct facility finance, which provides autonomy to frontline health facilities to allocate operating budgets without structured financial incentives. For example, providing operating funds to public health facilities in Nigeria had comparable effects to PFP on health care use, but at half the cost (Khanna et al. 2021). A similar conclusion was seen in Zambia (Friedman et al. 2016). Greater efficiency in health service spending and better outcomes may be achieved by reallocating resources within a constant budget envelope toward direct facility financing, supportive supervision, and overcoming financial barriers to accessing health care.

Digitalization also holds promise for increased public spending efficiency. One way it does so is that digital transformation can reduce leakages from public spending. In India, a reform to the workfare transfer system reduced administration costs and improved transparency, resulting in persistent savings of almost 20 percent of program expenditure after a nationwide scale-up (Banerjee et al. 2020). Program expenditures dropped, because the official database dropped fake households and program officials' personal wealth fell. Investing in delivery systems is likely to be cost-effective not just for regular transfers but also for future crisis response. Digital platforms can enable timely and targeted support during a crisis, as demonstrated during the pandemic. Chapter 7 discusses in more detail the more general benefits of digitalization for the conduct of fiscal policy.

Conclusion

This chapter has highlighted the importance of choosing fiscal policies that bring long-run growth and benefits, and finding ways to comprehensively quantify the benefits and costs for policy analysis. Governments currently face difficult fiscal trade-offs. Considering these long-run benefits and choosing high-value policies will be essential to ensure that governments make choices in a way that benefits poverty reduction and shared prosperity in the long run. Without a focus on high-value fiscal policies, it will be hard to reverse the setback to progress, including the loss of learning and opportunities experienced by children described in part 1 of this report. Chapter 7 further discusses policy options and provides a set of simulations that underscore the importance of prioritizing faster growth.

Notes

1. Fiscal externalities can also be negative; for example, a policy can reduce labor supply and tax revenue or require increased spending on something else (for example, health care).

2. The mathematical formulation for the marginal value of public funds has been around for decades (see, for example, Mayshar 1990). Hendren and Sprung-Keyser (2020) highlight its empirical usefulness in the wake of an abundance of causal policy estimates.

3. This is done by assessing how much each affected individual or household is willing to pay for their observed benefit.

4. Children in beneficiary households (beneficiary households are those with children who are enrolled in preprimary programs that receive increased investment) will have benefits equal to the discounted gain in lifetime earnings that increased investments in preprimary education generate. Despite limited evidence on the direct impacts of preprimary education on children's lifetime earnings, a sizable literature demonstrates that investments in preprimary education often lead to substantial increases in children's cognitive and noncognitive skills. Holla et al. (2021), for example, review more than 50 studies in a wide variety of contexts and find that investments in preprimary education increase cognitive skills by 0.086 standard deviation in low- and middle-income countries. These gains in skills are translated into gains in years of schooling using recent work by Evans and Yuan (2019). A 0.13 standard deviation increase in cognitive skills is equivalent to a 0.52–0.88 increase in years of schooling, which implies that a 0.086 standard deviation increase in cognitive skills is equivalent to a 0.34–0.52 increase in years of schooling. Translating these gains in years of schooling into gains in lifetime earnings via Mincer regressions from Montenegro and Patrinos (2021), the estimated gain in (discounted) lifetime earnings is between US$109 and US$186 in a low-income setting and US$628 and US$1,065 in a middle-income setting. Adults in beneficiary households (particularly females) may experience increased labor supply (see, for example, Berger and Black 1992;

Cascio 2009; Herbst 2010), in turn leading to increased earnings (at least in the short run). However, this increase in labor supply comes with a reduction in leisure time; thus, the net monetary benefit from increased labor supply is smaller than the increase in associated labor market income. It is assumed that the net monetary benefit of increased labor supply is zero; that is, increased earnings are fully offset by the monetary cost of decreased leisure time. The net cost of investments in preprimary education is assumed to be US$65 per child in program costs (Holla et al. 2021) and a discounted gain in consumption tax revenue between US$3 and US$6 in low-income countries and US$47 and US$80 in middle-income countries (using the same calculation method as the cash transfer example). The MVPF is thus estimated to be between 1.8 and 3.1 in low-income settings and from 35.1 to infinity in middle-income settings.

5. The Abdul Latif Jameel Poverty Action Lab, headquartered at the Massachusetts Institute of Technology, is a global research center working to reduce poverty by ensuring that policy is informed by scientific evidence (https://www.povertyactionlab.org).

6. Average tax revenue as a percent of GDP for 2010 comes from World Bank Databank (https://data.worldbank.org/indicator/GC.TAX.TOTL.GD.ZS?end=2020&start=1972). The 2.3 percent of GDP was defined as follows: $0.17 \times 0.134 = 0.023$ of 2010 GDP.

7. Although learning effects can arise from temporary subsidies (Carter, Laajaj, and Yang 2021).

References

Arouna, Aminou, Jeffrey D. Michler, and Jourdain C. Lokossou. 2021. "Contract Farming and Rural Transformation: Evidence from a Field Experiment in Benin." *Journal of Development Economics* 151 (102626). https://doi.org/10.1016/j.jdeveco.2021.102626.

Asher, Sam, and Paul Novosad. 2020. "Rural Roads and Local Economic Development." *American Economic Review* 110 (3): 797–823.

Azevedo, Deven, Hendrik Wolff, and Akio Yamazaki. 2019. "Do Carbon Taxes Kill Jobs? Firm-Level Evidence from British Columbia." Clean

Economy Working Paper Series (March) 18-08, Smart Prosperity Institute, Ottawa, Canada.

Baird, Sarah, Joan Hamory Hicks, Michael Kremer, and Edward Miguel. 2016. "Worms at Work: Long-Run Impacts of a Child Health Investment." *Quarterly Journal of Economics* 131 (4): 1637–80.

Bandiera, Oriana, Michael Carlos Best, Adnan Qadir Khan, and Andrea Prat. 2021. "The Allocation of Authority in Organizations: A Field Experiment with Bureaucrats." *Quarterly Journal of Economics* 136 (4): 2195–242.

Banerjee, Abhijit, Esther Duflo, Clément Imbert, Santhosh Mathew, and Rohini Pande. 2020. "E-governance, Accountability, and Leakage in Public Programs: Experimental Evidence from a Financial Management Reform in India." *American Economic Journal: Applied Economics* 12 (4): 39–72.

Banuri, Sheheryar, and Philip Keefer. 2015. "Was Weber Right? The Effects of Pay for Ability and Pay for Performance on Pro-Social Motivation, Ability and Effort in the Public Sector." Policy Research Working Paper 7261, World Bank, Washington, DC.

Bari, Faisal, Kashif Malik, Muhammad Meki, and Simon R. Quinn. 2021. "Asset-Based Microfinance for Microenterprises: Evidence from Pakistan." CEPR Discussion Paper No. DP15768, Center for Economic and Policy Research, Washington, DC.

Battaglia, Marianna, Selim Gulesci, and Andreas Madestam. 2018. "Repayment Flexibility and Risk Taking: Experimental Evidence from Credit Contracts." CEPR Discussion Paper 13329, Center for Economic and Policy Research, Washington, DC.

Baum, Anja, Tewodaj Mogues, and Genevieve Verdier. 2020. "Getting the Most from Public Investment." Chapter 3 in *Well Spent: How Strong Infrastructure Governance Can End Waste in Public Investment*, edited by Gerd Fouad, Manal Fouad, Torban S. Hansen, and Genevieve Verdier. Washington, DC: International Monetary Fund.

Berger, Mark C., and Dan A. Black. 1992. "Child Care Subsidies, Quality of Care, and the Labor Supply of Low-Income, Single Mothers." *Review of Economics and Statistics* 74 (4): 635–42.

Bergstrom, Katy, William Dodd, and Juan Rios. 2022. "Welfare Analysis of Changing Notches: Evidence from Bolsa Família." Policy Research Working Paper 10117, World Bank, Washington, DC.

Bernard, Jean-Thomas, Maral Kichian, and Misbahul Islam. 2018. "Effects of B.C.'s Carbon Tax on GDP." USAEE/IAEE Research Paper Series 18-329, United States Association for Energy Economics, Dayton, OH; International Association for Energy Economics, Dallas, TX.

Bernard, Tanguy, Alain De Janvry, Samba Mbaye, and Elisabeth Sadoulet. 2017. "Expected Product Market Reforms and Technology Adoption by Senegalese Onion Producers." *American Journal of Agricultural Economics* 99 (4): 1096–115.

Best, Michael Carlos, Jonas Hjort, and David Szakonyi. 2019. "Individuals and Organizations as Sources of State Effectiveness." NBER Working Paper 23350, National Bureau of Economic Research, Cambridge, MA.

Bhula, Radhika, Meghan Mahoney, and Kyle Murphy. 2020. "Conducting Cost-Effectiveness Analysis (CEA)." Abdul Latif Jameel Poverty Action Lab, Massachusetts Institute of Technology, Cambridge, MA. www.povertyactionlab.org/resource/conducting-cost-effectiveness-analysis-cea.

Bloom, Nicholas, Renata Lemos, Raffaella Sadun, and John Van Reenen. 2015. "Does Management Matter in Schools?" *Economic Journal* 125 (584): 647–74.

Breeding, Mary, Tara Béteille, and David K. Evans. 2019. "Teacher Pay-for-Performance (PFP) Systems: What Works? Where? And How?" Teachers Thematic Group Working Paper, World Bank, Washington, DC.

Bridle, Leah, Jeremy Magruder, Craig McIntosh, and Tavneet Suri. 2019. "Experimental Insights on the Constraints to Technology Adoption." Working Paper, Agricultural Technology Adoption Initiative, Abdul Latif Jameel Poverty Action Lab, Massachusetts Institute of Technology, Cambridge, MA; and Center for Effective Global Action, University of California, Berkeley.

Brown, Christina, and Tahir Andrabi. 2021. "Inducing Positive Sorting through Performance Pay: Experimental Evidence from Pakistani Schools." Working Paper, University of California, Berkeley.

Carter, Michael, Rachid Laajaj, and Dean Yang. 2021. "Subsidies and the African Green

Revolution: Direct Effects and Social Network Spillovers of Randomized Input Subsidies in Mozambique." *American Economic Journal: Applied Economics* 13 (2): 206–29.

Cascio, Elizabeth U. 2009. "Maternal Labor Supply and the Introduction of Kindergartens into American Public Schools." *Journal of Human Resources* 44 (1): 140–70.

de Walque, Damien, Eeshani Kandpal, Adam Wagstaff, Jed Friedman, Sven Neelsen, Moritz Piatti-Fünfkirchen, Anja Sautmann, Gil Shapira, and Ellen Van de Poel. 2022. *Improving Effective Coverage in Health: Do Financial Incentives Work?* Washington, DC: World Bank.

Donaldson, D. 2018. "Railroads of the Raj: Estimating the Impact of Transport Infrastructure." *American Economic Review* 108 (4–5): 899–934.

Duflo, Esther, Pascaline Dupas, and Michael Kremer. 2021. "The Impact of Free Secondary Education: Experimental Evidence from Ghana." NBER Working Paper 28937, National Bureau of Economic Research, Cambridge, MA.

Duflo, Esther, Michael Kremer, and Jonathan Robinson. 2008. "How High Are Rates of Return to Fertilizer? Evidence from Field Experiments in Kenya." *American Economic Review* 98 (2): 482–88.

Dussaux, D. 2020. "The Joint Effects of Energy Prices and Carbon Taxes on Environmental and Economic Performance: Evidence from the French Manufacturing Sector." OECD Environment Working Paper 154, Organisation for Economic Co-operation and Development, Paris.

Evans, David K., and Fei Yuan. 2019. "Equivalent Years of Schooling: A Metric to Communicate Learning Gains in Concrete Terms." Policy Research Working Paper 8752, World Bank, Washington, DC.

FAO (Food and Agriculture Organization of the United Nations), UNDP (United Nations Development Programme), and UNEP (United Nations Environment Programme). 2021. *A Multi-Billion-Dollar Opportunity—Repurposing Agricultural Support to Transform Food Systems.* New York and Rome: United Nations.

Field, Erica, Rohini Pande, John Papp, and Natalia Rigol. 2013. "Does the Classic Microfinance Model Discourage Entrepreneurship among the Poor? Experimental Evidence from India." *American Economic Review* 103 (6): 2196–226.

Finkelstein, Amy, and Nathaniel Hendren. 2020. "Welfare Analysis Meets Causal Inference." *Journal of Economic Perspectives* 34 (4): 146–67.

Friedman, Jed, Jumana Qamruddin, Collins Chansa, and Ashis Kumar Das. 2016. "Impact Evaluation of Zambia's Health Results-Based Financing Pilot Project." Working paper, World Bank Group, Washington, DC.

Gentilini, Ugo. 2016. "Revisiting the 'Cash Versus Food' Debate: New Evidence for an Old Puzzle?" *World Bank Research Observer* 31 (1): 135–67.

Gerardino, Maria Paula, Stephan Litschig, and Dina Pomeranz. 2020. "Distortion by Audit: Evidence from Public Procurement." NBER Working Paper 23978, National Bureau of Economic Research, Cambridge, MA.

Gilligan, Daniel O., Naureen Karachiwalla, Ibrahim Kasirye, Adrienne M. Lucas, and Derek Neal. 2022. "Educator Incentives and Educational Triage in Rural Primary Schools." *Journal of Human Resources* 57 (1): 79–111.

Gollin, Douglas, Casper Worm Hansen, and Asger M. Wingender. 2021. "Two Blades of Grass: The Impact of the Green Revolution." *Journal of Political Economy* 129 (8): 2344–84.

Healy, Andrew, and Neil Malhotra. 2009. "Myopic Voters and Natural Disaster Policy." *American Political Science Review* 103 (3): 387–406.

Hendren, Nathaniel, and Ben Sprung-Keyser. 2020. "A Unified Welfare Analysis of Government Policies." *Quarterly Journal of Economics* 135 (3): 1209–318.

Herbst, Chris M. 2010. "The Labor Supply Effects of Child Care Costs and Wages in the Presence of Subsidies and the Earned Income Tax Credit." *Review of Economics of the Household* 8 (2): 199–230.

Hidrobo, Melissa, John Hoddinott, Amber Peterman, Amy Margolies, and Vanessa Moreira. 2014. "Cash, Food, or Vouchers? Evidence from a Randomized Experiment in Northern Ecuador." *Journal of Development Economics* 107: 144–56.

Holla, Alaka, Magdalena Bendini, Lelys Dinarte, and Iva Trako. 2021. "Is Investment in Preprimary Education Too Low? Lessons from (Quasi) Experimental Evidence across Countries." Policy Research Working Paper 9723, World Bank, Washington, DC.

Islam, Mahnaz, and Sabrin Beg. 2021. "Can a Rule-of-Thumb Tool Improve Fertilizer Management? Experimental Evidence from Bangladesh." *Economic Development and Cultural Change* 70 (1).

Jensen, Anders. 2022. "Employment Structure and the Rise of the Modern Tax System." *American Economic Review* 112 (1): 213–34.

Jones, Maria, Florence Kondylis, John Loeser, and Jeremy Magruder. 2022. "Factor Market Failures and the Adoption of Irrigation in Rwanda." *American Economic Review* 112 (7): 2316–52.

Karachiwalla, Naureen, and Albert Park. 2017. "Promotion Incentives in the Public Sector: Evidence from Chinese Schools." *Journal of Public Economics* 146: 109–28.

Khanna, Madhulika, Benjamin Loevinsohn, Elina Pradhan, Opeyemi Fadeyibi, Kevin McGee, Oluwole Odutolu, Gyorgy Bela Fritsche, Emmanuel Meribole, Christel MJ Vermeersch, and Eeshani Kandpal. 2021. "Decentralized Facility Financing versus Performance-Based Payments in Primary Health Care: A Large-Scale Randomized Controlled Trial in Nigeria." *BMC Medicine* 19 (1): 1–12.

Knowles, James C., Ernesto M. Pernia, and Mary Racelis. 1999. *Social Consequences of the Financial Crisis in Asia: The Deeper Crisis.* Asian Development Bank.

Kondylis, Florence, and John Loeser. 2021. "Intervention Size and Persistence." Policy Research Working Paper 9769, World Bank, Washington, DC.

Leaver, Clare, Owen Ozier, Pieter Serneels, and Andrew Zeitlin. 2021. "Recruitment, Effort, and Retention Effects of Performance Contracts for Civil Servants: Experimental Evidence from Rwandan Primary Schools." *American Economic Review* 111 (7): 2213–46.

Loyalka, Prashant, Sean Sylvia, Chengfang Liu, James Chu, and Yaojiang Shi. 2019. "Pay by Design: Teacher Performance Pay Design and the Distribution of Student Achievement." *Journal of Labor Economics* 37 (3): 621–62.

Martin, Ralf, Laure B. de Preux, and Ulrich J. Wagner. 2014. "The Impact of a Carbon Tax on Manufacturing: Evidence from Microdata." *Journal of Public Economics* 117: 1–14.

Mayshar, Joram. 1990. "On Measures of Excess Burden and Their Applications." *Journal of Public Economics* 43: 263–89.

McEwan, Patrick J. 2012. Cost-effectiveness analysis of education and health interventions in developing countries. *Journal of Development Effectiveness* 4(2): 189–213.

McKenzie, David. 2021. "Small Business Training to Improve Management Practices in Developing Countries: Reassessing the Evidence for 'Training Doesn't Work.'" *Oxford Review of Economic Policy* 37 (2): 276–301.

McKenzie, David, Christopher Woodruff, Kjetil Bjorvatn, Miriam Bruhn, Jing Cai, Juanita Gonzalez-Uribe, Simon Quinn, Tetsushi Sonobe, and Martin Valdivia. 2021. "Training Entrepreneurs." *VoxDevLit* 1 (2), August.

Metcalf, Gilbert E. 2019. "On the Economics of a Carbon Tax for the United States." *Brookings Papers on Economic Activity* (Spring): 405–84.

Metcalf, Gilbert E., and James H. Stock. 2020. "Measuring the Macroeconomic Impact of Carbon Taxes." *American Economic Association Papers and Proceedings* 110: 101–06.

Mohseni-Cheraghlou, Amin. 2016. "The Aftermath of Financial Crises: A Look on Human and Social Wellbeing." *World Development* 87: 88–106.

Montenegro, Claudio E., and Harry Anthony Patrinos. 2021. "A Data Set of Comparable Estimates of the Private Rate of Return to Schooling in the World, 1970–2014." *International Journal of Manpower*, October 27, 2021. https://www.emerald.com/insight/content/doi/10.1108/IJM-03-2021-0184/full/html.

Mullainathan, Sendhil, and Eldar Shafir. 2013. *Scarcity: Why Having Too Little Means So Much.* New York: Times Books.

Muralidharan, Karthik, and Abhijeet Singh. 2020. "Improving Public Sector Management at Scale? Experimental Evidence on School Governance in India." NBER Working Paper 28129, National Bureau of Economic Research, Cambridge, MA.

Muralidharan, Karthik, and Venkatesh Sundararaman. 2011. "Teacher Performance Pay: Experimental Evidence from India." *Journal of Political Economy* 119 (1): 39–77.

Quinn, Simon R., and Christopher Woodruff. 2019. "Experiments and Entrepreneurship in Developing Countries." *Annual Review of Economics* 11: 225–48.

Rasul, Imran, and Daniel Rogger. 2018. "Management of Bureaucrats and Public Service

Delivery: Evidence from the Nigerian Civil Service." *Economic Journal* 128 (608): 413–46.

Rasul, Imran, Daniel Rogger, and Martin J. Williams. 2018. "Management and Bureaucratic Effectiveness: Evidence from the Ghanaian Civil Service." Policy Research Working Paper 8595, World Bank, Washington, DC.

Rosenzweig, Mark R., and Christoper Udry. 2020. "External Validity in a Stochastic World: Evidence from Low-Income Countries." *Review of Economic Studies* 87 (1): 343–81.

Saenger, Christof, Maximo Torero, and Matin Qaim. 2014 "Impact of Third-Party Contract Enforcement in Agricultural Markets—A Field Experiment in Vietnam." *American Journal of Agricultural Economics* 96 (4) (July 1): 1220–38.

Schoder, Christian. 2021. "Regime-Dependent Environmental Tax Multipliers: Evidence from 75 Countries." Policy Research Working Paper 9640, World Bank, Washington, DC.

Shamdasani, Yogita. 2021. "Rural road infrastructure and agricultural production: Evidence from India." *Journal of Development Economics* 152 (2021) 102686.

Sosa, Mariano, and Matthew Wai-Poi. Forthcoming. "Fiscal Policy and Equity in Developing Countries: A Survey of International Patterns and Lessons." Background paper for *Poverty and Shared Prosperity 2022,* World Bank, Washington, DC.

Tsivanidis, Nick. 2019. "Evaluating the Impact of Urban Transit Infrastructure: Evidence from Bogotá's Transmilenio." Working paper, University of California, Berkeley.

Wingender, Philippe, and Florian Misch. 2021. *Revisiting Carbon Leakage.* Washington, DC: International Monetary Fund.

World Bank. 2017. *World Development Report 2017: Governance and the Law.* Washington, DC: World Bank.

World Bank. 2022. *Collapse and Recovery: How the COVID-19 Pandemic Eroded Human Capital and What to Do about It.* Washington, DC: World Bank.

Yamazaki, Akio. 2017. "Jobs and Climate Policy: Evidence from British Columbia's Revenue Neutral Carbon Tax." *Journal of Environmental Economics and Management* 83: 197–216.

Zárate, Román D. 2022. "Spatial Misallocation, Informality and Transit Improvements: Evidence from Mexico City." Policy Research Working Paper 9990, World Bank, Washington, DC.

Putting It All Together: Better Fiscal Policy for Reducing Poverty and Increasing Shared Prosperity

Summary

Part 1 of this report highlighted important recent challenges to global progress in poverty and inequality. Part II explores fiscal policy areas that could help meet those challenges. This chapter brings together the two parts of the report and suggests some fiscal policy priorities. It begins by describing how countries face very different needs, reflecting their circumstances going into the COVID-19 pandemic, as well as the impacts of the pandemic and subsequent crises (which were, in turn, influenced by the policies they adopted). These different needs translate into varying policy priorities that fiscal actions can help address.

This chapter outlines policy options for spending on higher-value policies that produce growth, for positioning fiscal policy to protect households against crises, and for raising revenue. Better fiscal policy for poverty reduction will also require better data and evidence—the type of evidence that has been presented throughout this report, as well as more evidence on key gaps such as spending data, costs of implementation, and the long-run impacts of fiscal policies.

Chapter 7 concludes by discussing whether better fiscal policy—that is, more progressive fiscal policy that produces higher growth—is by itself sufficient to meet the pressing needs outlined in part I. In doing so, it presents simulations of the likely impacts of dramatically more effective fiscal policy for poverty reduction until 2030. The results reveal that fiscal policy does make a difference and can even reverse, in the most optimistic scenarios, the setback in progress in 2020. However, the simulations are also sobering because they show that even heroic efforts to put in place better fiscal policy at the national level are not enough to get back on track to end extreme poverty. These results point to the need not just for better national policy making but also for more global action to end poverty.

Accelerating progress with better fiscal policy: Different options for different countries

Governments face the daunting task of deciding which fiscal policies are most suitable for achieving multiple goals. These goals include ensuring an inclusive recovery from the pandemic, supporting long-term growth, and preparing for ongoing and future crises. The current moment is especially challenging, with its record high debt, rising interest rates, and a medium-term outlook of poor growth and high inflation, all constraining the ability of a government to pursue the most appropriate policy mix. Finding ways to raise revenue and increase the efficiency of spending become paramount in this context. Policy makers seeking to raise revenue should consider more progressive forms of taxation, even in an informal economy, to avoid harming the poor and increasing inequality. Spending should aim at protecting vulnerable households today and spurring growth for tomorrow, all while focusing on efficiency and in some cases reducing the total level of spending.

This chapter discusses fiscal policy options for different types of countries by drawing on the analysis in the previous chapters. What follows highlights priorities for spending, both for today and for tomorrow, based on need and fiscal space. This chapter also looks at the feasible options for raising revenue, keeping in mind that the most urgent needs and the feasible policy choices available to policy makers vary considerably across countries.

Better debt management is also essential to increasing fiscal space for recovery from the pandemic and for responding to ongoing and future crises. This chapter does not dwell on options for better debt management because the *World Development Report 2022: Finance for an Equitable Recovery* discusses these measures in detail (World Bank 2022). The measures include proactively reducing exposure to risks that threaten to worsen public debt further, such as by pursuing regulatory reform in financial markets, improving debt transparency, and establishing a common framework inclusive of as many creditors as possible to manage debt restructuring or relief (World Bank 2022).

Illustrating that different countries have very different needs, figure 1.11 in chapter 1 reveals that, although some countries have recovered to their pre-COVID-19 poverty rates, others have struggled to recover, and, for some, poverty continues to increase. Recovery has been particularly elusive in lower-middle-income countries (LMICs) and low-income countries (LICs). The pre-COVID-19 trends in these countries were often very different: countries that have fully or partially recovered were more likely to have enjoyed growth and poverty reduction prior to the crisis, while those that have not recovered were already in a more difficult situation before the crisis, with high poverty rates and low growth (Reinhart 2022). Rising food and energy prices also affect countries very differently. Some countries have been badly affected by rising prices; in others, high prices have barely dented growth or poverty reduction; and, in still others, growth projections are increasing because of the rising prices of key exports. Although faster progress is needed on poverty reduction in all of these countries, the needs and policy priorities are very different across these groups.

As governments decide which fiscal policies are the most suitable for achieving an inclusive recovery and long-run growth, they must deal with rising fiscal deficits and debt burdens (a problem before the pandemic and exacerbated by it). High debt burdens reduce space for fiscal policy to support the recovery and respond to ongoing and future crises because a larger share of spending is taken up with debt repayments and borrowing to finance spending becomes more challenging. LICs and middle-income countries (MICs) carry significantly more debt today than two years ago and are more likely to be in debt distress—2020 saw more emerging economies experience country credit rating downgrades than over the entire 2010–19 period. According to Olaberria and Reinhart (2022), the ratio of government debt to revenue is much higher in LMICs and LICs because of their higher levels of debt going into the crisis.

Figure 7.1 shows that some countries with higher costs of borrowing (see the top left quadrant) are also those in most need of course correction to reverse poverty increases or to restart or accelerate poverty reduction. Because of the differences in both need and fiscal space across countries, the fiscal priorities will vary across countries.

The following sections describe the policy options available to countries to achieve the objectives of poverty reduction and broad-based growth. The exact options for a particular country depend on the characteristics of the economy and the fiscal system. The same policy can differ

FIGURE 7.1

Some countries are facing the dual challenge of stimulating recovery and coping with limited access to external finance

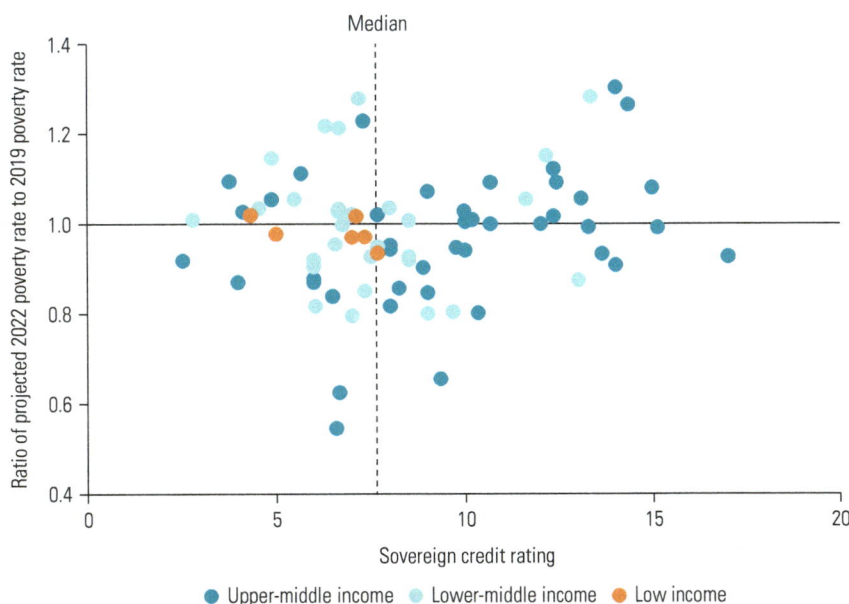

Sources: Original estimates based on data from Kose et al. 2017; Mahler, Yonzan, and Lakner, forthcoming; World Bank, Poverty and Inequality Platform, https://pip.worldbank.org.
Note: The figure shows the ratio of the projected poverty rate in 2022 to the poverty rate in 2019 for 79 low- and middle-income economies, sorted by sovereign credit rating. Each marker represents one economy. A ratio above 1 indicates that poverty is projected to increase from 2019 to 2022. Income-group appropriate poverty lines are used. Sovereign credit rating is the 2020 average of foreign currency long-term sovereign debt ratings by Moody's, Standard & Poor's, and Fitch Ratings converted to a numerical index from 1 (worst) to 21 (best). The sample excludes Kyrgyz Republic, Lebanon, and Ukraine, which are outliers with projected poverty in 2022 more than 1.6 times the poverty rate in 2019.

country by country, depending on the management of public funds, the capacity of tax administration and delivery systems, the structure of the economy, and initial endowments of wealth, health, and education. Although several characteristics of an economy determine the feasible set of policy options, one consistently discussed across chapters is the degree of an economy's formality. This characteristic affects the ability to tax and deliver benefits in both crisis and noncrisis times. It is strongly correlated with a country's income level, just as needs and costs of borrowing vary. Much of the policy discussion therefore distinguishes between policy options for LICs, LMICs, and upper-middle-income countries (UMICs). Distinguishing among them is not intended to suggest that specific policies should be used in only certain countries, but to highlight the very real differences in feasible policy options that countries face.

Spending for faster growth

Increasing spending for growth in the short run

There is no one answer to what spending best suits a country; the choice depends on the country's context and policy objectives. The evidence presented in chapters 5 and 6, however, points to reducing spending on subsidies and tax exemptions in favor of spending on cash transfers and policies aimed at addressing the market failures that constrain private investment. These options are more likely to increase growth. Key considerations include the following:

- *Targeted transfers are more cost-effective at redistribution than subsidies.* For subsidies and transfers, one consideration, in addition to their progressivity (see chapter 5), is the degree to which they reduce inequality (the points of the Gini index) per dollar spent—their "cost-effectiveness" at redistributing, as it were. For example, in 2012 subsidy spending in Indonesia was over 6 percent of gross domestic product (GDP) and social assistance spending less than 1 percent, but the least redistributive social assistance program had twice the cost-effectiveness of subsidies and the best program five times the cost-effectiveness (World Bank 2012). This finding led to the redirection of subsidy spending to infrastructure, health, and social protection. Similarly, in Jordan, spending on water and electricity subsidies amounted to more for each than the total direct transfers, but they are half as cost-effective as the least effective transfer program and a quarter that of the best (Rodriguez and Wai-Poi 2021). Nevertheless, targeted transfers have practical requirements and costs, such as for the data needed to assess eligibility and the potential social costs of differentiating eligibility and benefits.

- *Consumption subsidies vary in value and regressivity, but they are likely to be of lower value and more regressive than cash transfers.* When considering a subsidy, policy makers must answer several key questions: What is the policy objective? Is a subsidy the best instrument for achieving it? What externalities and distortions are being introduced? How difficult will it be later to remove the subsidy? Different subsidy types have different incidences and externalities. Fuel subsidies have high environmental externalities, and most benefits accrue to the rich. Utility subsidies also have negative externalities and leakage, but they are less regressive than fuel subsidies because they tend not to have indirect price effects (or at least not as large as those for fuel) because they are less likely to be inputs into production. A household or firm can consume only so much of utility subsidies, reducing their regressivity. Food subsidies are also less regressive than fuel subsidies—there are fewer indirect effects, and food makes up a large share of the consumption of the poor. Their incidence depends on their design. Chapter 6 points out that it is hard to justify putting in place distortionary subsidies that do not have positive externalities instead of cash transfers that have a higher value and are better targeted to those in need. However, such subsidies are widely used. One reason for their popularity may be that they benefit all households. This factor may point to the need for transfer programs that are somewhat less narrowly targeted. As a result, they may be more politically feasible, while also preventing the types of distortions that reduce the value of social spending via price subsidies.

- *Tax expenditures are large and often go to firms and better-off households.* There are many types of tax expenditures: value added tax exemptions and preferential rates, corporate income tax holidays, personal income tax exemptions and deductions, and so on. The beneficiaries of such tax expenditures vary. Some of these instruments may be progressive relative to income (that is, worth more to poorer households as a share of their income) but expensive and regressive in absolute terms (that is, the greatest share of benefits goes to richer households). Value added tax exemptions, in particular, act like subsidies.

- *Spending to address market failures is often of higher value than production subsidies and tax exemptions that do not produce positive externalities.* Agricultural input subsidies are large in low- and middle-income countries, but they are counterproductive in the long run because they distort incentives to invest in efficiency and often result in lasting damage to the natural resource base. Addressing the root cause of inefficiencies and constraints on productivity will bring larger gains in the long run. Experimental evidence from poor farmers in Sub-Saharan Africa and South Asia highlights the potential of well-designed extension and marketing support policies. Compared with tax exemptions to firms, recent evaluations of support of small and medium enterprises reveal that customized business services and management training can have a higher immediate and sustained return when implemented well (McKenzie 2021; McKenzie et al. 2021; Quinn and Woodruff 2019).

Spending for transformative growth in the long run

The benefits of high-value policies that usher in transformative growth often accrue in the long term. However, with their eye on immediate priorities and political cycles, governments can overlook the long-run growth benefits of these policies, which limit the potential of an economy to achieve inclusive growth tomorrow.

Investments in child health and education have large impacts on long-run growth. This type of spending can be transformative if well implemented because it places young people on a trajectory of higher lifetime earnings, thereby growing the economy and contributing to future revenue. For example, according to Hendren and Sprung-Keyser (2020), the average marginal value of public funds aimed at improving child health and education outcomes in the United States is infinite—they pay for themselves. Social spending programs to improve the welfare of adults tend to have a lower value in the long run (a marginal value of public funds of between 0.5 and 2.0). Impact evaluations suggest these findings hold in LICs and MICs, but implementation and context matter. For example, investments in education may need to be accompanied by policies that develop more labor market opportunities so that higher lifetime earnings can be realized.

Policies that produce transformative growth can be hard to identify. Examples include investment in research and development (R&D) that raises productivity, certain infrastructure projects, and policies associated with long-run climate-related benefits. Such policies can set an economy on a higher and more sustainable growth trajectory because they change the structure of the economy and increase productivity. Evidence from the Green Revolution finds that spending on agricultural R&D can have, for technology adopters, large impacts on agricultural growth, investments in schooling, capital accumulation, and reductions in fertility and migration (both locational and sectoral). The same spending can bring benefits to nonadopters through lower food prices, environmental benefits from lower land use, and a faster pace of structural transformation. Investments in public infrastructure also have the potential to bring transformative growth by reducing travel times and connecting new labor markets or by improving access to education and health services that increase earning opportunities in the long run. Evidence from public transit projects in Mexico and Colombia suggest that the gains in GDP can outweigh the direct costs. However, not all infrastructure investments will be of high value. The transformative potential of infrastructure policies depends on the country context, the efficiency of implementation, and how a particular project affects beneficiaries and nonbeneficiaries through different channels in the short and long run.

Positioning fiscal policy to protect households against future crises

Although the shock from the COVID-19 crisis was large and global in reach, every year climate-related and conflict-induced crises affect many households and hamper efforts to reduce poverty and build shared prosperity (World Bank 2020a). Countries can plan for the many crises that can be predicted (Clarke and Dercon 2016).

Waiting until a crisis occurs to plan and fund a fiscal response leads to a slow, inadequate recovery, with real consequences for the poor and those most affected by the crisis. By contrast, a well-targeted, timely response can fundamentally change the course of a disaster for poor or vulnerable households. Farmers who receive cash early in a drought can pay for supplemental irrigation to limit the impact of the drought on food production (Hill et al. 2019). In Bangladesh, households benefiting from a preapproved, funded action plan triggered by reaching the fore-casted flood level were more likely to evacuate household members, less likely to lose assets, and more likely to protect consumption (Pople et al. 2021). Even if this type of early response is not achieved, responding quickly to help households cope with their immediate income losses from a crisis can prevent short- and long-run increases in poverty from the crisis. In Mexico, when the costs of responding to disasters were covered by transfers from a contingent fund to municipalities, postdisaster mortality was reduced (del Valle 2021) and local economic recovery was accelerated (del Valle, de Janvry, and Sadoulet 2020). Often, however, the funding needs are not all met within a reasonable time frame. An assessment of financing for disaster response against needs (covering the 2015 earthquake in Nepal, the 2019 cyclones in Mozambique, the 2015 cyclone in Vanuatu, and the 2015 hurricane in Haiti) found that after 18 months an average of only 15 percent of needs had been met (Crossley et al. 2021).

Acting now on lessons from the COVID-19 crisis can strengthen the ability of governments to mitigate the welfare impacts of future crises. However, the experience of 2020 underscores that (1) in the medium term, fiscal policy cannot play the same protective role in countries with higher costs of borrowing and weaker delivery systems; and (2) it is crucial to supplement actions to strengthen the ability to respond to crises with other means of supporting poor house-holds to cope with shocks. Other crises have also shown that the costs of a crisis are typically not fully covered by public sources. Analysis in chapter 4 reveals that more households in LICs used savings or assets to manage the impacts of the COVID-19 crisis than received support from governments, thereby confirming other findings showing that in Sub-Saharan Africa savings and informal transfers are much more important sources of support than government transfers (see, for example, Nikoloski, Christiaensen, and Hill 2018).

While critical, planning for disasters does not replace but rather complements efforts in phys-ical risk reduction and emergency preparedness because these efforts can reduce the cost of disasters in the first place.

Steps to better financial preparedness for a crisis response

Financial planning help ensures that finance can be accessed quickly and cost-effectively in a crisis. Such planning includes designing comprehensive strategies based on the right data and information, developing risk financing instruments based on these strategic priorities, and implementing prearranged disbursement channels. A growing number of countries are develop-ing disaster risk finance strategies to do this.[1] Such a strategy outlines a government's priorities in dealing with the fiscal risks from disasters and serves as a reference for relevant stakeholders on managing these risks with tactical financial instruments.

Various risk financing instruments ensure better financial preparedness for disasters. These instruments, which can be designed to protect government budgets following shocks, may tar-get specific people or sectors, including the most vulnerable households, the agriculture sec-tor, and the infrastructure sector. For example, instruments can be used to fund infrastructure reconstruction or the additional costs associated with continuing service delivery (del Valle, de Janvry, and Sadoulet 2020). It is important that such instruments be combined in a cost-effective risk layering strategy that considers both time and cost. That will ensure that the volume of funding available at stages of the response matches actual needs in a cost-efficient manner in order to access cheaper sources of financing first. The benefits and costs of instruments are summarized in table 7.1. Examples of how these instruments have helped countries finance a crisis response follow.

- To implement its National Disaster Risk Finance and Insurance Strategy, the government of Indonesia established several instruments. A dedicated reserve fund, the Pooling Fund for Disasters (Pooling Fund untuk Bencana), ensures access to sufficient resources for disaster

TABLE 7.1

Comparison of risk financing instruments

Type of instrument	Advantages	Disadvantages	Best suited for
Ex ante			
Contingency/reserve fund	• Can be cheap, particularly for frequent shocks • Fast • Allows implementers to plan • Allows governments to learn from experiences of others because approach has been used in many contexts	• Requires fiscal discipline • High opportunity cost of funds given high rates of return on other government investments • Can be hard to defend annual allocations	Low-risk layer: frequent low-level events, such as annual flooding or localized drought or conflict
Contingent credit	• Can be cheap, particularly for mid-frequency shocks • Fast, if conditions are met • Allows implementers to plan • Can incentivize proactive actions to reduce risk (such as Cat DDO)	• Has conditionality • Entails opportunity cost of loan • Adds to country's debt burden; must be repaid	Middle-risk layer: higher-magnitude events such as widespread flooding or hurricanes that occur less frequently but cause damage that exhausts the resources of national contingencies
Market-based risk transfer instrument	• Leverages additional finance for infrequent events, making them more cost-efficient • Can be disbursed quickly • Allows implementers to plan • Supports fiscal discipline • Promotes risk diversification	• More expensive for frequent shocks • Can be vulnerable to criticism and "regret" • Can miss need • Requires a level playing field to negotiate • Entails trade-off between the cost of premiums and the frequency or scale of payout	High-risk layer: extreme, less frequent events occurring less often than every 5–10 years, such as severe droughts, hurricanes, or earthquakes
Ex post			
Humanitarian assistance	• Flexible; can respond to need • Does not have to be repaid	• Can be slow, so the hazard impact increases • Can be unreliable • Undermines planning	Only as a last resource
Other ex post instruments (such as budget reallocation)	• Offers lessons from experience, because approach has been used in many contexts • Can respond to materialized need	• Can have a negative impact on long-term development/investment programs • Can be expensive • Can be slow to mobilize funding	Primarily as a last resource

Source: World Bank, Disaster Risk Financing and Insurance Program.
Note: Cat DDO = Catastrophe Deferred Drawdown Option.

response and streamlines the execution and transparency of spending (World Bank 2021a). Its more than US$2 billion in insurance coverage of public assets provides infrastructure reconstruction protection covering more than 5,000 buildings across multiple line ministries and agencies.

• Countries with World Bank Catastrophe Deferred Drawdown Options before the COVID-19 crisis had the quickest flow of funds from the multilateral system for the fiscal response: 80 percent of these World Bank funds had been disbursed by the end of April 2020, compared with less than 30 percent of other forms of budget support from the multilateral system and less than 5 percent of project financing (Yang et al. 2021).

- In 2021, the Philippines—still recovering from the pandemic—was hit by Typhoon Rai, triggering a US\$52.5 million payout of the Philippines catastrophe bond to allow financing for disaster response and recovery (Evans 2022). In 2018, the Pacific Alliance countries (Chile, Colombia, Mexico, and Peru) jointly sponsored a US\$1.36 billion catastrophe bond to reduce their fiscal vulnerability to natural disasters. Peru received a US\$60 million payout in 2019 for an event that triggered the instrument (World Bank, n.d).

- In 2020, the Turkish Catastrophe Insurance Pool paid out more than US\$60 million to 58,591 households affected by two major earthquakes that year.[2] More than half of the households in Türkiye are insured by this pool.[3]

So why are these instruments so little used? It is not easy for governments to allocate funds to preparation for the next crisis when they are facing pressing needs today. Psychologists have long noted that people tend to be optimistic about the likelihood a bad event will befall them (the "it won't happen to me" heuristic). Governments thus find it hard to push for preparing for the low-probability, worst-case scenario. Even if the cost of preparation is small, the psychological cost-benefit assessment may not resolve in its favor. When the cost of preparation is large, choosing to fund tomorrow's disaster over urgent development needs today becomes even more difficult.

Meanwhile, many incentives are stacked against preparing for crises. Incentives differ by crisis and by country. Almost universally, however, political incentives are aligned with a big show of support in a crisis instead of preparing for a disaster. This approach wins more votes in the United States and Mexico (Healy and Malhotra 2009), and these political disincentives flow through to bureaucracies. The international humanitarian and development system also does not incentivize allocation of financing to a crisis response ex ante. Humanitarian and development partners consistently step in with finance when a predictable crisis is well developed and large welfare costs are already evident. This practice reduces the incentives for the governments, particularly governments in LICs, to proactively plan for these needs (Clarke and Dercon 2016).

Loans and grants to countries are an opportunity to incentivize proactive financing that prioritizes the right risks, responds to clear needs in a transparent and objective way, and complements ongoing initiatives and aligns with government strategic priorities. Some recent changes highlight steps in this direction. The International Development Association has now allocated US\$1 billion for early response financing. The Crisis Response Window for Early Response Financing can disburse funds based on predetermined triggers, and they do not count toward a country's International Development Association allocation. The World Bank's Global Risk Financing Facility makes funds available to match government contributions to investments in risk finance instruments.[4] And the United Nations' Central Emergency Response Fund is supporting anticipatory action pilots in which a response plan is financed before a crisis and disbursed according to pre-agreed triggers. These approaches need to move beyond the pilot scale to become part of mainstream financing by the international system.

Preplanning is important, but the urgency of financing needs might go well beyond what can be prepared for cost-effectively in advance. Governments will likely continue to rely on ex post financing in major disasters, even when prearranged finance is in place. Therefore, it is also important to strengthen ex post financing. As described in chapter 4, the scale of the fiscal response to the COVID-19 crisis was essential for impact, and this scale was determined in large part by the cost of borrowing. Better debt management in advance of a crisis is necessary for better crisis preparedness.

In addition to better debt management, a more transparent and more disciplined approach to budget cuts can minimize their costs. Budget reallocations should be rule based and, to the extent possible, predictable and conducted in a consultative way to maintain budget credibility and minimize opportunity cost without compromising the speed with which reallocations can be made. Tracking the historical response needs and costs is fundamental to understanding the requirements of the next shock and helps put the right instruments in place. Currently, very few countries systematically track disaster-related expenditures, and those that do have limited data on the use of the funds.

A fiscal system that can deliver support quickly in a crisis

Funding alone is not enough: a plan and operational preparedness—ensuring the flow of money to beneficiaries—are equally important. Impact has been demonstrated when financing and a plan have been put in place before a disaster *and* there is an automatic link between the availability of financing and the delivery of support—to municipalities in the case of Mexico (del Valle, de Janvry, and Sadoulet 2020) and to households in the case of Bangladesh (Pople et al. 2021). In both instances, eligibility for support was automatic once the pre-agreed trigger for action was met. According to *Public Expenditure Review: Disaster Response and Rehabilitation in the Philippines*, the release of funding from prearranged sources can be delayed by ineffective public financial management systems, such as complex approval processes (World Bank 2020b).

Why are automatic criteria and preapprovals important? Without preapprovals, public financial management systems and bureaucratic approvals can hinder the quick transfer of funds and implementation of response plans. The African Risk Capacity (ARC) Group provides its member governments in Africa with fast financing of drought responses using a parametric insurance policy and contingency planning support for governments to optimize use of the funds. In some cases, ARC policies have resulted in swift payments to farmers. For example, in Mauritania, ARC payouts allowed the distribution of support to households to start two months earlier than usual. However, in the early years of ARC, three out of four cases missed the target payout time of 120 days because of bureaucratic delays (OPM 2017; Vyas et al. 2019). Preplanned procurement for disaster response and recovery can facilitate implementation and disbursement and also generate savings and cost efficiencies, as evidenced in the Caribbean (Rafuse, Bruce, and Arnold 2020).

Delivery systems that automatically target and meet needs are an important component of support systems. The COVID-19 response highlights the challenge in quickly identifying needs and targeting timely support to meet those needs. Automatic stabilizers can deliver support to those in need quickly and with accurate targeting. Unemployment insurance and employment guarantee programs use self-selection to allow accurate targeting of those affected by all types of economic shocks. Public health, disability, and agricultural insurance increase support through pre-agreed rules for assessing need when specific shocks occur. Extending these programs where possible is essential to ensuring that households receive support quickly. Although schemes will remain challenging to implement in contexts in which a large share of the workforce is informal or self-employed, examples of two that are operating well in these settings follow.

- The government of Kenya has mobilized private sector financing and disbursement channels to reach vulnerable pastoralists. Its Kenya Livestock Insurance Program was launched in 2015 and implemented through a public-private partnership between the government and insurance companies. The program offers drought insurance that is fully subsidized by the government to some 30,000 households. Insurance companies pay claims directly to the beneficiaries when a payout is triggered by drought. The government is now moving toward a partially subsidized program, and similar programs are being prepared in Ethiopia and Somalia.

- In India, the Mahatma Gandhi National Rural Employment Guarantee Act has played a role in mitigating the impact of rainfall shocks in the past (Gehrke 2019) and was also used to mitigate income losses during COVID-19, particularly later in the crisis when concerns around social distancing eased (Gelb et al. 2021). The government of India increased the budget for additional workdays between April and September 2020, and states that were able to increase total workdays under the act by one day per rural person in a district reduced job losses by 7 percent in rural areas over the baseline employment rate (Afridi, Mahajan, and Sangwan 2022).

In the absence of automatic stabilizers, cash transfer programs can be made adaptive so that they scale up automatically in a crisis. In adaptive social protection programs, it is clear in advance how the number of beneficiaries will be increased on the basis of predictable crises, such as a one-in-five-years drought that increases the need for cash transfers in a rural area. The rules covering when to scale up (that is, what kind of event is used as a trigger), for whom, for what size event and duration, and for what method of financing are documented in the operational manuals of these programs. In Malawi, the government is implementing an adaptive social protection program in preselected districts, combining contingent financing with risk transfer (MEPDPSR 2021). Precrisis investments in the beneficiary registry, data collection repositories, and payment systems are needed to make this work. Gentilini (2022) provides a comprehensive assessment of what the COVID-19 response taught about the investments needed.

To increase the degree to which adaptive cash transfers can scale up automatically, further innovation in state-contingent targeting is needed. Data in social registries and PMT formulas collected and designed during noncrisis times cannot by themselves identify the newly poor in a crisis. Data that reflect the severity of the crisis on the ground in real time are needed as a complement. Nascent examples have demonstrated two promising approaches. The first approach involves combining preexisting vulnerability data with crisis-specific triggers, including geographic targeting of anticipatory action in response to a natural hazard. The second entails complementing existing population registers with individual-level data that are passively collected during a crisis, such as the phone-based targeting method used in Togo (see box 4.1 in chapter 4). The value of digital payment systems in expanding support to new beneficiaries was also a notable part of Togo's impressive COVID-19 support. Recent crises have highlighted multiple sources of real-time data that can effectively track economic outcomes during crises. Examples of such sources are emissions data and Google mobility data during the COVID-19 pandemic and data on flood extent, soil moisture, or greenness during climate crises.

Fiscal priorities for countries where building fiscal systems to respond will take time

The coverage of social assistance remains low in many countries, particularly LICs and LMICs. Although coverage may increase in coming years, it will take time before it is large enough to be a reliable source of support for poor and vulnerable households in a crisis (see figure 4.16 in chapter 4). In the meantime, during a crisis these households will be relying on savings, assets, loans, and informal transfers from friends and family. In these contexts, fiscal policy can support the development and use of these financial strategies. A review of evaluations of interventions that support household access to financial instruments—mobile money transfers, savings, credit, and insurance—reveals that (1) interventions that extend the geographic reach of informal risk sharing improve the ability of households to protect their welfare against disasters; (2) heavily subsidized insurance produces welfare benefits, or at least the belief that welfare that is better protected produces welfare gains; (3) interventions to increase savings may help households manage shocks (there is little evidence on this); and (4) there is one study that highlights the promising potential benefits of contingent credit (Hill, Peredo, and Tarazona 2021).

Examples of fiscal policies that help support these strategies are progressive taxation policy on digital transfers (discussed later) and other mobile money products (such as insurance), as well as investments in financial inclusion and reaching households not yet benefiting from mobile money.

Another example is subsidizing the development of insurance options that work well for nonpoor but still vulnerable households that need protection but do not qualify for a cash transfer program. The benefits and costs of each intervention will need to be assessed in each country context, and often in comparison with alternative interventions.

Supporting firms during the pandemic has been a way to protect jobs and markets for goods and services, helping to avoid the loss of potentially productive firms and preserve the long-term relationships between firms and workers that would be difficult to rebuild (World Bank 2021b). Interventions that support access to financial protection for firms have a role as well. In Rwanda, the government is financing a risk-sharing mechanism—a "bridge lending window"— to increase lending from the financial sector (banks and multilateral financial institutions) to vulnerable micro, small, and medium enterprises exposed to climate shocks. In such an event, MSMEs can use funds from the bridge lending window to meet loan repayments for a fixed period (say, six months), reducing default rates, and then pay back the lending window funds over a longer period. The Rwandan government is also exploring the option to take out an insurance product to protect the bridge lending window in the event of a catastrophic climate event that would increase requests by micro, small, and medium enterprises for support.

Raising revenue

This chapter does not review options for better debt management because the *World Development Report 2022* discusses those measures in detail (World Bank 2022). Instead, the chapter considers how to increase mobilization of domestic resources in a way that reduces inequality while not increasing poverty. In its discussion of the short-term impacts of fiscal policy, this section builds on chapter 5. The discussion is also informed by evidence on the long-run value of fiscal decisions, as discussed in chapter 6. The patterns of and lessons from international experience suggest a series of short- and medium-term actions:

- *Short term.* Use tax and transfer strategies appropriate to the country context to increase progressivity where possible. Such strategies exist for all levels of country income and administrative capacity.

- *Short term.* Explore new (or underused) tax instruments that address externalities and can be progressive (property, green, health, and digital taxes).

- *Medium term.* Strengthen direct taxation capacity (personal income, property, and corporate income taxes) and direct transfer capacity, in part through digitalization and better use of data.

Increasing progressivity while raising revenue through tax and transfer strategies

Although richer countries tend to redistribute more through fiscal policy (as discussed in chapter 5), progressive fiscal policy is possible at all income levels. Richer countries use taxes and transfers to reduce poverty and inequality to a greater extent than poorer countries. In richer countries, revenues rely more on progressive direct taxation and create more fiscal space for social spending. Meanwhile, these countries' administrative capacity allows them to accurately observe income, both limiting tax evasion and more accurately targeting support to poorer households. MICs can also reduce inequality by using fiscal instruments for the purposes for which they are better suited—indirect taxes for revenue generation and direct transfers for income support for the poor—while avoiding costly and regressive subsidies and indirect tax exemptions. In this way, countries can both generate sufficient revenues and reduce poverty and inequality. The poorest countries are particularly constrained in their revenue-generating capacity, space for spending, and ability to target. Even so, the short-term burden of taxes on the poor can be minimized through well-designed social assistance.

Table 7.2 describes tax and transfer strategies that can promote the progressivity of fiscal policy for countries at all income levels while still generating the additional revenue needed during fiscal consolidation. For high-income countries (HICs) and those UMICs aspiring to HIC status, broadening the direct tax base by means of changes to tax schedules and investments in administrative capacity is key, as is targeting direct income support to the households that need it most. Such an approach combines the most progressive fiscal instruments on both the tax and spending sides. For LMICs and UMICs without sufficient administrative capacity or sufficiently formal economies to sustain a broad direct tax base, medium-term investments in strengthening administrative capacity are important. In the shorter term, indirect taxes are best focused on revenue generation (eliminating costly and regressive exemptions), and direct transfers can be used to offset the burden on poorer households, although targeting errors are inevitable in less formal economies. LICs could also adopt this approach of maximizing revenue through indirect taxation while building targeted direct transfers to support the poor.

Patterns in the international experience suggest a series of short- and medium-term actions, as noted previously. In the short term, a country can assess whether the tax and transfer strategy is appropriate for its income level and administrative capacity and move toward a more suitable strategy if necessary. This process could include the exploration of new tax instruments (such as

TABLE 7.2

Progressive fiscal policy strategies are available to all countries

LICs: Increase revenue, build safety nets	LMICs and UMICs: Broad indirect taxation with targeted direct transfers	HICs and aspiring UMICs: Direct taxation and targeted direct transfers
Indirect and trade taxes are inevitable. • Taxes are not progressive and will burden households but they are the main revenue-generation instruments. But health taxes can raise important short-term revenue directly and long-term revenue indirectly, as well as reduce long-term public health spending Investments in social assistance can help reduce inequality and offset the burden of indirect taxation for the poorest. Investments are needed in tax administrative capacity for collecting direct taxes (such as PIT, property tax).	Indirect taxes have a revenue and regressivity trade-off. • But exemptions are generally an inefficient way to help the poor; "personalized VAT" schemes are difficult. Indirect taxes combined with targeted transfers can be progressive. • Each instrument should be used for its best purpose (raising revenue, supporting the poor). But indirect taxes have some limitations. • Indirect taxes create a greater burden to offset, while targeting has more errors because of data constraints and so transfers are less effective. • If the prices of basic goods are high, the VAT is a greater burden on the poor. Political economy issues are raised in closing exemptions/raising rates, targeting errors, and coverage rates. Indirect tax revenue should be augmented with progressive health tax revenue. Investing should continue in the capacity for direct taxation and expanding the PIT and property tax base.	Direct taxation is progressive. • It raises revenue from those who can most afford to pay, which can then be used for progressive spending. Use of progressive health tax revenue should continue. Targeted direct transfers are progressive. • They are the most cost-effective way of reducing poverty and inequality. • Richer countries with more formal economies and more data can target more precisely (eligibility and benefit levels).

Source: World Bank.

Note: HIC = high-income country; LIC = low-income country; LMIC = lower-middle-income country; PIT = personal income tax; UMIC = upper-middle-income country; VAT = value added tax.

green, health, or digital taxes) that raise revenue and can be designed in a progressive fashion. Short-term action could also include redirecting spending more toward cost-effective, targeted direct transfers and less toward subsidies and tax expenditures.

Over the medium term, all countries should invest in their direct tax capacity. Administrative constraints explain part of the low revenue collection of direct taxes, especially in LICs. Nevertheless, many countries already have the capacity to raise more direct tax revenue. Beyond income tax withholding by firms, consolidation of increasingly digitized data sources might allow expanding the tax base to capital and mixed income (discussed further later in this chapter). Furthermore, international tax agreements for automatic exchanges of information and greater transparency of wealth held offshore could reduce the movement of reported income across borders and the extent of international tax avoidance, thereby permitting more progressive taxation of domestic income.

Introducing new forms of progressive taxation

Property taxes can raise revenues progressively, but they are complex to administer and take time to implement at scale. New technology can help. On average, property tax revenue in countries that are not members of the Organisation for Economic Co-operation and Development (OECD) is just 0.3 percent of GDP, as opposed to close to 2.0 percent in OECD member countries. This finding may be surprising because historically property taxation has been an important source of revenue in OECD countries and the property tax base is visible and immobile. However, the data requirements (accurate land and building databases) are significant; their administration requires greater capacity than that for even personal income tax, and initially the costs of administration are greater than the revenue raised. Many countries thus start with a *land* tax, which itself requires governments to invest in their regulatory framework and institutional capacity. The revenue raised from successful land taxes can then, in part, be reinvested in the capacity to administer a *property* tax. Meanwhile, administrative constraints arising from outdated cadasters and property valuation can be partially resolved via data and technological improvements, even in countries with limited tax capacity:

- *Update cadasters.* Satellite imaging and drones can be used to extend and update cadasters. For example, in Kigali, Rwanda, high-resolution satellite images for measuring building footprints and heights are combined with data from the statistical agency to build accurate cadastral records and extend their coverage at a low cost (Ali, Deininger, and Wild 2020).

- *Improve and simplify valuation.* Area-based valuation, which uses easily observable characteristics of a property, combined with local data on rental and sales values, can simplify the complicated process of valuation. Such data are increasingly available in urban areas with active rental and resale markets.

- *Encourage local government and central administrations to share the tax collection effort.* Property taxes are often local, funding local public goods and building trust. But higher-capacity central governments need to assist local governments in valuation, cadastral updates, and data sharing. Relying on the central government for valuation also limits the possibility of corruption.

- *Enhance social acceptance and trust.* Property taxes are unpopular—taxpayers frequently do not believe they have any benefits, and their lump sum nature can make them seem unfair to illiquid taxpayers. Increasing transparency, demonstrating that taxes fund local public goods, and, in some cases, earmarking revenue for popular projects can improve the social contract (Dom et al. 2022). Another frequent criticism is that, by taxing wealth, these taxes do not consider the capacity to pay and liquidity constraints. This criticism can be alleviated by spreading payments over time, withholding taxes from direct deposits, and building exemptions for specific situations.

New fiscal instruments could raise additional revenue. Examples are green taxes, health taxes, taxation of the digital sector, and improved inheritance, wealth, and capital gains taxation. These tax instruments may not be appropriate for every context, but they should be explored.

- *The climate urgency implies that fiscal policies that reduce carbon emissions and encourage clean energy use should be considered.* Excise taxes on fossil fuel consumption and electricity could raise revenue, but any reform needs to carefully consider their distributional implications, and, like the removal of value added tax exemptions, design compensation mechanisms for the poor. Carbon taxes present several advantages. First, they can initially be applied to a small group of heavy-polluting firms (which often produce upstream), thereby facilitating tax administration. Second, beyond their impact on carbon reduction, these taxes tend to generate other positive externalities, such as less air pollution. Third, their design needs to consider their impact on competitiveness, employment, and abatement possibilities. Employment effects are difficult to identify, but studies find, if anything, positive impacts and progressive reallocation of jobs. Furthermore, carbon taxes do not distort the choice between the formal and the informal sector when collected upstream from large formal firms, and some of the new revenue collected could be used to lower labor taxation (Schroder 2021). Much of the existing analysis is focused on HICs (Azevedo, Wolff, and Yamazaki 2019; Dussaux 2020; Goulder et al. 2019; Martin, de Preux, and Wagner 2014; Metcalf and Stock 2020; Schroder 2021; Yamazaki 2017), but cross-country analysis suggests that carbon taxes can raise revenue without increasing inequality in LICs and MICs (Dorband et al. 2019).

- *Health taxes, such as on tobacco, alcohol, and sugar-sweetened beverages, are increasingly being adopted, with often net positive effects on long-term health and public finances.* Although health taxes can affect the poor more in the short term, they are progressive over the long term because poorer households benefit more from lower out-of-pocket spending and higher lifetime earnings. Shorter-term revenue averages around 0.4 percent of GDP for tobacco and for alcohol and 0.1 percent for sugar-sweetened beverages (OECD chapter, in Lauer et al., forthcoming). In Indonesia, however, tobacco excise taxes made up 10.6 percent of all revenue in 2020 (1.1 percent of GDP), and they could grow quickly (Ross 2021). In the Philippines, reforms saw alcohol excise taxes grow in contribution from 0.2 percent to 0.4 percent of GDP by 2019, and for tobacco from 0.3 percent to 0.8 percent of GDP. Moreover, the long-term savings to public health spending may even exceed the short-term revenue. Thus, if revenue declines over time as consumption falls, the health spending savings will continue to increase, implying that the fiscal gains can be significant and sustained.

- *The digital sector and online purchases often avoid taxation because of outdated legislation.* Although some aspects of the digital economy could complicate the administrative process of collecting taxes, especially when they occur across borders, other aspects are simplifying the process (Lucas-Mas and Junquera-Varela 2021). For example, large online platforms concentrating economic activity and transactions can act as withholding agents. With appropriate adjustment of legal frameworks and investments in the capacity to monitor this expanding sector, the digital economy might serve as a chance to improve tax collection.

- *Taxation of inheritance and wealth raises little revenue outside of OECD countries.* Taxes on capital transmission and on capital stock (wealth taxes) are often unpopular, can be hard to administer, and may slow capital accumulation, at least in OECD countries (Jakobsen et al. 2020). Yet these taxes are very progressive, and the widening of income and wealth inequality in many countries could call for their expansion. Currently, low- and middle- income countries do not rely much on this form of taxation, but in OECD countries there is an active debate, especially on the expansion of inheritance taxes, which could reduce inequality of opportunity and reduce social mobility (OECD 2021). Despite the uncertainty, UMICs with greater institutional capacity and accumulated wealth could consider further reliance on taxes on inheritance and possibly wealth.

- *Taxes on capital gains (appreciation of property or shares).* These taxes are progressive and can raise revenue, especially in places where real estate values have increased substantially. Yet capital gains taxes face their own challenge: they can discourage investment, can lock capital owners into their position (because they are untaxed until realization of the gains), and can require that transactions be recorded and administered efficiently. The government thus needs to work closely with third parties, such as public notaries, to ensure compliance. Many countries apply low rates to capital gains, and some UMICs might consider revising this practice.

Increasing the progressivity of personal income tax and corporate income tax

As discussed in chapter 6, the degree of progressivity of the tax code is a choice that will, in part, reflect the social welfare weights a country gives its income groups. However, hastening poverty reduction will often benefit from increasing the progressivity of the personal income tax and corporate income tax. Corporate income taxes (CITs) contribute about 2 percent of GDP, but more could be raised in many countries. The CIT acts as a complement to the personal income tax, is progressive, and is administratively simple to collect. Although tax competition to attract investments has led to a drop in the statutory CIT rates worldwide, the macroeconomic effective tax rate on corporate profits has risen over the last 20 years in several MICs, especially in large economies (Bachas et al. 2022). Thus, the race to the bottom in corporate taxation is not inevitable, and governments can undertake measures to raise CIT revenue.

- *Reassess corporate tax incentives.* Many countries provide large firms with generous tax incentives, leading to a reduction in effective tax rates at the top of the firm size distribution. A cost-benefit analysis of these tax provisions would help justify those that are productive and remove those that are inefficient and inequitable (Kronfol and Steenbergen 2020).

- *Increase firm formalization.* Governments should not try aggressively to formalize small firms, which often display low productivity and whose reported income is very elastic to the tax rate (Bachas and Soto 2021). However, formalizing productive medium-size informal firms, which compete with formal ones, would raise revenue and level the playing field (Ulyssea 2018).

- *The new international corporate tax infrastructure is projected to yield little additional revenue. Countries should continue to train personnel and adapt legislation to limit tax avoidance.* The OECD-led reform of the corporate tax architecture (scheduled for implementation by 2023 in 136 countries) includes both rule revisions to determine where economic activity takes place and how to allocate profits across jurisdictions and the establishment of a global minimum corporate tax of 15 percent to prevent excessive use of tax havens. Its adoption would represent a step forward for equitable taxation of multinational enterprises globally. As currently designed, however, the reform benefits OECD countries and large economies because the distribution of revenue depends on the location of such enterprises' headquarters, and the rules permit substantial exemptions. For low- and middle- income countries, the new framework is projected to raise CIT collection by only a few percent of baseline (Barake et al. 2021). To raise further revenue, these countries will need to continue to improve their legal arsenal, train personnel, and adopt the OECD/G20 Base Erosion and Profit Shifting framework to limit tax avoidance by multinational enterprises. The momentum for global CIT reform might encourage additional exchanges of information across jurisdictions and reduce the role of tax havens and unfavorable tax treaties.

Finally, ongoing investments in data and technology can improve revenue collection and the ability to increase the progressivity of taxation. Because taxation is first and foremost about precise information on income, the digitalization of large quantities of data on transactions, tax and transfer histories, and third parties (such as procurement, financial, and utilities) promises to improve government fiscal capacity. Digitalization can help countries detect unregistered firms, improve the assessment of taxes to be paid, and detect fraud. E-filing and prefiled tax returns can reduce taxpayer compliance costs and the need for tax official interventions.[5] Furthermore, new data could permit more precise targeting of beneficiaries of social assistance and social insurance programs.[6] Box 7.1 discusses the potential benefits of investments in digital technology in more detail, as well as some of its limitations.

A concrete example of technological change enhancing fiscal capacity is the increasing use of digital payment methods. When combined with the adoption of electronic billing machines, which directly report taxable sales to the tax administration, the declining use of cash improves the capacity to detect tax evasion and illicit transactions, and it could solve the main weakness of the value added tax by providing information on end-consumer transactions. The Republic of Korea is an example of a successful digital transition supported by tax incentives (Sung, Awasthi, and Lee 2017). Policy makers should, however, remain cautious in their approach to the digital sector—putting restrictions on cash can come at a high efficiency cost, especially for poorer households (Alvarez et al. 2022), and formalizing very small firms could be regressive. Furthermore, as mobile money services and transactions expand, governments are increasingly tempted to tax both mobile money providers and transactions directly. This taxation could hurt technology adoption and reduce financial integration over time.

Nevertheless, data and technology are not a panacea: their use and adoption need to be adapted to each country and combined with investments in the skills of the bureaucracy. Data need to be centralized, merged, and harmonized. At the same time, an adequate legislative and regulatory environment will both facilitate data sharing and ensure data protection and privacy. In practice, data integration often faces constraints stemming from lack of centralized systems to host data, missing digital IDs, lack of collaboration across government institutions, and an inadequate information technology infrastructure. Governments must, then, hire well-trained personnel and phase in technologies customized for each country and tailored to their segments of taxpayers (such as large firms versus small and medium enterprises). For example, tax administrations could build a data lab or a policy studies unit to ensure the quality, security, and usability of data merged across sources. The *World Development Report 2021: Data for Better Lives* describes what governments can do to improve the role of data in public administration (World Bank 2021c). Among other things, governments could create an efficient Integrated National Data System that includes relevant stakeholders in the data life cycle and in the governance structures of the system. Data labs for tax administrations can benefit from the system to foster data production, protection, exchange, planning, and decision-making.

Political economy considerations

Some of the recommendations in this section on how fiscal policy could increase equity in the context of countries' administrative capacity can be implemented through administrative reforms such as greater enforcement of property taxation. Others will require tax reforms supported by a broad political consensus. Although the recommended reforms represent a move toward a progressive revenue base, they will produce winners and losers, and the losers may

Digitalization can improve the efficiency of fiscal administration, but not without challenges

Digitalization of a developing economy's tax system could increase the efficiency of fiscal administration, in part through higher data quality and better access to the data generated by digital systems. For example, the use of geographic information system mapping has increased the quality of cadastral data collection and planning in Georgia by simplifying the process for authorities and citizens and eliminating fraud (National Agency of Public Registry of Georgia 2015). This method was also used in India, beginning in the 1980s, to create digital images for the cadastral map, which helps to identify unreported property across the country. The creation of a cadastral map facilitates land management and planning, as well as land registration and insurance of land titles to reduce land disputes (Mondal, Bandyopadhyay, and Chakravarty 2015).

Digitalization in the tax system can boost government revenue. Peru's e-invoicing system, introduced in 2013, contains billing and payment data in a machine-readable format that can be imported directly into the accounts payable system and shared with tax authorities. In one quarter alone, e-invoicing was associated with average increase of 15 percent in taxable sales and 11 percent in taxable purchases. Value added tax liabilities also increased the first year by 11.6 percent. E-invoicing has reduced the cost for small and medium enterprises from US$0.56 to US$0.20 per invoice and helped eliminate data entry errors (Bellon et al. 2022). The iTax system in Kenya enables user registration, electronic filing, and tax payment online. This expansion of the tax base and increased ease of tax payment increased tax collection from US$6.82 billion in 2011/12 to US$8.94 billion in 2013/14, reaching the highest increase of US$10 billion for the first time in 2014/15 (Ndung'u 2019).

Digitalization can also have a positive impact on the fiscal spending side through ease of cash payment, improved digital tools, and data transparency. Use of fingerprint-based biometric automated teller machines enabled the South African government to identify and remove the 650,000 social grants being delivered to noneligible citizens, saving it US$65 million annually. This system also ensures that payments cease even when an individual's death is not registered. Recipients must confirm their participation in the program through monthly fingerprint verification or voice recognition (Kanbur 2017).

Although digitalization can effectively improve the conduct of fiscal policy, it also may come with significant challenges for low- and middle-income countries. System design and implementation are some of the issues. In South Africa, where e-filing replaced paper filing for VAT and employment taxes, tax compliance costs (TCC) for small and medium enterprises fell, on average, by 22.4 percent and hours spent on tax compliance fell by 21.8 percent from 2006 to 2008. Meanwhile, Nepal saw a 34 percent increase in TCC from 2009 to 2011, while in Ukraine there was up to a 25 percent increase in TCC within the time frame of 2006 and 2009. These differences were driven by variations in policy implementation, timelines, and TCC measurement. For example, although South African small and medium enterprises were only required to file taxes electronically, in Nepal and Ukraine companies were also required to provide hard copies of documents, resulting in the possibility of double reporting. Notably, the TCC success rate in South Africa was measured three to four years after its policy implementation, whereas in Nepal and Ukraine results were measured after only one year, without possibly accounting for the learning curve of firms (Yilmaz and Coolidge 2013).

need to be compensated or convinced of the value of the reforms via a robust social contract. Tax reforms intended to change distributional outcomes can often be blocked by elites and specific lobbying groups, and these political constraints represent one of the key barriers to progressive taxation (Prichard 2019).

Two specific political constraints are (1) low taxpayer morale and low compliance norms; and (2) resistance from interest groups and elites opposing tax reforms. An expanding literature has studied the issue of tax morale and information, suggesting that a lack of trust in institutions and the perception that various tax revenues are not well used and do not reach intended users often hinder demand for more revenue collection (Dom et al. 2022). The use of behavioral science may in certain contexts help to increase tax compliance (see box 7.2). Furthermore, multiple studies show that taxpayers are poorly informed about the redistributive role of the tax system, although information on the (positive) distributional impacts of fiscal policy may increase citizens' willingness to pay taxes (Hoy, forthcoming). Understanding the determinants of successful tax reforms, which can overcome entrenched interests, is more difficult, and there are no one-size-fits-all recommendations. Successful tax reforms are usually achieved after extensive consultation and a political pact that explains both the equity and efficiency goals of the reform. Favorable conditions are more easily reached during political transitions and following important events that reinforce the need for state intervention, such as the COVID-19 pandemic. Martinez-Vazquez, Sanz-Arcega, and Tránchez-Martín (2022) reviews the experiences of countries that substantially increased their tax revenue in the past few decades. Some successful cases arose from expanding the tax base combined with simplifying tax collection, especially for corporate taxation by reducing the number of tax levies and harmonizing rates. For example, over a decade, Cambodia, Georgia, and Paraguay raised their tax revenue as a share of GDP by more than 5 percent.

BOX 7.2

Nudging tax compliance: How behavioral science tools can improve compliance at low financial and political costs

A wealth of recent studies across the world, including of low- and middle- income countries, have demonstrated that *nudging* taxpayers or applying insights from behavioral science to improve the way tax administrations communicate with taxpayers can lead to more honest and timelier tax declarations and payments (Dalton and Manning 2021; Hallsworth et al. 2017; Mascagni, Nell, and Monkam 2017). Nudging is best described as an intervention that alters the choice architecture (that is, how information or options are presented) in a way that promotes certain behaviors over others without significantly altering economic incentives. In this context, presenting information to taxpayers about their obligations in ways that induce *voluntary* compliance instead of *enforcing* compliance through costly audits, fines, or business closures has shown positive impacts. Various studies point to the effective use of targeted notifications centered around deterrence (Hernandez et al. 2017), national pride (Hallsworth et al. 2017), and public goods provision (Mascagni, Nell, and Monkam 2017).

A recent tax experiment in Albania tested this approach in the context of the COVID-19 pandemic. The General Directorate of Taxation, with technical assistance from the World Bank, explored the impact of behaviorally informed notifications to improve compliance among firms (employers and their employees) suspected of underdeclaring their personal income tax withholding on monthly tax returns. The exercise tested whether using a soft tone (positive reinforcement and highlighting the benefits of compliance) or a strong tone (warnings about the costs of noncompliance) was effective in reducing the withholding of payments. During the first month of COVID-19 lockdown in Albania, soft-tone letters were sent to some employers and employees and strong-tone letters to others. The impact of these letters was substantial. For employers receiving soft-tone letters, the study found large, statistically significant increases in subsequent payroll declarations (by as much as 10 percent relative to business as usual). Strong-tone letters induced no change in behavior relative to the group that received no notification (Karver, Shijaku, and Ungerer 2022).

Note: Box was prepared by Jonathan Karver, Abigail Dalton, Renos Vakis, Ana Maria Muñoz, and Zeina Afif.

Data and evidence for better fiscal decision-making

Data and evidence gaps that need to be filled to improve understanding of the distributional impact of fiscal policy have been highlighted throughout this report. This section summarizes the needs identified. Addressing these needs can help improve the quality of fiscal decision-making, or at least the evidence base on which decisions are made. Improving data and evidence is also important for increasing the transparency of government fiscal choices.

Many of the investments needed to improve data and evidence for fiscal decision-making particularly pay off during a crisis. Chapter 4 highlights the importance of good data to designing and targeting support in a crisis. For example, in South Africa the government's ability to make evidence-based decisions during the COVID-19 pandemic was enabled by investments in data infrastructure (box 7.3). The data system allowed policy makers to leverage various data to improve the targeting of cash transfers. Nationally representative survey data enabled projections of how many people would be eligible for the transfers and the likely cost under different designs. Fiscal incidence analysis determined who was benefiting from existing transfers. Administrative data from the tax authority, the register of recipients of social grants, and the government payroll were used to identify individuals and households that needed benefits. In addition, evidence on the impact of cash transfers was instrumental in encouraging their use instead of food parcels or vouchers.

BOX 7.3

Using evidence and data to expand COVID-19 social protection in South Africa

At the onset of the pandemic, millions of informal workers in South Africa lost their livelihoods and were unable to access support. Despite an extensive social protection system for the elderly, children, and the disabled, there was no safety net for able-bodied people of working age, and the existing social protection system was largely structured around food parcels to the destitute. Recipients had to file paperwork to prove eligibility and collect grants in person. By July 2020, while severe lockdown restrictions were in place, roughly 9.8 million households were unable to buy enough food to cover basic needs (Bassier and Leibbrandt 2020).

The government of South Africa drew on scientific advice, data, and evidence to respond to this immense challenge. In May 2020, the government announced the biggest expansion of the social safety net since the early 2000s, leading to US$6 billion in additional spending on poverty relief during 2020 and 2021, which reached 28.5 million people. Independent analysis estimates that the expansion led to 5.5 million fewer people living in food poverty between April and June 2020 and reached many poor households affected by informal job losses—almost half of job losers in the bottom 50 percent of the income distribution were covered by the new grant (Jain et al. 2020). The new verification process implemented was effective in targeting the poor: four persons in the bottom 20 percent of earners received the grant for every one person receiving it in the top 20 percent.

So what data and evidence helped the government of South Africa design and implement these policies so rapidly? The government formed an advisory group of experts from the Southern Africa Labour and Development Research Unit at the University of Cape Town, the Centre for the Study of African Economies at the University of Oxford, the DevLab at Duke University in the United States, and independent experts. The government commissioned this group to review international evidence and simulate the likely costs and impacts of various policy options.

Two complementary forms of evidence were used to inform the response: (1) international evidence from randomized controlled trials in other settings on the effects of cash grants and

(continued)

BOX 7.3

Using evidence and data to expand COVID-19 social protection in South Africa *(continued)*

(2) local evidence from nationally representative data on the likely number of people who would be eligible for a grant and the likely cost to the state.

Researchers at Oxford and Duke collated evidence on the speed of delivery, cost-effectiveness, and targeting of cash transfers relative to food parcels or vouchers, as well as the potential multiplier effects benefiting the informal economy. These were important in convincing policy makers to adopt cash transfers more widely (Orkin et al. 2022). The lessons from recent evidence included the following:

- Cash transfers are often more cost-effective and simpler to distribute than food parcels, but they achieve similar improvements in nutrition when markets function well (Gentilini 2014).

- Cash transfer recipients often work the same or more hours, in contrast to the assumption that providing welfare to able-bodied unemployed people would discourage them from working (Orkin et al. 2022). Regular cash payments can also improve people's ability to generate income, enabling them to search for work, start businesses, or buy agricultural inputs.

- Governments in other countries gave priority to expanding access to social assistance by providing support remotely, even if a small number of applications were approved in error (Gerard, Imbert, and Orkin 2020).

- Cash transfers can have multiplier effects in local economies, where they are often spent (Egger et al., forthcoming). The beneficiaries of the spending enabled by transfers are different from those for food vouchers (which must be spent in large supermarket chains) and cash (which can be spent anywhere, including informal businesses in local communities, which were especially in need of support during lockdowns).

To project the numbers of people who would be eligible for the cash grant and its likely cost, the University of Cape Town researchers were able to use a pre-COVID-19 nationally representative survey, the National Income Dynamics Survey, and build on prepandemic Commitment to Equity analysis to model the extent to which top-ups through the existing transfer system would reach those likely to lose jobs and on how many applicants there might be for the unemployment transfer (Goldman et al. 2021). Before the pandemic, it was difficult to find funding for the National Income Dynamics Survey, but the investment paid for itself many times over in just this crisis. Researchers also used the sample frame to conduct phone surveys during the pandemic and track the impacts of the transfer extensions on poverty and hunger.[a]

To rapidly assess the eligibility of applicants for the grant without requiring in-person applications, the National Treasury and Department of Social Development used the national population register, firm-level tax data on employment, unemployment insurance data, and data on social grant receipts. Funding from the United Nations University World Institute for Development Economics Research had helped establish a tax database that could be cross-referenced with the population register to identify formal workers. This database enabled a new grant to be rolled out to more than 10 million people in a matter of weeks.

The evidence and recommendations were distributed across the government to build support for policy reform. Crucially, the government's ability to make evidence-based decisions and move forward with the expansion was enabled by prior investments in high-quality evidence, surveys, and data infrastructure.

Sources: Orkin et al. 2022; personal communication with Kate Orkin, University of Oxford, and Saul Musker, director, Private Office of the President, South Africa.
a. Coronavirus Rapid Mobile Survey (https://cramsurvey.org).

So what are some of the key data and evidence gaps? Chapter 5 highlights the gaps in both tax and spending data. Although analysis by the Commitment to Equity (CEQ) Institute at Tulane University captures the two main tax instruments in most countries—consumption and personal income taxes—household surveys often miss the richest households (see box 2.2 in chapter 2). Also, CEQ data do not consider important taxes that are part of a government budget, such as those on corporate profits, property, or international trade (tariffs). Survey and administrative data can be used to fill these gaps. However, survey data must be more comprehensive to include this missing information, and administrative data must be more disaggregated and comparable across varying government and private sector systems. Moreover, administrative and survey data can be combined to provide the information needed for a more comprehensive fiscal incidence analysis. Several studies describe various methods for combining administrative and survey data (see, for example, Medalia et al. 2019; Meyer and Mittag 2019). These methods are based on methodological assumptions that preserve the representativeness of survey data in the combined data set and have also been found to improve program targeting in addition to producing more accurate distributional estimates (Meyer and Mittag 2019).

Fiscal incidence analysis is conducted largely for social spending, but not as much for spending designed to increase growth (in the short or long run), such as investments in agricultural R&D, agricultural subsidies, agricultural extensions, and tax exemptions aimed at firms. A better understanding of the distributional impacts of these spending categories will require better disaggregated spending data, as well as innovations in reporting. Global databases on government spending classify a huge portion of spending as "other spending" in order to capture the difference between spending in the categories explicitly defined and total government spending. Greater disaggregation of data in this "other" category is important.

In addition, methodological improvements that allow CEQ-type analysis to assess the trade-offs between the impacts of present and future fiscal spending are needed. Analyses that consider dynamic trade-offs as opposed to point-in-time analyses will help policy makers choose between public spending with immediate benefits, such as direct cash transfers, and those with benefits only over time, such as public education, infrastructure, and agricultural R&D (World Bank 2018).

Better data on costs are also needed to improve the prioritization of high-value fiscal spending. Although methods that assess the value of different policies are well established, cost and impact data on fiscal programs are not widely available. Several approaches and tools can be leveraged across countries to retrieve the comprehensive cost and impact data needed by governments when making fiscal policy choices. Examples are the quick costing tool developed by the World Bank's Partnership for Economic Inclusion to analyze self-reported cost data from 34 economic inclusion programs (Varghese Paul, Vasudeva Dutta, and Chaudhary 2021); the cost-effectiveness analyses of education-focused programs from the Abdul Latif Jameel Poverty Action Lab at the Massachusetts Institute of Technology (Dhaliwal et al. 2012); and the tools developed by several research programs under the World Bank's Strategic Impact Evaluation Fund.

Chapter 6 highlighted the value of investments in evaluations of impact. A comprehensive understanding of the impacts of fiscal policies on identified beneficiaries will help determine the growth effects of policy. Even short-run evaluations that use good proxy indicators of long-run outcomes will be highly useful (Athey et al. 2019). For targeted programs, understanding impacts on nonbeneficiaries is also important, and more impact evaluations can include this as a key component of evaluation design.

Can better fiscal policy put progress back on track? The need for global action

As this chapter has set out, correcting course on poverty and inequality reduction likely requires fiscal policy that is better targeted, more strongly focused on supporting growth, and able to protect any gains from subsequent crises. The following points provide some indications of what gains are realistic to expect on each of these fronts.

- *Protecting progress.* During the COVID-19 crisis, poverty would have been, on average, 2.0 percentage points lower for UMICs and 1.5 percentage points lower for LICs and LMICs if all countries in each income category had performed as well as the top performers in their income category in preventing poverty increases.[7] Policies that increase the protective power of fiscal policy by improving access to finance in a crisis and the readiness of delivery systems could reduce the poverty increase during a crisis by 50 percent for UMICs and 60 percent for LICs and LMICs if these best performers are an attainable benchmark.

- *Better targeted.* Tax and transfer reform in poorer countries can also make a difference. If each country was able to reach the level of poverty reduction achieved through taxes and transfers by the top quintile for their income category, poverty would fall by 1.6 percentage points in UMICs and 0.9 percentage point in LICs and LMICs.[8] If fiscal policy became more progressive, thereby moving toward the top performers in terms of reducing inequality, the change in inequality achieved through fiscal policy could be substantial. In concrete terms, the Gini coefficient for UMICs would fall by 6.4 percent and for LICs and LMICs by 5.2 percent. As chapter 5 noted, this decline in inequality would not necessarily result in more poverty reduction.

- *More supportive of growth.* Although there are complex trade-offs in fiscal decision-making, investments in areas such as health, education, infrastructure, and R&D can bring sustained economic growth if not financed by deficits or highly distortionary taxes (Moreno-Dodson 2012). For example, in India, connecting a district to the Indian railroad network increased agricultural income growth by 16 percent (Donaldson 2018). Globally, the R&D that led to the Green Revolution resulted in GDP per capita that was 17 percent higher in 2010 than it would have been had the Green Revolution been delayed by 10 years (Gollin, Hansen, and Wingender 2021). When these increases in growth benefit households at the bottom of the income distribution, the impact on poverty is large. However, not all spending brings such high returns, and the literature on fiscal spending and growth estimates that capital spending would have a wide range of impacts on subsequent growth. However, these examples, and others discussed in chapter 6, point to the poverty reduction potential of growth-oriented fiscal policy.

To assess how much of a difference fiscal policy can make in global progress on poverty reduction, the simulations of poverty to 2030 conducted at the end of chapter 1 are revisited here, considering these possible fiscal levers for poverty reduction. How fiscal policy may protect against shocks is not included in the simulations of projected future progress because historical growth trends are used as a baseline, abstracting from the possibility of shocks.

Although the experience of the last two years has certainly demonstrated the undeniable nature of shocks when they occur, the improvements in poverty reduction that come from more protective fiscal policy are not modeled in the simple exercise here. Instead, the simulations either model reductions in the Gini coefficient that correspond to movement of each country toward being a best performer in its income category in terms of tax and transfer progressivity, or model an increase in the per capita growth rate. Increases in tax and transfer progressivity are modeled as reductions in the Gini coefficient commensurate with movement of each country from its current level of progressive fiscal policy to the top quintile in its income category.[9] As discussed in chapter 5, this achievement will not necessarily translate into an immediate reduction in poverty because not all spending benefits household income in the short run. Here it is assumed that the income gained from increased progressivity is split between immediate transfers and long-term spending at the same rate currently experienced by countries in that income level, and that immediate transfers are distributed equally across all households through a universal transfer. Although inequality is reduced in this simulation, this simulation does not necessarily entail a reduction in poverty.

The impact of fiscal policy on growth is based on the wider literature. This literature does not provide one estimate of the impacts of better fiscal policy on growth because this relationship has many determinants and mediating factors. However a 0.6 percentage point increase is the midpoint of the estimates from the early literature on the growth impacts of a 1 percent of GDP increase in capital spending when undertaken prudently—that is, not deficit financed (Adam and Bevan 2005; Morozumi and Veiga 2016).[10] More recent work suggests that even this midpoint estimate of how fiscal choices translate into growth is quite high, and that the average output elasticity of public capital spending is likely closer to 0.2 (Bom and Ligthart 2014; Calderón, Moral-Benito, and Servén 2015; Núñez-Serrano and Velázquez 2017). Because these fiscal simulations attempt to provide an upper bound of the progress expected from successful fiscal policy, they maintain a relatively optimistic output elasticity of capital spending of 0.6.

The results of the simulations (figure 7.2) reveal that fiscal policy can help countries recover from the losses of 2020. Indeed, the arguably heroic efforts modeled here—shifting a country's progressivity of spending toward the top performers and raising an additional 1 percent of GDP in a minimally distortionary way while directing it toward productive capital spending—would see the setbacks of 2020 fully recovered by 2026 and a return to the prepandemic poverty projections years earlier than otherwise expected. However, even both efforts would not be enough to put the world on track to ending extreme poverty by 2030. The 3 percent target is well beyond the reach of what can be achieved through national policies alone, even if highly optimistic scenarios are considered. Although the potential of fiscal policies to reverse the 2020 setback should be noted, full reversal of the setback before 2030 would require optimistic projections unlikely to be realized. Furthermore, the 3 percent target was challenging to meet through national policy reform even before the 2020 setback. Now it is even further out of reach through national action alone.

Beneath the global numbers, the simulations highlight countries for which these changes have very different implications. To summarize the diversity, the proportion of countries that

Improving fiscal policy can help recover the losses of 2020, but it requires historic efforts and does not result in ending extreme poverty by 2030

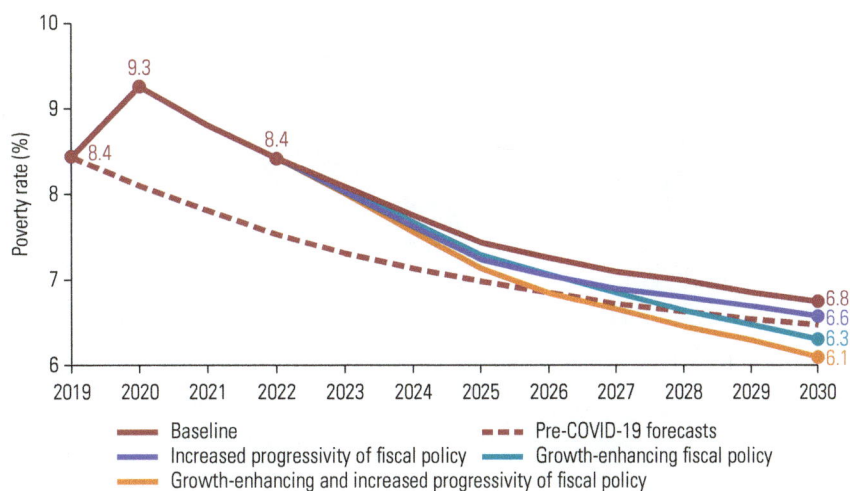

Source: Original estimates based on Mahler, Yonzan, and Lakner, forthcoming; World Bank, Poverty and Inequality Platform, https://pip .worldbank.org.
Note: The figure shows the projected poverty rate from 2022 to 2030 under assumptions of growth-enhancing fiscal policy, increased progressivity of fiscal policy, and both growth-enhancing and more progressive fiscal policy together.

reach the prepandemic poverty projection by 2030 are calculated separately for LICs, LMICs, and UMICs in figure 7.3. Clearly, extensive fiscal reform of the nature modeled here will return over 90 percent of UMICs to the prepandemic trajectory. Indeed, a switch to a more progressive spending profile alone will enable almost 90 percent of UMICs to reach the prepandemic trajectory, whereas the same goal would be attained by almost 75 percent of UMICs by means of the growth-enhancing policy alone. The effectiveness of the policies declines, however, with country income level. Among LICs, increased progressivity of fiscal policy will help only 25 percent of countries return to their prepandemic trajectory, while growth-enhancing policy will help less than half of them reach this benchmark. Taking the two ambitious fiscal reforms together will only move half of LICs to the benchmark. Especially for the poorest countries, fiscal actions alone will not return many countries to the pre-2020 course, let alone reach the more ambitious global target of 3 percent.

These simulations highlight the potential of better fiscal policies to help address the poverty and inequality challenges of today, but also the limit to what can be achieved by national policy making. More is likely needed than can be achieved by ambitious fiscal policy reform alone. Other national policy reforms that stimulate growth, particularly the income growth of households at the bottom of the income distribution, will likely be needed. The simulations also point to the importance of global action to address the unprecedented setback posed by the COVID-19 crisis and compounding crises since then.

The need for global action occurs at a moment when coordinated global action seems particularly elusive. Countries in all income categories are facing challenging economic times, and global cooperation is strained. However, the analysis in this report has shown that, although the continuing crises make 2022 a difficult moment for a new commitment to global action, it can still be an opportune time. And there is good precedent for global cooperation in these moments. After all, the Bretton Woods conference that established the International Monetary Fund and the International Bank for Reconstruction and Development was held while World War II was still being fought.

FIGURE 7.3

Many countries cannot recover the losses of 2020 by 2030, despite historic fiscal efforts

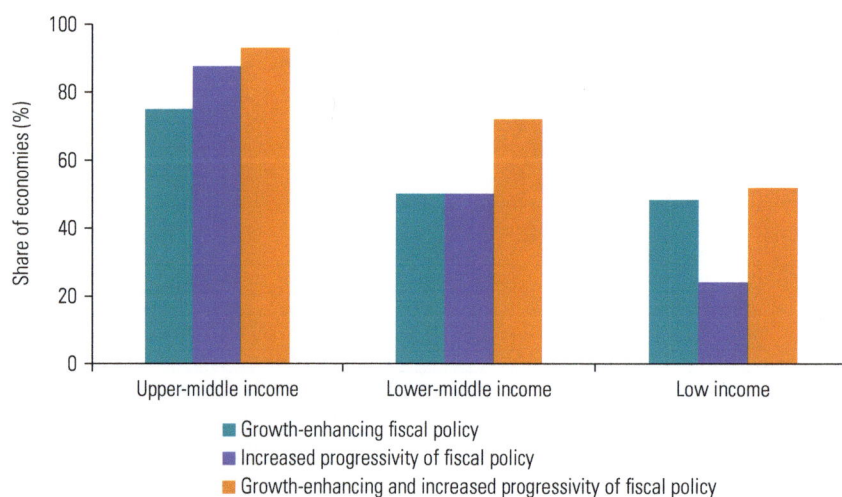

Legend:
- Growth-enhancing fiscal policy
- Increased progressivity of fiscal policy
- Growth-enhancing and increased progressivity of fiscal policy

Source: Original estimates based on Mahler, Yonzan, and Lakner, forthcoming.
Note: The figure shows the share of economies in each income group that can reach pre-COVID-19 poverty forecasts by 2030 under assumptions of growth-enhancing fiscal policy, increased progressivity of fiscal policy, and both growth-enhancing and more progressive fiscal policy together.

Notes

1. For example, in Sub-Saharan Africa alone, Kenya, Malawi, and Senegal, with strategies being developed in Benin, Eswatini, Ethiopia, Lesotho, Madagascar, Niger, and Sierra Leone.
2. DASK, Turkish Catastrophe Insurance Pool, "Compensation Payments," https://dask.gov.tr/en/compensation-payments.
3. DASK, Turkish Catastrophe Insurance Pool, "Interactive Earthquake Map," https://dask.gov.tr/en/interactive-earthquake-map.
4. World Bank, Global Risk Financing Facility (dashboard), https://globalriskfinancing.org/.
5. From unpublished work by Fuchs and Wai-Poi, developed further in Sosa and Wai-Poi (forthcoming).
6. For applications, see Rodriguez and Wai-Poi (2021) for Jordan and Wai-Poi et al. (forthcoming) for Vietnam. Sosa and Wai-Poi (forthcoming)

approximate impacts across a wider range of countries, with grouped decile data.

7. This is the poverty rate at the poverty line relevant for that income category.
8. Using the poverty line relevant for that income category.
9. For countries where no CEQ data are available (and therefore no information on the progressivity of a country's fiscal policy is available), the median level of progressivity for the income category is used.
10. Adam and Bevan (2005) suggest that a 1 percent GDP increase in fiscal spending can increase growth by 0.6 percentage point, on average, with a range from 0.1 to 1.1 percentage points. This increase in spending cannot be deficit financed if it is to spur growth. Morozumi and Veiga (2016) indicate that the growth effects of fiscal spending arise with changes to capital spending, but not current spending.

References

Adam, Christopher S., and David L. Bevan. 2005. "Fiscal Deficits and Growth in Developing Countries." *Journal of Public Economics* 89 (4): 571–97.

Afridi, Farzana, Kanika Mahajan, and Nikita Sangwan. 2022. "Employment Guaranteed? Social Protection during a Pandemic." *Oxford Open Economics* 1 (1): 1–15.

Ali, Daniel Ayalew, Klaus Deininger, and Michael Wild. 2020. "Using Satellite Imagery to Create Tax Maps and Enhance Local Revenue Collection." *Applied Economics* 52 (4): 415–29.

Alvarez, Fernando, David Argente, Rafael Jimenez, and Francesco Lippi. 2022. "Cash: A Blessing or a Curse?" *Journal of Monetary Economics* 125: 85–128.

Athey Susan, Raj Chetty, Guido W. Imbens, and Hyunseung Kang. 2019. "The Surrogate Index: Combining Short-Term Proxies to Estimate Long-Term Treatment Effects More Rapidly and Precisely." NBER Working Paper 26463, National Bureau of Economic Research, Cambridge, MA.

Azevedo, Deven, Hendrik Wolff, and Akio Yamazaki. 2019. "Do Carbon Taxes Kill Jobs? Firm-Level Evidence from British Columbia." Clean Economy Working Paper 18-08, Smart

Prosperity Institute, University of Ottawa, Ontario.

Bachas, Pierre, and Mauricio Soto. 2021. "Corporate Taxation under Weak Enforcement." *American Economic Journal: Economic Policy* 13 (4): 36–71.

Bachas, Pierre, Matthew H. Fisher-Post, Anders Jensen, and Gabriel Zucman. 2022. "Globalization and Factor Income Taxation." NBER Working Paper 29819, National Bureau of Economic Research, Cambridge, MA.

Barake, Mona, Theresa Neef, Paul-Emmanuel Chouc, and Gabriel Zucman. 2021. "Revenue Effects of the Global Minimum Tax: Country-by-Country Estimates." EU Tax Observatory Note 2, EUTAX, Paris School of Economics.

Bassier, Ihsaan, and Murray Leibbrandt. 2020. "Note: Extension of Grants in October, 16 September 2020." Presidency of the Republic of South Africa.

Bellon, Matthieu, Jillie Chang, Era Dabla-Norris, Salma Khalid, Frederico Lima, Enrique Rojas, and Pilar Villena. 2022. "Digitalization to Improve Tax Compliance: Evidence from VAT E-Invoicing in Peru." *Journal of Public Economics* 210: 104661. https://www.sciencedirect.com/science/article/pii/S0047272722000639?via%3Dihub.

Bom, P. R., and J. E. Ligthart. 2014. "What Have We Learned from Three Decades of Research on the Productivity of Public Capital? *Journal of Economic Surveys* 28: 889–916.

Calderón, César, Enrique, Moral-Benito, and Luis Servén. 2015. "Is Infrastructure Capital Productive? A Dynamic Heterogeneous Approach." *Journal of Applied Economics* 30: 177–98.

Clarke, Daniel J., and Stefan Dercon. 2016. *Dull Disasters? How Planning Ahead Will Make a Difference.* Oxford, UK: Oxford University Press.

Crossley, Elle, Debbie Hillier, Michèle Plichta, Niklas Rieger, and Scott Waygood. 2021. "Funding Disasters: Tracking Global Humanitarian and Development Funding for Response to Natural Hazards." Working Paper 8, Centre for Disaster Protection and Development Initiatives, London.

Dalton, Abigail, and Lauren Manning. 2021. "Behavioral Insights for Tax Compliance." eMBeD brief, World Bank, Washington, DC.

del Valle, Alejandro. 2021. "Saving Lives with Pre-Financed Rules-Based Disaster Aid: Evidence from Mexico." medRxiv.

del Valle, Alejandro, Alain de Janvry, and Elisabeth Sadoulet. 2020. "Rules for Recovery: Impact of Indexed Disaster Funds on Shock Coping in Mexico." *American Economic Journal: Applied Economics* 12 (4): 164–95.

Dhaliwal, Iqbal, Esther Duflo, Rachel Glennerster, and Caitlin Tulloch. 2012. "Comparative Cost-Effectiveness Analysis to Inform Policy in Developing Countries: A General Framework with Applications for Education." Abdul Latif Jameel Poverty Action Lab (J-PAL), Massachusetts Institute of Technology, Cambridge, MA. https://www.povertyactionlab .org/sites/default/files/research-paper/EA%20 in%20Education%202013.01.29.pdf.

Dom, Roel, Anna Custers, Stephen Davenport, and Wilson Prichard. 2022. *Innovations in Tax Compliance: Building Trust, Navigating Politics, and Tailoring Reform.* Washington, DC: World Bank.

Donaldson, D. 2018. "Railroads of the Raj: Estimating the Impact of Transport Infrastructure." *American Economic Review* 108(4-5): 899–934.

Dorband, Ira, Michael Jakob, Matthias Kalkuhl, and Jan Christoph Steckel. 2019. "Poverty and Distributional Effects of Carbon Pricing in Low- and Middle-Income Countries: A Global Comparative Analysis." *World Development* 115: 246–57.

Dussaux, Damien. 2020. "The Joint Effects of Energy Prices and Carbon Taxes on Environmental and Economic Performance: Evidence from the French Manufacturing Sector." OECD Environment Working Paper 154, Organisation for Economic Co-operation and Development, Paris.

Egger, Dennis, Johannes Haushofer, Edward Miguel, Paul Niehaus, and Michael W. Walker. Forthcoming. "General Equilibrium Effects of Cash Transfers: Experimental Evidence from Kenya." *Econometrica.*

Evans, Steve. 2022. "Philippines Cat Bond Payout a 'Tangible Result', Says Finance Secretary." *Artemis*, January 25, 2022. https://www.artemis .bm/news/philippines-cat-bond-payout-a-tangible -result-says-finance-secretary/.

Gehrke, Esther. 2019. "An Employment Guarantee as Risk Insurance? Assessing the Effects of the NREGS on Agricultural Production Decisions." *World Bank Economic Review* 33 (2): 413–35.

Gelb, Alan, Anurodh Giri, Anit Mukherjee, Kritika Shukla, Mitul Thapliyal, and Brian Webster. 2021. "Social Assistance and Information in the Initial Phase of the COVID-19 Crisis: Lessons from a Household Survey in India." Policy Paper 217, Center for Global Development, Washington, DC.

Gentilini, Ugo. 2014. "Our Daily Bread: What Is the Evidence on Comparing Cash versus Food Transfers?" Social Protection and Labor Discussion Paper 1420, World Bank, Washington, DC.

Gentilini, Ugo. 2022. "Cash Transfers in Pandemic Times: Evidence, Practices, and Implications from the Largest Scale Up in History." World Bank, Washington, DC.

Gerard, François, Clément Imbert, and Kate Orkin. 2020. "Social Protection Response to the COVID-19 Crisis: Options for Developing Countries." *Oxford Review of Economic Policy* 36 (Supplement 1): S281–S296.

Goldman, Maya, Ihsaan Bassier, Joshua Budlender, Lindi Mzankomo, Ingrid Woolard, and Murray V. Leibbrandt. 2021. "Simulation of Options to Replace the Special COVID-19 Social Relief of Distress Grant and Close the Poverty Gap at the Food Poverty Line." UNU-WIDER Working

Paper 2021/165, United Nations University World Institute for Development Economics Research, Helsinki.

Gollin, Douglas, Casper Worm Hansen, and Asger M. Wingender. 2021. "Two Blades of Grass: The Impact of the Green Revolution." *Journal of Political Economy* 129 (8): 2344–84.

Goulder, Lawrence H., Marc A. C. Hafstead, GyuRim Kim, and Xianling Long. 2019. "Impacts of a Carbon Tax across US Household Income Groups: What Are the Equity-Efficiency Trade-Offs?" *Journal of Public Economics* 175: 44–64.

Hallsworth, Michael, John A. List, Robert D. Metcalfe, and Ivo Vlaev. 2017. "The Behavioralist as Tax Collector: Using Natural Field Experiments to Enhance Tax Compliance." *Journal of Public Economics* 148: 14–31.

Healy, Andrew, and Neil Malhotra. 2009. "Myopic Voters and Natural Disaster Policy." *American Political Science Review* 103 (3): 387–406.

Hendren, Nathaniel, and Ben Sprung-Keyser. 2020. "A Unified Welfare Analysis of Government Policies." *Quarterly Journal of Economics* 135 (3): 1209–1318.

Hernandez, Marco, Julian Jamison, Ewa Korczyc, Nina Mazar, and Roberto Sormani. 2017. "Applying Behavioral Insights to Improve Tax Collection: Experimental Evidence from Poland." World Bank, Washington, DC.

Hill, Ruth Vargas, Alejandra Campero Peredo, and Marcela Tarazona. 2021. "The Impact of Pre-arranged Disaster Finance: Evidence Gap Assessment." Working Paper 7, Centre for Disaster Protection, London.

Hill, Ruth Vargas, Neha Kumar, Nicholas Magnan, Simrin Makhija, Francesca de Nicola, David J. Spielman, and Patrick S. Ward. 2019. "Ex Ante and Ex Post Effects of Hybrid Index Insurance in Bangladesh." *Journal of Development Economics* 136: 1–17.

Hoy, Christopher. Forthcoming. "How Does the Progressivity of Taxes and Government Transfers Impact People's Willingness to Pay Tax? Experimental Evidence across Developing Countries" Policy Research Working Paper, World Bank, Washington DC.

Jain, Ronak, Joshua Budlender, Rocco Zizzamia, and Ihsaan Bassier. 2020. "The Labor Market and Poverty Impacts of COVID-19 In South Africa." SALDRU Working Paper 264, Southern Africa Labour and Development Research Unit, University of Cape Town.

Jakobsen, Katrine, Kristian Jakobsen, Henrik Kleven, and Gabriel Zucman. 2020. "Wealth Taxation and Wealth Accumulation: Theory and Evidence from Denmark." *Quarterly Journal of Economics* 135 (1): 329–88. https://doi.org/10.1093/qje/qjz032.

Kanbur, Ravi. 2017. "The Digital Revolution and Targeting Public Expenditure for Poverty Reduction." Discussion Paper DP12089, Centre for Economic Policy Research, London. https://ssrn.com/abstract=2988847.

Karver, Jonathan, Hilda Shijaku, and Christoph Ungerer. 2022. "Nudging in the Time of the Coronavirus: Evidence from an Experimental Tax Trial in Albania at the Onset of a Global Pandemic." Policy Research Working Paper 9961, World Bank, Washington, DC.

Kose, M. Ayhan, Sergio Kurlat, Franziska Ohnsorge, and Naotaka Sugawara. 2017. "A Cross-Country Database of Fiscal Space." Policy Research Working Paper 8157, World Bank, Washington, DC.

Kronfol, Hania, and Victor Steenbergen. 2020. *Evaluating the Costs and Benefits of Corporate Tax Incentives: Methodological Approaches and Policy Considerations. Finance, Competitiveness and Innovation in Focus.* Washington, DC: World Bank.

Lauer, Jeremy A., Franco Sassi, Agnes Soucat, and Angeli Vigo. Forthcoming. *Health Taxes: Policy and Practice.* Geneva: World Health Organization and Imperial's Centre for Health Economics and Policy Innovation.

Lucas-Mas, Cristian Óliver, and Raúl Félix Junquera-Varela. 2021. *Tax Theory Applied to the Digital Economy: A Proposal for a Digital Data Tax and a Global Internet Tax Agency.* Washington, DC: World Bank.

Mahler, Daniel Gerszon, Nishant Yonzan, and Christoph Lakner [randomized order]. Forthcoming. "The Impact of COVID-19 on Global Inequality and Poverty." World Bank, Washington DC.

Martin, Ralf, Laure B. de Preux, and Ulrich J. Wagner. 2014. "The Impact of a Carbon Tax on Manufacturing: Evidence from Microdata." *Journal of Public Economics* 117: 1–14.

Martinez-Vazquez, Jorge, Eduardo Sanz-Arcega, and José Manuel Tránchez-Martín. 2022.

"Tax Revenue Management and Reform in the Digital Era in Developing and Developed Countries." International Center for Public Policy Working Paper 2201, International Center for Public Policy, Andrew Young School of Policy Studies, Georgia State University, Atlanta.

Mascagni, Giulia, Christopher Nell, and Nara Monkam. 2017. "One Size Does Not Fit All: A Field Experiment on the Drivers of Tax Compliance and Delivery Methods in Rwanda." ICTD Working Paper 58, International Centre for Tax and Development, Brighton, UK.

McKenzie, David. 2021. "Small Business Training to Improve Management Practices in Developing Countries: Reassessing the Evidence for 'Training Doesn't Work.'" *Oxford Review of Economic Policy* 37 (2): 276–301.

McKenzie, David, Christopher Woodruff, Kjetil Bjorvatn, Miriam Bruhn, Jing Cai, Juanita Gonzalez-Uribe, Simon Quinn, et al. 2021. "Training Entrepreneurs." *VoxDevLit* 1 (2).

Medalia, Carla, Bruce D. Meyer, Amy B. O'Hara, and Derek Wu. 2019. "Linking Survey and Administrative Data to Measure Income, Inequality, and Mobility." *International Journal of Population Data Science* 4 (1): 939.

MEPDPSR (Ministry of Economic Planning and Development and Public Sector Reforms). 2021. "Social Support for Resilient Livelihoods, Scalable Handbook." Ministry of Economic Planning and Development and Public Sector Reforms, Government of Malawi, Lilongwe. https://nlgfc.gov.mw/index.php/the-star/documents /file/114-scalable-handbook-ssrlp.

Metcalf, Gilbert E., and James H. Stock. 2020. "Measuring the Macroeconomic Impact of Carbon Taxes." *American Economic Review Papers and Proceedings* 110: 101–06.

Meyer, Bruce D., and Nikolas Mittag. 2019. "Using Linked Survey and Administrative Data to Better Measure Income: Implications for Poverty, Program Effectiveness, and Holes in the Safety Net." *American Economic Journal: Applied Economics* 11 (2): 176–204.

Mondal, Sonjay, Jatisankar Bandyopadhyay, and Debashish Chakravarty. 2015. "Land Information System Using Cadastral Techniques, Mining Area of Raniganj,

Barddhaman District, India." *International Journal of Remote Sensing Applications* 5: 45–53.

Moreno-Dodson, Blanca, ed. 2012. *Is Fiscal Policy the Answer? A Developing Country Perspective.* Washington, DC: World Bank.

Morozumi, Atsuyoshi, and Francisco José Veiga. 2016. "Public Spending and Growth: The Role of Government Accountability." *European Economic Review* 89 (2016): 148–71.

National Agency of Public Registry of Georgia. 2015. "Land Cadastre Reform in Georgia." Tbilisi, Georgia.

Ndung'u, Njuguna. 2019. *Digital Technology and State Capacity in Kenya.* Washington, DC: Center for Global Development. https://www .cgdev.org/sites/default/files/digital-technology -and-state-capacity-kenya.pdf.

Nikoloski, Zlatko, Luc Christiaensen, and Ruth Hill. 2018. "Coping with Shocks: The Realities of African Life." In *Agriculture in Africa: Telling Myths from Facts,* edited by Luc Christiaensen and Lionel Demery, 123–34. Directions in Development Series. Washington, DC: World Bank.

Núñez-Serrano, Juan A., and Francisco J. Velázquez. 2017. "Is Public Capital Productive? Evidence from a Meta-analysis." *Applied Economic Perspectives and Policy* 39: 313–45.

OECD (Organisation for Economic Co-operation and Development). 2021. *Inheritance Taxation in OECD Countries.* OECD Tax Policy Studies, No. 28. Paris: OECD Publishing. https://doi .org/10.1787/e2879a7d-en.

Olaberria, Eduardo, and Carmen M. Reinhart. 2022. "The Reversal Problem: Development Going Backwards." World Bank, Washington, DC.

OPM (Oxford Policy Management). 2017. "Independent Evaluation of the African Risk Capacity." Formative Phase 1 Report, OPM, Oxford, UK.

Orkin, Kate, Marta Grabowska, Brynde Kreft, Alice Cahill, Robert Garlick, and Yasmine Bekkouche. 2022. "Designing Social Protection to Improve Employment, Earnings and Productivity in Lower- and Middle-Income Countries." Working paper, University of Oxford, Oxford, UK. https://mbrg.bsg.ox.ac.uk/sites/default/files /2022-02/cash-policy-2.2.pdf.

Pople, Ashley, Ruth Hill, Stefan Dercon, and Ben Brunckhorst. 2021. "Anticipatory Cash Transfers in Climate Disaster Response." Working Paper 6, Centre for Disaster Protection, London.

Prichard, W. 2019. "Tax, Politics, and the Social Contract in Africa." In *Oxford Research Encyclopedia of Politics*. Oxford, UK: Oxford University Press.

Quinn, Simon R., and Christopher Woodruff. 2019. "Experiments and Entrepreneurship in Developing Countries." *Annual Review of Economics* 11: 225–48.

Rafuse, Bill, Stacey Bruce, and Ainsley Arnold. 2020. "Lessons from the Effects of Hurricanes Irma and Maria on the PFM Systems and Operational Issues in Caribbean Governments." Unpublished manuscript, International Monetary Fund Caribbean Regional Technical Assistance Centre (CARTAC), Barbados.

Reinhart, Carmen M. 2022. "From Health Crisis to Financial Distress." *IMF Economic Review* 70 (1): 4–31.

Rodriguez, Laura, and Matthew Wai-Poi. 2021. *Fiscal Policy, Poverty, and Inequality in Jordan: The Role of Taxes and Public Spending*. Washington, DC: World Bank.

Ross, H. 2021. *Lost Funds: A Study on the Tobacco Tax Revenue Gap in Selected ASEAN Countries*. Bangkok: Southeast Asia Tobacco Control Alliance.

Schroder, Christian. 2021. "Regime-Dependent Environmental Tax Multipliers: Evidence from 75 Countries." Policy Research Working Paper 9640, World Bank, Washington, DC.

Sosa, Mariano, and Matthew Wai-Poi. Forthcoming. "Fiscal Policy and Equity in Developing Countries: A Survey of International Patterns and Lessons." Background paper prepared for this report, World Bank, Washington, DC.

Sung, Myung Jae, Rajul Awasthi, and Hyung Chul Lee. 2017. "Can Tax Incentives for Electronic Payments Reduce the Shadow Economy? Korea's Attempt to Reduce Underreporting in Retail Businesses." Policy Research Working Paper 7936, World Bank, Washington, DC.

Ulyssea, Gabriel. 2018. "Firms, Informality, and Development: Theory and Evidence from Brazil." *American Economic Review* 108 (8): 2015–47.

Varghese Paul, Boban, Puja Vasudeva Dutta, and Sarang Chaudhary. 2021. "Assessing the Impact and Cost of Economic Inclusion Programs: A Synthesis of Evidence." Policy Research Working Paper 9536, World Bank, Washington, DC.

Vyas, S., V. Seifert, L. Schäfer, and S. Kreft. 2019. "Climate Risk Insurance Solutions: Understanding the Drivers of Cost-Effectiveness; A Multi-Criteria Assessment Framework and Key Performance Indicators." Discussion Paper Series, Munich Climate Insurance Initiative, Bonn, Germany.

Wai-Pol, Matthew, Michal Myck, Kajetan Trzcinski, Monika Oczkowska, and Jon Jellema. Forthcoming. Vietnam CEQ technical working paper (title to come), World Bank, Washington, DC.

World Bank. 2012. *Protecting the Poor and Vulnerable in Indonesia*. Washington, DC: World Bank.

World Bank. 2018. *Fiscal Incidence Analysis for Kenya: Using the Kenya Integrated Household Budget Survey 2015–16*. Washington, DC: World Bank.

World Bank. 2020a. *Poverty and Shared Prosperity 2020: Reversals of Fortune*. Washington, DC: World Bank.

World Bank. 2020b. *Public Expenditure Review: Disaster Response and Rehabilitation in the Philippines*. 2020. Washington, DC: World Bank. https://openknowledge.worldbank.org/bitstream /handle/10986/35064/Disaster-Response-and -Rehabilitation-in-the-Philippines-Public-Expenditure -Review-Technical-Report.pdf?sequence=1&is Allowed=y.

World Bank. 2021a. "Disaster Risk Financing for Agriculture." Factsheet 8, Disaster Risk Financing and Insurance, World Bank, Washington, DC.

World Bank. 2021b. "Supporting Firms in Restructuring and Recovery. Equitable Growth, Finance and Institutions Insight." Working paper, World Bank, Washington, DC.

World Bank. 2021c. *World Development Report 2021: Data for Better Lives*. Washington, DC: World Bank.

World Bank. 2022. *World Development Report 2022: Finance for an Equitable Recovery*. Washington, DC: World Bank.

World Bank. No date. "Building Sovereign Financial Resilience in Middle-Income Countries." Factsheet 5, Disaster Risk Financing and Insurance Program, World Bank, Washington,

DC. https://www.financialprotectionforum.org /sites/default/files/SECO%20Factsheet%2005 _Final_Updated.pdf.

Yamazaki, Akio. 2017. "Jobs and Climate Policy: Evidence from British Columbia's Revenue Neutral Carbon Tax." *Journal of Environmental Economics and Management* 83: 197–216.

Yang, Yi, Dillan Patel, Ruth Vargas Hill, and Michèle Plichta. 2021. "Funding COVID-19 Response: Tracking Global Humanitarian and Development Funding to Meet Crisis Needs." Working Paper 5, Centre for Disaster, London.

Yilmaz, Fatih, and Jacqueline Coolidge. 2013. "Can E-Filing Reduce Tax Compliance Costs in Developing Countries?" Policy Research Working Paper 6647, World Bank, Washington, DC. https://openknowledge.worldbank.org /handle/10986/16861.